SOURCES
of the
WESTERN
TRADITION

BRIEF EDITION

VOLUME I: FROM ANCIENT TIMES
TO THE ENLIGHTENMENT

Marvin Perry

Baruch College, City University of New York

HOUGHTON MIFFLIN COMPANY   BOSTON   NEW YORK

Senior Sponsoring Editor: Nancy Blaine
Senior Development Editor: Julie Dunn
Senior Project Editor: Jane Lee
Editorial Assistant: Kristen Truncellito
Senior Art and Design Coordinator: Jill Haber
Senior Photo Editor: Jennifer Meyer Dare
Senior Composition Buyer: Chuck Dutton
Senior Manufacturing Coordinator: Marie Barnes
Marketing Manager: Sandra McGuire
Marketing Assistant: Molly Parke

Cover image: *Three Actors on Stage.* Scene from a comedy (Atelian farce): Man at left wearing a slave's mask and two women. Wall painting from Pompeii. Credit: Museo Archeologico Nazionale, Naples, Italy/Erich Lessing/Art Resource, N.Y.

Text Credits:

Chapter 1
Section 1 p. 4: From *The Epic of Gilgamesh,* translated by N. K. Sandars (Penguin Classics, 1960, third edition, 1972). Copyright © N. K. Sandars, 1950, 1964, 1972. Reproduced by permission of Penguin Books Ltd. *Section 2* p. 8: From *Babylonian and Assyrian Laws, Contracts, and Letters,* ed. C. M. W. Johns (New York: Charles Scribner's Sons, 1904), pp. 44–67. *Section 3* pp. 11–13: Erman, Adolph, *The Ancient Egyptians.* Reprinted with permission of Methuen & Co. *Section 4* p. 14: From James Pritchard, *Ancient Near East Texts Relating to the Old Testament,* Third Edition with Supplement. Copyright © 1950, 1955, 1969, renewed 1978 by Princeton University Press. Reprinted by permission of Princeton University Press. *Section 5* pp. 16–17: From *The Intellectual Adventure of Ancient Man: An Essay on Speculative Thought in the Ancient Near East,* by Henri Frankfort, H. A. Frankfort, John A. Wilson, Thorkild Jacobsen, and William A. Irwin (eds.). Reprinted with permission of The University of Chicago Press.

Credits are continued on page 265.

Printed in the U.S.A.

Library of Congress Control Number: 2005924529

ISBN: 0-618-53901-8

123456789-MP-09 08 07 06 05

Contents

CHAPTER 4   *Early Christianity* 102

PART TWO: THE MIDDLE AGES 121

CHAPTER 5   *The Early Middle Ages* 121

CHAPTER 6   *The High and Late Middle Ages* 139

PART THREE: EARLY MODERN EUROPE   175

CHAPTER 7 *The Renaissance and Reformation   175*

CHAPTER 8 *Early Modern Society and Politics   206*

CHAPTER 9 *Intellectual Revolutions   227*

Thematic Contents

RELIGION

WOMEN

Preface

Teachers of the Western Civilization survey have long recognized the pedagogical value of primary sources, which are the raw materials of history. *Sources of the Western Tradition: Brief Edition* is an abridged version of the best-selling *Sources of the Western Tradition,* now in its sixth edition. This abridgment is intended for instructors who find traditional readers contain more selections than they can profitably utilize in a crowded curriculum or are discouraged by their cost. Although many selections have been dropped, this brief edition continues to contain a wide assortment of carefully selected and edited documents, principally primary sources, that fit the need of the survey and supplement standard texts.

I have based my choice of documents for the two volumes on several criteria. In order to introduce students to those ideas and values that characterize the Western tradition, *Sources of the Western Tradition* emphasizes primarily the works of the great thinkers. While focusing on the great ideas that have shaped the Western heritage, however, the reader also provides a balanced treatment of political, economic, and social history. I have tried to select documents that capture the characteristic outlook of an age and that provide a sense of the movement and development of Western history. The readings are of sufficient length to convey their essential meaning, and I have carefully extracted those passages that focus on the documents' main ideas.

An important feature of the reader is the grouping of several documents that illuminate a single theme; such a constellation of related readings reinforces understanding of important themes and invites comparison, analysis, and interpretation. For example, in Volume I, Chapter 7, The Renaissance and Reformation, Section 1, "The Humanists' Fascination with Antiquity," contains two interrelated readings: "The Father of Humanism," by Petrarch, and "Study of Greek Literature and a Humanist Educational Program," by Leonardo Bruni. In Volume II, Chapter 3, Era of the French Revolution, Section 3, "Expansion of Human Rights," contains three readings: *Vindication of the Rights of Woman,* by Mary Wollstonecraft; "Address to the National Assembly in Favor of the Abolition of the Slave Trade," by the Society of the Friends of Blacks; and "Petition of the Jews of Paris, Alsace, and Lorraine to the National Assembly, January 28, 1790."

The brief edition retains the overriding concern of the complete edition: making the documents accessible so that students can comprehend and interpret them on their own. To facilitate this aim, I have preserved the pedagogical features of the complete edition that have been successful in its six editions. Introductions of three types explain the historical setting, the authors' intent, and the meaning and significance of the readings. First, introductions to each chapter—nine in Volume I and eleven in Volume II—provide comprehensive overviews to periods. Second, introductions to each numbered section or grouping treat the historical background for the reading(s) that follow(s). Third, each reading has a brief headnote that provides specific details about that reading.

Within some readings, interlinear notes, clearly set off from the text of the document, serve as transitions and suggest the main themes of the passages that follow. Used primarily in longer extracts of the great thinkers, these interlinear notes help to guide students through the readings.

To aid students' comprehension, brief, bracketed editorial definitions or notes that explain unfamiliar or foreign terms are inserted into the running text. When terms or concepts in the documents require fuller explanations, these appear at the bottom of pages as editor's footnotes. Where helpful, I have retained the notes of authors, translators, or editors from whose works the documents were acquired. (The latter have asterisks, daggers, et cetera, to distinguish them from my numbered explanatory notes.) The review questions that appear at the ends of sections enable students to check their understanding of the documents; sometimes the questions ask for comparisons with other readings, linking or contrasting key concepts.

For ancient sources, I have generally selected recent translations that are both faithful to the text and readable. For some seventeenth- and eighteenth-century English documents, the archaic spelling has been retained, when this does not preclude comprehension, in order to show students how the English language has evolved over time.

The brief edition retains a new feature of the sixth edition of the complete edition—a thematic table of contents for each volume. All of the documents in the book have been grouped together under broad, thematic categories to assist instructors in selecting sources that best fit the needs of their course. The thematic listing also provides students with potential research and essay topics. Many of the documents will be cross-listed under two or more categories—for instance, in Volume I, Saint Augustine's *The City of God* appears under "Religion," "Philosophy," "Social and Economic Conditions," and "Government and Politics." Chapter numbers appear to the left of the documents so that they can be easily referenced in class.

I am grateful to the staff of Houghton Mifflin Company who lent their talents to the project. I would like to thank Nancy Blaine, Senior Sponsoring Editor, for suggesting a brief edition of *Sources of the Western Tradition* and Julie Swasey, Senior Development Editor, for guiding the brief edition from its inception; Jane Lee, Senior Project Editor, for her careful attention to detail; and Ellen Whalen for her superb copyediting skills. Although George W. Bock and Angela Von Laue did not work on this brief edition, their excellent contribution to the larger edition has, no doubt, contributed to the quality of this new format.

Prologue
Examining Primary Sources

When historians try to reconstruct and apprehend past events, they rely on primary or original sources—official documents prepared by institutions and eyewitness reports. Similarly, when they attempt to describe the essential outlook or world-view of a given era, people, or movement, historians examine other types of primary sources—the literature, art, philosophy, and religious expressions of the time. These original sources differ from secondary or derivative sources—accounts of events and times written at a later date by people who may or may not have had access to primary sources. *Sources of the Western Tradition* consists principally of primary sources, which are the raw materials of history; they provide historians with the basic facts, details, and thinking needed for an accurate reconstruction of the past.

Historians have to examine a document with a critical spirit. The first question asked is: Is the document authentic and reliable? An early illustration of critical historical awareness was demonstrated by the Renaissance thinker Lorenzo Valla (c. 1407–1457) in *Declamation Concerning the False Decretals of Constantine*. The so-called Donation of Constantine, which was used by popes to support their claim to temporal authority, stated that the fourth-century Roman emperor Constantine had given the papacy dominion over the western Empire. By showing that some of the words in the document were unknown in Constantine's time and therefore could not have been used by the emperor, Valla proved that the document was forged by church officials several hundred years after Constantine's death. A more recent example of the need for caution is shown by the discovery of the "Hitler Diaries" in the mid-1980s. Several prominent historians "authenticated" the manuscript before it was exposed as a forgery—the paper dated from the 1950s and Hitler died in 1945. Nor can all eyewitness accounts be trusted, something Thucydides, the great Greek historian, noted 2,400 years ago.

[E]ither I was present myself at the events which I have described or else I heard of them from eye-witnesses whose reports I have checked with as much thoroughness as possible. Not that even so the truth was easy to discover: different eye-witnesses give different accounts of the same events, speaking out of partiality for one side or the other or else from imperfect memories.

An eyewitness's personal bias can render a document worthless. For example, in *The Auschwitz Lie* (1973), Thies Christophersen, a former SS guard at Auschwitz-Birkenau, denied the existence of gas chambers and mass killings in the notorious Nazi death camp, which he described as a sort of resort where prisoners, after work, could swim, listen to music in their rooms, or visit a brothel. Years later he was captured on videotape—he mistakenly thought the interviewers were fellow neo-Nazis—confessing that he had lied about the gas chambers because of loyalty to the SS and his desire to protect Germany's honor.

After examining the relevant primary sources and deciding on their usefulness, historians have to construct a consistent narrative and provide a plausible interpretation. Ideally, this requires that they examine documentary evidence in a wholly neutral, detached, and objective way. But is it possible to write history without being influenced by one's own particular viewpoint and personal biases?

No doubt several historians examining the same material might draw differing conclusions and each could argue his or her position persuasively. This is not surprising, for history is not an exact science and historians, like all individuals, are influenced by their upbringing and education, by their thoughts and feelings. Conflicting interpretations of historical events and periods are expected and acceptable features of historiography. But what is not acceptable is the deliberate distortion and suppression of evidence in order to substantiate one's own prejudices.

A flagrant example of writers of history misusing sources and distorting evidence in order to fortify their own prejudices is the recent case of British historian David Irving, author of numerous books on World War II, several of them well reviewed. Increasingly Irving revealed an undisguised admiration for Hitler and an antipathy toward Jews, which led him to minimize and disguise atrocities committed by the Third Reich. Addressing neo-Nazi audiences in several lands, he asserted that the Holocaust is "a major fraud. . . . There were no gas chambers. They were fakes and frauds." In *Lying About Hitler: History, Holocaust and the David Irving Trial* (2001), Richard J. Evans, a specialist in modern German history with a broad background in archival research, exposed instance after instance of how Irving, in his attempt to whitewash Hitler, misquoted sources, "misrepresented data, . . . skewed documents [and] ignored or deliberately suppressed material when it ran counter to his arguments. . . . [W]hen I followed Irving's claims and statements back to the original documents on which they purported to rest . . . Irving's work in this respect was revealed as a house of cards, a vast apparatus of deception and deceit."

The sources in this anthology can be read on several levels. First, they enhance understanding of the historical period in which they were written, shedding light on how people lived and thought and the chief concerns of the time. Several of the sources, written by some of humanity's greatest minds, have broader implications. They are founts of wisdom, providing insights of enduring value into human nature and the human condition. The documents also reveal the evolution of those core ideas and values—reason, freedom, and respect for human dignity—that constitute the Western heritage. Equally important, several documents reveal the precariousness of these values and the threats to them. It is the hope of the editor that an understanding of the evolution of the Western tradition will foster a renewed commitment to its essential ideals.

The documents in these volumes often represent human beings struggling with the vital questions of their day. As such they invite the reader to react actively and imaginatively to the times in which they were produced and to the individuals who produced them. The documents should also be approached with a critical eye. The reader has always to raise several pointed questions regarding the author's motivation, objectivity, logic, and accuracy. In addition, depending on the content of a particular document, the reader should consider the following questions: What does the document reveal about the times in which it was written? About the author? About the nature, evolution, and meaning of the Western tradition? About human nature and human relations? About good and evil? About progress? About war and peace? About gender relations? About life and death? Doubtless other questions will come to mind. In many instances, no doubt, the documents will impel readers to reflect on current issues and their own lives.

CHAPTER I

The Ancient Near East

STROLL IN THE GARDEN, Eighteenth Dynasty, c. 1350 B.C. This relief portrays members of the Egyptian royal family. *(Limestone, 24 cm high. Ägyptisches Museum und Papyrussammlung, Staatliche Museum zu Berlin. [Farabb. s.S. 91])*

The world's first civilizations arose some five thousand years ago in the river valleys of Mesopotamia (later Iraq) and Egypt. In these Near Eastern lands people built cities, organized states with definite boundaries, invented writing, engaged in large-scale trade, practiced specialization of labor, and erected huge monuments: all activities that historians associate with civilization. Scholars emphasize the fact that civilizations emerged in the river valleys—the Tigris and Euphrates in Mesopotamia and the Nile in Egypt. When they overflowed their banks, these rivers deposited fertile soil, which could provide a food surplus required to sustain life in cities. The early inhabitants of these valleys drained swamps and built irrigation works, enabling them to harness the rivers for human advantage. In the process they also strengthened the bonds of cooperation, a necessary ingredient of civilization.

Religion and myth were the central forces in these early civilizations. They pervaded all phases of life, providing people with satisfying explanations for the operations of nature and the mystery of death and justifying traditional rules of morality. Natural objects—the sun, the river, the mountain—were seen as either gods or as the abodes of gods. The political life of the Near East was theocratic: that is, people regarded their rulers either as divine or as representatives of the gods and believed that law originated with the gods. Near Eastern art and literature were dominated by religious themes.

Although the cultural patterns of both civilizations were similar—in both, religion and theocratic kingship played a dominant role—there were significant differences between the two. Whereas in Egypt the pharaoh was considered divine, rulers in Mesopotamia were regarded as exceptional human beings whom the gods had selected to act as their agents. Second, the natural environment of the Egyptians fostered a sense of security and an optimistic outlook toward life. Natural barriers—deserts, the Mediterranean Sea, and cataracts in the Nile—protected Egypt from invasion, and the overflowing of the Nile was regular and predictable, ensuring a good harvest. In contrast, Mesopotamia, without natural barriers, suffered from frequent invasions, and the Tigris and Euphrates rivers were unpredictable. Sometimes there was insufficient overflow, and the land was afflicted with drought; at other times, rampaging floods devastated the fields. These conditions promoted a pessimistic outlook, which pervaded Mesopotamian civilization.

Egyptians, Mesopotamians, and other Near Eastern peoples developed a rich urban culture and made important contributions to later civilizations. They established bureaucracies, demonstrated creativity in art and literature, fashioned effective systems of mathematics, and advanced the knowledge of architecture, metallurgy, and engineering. The wheel, the plow, the phonetic alphabet, and the calendar derive from the Near East. Both the Hebrews (Jews) and the Greeks, the principal sources of Western civilization, had contact with these older civilizations and adopted many of their cultural forms. But, even more important for the shaping of Western civilization was how the Hebrews and the Greeks broke with the essential style of Near Eastern society and conceived new outlooks, new points of departure for the human mind.

The Hebrews borrowed elements from the older civilizations of the Near East. Thus there are parallels between Babylonian literature and biblical accounts of the Creation, the Flood, and the Tower of Babel. Nevertheless, Israelite religion marks a profound break with the outlook of the surrounding civilizations of the Near East.

There are two fundamental characteristics of ancient Near Eastern religion. First, the Near Eastern mind saw gods everywhere in nature; the moon and stars, rivers and mountains, thunder and wind storms were either gods or the dwelling places of gods. The Near Eastern mind invented myths—stories about the gods' birth, deeds, death, and resurrection. Second, Near Eastern gods were not fully sovereign. They were not eternal but were born or created; their very existence and power depended on some prior realm. They grew old, became ill, required food, and even died—all limitations on their power. The gods were subject to magic and destiny—forces that preceded them in time and surpassed them in power—and if the gods did wrong, destiny, or fate, punished them.

Hebrew religious thought evolved through the history and experience of the Jewish people. Over the centuries the Hebrew view of God came to differ markedly from Near Eastern ideas about the gods and the world. For the Hebrews, God was not only one, he was also *transcendent*—above nature. This means that natural objects were not divine, holy, or alive, but were merely God's creations. In contrast to the Near Eastern gods, Yahweh was fully *sovereign,* absolutely free; there were no limitations whatsoever on his power. He was eternal and the source of all in the universe; he did not answer to fate but himself determined the consequences of wrongdoing; he was not subject to any primordial power or to anything outside or above him.

The Hebrew conception of God led to a revolutionary view of the human being. The Hebrews believed that God had given the individual moral autonomy—the capacity to choose between good and evil. Therefore, men and women had to measure their actions by God's laws and were responsible for their own behavior. Such an outlook led people to become aware of themselves—their moral potential and personal worth. From the Hebrews came a fundamental value of the Western tradition—the inviolable worth and dignity of the individual.

1 Mesopotamian Protest Against Death

The *Epic of Gilgamesh,* the greatest work of Mesopotamian literature, was written about 2000 B.C. It utilized legends about Gilgamesh, probably a historical figure who ruled the city of Uruk about 2600 B.C. The story deals with a profound theme—the human protest against death. In the end, Gilgamesh learns to accept reality: there is no escape from death. While the *Epic of Gilgamesh* is an expression of the pessimism that pervaded Mesopotamian life, it also reveals the Mesopotamians' struggle to come to terms with reality.

EPIC OF GILGAMESH[1]

Human Ninsun
Gilgamesh
Aruru
(creation goddess)
↓
creates
↓
Enkidu

The *Epic of Gilgamesh* involves the gods in human activities. Because King Gilgamesh, son of a human father and the goddess Ninsun, drives his subjects too hard, they appeal to the gods for help. The gods decide that a man of Gilgamesh's immense vigor and strength requires a rival with similar attributes with whom he can contend. The creation goddess, Aruru, is instructed to create a man worthy of Gilgamesh. From clay she fashions Enkidu in the image of Anu, the god of the heavens and father of all the gods. Enkidu is a powerful man who roams with the animals and destroys traps set by hunters, one of whom appeals to King Gilgamesh. The two of them, accompanied by a harlot, find Enkidu at a watering place frequented by animals. The harlot removes her clothes and seduces Enkidu, who spends a week with her, oblivious to everything else. After this encounter, the bond between Enkidu and the animals is broken. He now enters civilization and is befriended by Gilgamesh, with whom he slays the terrible monster Humbaba.

Returning to Uruk after the encounter with Humbaba, Gilgamesh washes away the grime of battle and dons his royal clothes; thus arrayed he attracts the goddess of love, Ishtar, patroness of Uruk, who proposes marriage, but because of Ishtar's previous marriages and infidelities, Gilgamesh refuses. Ishtar falls into a bitter rage and appeals to her father, the god Anu, to unleash the fearful Bull of Heaven on Gilgamesh. However, Gilgamesh and Enkidu together slay the beast. To avenge the deaths of Humbaba and the Bull of Heaven, the gods decide that Enkidu shall die. In the following passage, Enkidu dreams of his impending death and the House of Darkness, from which no one returns.

When the daylight came Enkidu got up and cried to Gilgamesh, "O my brother, such a dream I had last night. Anu, Enlil, Ea and heavenly Shamash took counsel together, and Anu said to Enlil, 'Because they have killed the Bull of Heaven, and because they have killed Humbaba who guarded the Cedar Mountain one of the two must die.'. . ."

So Enkidu lay stretched out before Gilgamesh: his tears ran down in streams and he said to Gilgamesh, "O my brother, so dear as you are to

---

[1]Throughout the text, titles original to the source appear in italics. Titles of poems and essays have quotation marks. Titles added by the editors are not italicized.

me, brother, yet they will take me from you." Again he said, "I must sit down on the threshold of the dead and never again will I see my dear brother with my eyes."

. . . In bitterness of spirit he poured out his heart to his friend. "It was I who cut down the cedar, I who levelled the forest, I who slew Humbaba and now see what has become of me. Listen, my friend, this is the dream I dreamed last night. The heavens roared, and earth rumbled back an answer; between them stood I before an awful being, the sombre-faced man-bird; he had directed on me his purpose. His was a vampire face, his foot was a lion's foot, his hand was an eagle's talon. He fell on me and his claws were in my hair, he held me fast and I smothered; then he transformed me so that my arms became wings covered with feathers. He turned his stare towards me, and he led me away to the palace of Irkalla, the Queen of Darkness, to the house from which none who enters ever returns, down the road from which there is no coming back.

"There is the house whose people sit in darkness; dust is their food and clay their meat. They are clothed like birds with wings for covering, they see no light, they sit in darkness. I entered the house of dust and I saw the kings of the earth, their crowns put away for ever; rulers and princes, all those who once wore kingly crowns and ruled the world in the days of old. They who had stood in the place of the gods like Anu and Enlil, stood now like servants to fetch baked meats in the house of dust, to carry cooked meat and cold water from the water-skin. In the house of dust which I entered were high priests and acolytes, priests of the incantation and of ecstasy; there were servers of the temple, and there was Etana, that king of Kish whom the eagle carried to heaven in the days of old. I saw also Samuqan, god of cattle, and there was Ereshkigal the Queen of the Underworld; and Belit-Sheri squatted in front of her, she who is recorder of the gods and keeps the book of death. She held a tablet from which she read. She raised her head, she saw me and spoke: 'Who has brought this one here?' Then I awoke like a man drained of blood who wanders alone in a waste of rushes; like one whom the bailiff has seized and his heart pounds with terror."

Gilgamesh had peeled off his clothes, he listened to his words and wept quick tears, Gilgamesh listened and his tears flowed. . . .

This day on which Enkidu dreamed came to an end and he lay stricken with sickness. One whole day he lay on his bed and his suffering increased. He said to Gilgamesh, the friend on whose account he had left the wilderness, "Once I ran for you, for the water of life, and I now have nothing." A second day he lay on his bed and Gilgamesh watched over him but the sickness increased. A third day he lay on his bed, he called out to Gilgamesh, rousing him up. Now he was weak and his eyes were blind with weeping. Ten days he lay and his suffering increased, eleven and twelve days he lay on his bed of pain. Then he called to Gilgamesh, "My friend, the great goddess cursed me and I must die in shame. I shall not die like a man fallen in battle; I feared to fall, but happy is the man who falls in the battle, for I must die in shame." And Gilgamesh wept over Enkidu. With the first light of dawn he raised his voice and said to the counsellors of Uruk:

"Hear me, great ones of Uruk,
I weep for Enkidu, my friend,
Bitterly moaning like a woman mourning
I weep for my brother.
O Enkidu, my brother,
You were the axe at my side,
My hand's strength, the sword in my belt,
The shield before me,
A glorious robe, my fairest ornament;
An evil Fate has robbed me.

. . .

All the people of Eridu
Weep for you Enkidu.

. . .

What is this sleep which holds you now?
You are lost in the dark and cannot hear me."

He touched his heart but it did not beat, nor did he lift his eyes again. When Gilgamesh touched his heart it did not beat. So Gilgamesh laid a veil, as one veils the bride, over his friend.

He began to rage like a lion, like a lioness robbed of her whelps. This way and that he paced round the bed, he tore out his hair and strewed it around. He dragged off his splendid robes and flung them down as though they were abominations.

In the first light of dawn Gilgamesh cried out, "I made you rest on a royal bed, you reclined on a couch at my left hand, the princes of the earth kissed your feet. I will cause all the people of Uruk to weep over you and raise the dirge of the dead. The joyful people will stoop with sorrow; and when you have gone to the earth I will let my hair grow long for your sake, I will wander through the wilderness in the skin of a lion." The next day also, in the first light, Gilgamesh lamented; seven days and seven nights he wept for Enkidu, until the worm fastened on him. Only then he gave him up to the earth, for the Anunnaki, the judges [of the dead],[2] had seized him. . . .

In his despair, Gilgamesh is confronted with the reality of his own death. Yearning for eternal life, he seeks Utnapishtim, legendary king of the city of Shurrupak, a man to whom the gods had granted everlasting life.

Bitterly Gilgamesh wept for his friend Enkidu; he wandered over the wilderness as a hunter, he roamed over the plains; in his bitterness he cried, "How can I rest, how can I be at peace? Despair is in my heart. What my brother is now, that shall I be when I am dead. Because I am afraid of death I will go as best I can to find Utnapishtim whom they call the Faraway, for he has entered the assembly of the gods." So Gilgamesh travelled over the wilderness, he wandered over the grasslands, a long journey, in search of Utnapishtim, whom the gods took after the deluge; and they set him to live in the land of Dilmun, in the garden of the sun; and to him alone of men they gave everlasting life. . . .

In the garden of the gods, Gilgamesh speaks with Siduri, the divine winemaker, who tells him that his search for eternal life is hopeless.

". . . My friend who was very dear to me and who endured dangers beside me, Enkidu my brother, whom I loved, the end of mortality has overtaken him. I wept for him seven days and nights till the worm fastened on him. Because of my brother I am afraid of death, because of my brother I stray through the wilderness and cannot rest. But now, young woman, maker of wine, since I have seen your face do not let me see the face of death which I dread so much."

She answered, "Gilgamesh, where are you hurrying to? You will never find that life for which you are looking. When the gods created man they allotted to him death, but life they retained in their own keeping. As for you, Gilgamesh, fill your belly with good things; day and night, night and day, dance and be merry, feast and rejoice. Let your clothes be fresh, bathe yourself in water, cherish the little child that holds your hand, and make your wife happy in your embrace; for this too is the lot of man."

But Gilgamesh said to Siduri, the young woman, "How can I be silent, how can I rest, when Enkidu whom I love is dust, and I too shall die and be laid in the earth. You live by the sea-shore and look into the heart of it; young woman, tell me now, which is the way to Utnapishtim, the son of Ubara-Tutu? What directions are there for the passage; give me, oh, give me directions, I will cross the Ocean if it is possible; if it is not I will wander still farther in the wilderness." . . .

---

[2]Throughout the text, words in brackets have been added as glosses by the editors. Brackets around glosses from the original sources have been changed to parentheses to distinguish them.

Siduri instructs Gilgamesh how to reach Utnapishtim. Ferried across the "waters of death" by a boatman, Gilgamesh meets Utnapishtim. But he, too, cannot give Gilgamesh the eternal life for which he yearns.

. . . "Oh father Utnapishtim, you who have entered the assembly of the gods, I wish to question you concerning the living and the dead, how shall I find the life for which I am searching?"

Utnapishtim said, "There is no permanence. Do we build a house to stand for ever, do we seal a contract to hold for all time? Do brothers divide an inheritance to keep for ever, does the flood-time of rivers endure? It is only the nymph of the dragon-fly who sheds her larva and sees the sun in his glory. From the days of old there is no permanence. The sleeping and the dead, how alike they are, they are like a painted death. What is there between the master and the servant when both have fulfilled their doom? When the Anunnaki, the judges, come together, and Mammetun the mother of destinies, together they decree the fates of men. Life and death they allot but the day of death they do not disclose."

The tale concludes with one of several Near Eastern flood stories that preceded the account of Noah in Genesis.

REVIEW QUESTIONS

1. Describe the condition of the dead as envisioned in Enkidu's dream.
2. Describe the stages of Gilgamesh's reaction to Enkidu's death. Do these seem plausible psychologically? Explain.
3. What philosophic consolation did the goddess Siduri and Utnapishtim offer Gilgamesh?
4. Historians often comment on the pessimism or sense of the tragic that is reflected in Mesopotamian literature. To what extent is this true in the story of Gilgamesh?

2 Mesopotamian Concepts of Justice

A significant source of information about the life of the ancient peoples of Mesopotamia is a code of laws issued about 1750 B.C. by the Babylonian king Hammurabi (1792–1750 B.C.). Discovered by archaeologists in 1901, the code was inscribed on a stone that shows the king accepting the laws from the sun god, Shamash, who was also the Babylonian god of justice.

These laws offer striking insights into the moral values, class structure, gender relationships, and roles of kingship and religion in Babylonian society. The 282 laws cover a range of public and private matters: marriage and family relations, negligence, fraud, commercial contracts, duties of public officials, property and inheritance, crimes and punishments, and techniques of legal procedure. The prologue to the code reveals the Mesopotamian concept of the priest-king—a ruler chosen by a god to administer his will on earth. In it, Hammurabi asserted that he had a divine duty to uphold justice in the land, to punish the wicked, and to further the welfare of the people.

CODE OF HAMMURABI

Two distinct approaches to choice of punishment for crime are found in Hammurabi's code with its numerous laws. In some instances, the guilty party is required to pay a monetary compensation to the victim, a tradition traceable to the earliest known Sumerian laws. Another approach, also found in the later Hebrew codes of law, is the principle of exact retaliation: "an eye for an eye, a tooth for a tooth."

Another feature of Hammurabi's code is that the penalties vary according to the social status of the victim. Three classes are represented: free men and women (called *patricians* in the reading here); commoners (or *plebeians*), not wholly free, but dependents of the state or perhaps serfs on landed estates; and slaves. The patricians are protected by the law of retaliation. People of the lower classes receive only monetary compensation if they are victims of a crime.

196. If a man has knocked out the eye of a patrician, his eye shall be knocked out.

197. If he has broken the limb of a patrician, his limb shall be broken.

198. If he has knocked out the eye of a plebeian or has broken the limb of a plebeian, he shall pay one mina[1] of silver.

199. If he has knocked out the eye of a patrician's servant, or broken the limb of a patrician's servant, he shall pay half his value.

200. If a patrician has knocked out the tooth of a man that is his equal, his tooth shall be knocked out.

201. If he has knocked out the tooth of a plebeian, he shall pay one-third of a mina of silver. . . .

209. If a man has struck a free woman with child, and has caused her to miscarry, he shall pay ten shekels[2] for her miscarriage.

210. If that woman die, his daughter shall be killed.

211. If it be the daughter of a plebeian, that has miscarried through his blows, he shall pay five shekels of silver.

212. If that woman die, he shall pay half a mina of silver.

213. If he has struck a man's maid and caused her to miscarry, he shall pay two shekels of silver.

214. If that woman die, he shall pay one-third of a mina of silver.

Many laws relating to business transactions show the importance of trade in Mesopotamian society and the willingness of the government to intervene in order to regulate the practices of the marketplace.

---

218. If a surgeon has operated with the bronze lancet on a patrician for a serious injury, and has caused his death, or has removed a cataract for a patrician, with the bronze lancet, and has made him lose his eye, his hands shall be cut off.

219. If the surgeon has treated a serious injury of a plebeian's slave, with the bronze lancet, and has caused his death, he shall render slave for slave.

220. If he has removed a cataract with the bronze lancet, and made the slave lose his eye, he shall pay half his value.

221. If a surgeon has cured the limb of a patrician, or has doctored a diseased bowel, the

---

[1]The mina was a weight of silver used to express monetary value. (Throughout the text, the editors' notes carry numbers, whereas notes from the original sources are indicated by asterisks, daggers, et cetera. An exception is made for editorial notes pertaining to Scriptures, which have symbols rather than numbers.)

[2]The shekel, also a weight of monetary value, was worth far less than the mina.

patient shall pay five shekels of silver to the surgeon.

222. If he be a plebeian, he shall pay three shekels of silver.

223. If he be a man's slave, the owner of the slave shall give two shekels of silver to the doctor. . . .

228. If a builder has built a house for a man, and finished it, he shall pay him a fee of two shekels of silver, for each *SAR*[3] built on.

229. If a builder has built a house for a man, and has not made his work sound, and the house he built has fallen, and caused the death of its owner, that builder shall be put to death.

230. If it is the owner's son that is killed, the builder's son shall be put to death.

231. If it is the slave of the owner that is killed, the builder shall give slave for slave to the owner of the house.

232. If he has caused the loss of goods, he shall render back whatever he has destroyed. Moreover, because he did not make sound the house he built, and it fell, at his own cost he shall rebuild the house that fell. . . .

271. If a man has hired oxen, a wagon, and its driver, he shall pay one hundred and sixty *KA*[4] of corn daily. . . .

275. If a man has hired a boat, its hire is three *ŠE*[5] of silver daily.

The outcome of some procedures depended upon the will of the gods: for example, an accused woman could place her fate in the hands of a god by plunging into a river, canal, or reservoir; if she did not drown, she was declared innocent. In other cases, legal culpability could be removed by invoking a god to bear witness to the truth of one's testimony. The law was particularly harsh on perjurers and those who made grave charges that they could not prove in court.

1. If a man has accused another of laying a *nêrtu* (death spell?) upon him, but has not proved it, he shall be put to death.

2. If a man has accused another of laying a *kišpu* (spell) upon him, but has not proved it, the accused shall go to the sacred river, he shall plunge into the sacred river, and if the sacred river shall conquer him, he that accused him shall take possession of his house. If the sacred river shall show his innocence and he is saved, his accuser shall be put to death. He that plunged into the sacred river shall appropriate the house of him that accused him.

3. If a man has borne false witness in a trial, or has not established the statement that he has made, if that case be a capital trial, that man shall be put to death.

4. If he has borne false witness in a civil law case, he shall pay the damages in that suit. . . .

9. If a man has lost property and some of it be detected in the possession of another, and the holder has said, "A man sold it to me, I bought it in the presence of witnesses"; and if the claimant has said, "I can bring witnesses who know it to be property lost by me"; then the alleged buyer on his part shall produce the man who sold it to him and the witnesses before whom he bought it; the claimant shall on his part produce the witnesses who know it to be his lost property. The judge shall examine their pleas. The witnesses to the sale and the witnesses who identify the lost property shall state on oath what they know. Such a seller is the thief and shall be put to death. The owner of the lost property shall recover his lost property. The buyer shall recoup himself from the seller's estate.

The laws concerned with family relationships placed great power in the hands of husbands and fathers, yet the code tried to protect women and children from neglect and mistreatment. Divorce initiated by either husband or wife was permitted under specific circumstances.

---

[3]*SAR* was a measure of land.
[4]*KA* stood for a bulk measure.
[5]*ŠE* was another monetary weight of silver.

141. If a man's wife, living in her husband's house, has persisted in going out, has acted the fool, has wasted her house, has belittled her husband, he shall prosecute her. If her husband has said, "I divorce her," she shall go her way; he shall give her nothing as her price of divorce. If her husband has said, "I will not divorce her," he may take another woman to wife; the wife shall live as a slave in her husband's house.

142. If a woman has hated her husband and has said, "You shall not possess me," her past shall be inquired into, as to what she lacks. If she has been discreet, and has no vice, and her husband has gone out, and has greatly belittled her, that woman has no blame, she shall take her marriage-portion and go off to her father's house.

143. If she has not been discreet, has gone out, ruined her house, belittled her husband, she shall be drowned. . . .

148. If a man has married a wife and a disease has seized her, if he is determined to marry a second wife, he shall marry her. He shall not divorce the wife whom the disease has seized. In the home they made together she shall dwell, and he shall maintain her as long as she lives. . . .

168. If a man has determined to disinherit his son and has declared before the judge, "I cut off my son," the judge shall inquire into the son's past, and, if the son has not committed a grave misdemeanor such as should cut him off from sonship, the father shall (not) disinherit his son.

169. If he has committed a grave crime against his father, which cuts him off from sonship, for the first offence he shall pardon him. If he has committed a grave crime a second time, the father shall cut off his son from sonship. . . .

195. If a son has struck his father, his hands shall be cut off.

One of the most unusual features of the law dealt with the failure of the government officials of a city or a district to prevent banditry. The code held the governor responsible for the breach of the peace and required him to compensate the bandit's victim. Government officials found guilty of extortion, bribery, or use of public employees for private purposes were severely punished.

---

23. If the highwayman has not been caught, the man that has been robbed shall state on oath what he has lost and the city or district governor in whose territory or district the robbery took place shall restore to him what he has lost.

24. If a life (has been lost), the city or district governor shall pay one mina of silver to the deceased's relatives. . . .

34. If either a governor, or a prefect, has appropriated the property of a levymaster,[6] has hired him out, has robbed him by high-handedness at a trial, has taken the salary which the king gave to him, that governor, or prefect, shall be put to death. . . .

---

[6]A levymaster was a military official.

REVIEW QUESTIONS

1. What does Hammurabi's code reveal about the social structure of Babylonian society?
2. Explain the role of religion in the administration of law in Babylonia.
3. How did Hammurabi seek to regulate business practices among the Babylonian people?
4. What do the laws indicate about the status of women in Babylonian society?
5. How did Hammurabi try to control corrupt practices among the government officials of Babylonia?

3 Divine Kingship in Egypt

Theocratic monarchy, in which the ruler was considered either a god or a representative of the gods, was the basic political institution of ancient Near Eastern civilization. Kings were believed to rule in accordance with divine commands, and law was viewed as god-given. Theocracy as a form of government that subordinates the individual to the gods and their earthly representatives is compatible with mythical thought that sees nature and human destiny controlled by divine beings.

The theocratic mind of the Near East did not conceive the idea of political freedom. Mesopotamians and Egyptians were not free citizens but subjects who obeyed unquestioningly the edicts of their god-kings or priest-kings. Nor did Near Easterners arrive at a systematically rational way of analyzing the nature and purpose of government and the merits or demerits of political institutions. To them the power of their gods and rulers was absolute and not an issue for discussion or reflection.

Divine kingship was the basic political institution of ancient Egyptian civilization. The Egyptians believed their king or pharaoh to be both a god and a man, the earthly embodiment of the god Horus. He was regarded as a benevolent protector who controlled the flood waters of the Nile, kept the irrigation system in working order, maintained justice in the land, and expressed the will of the gods by his words. It was expected that when the pharaoh died and joined his fellow gods, he would still help his living subjects. The Egyptians rejoiced in the rule of their all-powerful god-king.

HYMNS TO THE PHARAOHS

The first reading is a hymn to the new god-king Ramesses IV (c. 1166 B.C.). The second reading is a hymn to a deceased pharaoh, perhaps Unnos (c. 2600 B.C.).

TO RAMESSES IV

What a happy day! Heaven and earth rejoice, (for) thou art the great lord of Egypt.

They that had fled have come again to their towns, and they that were hidden have again come forth.

They that hungered are satisfied and happy, and they that thirsted are drunken.

They that were naked are clad in fine linen, and they that were dirty have white garments.

They that were in prison are set free, and he that was in bonds is full of joy.

They that were at strife in this land are reconciled. High Niles [beneficial floods] have come from their sources, that they may refresh the hearts of others.

Widows, their houses stand open, and they suffer travellers to enter.

Maidens rejoice and repeat their songs of gladness (?). They are arrayed in ornaments and say (?): "——— he createth generation on generation. Thou ruler, thou wilt endure for ever."

The ships rejoice on the deep ———.
They come to land with wind or oars,

They are satisfied . . . when it is said:

"King Hekmaatrē-Beloved-of-Amūn[1] again
    weareth the crown.

The son of [the sun-god] Rē, Ramesses, hath re-
    ceived the office of his father."

All lands say unto him:

"Beautiful is Horus on the throne of Amūn who
    sendeth him forth,

(Amūn) the protector of the Prince, who bringeth
    every land."

TO A DECEASED PHARAOH

The King has not died the death: he has become
one who rises (like the morning sun) from the
horizon. He rests from life (like the setting sun)
in the West, but he dawns anew in the East.
O King, you have not departed dead: you have
departed living! Have you said that he would
die?—nay, he dies not: this king lives for ever.

_____

[1]Hekmaatrē was another name of this pharaoh.

He has escaped his day of death. O lofty one
among the imperishable stars!—you shall not
ever perish. Loose the embalming bandages!—
they are not bandages (at all): they are the tresses
of the goddess Nephthys (as she leans down over
you). Men fall, and their name ceases to be:
therefore God takes hold of this king by his arm,
and leads him to the sky, that he may not die
upon earth amongst men. This king flies away
from you, you mortals. He is not of the earth, he
is of the sky. He flies as a cloud to the sky, he
who was like a bird at the masthead. He goes up
to heaven like the hawks, and his feathers are like
those of the wild geese; he rushes at heaven like a
crane, he kisses heaven like the falcon, he leaps to
heaven like the locust. He ascends to the sky!
He ascends to the sky on the wind, on the wind!
The stairs of the sky are let down for him that he
may ascend thereon to heaven. O gods, put your
arms under the king: raise him, lift him to the
sky. To the sky! To the sky! To the great throne
amongst the gods!

GUIDELINES FOR THE RULER

**Generally, pharaohs were mindful of their responsibilities. To prepare his son to
rule, a pharaoh or his vizier (a high executive officer) might compile a list of instructions, like the ones that follow. These instructions were most likely composed by a vizier of King Issi (c. 2400 B.C.).**

If thou art a leader and givest command to the
multitude, strive after every excellence, until
there be no fault in thy nature. Truth is good
and its worth is lasting, and it hath not been
disturbed since the day of its creator,* whereas
he that transgresseth its ordinances is punished.
It lieth as a (right) path in front of him that
knoweth nothing. Wrong-doing (?) hath never
yet brought its venture to port. Evil indeed win-
neth wealth, but the strength of truth is that it

endureth, and the (upright) man saith: "It is the
property of my father.". . .†

_____

The following excerpts come from the instructions of Amenemhet I (1991–1962 B.C.),
who prepared them for his son.

_____

I gave to the poor and nourished the orphan,
I caused him that was nothing to reach the goal,
even as him that was of account. . . .

_____

*Rē [the sun god], who brought truth into the world.

_____

†That my father brought me up in the ways of truth is the
best thing that he has bequeathed me.

None hungered in my years, none thirsted in them. Men dwelt in (peace) through that which I wrought; . . . all that I commanded was as it should be. . . .

These instructions were prepared for King Merikare (c. 2050 B.C.) by his father.

Be not evil, it is good to be kindly. Cause thy monument‡ to endure through the love of thee. . . . Then men thank God on thine account, men praise thy goodness and pray for thine health. . . . But keep thine eyes open, one that is trusting will become one that is afflicted. . . .

Do right so long as thou abidest on the earth. Calm the weeper, oppress no widow, expel no man from the possessions of his father. . . . Take heed lest thou punish wrongfully.

Exalt not the son of one of high degree more than him that is of lowly birth, but take to thyself a man because of his actions.

---

‡The remembrance of thee.

REVIEW QUESTIONS

1. What were the duties expected of an Egyptian king?
2. Discuss the role of religion in sustaining the authority of rulers over their subjects.

4 Religious Inspiration of Akhenaten

Pharaoh Amenhotep IV (1369–1353 B.C.) was a religious mystic who conceived of divinity in a manner approaching monotheism. He suppressed the worship of the many gods of Egypt and insisted that only Aton—the sun god—and himself, the king and son of Aton, be worshiped by the Egyptians. Aton was viewed as the creator of the world, a god of love, peace, and justice. To promote the exclusive worship of Aton and himself, Amenhotep changed his name to Akhenaten ("It is well with Aton"), and near modern Tell El-Amarna he built a new capital city, Akhetaten, which became the center of the new religious cult. The new religion perished quickly after Akhenaten's death. There is no evidence that this step toward a monotheistic conception of the divine had any later influence on the Hebrews.

The masses of Egypt were not influenced by Akhenaten's religious inspiration, and he was resisted by the priests, who clung to traditional beliefs. His immediate successors abandoned the new capital and had the monuments to Aton destroyed.

HYMN TO ATON

Akhenaten's religious outlook inspired remarkable works of art and literature. In the following hymn, Akhenaten glorifies Aton in words that are reminiscent of Psalm 104.

Thou appearest beautifully on the horizon of
heaven,
Thou living Aton, the beginning of life!
When thou art risen on the eastern horizon,
Thou hast filled every land with thy beauty.
Thou art gracious, great, glistening, and high
over every land;
Thy rays encompass the lands to the limit of
all that thou hast made. . . .
At daybreak, when thou arisest on the horizon,
When thou shinest as the Aton by day,
Thou drivest away the darkness and givest thy
rays.
The Two Lands[1] are in festivity *every day,*
Awake and standing upon (their) feet,
For thou hast raised them up.
Washing their bodies, taking (their) clothing,
Their arms are (raised) in praise at thy appear-
ance.
All the world, they do their work.

All beasts are content with their pasturage;
Trees and plants are flourishing.
The birds which fly from their nests,
Their wings are (stretched out) in praise to
thy *ka.*[2]
All beasts spring upon (their) feet.
Whatever flies and alights,
They live when thou hast risen (for) them.
The ships are sailing north and south as well,
For every way is open at thy appearance.
The fish in the river dart before thy face;
Thy rays are in the midst of the great green sea.

Creator of seed in women,
Thou who makest fluid into man,
Who maintainest the son in the womb of his
mother,
Who soothest him with that which stills his
weeping,
Thou nurse (even) in the womb,
Who givest breath to sustain all that he had
made!
When he descends from the womb to *breathe*

On the day when he is born,
Thou openest his mouth completely,
Thou suppliest his necessities.
When the chick in the egg speaks within the
shell,
Thou givest him breath within it to maintain
him.
When thou hast made him his fulfillment
within the egg, to break it,
He comes forth from the egg to speak at his
completed (time);
He walks upon his legs when he comes forth
from it.

How manifold it is, what thou hast made!
They are hidden from the face (of man).
O sole god, like whom there is no other!
Thou didst create the world according to thy
desire,
Whilst thou wert alone:
All men, cattle, and wild beasts,
Whatever is on earth, going upon (its) feet,
And what is on high, flying with its wings.

The countries of Syria and Nubia,[3] the *land* of
Egypt,
Thou settest every man in his place,
Thou suppliest their necessities:
Everyone has his food, and his time of life is
reckoned.
Their tongues are separate in speech,
And their natures as well;
Their skins are distinguished,
As thou distinguishest the foreign peoples.
Thou makest a Nile in the underworld,[4]
Thou bringest it forth as thou desirest
To maintain the people (of Egypt)
According as thou madest them for thyself,
The lord of all of them, wearying (himself)
with them,
The lord of every land, rising for them,
The Aton of the day, great of majesty.

---

[1]The Two Lands were the two political divisions of Egypt,
Upper and Lower Egypt. They were usually governed by
the same king.
[2]The *ka* was a protective and guiding spirit, which each person was thought to have.

[3]Syria was an ancient country, larger than modern Syria,
north of modern Israel and Jordan; Nubia was a kingdom
located south of the first cataract of the Nile. It is now in
Sudan.
[4]The Egyptians believed that the source of their Nile was in
a huge body of water, which they called Nun, under the
earth.

1. Why was the sun a likely choice for a god conceived as one and universal?
2. What were some of the gifts of Aton to humanity?
3. What does the poem reveal about Akhenaten's view of the world and its peoples?

5 The Myth-Making Outlook of the Ancient Near East

The civilizations of the ancient Near East were based on a way of thinking that is fundamentally different from the modern scientific outlook. The peoples of Mesopotamia and Egypt interpreted nature and human experience through myths, which narrated the deeds of gods who in some distant past had brought forth the world and human beings. These myths made the universe and life intelligible for Near Eastern people.

The difference between scientific thinking and mythical thinking is profound. The scientific mind views physical nature as an *it*—inanimate, impersonal, and governed by universal law. The myth-making (mythopoeic) mind sees nature as personified—alive, with individual wills, gods, and demons who manipulate things according to their desires. The scientific mind holds that natural objects obey universal rules; hence the location of planets, the speed of objects, and the onset of a hurricane can be predicted. The myth-making mind has no awareness of repetitive laws inherent in nature; rather it attributes all occurrences to the actions of gods, whose behavior is often unpredictable. The scientific mind appeals to reason—it analyzes nature logically and systematically and searches for general principles that govern the phenomena. The myth-making mind explains nature and human experience by narrating stories about the gods and their deeds. Myth is an expression of the poetic imagination; it proclaims a truth that is emotionally satisfying, not one produced by intellectual analysis and synthesis. It gives order to human experiences and justifies traditional rules of morality. Mythical explanations of nature and human experience, appealing essentially to the imagination, enrich perception and feeling; they make life seem less overwhelming and death less frightening.

PERSONIFICATION OF NATURAL OBJECTS

The mythopoeic mind accounts for causation by personifying inanimate substances. To explain through personification is to seek the *who* behind events, to attribute these events to the will of a god (or to an object suffused with divine presence). Thus if a river did not rise, it was because it refused to do so; either the river or the gods were angry at the people.

The following excerpts from Mesopotamian literature are examples of personification. While we regard table salt as an ordinary mineral, to the Mesopotamians it was alive, a fellow being. In one passage, a person appeals to salt to end his bewitchment. In the second, an afflicted person who believes himself bewitched calls on fire to destroy his enemies.

O SALT

O Salt, created in a clean place,
For food of gods did *Enlil* [father of the
    Sumerian gods] destine thee.
Without thee no meal is set out in *Ekur,*
Without thee god, king, lord, and prince do
    not smell incense.
I am so-and-so, the son of so-and-so,
Held captive by enchantment,
Held in fever by bewitchment.
O Salt, break my enchantment! Loose my spell!
Take from me the bewitchment!—And as My
    Creator
I shall extol thee.

SCORCHING FIRE

Scorching Fire, warlike son of Heaven,
Thou, the fiercest of thy brethren,
Who like Moon and Sun decidest lawsuits—
Judge thou my case, hand down the verdict.
Burn the man and woman who bewitched me;
Burn, O Fire, the man and woman who be-
    witched me;
Scorch, O Fire, the man and woman who be-
    witched me;
Burn them, O Fire;
Scorch them, O Fire;
Take hold of them, O Fire;
Consume them, O Fire;
Destroy them, O Fire.

ENUMA ELISH
THE BABYLONIAN GENESIS

The Mesopotamian creation epic *Enuma Elish* (Poem of Creation) is another example of mythical thinking. Marduk, the chief god of Babylon, slays Tiamat, a primal mother identified with the salt sea, and then proceeds to construct the cosmos from her carcass.

"Stand thou up, that I and thou meet in
    single combat!"
When Tiamat heard this,
She was like one possessed; she took leave of
    her senses.
In fury Tiamat cried out aloud.
To the roots her legs shook both together.
She recites a charm, keeps casting her spell,
While the gods of battle sharpen their
    weapons.
Then joined issue Tiamat and Marduk, wisest
    of gods.

They strove in single combat, locked in
    battle.
The lord spread out his net to enfold her,
The Evil Wind, which followed behind, he let
    loose in her face.
When Tiamat opened her mouth to consume
    him,
He drove in the Evil Wind that she close not
    her lips.
As the fierce winds charged her belly,
Her body was distended and her mouth was
    wide open.

He released the arrow, it tore her belly,
It cut through her insides, splitting the heart.
Having thus subdued her, he extinguished her
    life.
He cast down her carcass to stand upon it.
After he had slain Tiamat, the leader,
Her band was shattered, her troupe broken
    up;
And the gods, her helpers who marched at her
    side,
Trembling with terror, turned their backs
    about,
In order to save and preserve their lives.
Tightly encircled, they could not escape.
He made them captives and he smashed their
    weapons.
Thrown into the net, they found themselves
    ensnared;
Placed in cells, they were filled with wailing;
Bearing his wrath, they were held imprisoned.

———

When he had vanquished and subdued his
    adversaries. . . .
[Marduk] turned back to Tiamat whom he had
    bound.
The lord trod on the legs of Tiamat,
With his unsparing mace he crushed her skull.
When the arteries of her blood he had severed,
The North Wind bore (it) to places undis-
    closed.
On seeing this, his fathers were joyful and
    jubilant,
They brought gifts of homage, they to him.
Then the lord paused to view her dead body,

That he might divide the monster and do artful
    works.
He split her like a shellfish into two parts:
Half of her he set up and ceiled it as sky,
Pulled down the bar and posted guards.
He bade them to allow not her waters to escape.
He crossed the heavens and surveyed the
    regions.

———

[There] He constructed stations for the great gods.
Fixing their astral likenesses as constellations.
He determined the year by designating the
    zones:
He set up three constellations for each of the
    twelve months.

———

In her [Tiamat's] belly he established the
    zenith.
The Moon he caused to shine, the night (to
    him) entrusting.
He appointed him a creature of the night to
    signify the days. . . .
When Marduk hears the words of the gods.
His heart prompts (him) to fashion artful
    works.
Opening his mouth, he addressed [the god] Ea
To impart the plan he had conceived in his
    heart:
"Blood I will mass and cause bones to be.
I will establish a savage, 'man' shall be his
    name.
Verily, savage-man I will create.
He shall be charged with the service of the gods
    That they might be at ease!"

REVIEW QUESTIONS

1. What is myth? How does mythical thinking differ from scientific thinking?
2. It has been said that humans are myth-making animals and that all human societies
   sustain themselves by creating myths. Discuss.
3. On what occasions might the ancient Mesopotamians have turned to the gods for
   help?
4. How did the Babylonians explain the creation of the heavens?

6 God's Greatness and Human Dignity

The Hebrew Scriptures, which form the Old Testament of the Christian Bible, are a collection of thirty-nine books written over several centuries by several authors. It is a record of more than a thousand years of ancient Jewish history and religious development.

The Hebrew view of God produced a remarkable new concept of human dignity. In God's plan for the universe, the Hebrews believed, human beings are the highest creation, subordinate only to God. Of all God's creatures, only they have been given the freedom to choose between good and evil. To human beings God granted dominion over the earth and the seas.

The Psalms in the Hebrew Scriptures contain 150 hymns extolling Yahweh, some of them written by King David, who ruled c. 1000–961 B.C. In addition to his great success as a warrior and administrator, David was renowned as a harpist and composer.

PSALM 8

In the following song, the psalmist rejoices in the greatness of God. He marvels in the Lord's love for human beings, expressed in their having been given dominion over the earth and its creatures.

O LORD, our Lord,
how majestic is thy name in all the earth!

Thou whose glory above the heavens is
    chanted
    ²by the mouth of babes and infants,
thou hast founded a bulwark because of thy
    foes,
    to still the enemy and the avenger.

³When I look at thy heavens, the work of thy
    fingers,
    the moon and the stars which thou hast
    established;
⁴what is man that thou art mindful of him,

and the son of man that thou dost care for
    him?
⁵Yet thou hast made him little less than God,
    and dost crown him with glory and honor.
⁶Thou hast given him dominion over the works
    of thy hands;
    thou hast put all things under his feet,
⁷all sheep and oxen,
    and also the beasts of the field,
⁸the birds of the air, and the fish of the sea,
    whatever passes along the paths of the sea.

⁹O LORD, our Lord,
    how majestic is thy name in all the earth!

REVIEW QUESTION

1. What does the psalm reveal about the Hebrew view of God? Of human beings?
   Of nature?

7 Humaneness of Hebrew Law

The new awareness of the individual that was produced by the Hebrew concept of God found expression in Hebrew law, which was recorded in the Torah, the first five books of the Scriptures. For the Hebrews, the source of law was, of course, God, and because God is good, his law must be concerned with human welfare. Israelite law incorporated the legal codes and oral traditions of the older civilizations of the Near East. In contrast to the other law codes of the Near East, however, Hebrew laws were more concerned with people than with property; they expressed a humane attitude toward slaves and rejected the idea (so clearly demonstrated in the Code of Hammurabi) of one law for nobles and another for commoners.

EXODUS
THE TEN COMMANDMENTS

Together with the covenant, Moses received the Ten Commandments, which specified God's moral laws. Exodus 20 sets forth the Ten Commandments.

17 Then Moses brought the people out of the camp to meet God; and they took their stand at the foot of the mountain. 18And Mount Sinai was wrapped in smoke, because the LORD descended upon it in fire; and the smoke of it went up like the smoke of a kiln, and the whole mountain quaked greatly. 19And as the sound of the trumpet grew louder and louder, Moses spoke, and God answered him in thunder. 20And the LORD came down upon Mount Sinai, to the top of the mountain; and the LORD called Moses to the top of the mountain, and Moses went up. (Exodus 19)

1 And God spoke all these words, saying,

2 "I am the LORD your God, who brought you out of the land of Egypt, out of the house of bondage.

3 "You shall have no other gods before me.

4 "You shall not make yourself a graven image, or any likeness of anything that is in heaven above, or that is in the earth beneath, or that is in the water under the earth; 5you shall not bow down to them or serve them; for I the LORD your God am a jealous God, visiting the iniquity of the fathers upon the children to the third and the fourth generation of those who hate me, 6but showing steadfast love to thousands of those who love me and keep my commandments.

7 "You shall not take the name of the LORD your God in vain; for the LORD will not hold him guiltless who takes his name in vain.

8 "Remember the sabbath day, to keep it holy. 9Six days you shall labor, and do all your work; 10but the seventh day is a sabbath to the LORD your God; in it you shall not do any work, you, or your son, or your daughter, your manservant, or your maidservant, or your cattle, or the sojourner who is within your gates; 11for in six days the LORD made heaven and earth, the sea, and all that is in them, and rested the seventh day; therefore the LORD blessed the sabbath day and hallowed it.

12 "Honor your father and your mother, that your days may be long in the land which the LORD your God gives you.

13 "You shall not kill.

14 "You shall not commit adultery.

15 "You shall not steal.

16 "You shall not bear false witness against your neighbor.

17 "You shall not covet your neighbor's house; you shall not covet your neighbor's wife, or his manservant, or his maidservant, or his ox, or his ass, or anything that is your neighbor's."

18 Now when all the people perceived the thunderings and the lightnings and the sound of the trumpet and the mountain smoking, the people were afraid and trembled; and they stood afar off, [19]and said to Moses, "You speak to us, and we will hear; but let not God speak to us, lest we die." [20]And Moses said to the people, "Do not fear; for God has come to prove you, and that the fear of him may be before your eyes, that you may not sin."

21 And the people stood afar off, while Moses drew near to the thick cloud where God was. (Exodus 20)

LEVITICUS
NEIGHBOR AND COMMUNITY

To the Hebrews, laws governing economic, social, and political relationships gave practical expression to God's universal standards of morality. Leviticus, the third book in the Scriptures, contains laws governing actions dealing with neighbors and the community.

9 "When you reap the harvest of your land, you shall not reap your field to its very border, neither shall you gather the gleanings after your harvest. [10]And you shall not strip your vineyard bare, neither shall you gather the fallen grapes of your vineyard; you shall leave them for the poor and for the sojourner: I am the LORD your God.

11 "You shall not steal, nor deal falsely, nor lie to one another. [12]And you shall not swear by my name falsely, and so profane the name of your God: I am the LORD.

13 "You shall not oppress your neighbor or rob him. The wages of a hired servant shall not remain with you all night until the morning. [14]You shall not curse the deaf or put a stumbling block before the blind, but you shall fear your God: I am the LORD.

15 "You shall do no injustice in judgment; you shall not be partial to the poor or defer to the great, but in righteousness shall you judge your neighbor. [16]You shall not go up and down as a slanderer among your people, and you shall not stand forth against the life of your neighbor: I am the LORD.

17 "You shall not hate your brother in your heart, but you shall reason with your neighbor, lest you bear sin because of him. [18]You shall not take vengeance or bear any grudge against the sons of your own people, but you shall love your neighbor as yourself: I am the LORD. . . .

33 "When a stranger sojourns with you in your land, you shall not do him wrong. [34]The stranger who sojourns with you shall be to you as the native among you, and you shall love him as yourself. . . ." (Leviticus 19)

DEUTERONOMY
JUDGES, WITNESSES, AND JUSTICE

The book of Deuteronomy was composed in the seventh century B.C., some six centuries after the exodus from Egypt. Written as though it were a last speech of Moses advising the people how to govern themselves as they entered the land of Canaan, Deuteronomy reflects the new problems faced by the Hebrews who had already established a kingdom and lived in a settled urban society. In presenting their reform program, the authors of Deuteronomy linked their message to the authority of Moses. The central theme of these verses is the attainment of justice.

---

18 "You shall appoint judges and officers in all your towns which the LORD your God gives you, according to your tribes; and they shall judge the people with righteous judgment. ¹⁹You shall not pervert justice; you shall not show partiality; and you shall not take a bribe, for a bribe blinds the eyes of the wise and subverts the cause of the righteous. ²⁰Justice, and only justice, you shall follow, that you may live and inherit the land which the LORD your God gives you." (Deuteronomy 16)

---

15 "A single witness shall not prevail against a man for any crime or for any wrong in connection with any offence that he has committed; only on the evidence of two witnesses, or of three witnesses, shall a charge be sustained. ¹⁶If a malicious witness rises against any man to accuse him of wrongdoing, ¹⁷then both parties to the dispute shall appear before the LORD, before the priests and the judges who are in office in those days; ¹⁸the judges shall inquire diligently, and if the witness is a false witness and has accused his brother falsely, ¹⁹then you shall do to him as he had meant to do to his brother; so you shall purge the evil from the midst of you." (Deuteronomy 19)

---

15 "You shall not give up to his master a slave who has escaped from his master to you; ¹⁶he shall dwell with you, in your midst, in the place which he shall choose within one of your towns, where it pleases him best; you shall not oppress him." (Deuteronomy 23)

---

14 "You shall not oppress a hired servant who is poor and needy, whether he is one of your brethren or one of the sojourners who are in your land within your towns; ¹⁵you shall give him his hire on the day he earns it, before the sun goes down (for he is poor, and sets his heart upon it); lest he cry against you to the LORD, and it be sin in you.

16 "The fathers shall not be put to death for the children, nor shall the children be put to death for the fathers; every man shall be put to death for his own sin.

17 "You shall not pervert the justice due to the sojourner or to the fatherless, or take a widow's garment in pledge; ¹⁸but you shall remember that you were a slave in Egypt and the LORD your God redeemed you from there; therefore I command you to do this.

19 "When you reap your harvest in your field, and have forgotten a sheaf in the field, you shall not go back to get it; it shall be for the sojourner, the fatherless, and the widow; that the LORD your God may bless you in all the work of your hands. ²⁰When you beat your olive trees, you shall not go over the boughs again; it shall be for the sojourner, the fatherless, and the widow. ²¹When you gather the grapes of your vineyard, you shall not glean it afterward; it shall be for the sojourner, the fatherless, and the widow. ²²You shall remember that you were a slave in the land of Egypt; therefore I command you to do this." (Deuteronomy 24)

REVIEW QUESTIONS

1. What were the terms of the covenant between God and the Hebrews?
2. The belief that some laws were divine in origin was shared by many Near Eastern peoples, including the Hebrews. How has this belief shaped subsequent Western civilization?
3. Show how an awareness of social justice pervaded Hebrew law.
4. How did the legal procedures of Hebrew law try to ensure fair treatment of all ranks of society?

---

8   The Age of Classical Prophecy

Ancient Jewish history was marked by the rise of prophets—spiritually inspired persons who believed that God had chosen them to remind the Jews of their duties to God and his law. These prophets carried God's message to the leaders and the people and warned of divine punishments for disobedience to God's commandments.

The prophetic movement—the age of classical prophecy—which emerged in the eighth century B.C., creatively expanded Hebrew religious thought. Prophets denounced exploitation of the poor, the greed of the wealthy, and the oppressive behavior of the powerful as a betrayal of Yahweh, a violation of his moral laws. They insisted that the core of Hebrew faith was not ritual but morality. Their concern for the poor and their attack on injustice received reemphasis in the Christian faith and thus became incorporated into the Western ideal of social justice.

AMOS AND ISAIAH SOCIAL JUSTICE

By the eighth century a significant disparity existed between the wealthy and the poor. Small farmers in debt to moneylenders faced the loss of their land or even bondage. Amos, a mid-eighth-century prophet, felt a tremendous compulsion to speak out in the name of God against these injustices.

²¹"I hate, I despise your feasts,
   and I take no delight in your solemn
      assemblies.
²²Even though you offer me your burnt
      offerings and cereal offerings,
   I will not accept them,
and the peace offerings of your fatted beasts
   I will not look upon.
²³Take away from me the noise of your songs;
   to the melody of your harps I will not listen.
²⁴But let justice roll down like waters,
   and righteousness like an everflowing
      stream." (Amos 5)

The prophets' insistence that rituals were not the essence of the law and their passion for righteousness are voiced in the Scriptures by Isaiah of Jerusalem, who lived in the mid-eighth century B.C. Scholars agree that Isaiah of Jerusalem did not write all sixty-six chapters that make up the Book of Isaiah. Some material appears to have been written by his disciples and interpreters, and Chapters 40 to 55, composed two centuries later, are attributed to a person given the name Second Isaiah. The following verses come from Isaiah of Jerusalem.

---

¹¹"What to me is the multitude of your
    sacrifices?
  says the LORD;
I have had enough of burnt offerings of rams
    and the fat of fed beasts;
I do not delight in the blood of bulls, or of
    lambs, or of he-goats. . . .
¹³Bring no more vain offerings;
    incense is an abomination to me.
New moon and sabbath and the calling of
    assemblies—
    I cannot endure iniquity and solemn
      assembly.
¹⁴Your new moons and your appointed feasts
    my soul hates;
they have become a burden to me,
    I am weary of bearing them.
¹⁵When you spread forth your hands,
    I will hide my eyes from you;

even though you make many prayers,
    I will not listen;
    your hands are full of blood.
¹⁶Wash yourselves; make yourselves clean;
    remove the evil of your doings
    from before my eyes;
cease to do evil,
¹⁷   learn to do good;
seek justice,
    correct oppression;
defend the fatherless,
    plead for the widow."
    (Isaiah 1)

Isaiah denounced the rich and the powerful for exploiting the poor.

---

¹³The LORD has taken his place to contend,
    he stands to judge his people.
¹⁴The LORD enters into judgment
    with the elders and princes of his people:
"It is you who have devoured the vineyard,
    the spoil of the poor is in your houses.
¹⁵What do you mean by crushing my people,
    by grinding the face of the poor?"
    says the Lord GOD of hosts.
    (Isaiah 3)

ISAIAH
PEACE AND HUMANITY

Isaiah of Jerusalem envisioned the unity of all people under God. This universalism drew out the full implications of Hebrew monotheism. In Isaiah's vision all peoples would live together in peace and harmony. Some of these lines are inscribed on the building that houses the United Nations in New York City.

²It shall come to pass in the latter days
    that the mountain of the house of the LORD
shall be established as the highest of the
    mountains,
    and shall be raised above the hills;

and all the nations shall flow to it,
³   and many peoples shall come, and say:
"Come, let us go up to the mountain of the
    LORD,
    to the house of the God of Jacob;

that he may teach us his ways
and that we may walk in his paths."
For out of Zion shall go forth the law,
and the word of the LORD from Jerusalem.
⁴He shall judge between the nations,
and shall decide for many peoples;

and they shall beat their swords into
plowshares,
and their spears into pruning hooks;
nation shall not lift up sword against nation,
neither shall they learn war any more.
(Isaiah 2)

REVIEW QUESTIONS

1. For the Hebrew prophets, ethical conduct was preferable to ritual acts as a way to worship God. Discuss.
2. How have the teachings of the Hebrew prophets influenced modern Western concepts of human dignity and social justice?

CHAPTER 2
The Greeks

SOPHOCLES (c. 496–406). The great Athenian dramatist wrote 123 tragedies, only seven of which have survived. *(The Granger Collection, New York.)*

Hebrew ethical monotheism, which gave value to the individual, is one source of Western civilization. Another source derives from the ancient Greeks, who originated scientific and philosophic thought, created democracy, and developed a humanistic outlook. From about 750 B.C. to 338 B.C. the Greek world consisted of small, independent, and self-governing city-states. Within this political-social context, the Greeks made their outstanding contributions to civilization.

In contrast to the Egyptians and Mesopotamians, the Greeks developed rational-scientific, rather than mythical, interpretations of nature and the human community. In trying to understand nature, Greek philosophers proposed physical explanations: that is, they gradually omitted the gods from their accounts of how nature came to be the way it is. Greek intellectuals also analyzed government, law, and ethics in logical and systematic ways. It was the great achievement of Greek thinkers to rise above magic, miracles, mystery, and custom and to assert that reason was the avenue to knowledge. The emergence of rational attitudes did not, of course, end traditional religion, particularly for the peasants, who remained devoted to their ancient cults, gods, and shrines. But what distinguishes the Greeks is that alongside an older religious-mythical tradition arose a philosophic-scientific view of the natural world and human culture.

The Greeks, who defined human beings by their capacity to use reason, also defined the principle of political liberty. Egyptians and Mesopotamians were subject to the authority of god-kings and priest-kings; the common people did not participate in political life, and there was no awareness of individual liberty. In contrast, many Greek city-states, particularly Athens, developed democratic institutions and attitudes. In the middle of the fifth century B.C., when Athenian democracy was at its height, adult male citizens were eligible to hold public office and were equal before the law; in the assembly, which met some forty times a year, they debated and voted on the key issues of state. Whereas Mesopotamians and Egyptians believed that law had been given to them by the gods, the Greeks came to understand that law was a human creation, a product of human reason. The Athenians abhorred rule by absolute rulers and held that people can govern themselves. While expressing admiration for the Greek political achievement, modern critics also point out several limitations of Greek democracy, notably slavery and the inability of women to participate in political life.

The Greeks originated the Western humanist tradition. They valued the human personality and sought the full cultivation of human talent. In the Greek view, a man of worth pursued excellence: that is, he sought to mold himself in accordance with the highest standards and ideals. Greek art, for example, made the human form the focal point of attention and exalted the nobility, dignity, self-assurance, and beauty of the human being.

Alexander the Great's conquest of the Near East marks a second stage in the evolution of Greek civilization (Hellenism). The first stage, the *Hellenic Age,* began about 800 B.C. with the earliest city-states and lasted until Alexander's death in 323 B.C.; at that time Greek civilization entered the *Hellenistic Age,* which lasted until 30 B.C., when Egypt, the last Hellenistic kingdom, lost its independence to Rome.

The Hellenistic Age inherited many cultural achievements of the earlier Hellenic Age, but crucial differences exist between the two eras. The self-sufficient and independent *polis* (city-state), the center of life in the Hellenic Age, was diminished in power and importance by larger political units, kingdoms headed by absolute monarchs. Although Greek cities continued to exercise considerable control over domestic affairs, they had lost to powerful monarchs their freedom of action in foreign affairs.

A second characteristic of the Hellenistic Age was cosmopolitanism, an intermingling of peoples and cultural traditions. In the Hellenic Age, the Greeks had drawn a sharp distinction between Greek and non-Greek. In the wake of Alexander's conquests, however, thousands of Greek soldiers, merchants, and administrators settled in Near Eastern lands, bringing with them Greek language, customs, and culture. Many upper-class citizens of Near Eastern cities, regardless of their ethnic backgrounds, came under the influence of Greek civilization. At the same time, Mesopotamian, Egyptian, and Persian ways, particularly religious practices and beliefs, spread westward into regions under the sway of Greek civilization.

---

1 Homer: The Educator of Greece

The poet Homer, who probably lived during the eighth century B.C., helped shape the Greek outlook. His great epics, *The Iliad* and *The Odyssey,* contain the embryo of the Greek humanist tradition: the concern with man and his achievements. "To strive always for excellence and to surpass all others"—in these words lies the essence of the Homeric hero's outlook. In the warrior-aristocratic world of Homer, excellence is primarily interpreted as bravery and skill in battle. The Homeric hero is driven to demonstrate his prowess, to assert himself, to win honor, and to earn a reputation.

The Iliad deals in poetic form with the Trojan War, which probably was waged in the thirteenth century B.C., between the Mycenaean Greeks and the Trojans of Asia Minor. At the outset Homer states his theme: the wrath of Achilles that brought so much suffering to the Greeks. Agamemnon, their king, has deprived the great warrior Achilles of his rightful prize, the captive girl Briseis.

Achilles will not submit to this grave insult to his honor and refuses to join the Greeks in combat against the Trojans. In this way he intends to make Agamemnon pay for his arrogance, for without the Greeks' greatest warrior, Agamemnon will have no easy victories. With Achilles on the sidelines, the Greeks suffer severe losses.

Destiny is at work: the "wicked arrogance" of Agamemnon and the "ruinous wrath" of Achilles have caused suffering and death among the Greek forces. For Homer, human existence has a pattern—a universal plan governs human affairs. People, even the gods, operate within a certain unalterable framework; their deeds are subject to the demands of destiny or necessity. Later Greek thinkers would express this idea of a universal order in philosophic and scientific terms.

Homer
THE ILIAD

The following passages from *The Iliad* illustrate the Homeric ideal of excellence. In the first, Hector of Troy, son of King Priam, prepares for battle. Hector's wife Andromache pleads with him to stay within the city walls, but Hector, in the tradition of the Homeric hero, feels compelled to engage in combat to show his worth and gain honor.

Hector looked at his son and smiled, but said nothing. Andromache, bursting into tears, went up to him and put her hand in his. "Hector," she said, "you are possessed. This bravery of yours will be your end. You do not think of your little boy or your unhappy wife, whom you will make a widow soon. Some day the Achaeans [Greeks] are bound to kill you in a massed attack. And when I lose you I might as well be dead. There will be no comfort left, when you have met your doom—nothing but grief. I have no father, no mother, now. My father fell to the great Achilles when he sacked our lovely town, Cilician Thebe[1] of the High Gates. . . . I had seven brothers too at home. In one day all of them went down to Hades' House.[2] The great Achilles of the swift feet killed them all. . . .

"So you, Hector, are father and mother and brother to me, as well as my beloved husband. Have pity on me now; stay here on the tower; and do not make your boy an orphan and your wife a widow. . . ."

"All that, my dear," said the great Hector of the glittering helmet, "is surely my concern. But if I hid myself like a coward and refused to fight, I could never face the Trojans and the Trojan ladies in their trailing gowns. Besides, it would go against the grain, for I have trained myself always, like a good soldier, to take my place in the front line and win glory for my father and myself. . . ."

As he finished, glorious Hector held out his arms to take his boy. But the child shrank back with a cry to the bosom of his girdled nurse, alarmed by his father's appearance. He was frightened by the bronze of the helmet and the horsehair plume that he saw nodding grimly down at him. His father and his lady mother had to laugh. But noble Hector quickly took his helmet off and put the dazzling thing on the ground. Then

---

[1]In *The Iliad* the Cilices lived in southern Asia Minor.
[2]Hades refers both to the god of the underworld and to the underworld itself.

he kissed his son, dandled him in his arms, and prayed to Zeus [the chief god] and the other gods: "Zeus, and you other gods, grant that this boy of mine may be, like me, pre-eminent in Troy; as strong and brave as I; a mighty king of Ilium [Troy]. May people say, when he comes back from battle, 'Here is a better man than his father.' Let him bring home the bloodstained armour of the enemy he has killed, and make his mother happy."

Hector handed the boy to his wife, who took him to her fragrant breast. She was smiling through her tears, and when her husband saw this he was moved. He stroked her with his hand and said: "My dear, I beg you not to be too much distressed. No one is going to send me down to Hades before my proper time. But Fate is a thing that no man born of woman, coward or hero, can escape. Go home now, and attend to your own work, the loom and the spindle, and see that the maidservants get on with theirs. War is men's business; and this war is the business of every man in Ilium, myself above all."

Many brave Greek warriors die in battle, including Achilles' best friend Patroclus, slain by the Trojan Hector. Achilles now sets aside his quarrel with Agamemnon (who has appealed to Achilles) and joins the battle. King Priam urges his son not to fight the mighty Achilles, but Hector, despite his fears, faces Achilles and meets his death. In this passage, the grief-stricken Priam goes to Achilles and requests Hector's body. Achilles responds with compassion. This scene shows that although Homer sees the essence of life as the pursuit of glory, he is also sensitive to life's brevity and to the suffering that pervades human existence.

. . . Big though Priam was, he came in unobserved, went up to Achilles, grasped his knees and kissed his hands, the terrible, man-killing hands that had slaughtered many of his sons. Achilles was astounded when he saw King Priam, and so were all his men. . . .

But Priam was already praying to Achilles. "Most worshipful Achilles," he said, "think of

your own father, who is the same age as I, and so has nothing but miserable old age ahead of him. No doubt his neighbours are oppressing him and there is nobody to save him from their depredations. Yet he at least has one consolation. While he knows that you are still alive, he can look forward day by day to seeing his beloved son come back from Troy; whereas my fortunes are completely broken. I had the best sons in the whole of this broad realm, and now not one, not one I say, is left. There were fifty when the Achaean expedition came. Nineteen of them were borne by one mother and the rest by other ladies in my palace. Most of them have fallen in action, and Hector, the only one I still could count on, the bulwark of Troy and the Trojans, has now been killed by you, fighting for his native land. It is to get him back from you that I have come to the Achaean ships, bringing this princely ransom with me. Achilles, fear the gods, and be merciful to me, remembering your own father, though I am even more entitled to compassion, since I have brought myself to do a thing that no one else on earth has done—I have raised to my lips the hand of the man who killed my son."

Priam had set Achilles thinking of his own father and brought him to the verge of tears. Taking the old man's hand, he gently put him from him; and overcome by their memories they both broke down. Priam, crouching at Achilles' feet, wept bitterly for man-slaying Hector, and Achilles wept for his father, and then again for Patroclus. The house was filled with the sounds of their lamentation. But presently, when he had had enough of tears and recovered his composure, the excellent Achilles leapt from his chair, and in compassion for the old man's grey head and grey beard, took him by the arm and raised him. Then he spoke to him from his heart: "You are indeed a man of sorrows and have suffered much. How could you dare to come by yourself to the Achaean ships into the presence of a man who has killed so many of your gallant sons? You have a heart of iron. But pray be seated now, here on this chair, and let us leave our sorrows, bitter though they are, locked up in our own hearts, for weeping is cold comfort and does little good. We men are wretched things, and the gods, who have no cares themselves, have woven sorrow into the very pattern of our lives."

REVIEW QUESTIONS

1. What glimpses do we get from Homer's *Iliad* of the respective roles of men and women in Greek society?
2. Homer's epic poems were studied and even memorized by Greek schoolchildren. What values would the poems have taught these youngsters to emulate?
3. What lessons about the human condition did Achilles draw from the tragic events of the Trojan War?

---

2 The Expansion of Reason

In the sixth century B.C., Greeks living in the city of Miletus in Ionia, the coast of Asia Minor, conceived a nonmythical way of viewing nature, a feat that marks the origins of philosophic and scientific thought. Traditionally, natural occurrences like earthquakes and lightning had been attributed to the gods. But early Greek thinkers, called cosmologists because they were interested in the nature and structure of the universe, were the first to see nature as a system governed by laws that the intellect could ascertain. The cosmologists sought physical rather than supernatural explanations for natural events. This new approach made possible a self-conscious and systematic investigation of nature and a critical appraisal of proposed theories; in contrast, the mythical view that the gods regulate nature did not invite analysis, discussion, and questioning.

The method of inquiry initiated by the Ionian natural philosophers found expression in other areas of Greek culture. Thus, in the Greek medical school headed by Hippocrates (c. 460–377 B.C.) on the island of Cos, doctors consciously attacked magical practices and beliefs, seeing them as hindrances to understanding causes and cures of disease. The historian Thucydides (c. 460–400 B.C.) sought logical explanations for human events, and the Sophists applied reason to traditional religion, law, and morality.

Hippocrates
THE SACRED DISEASE:
THE SEPARATION OF MEDICINE
FROM MYTH

In the following excerpt from "The Sacred Disease," a Hippocratic doctor rejects the belief that epilepsy is a sacred disease. Instead he maintains that epilepsy, like all other diseases, has a natural explanation and denounces as "charlatans and quacks" those who claim that gods cause the disease.

I. I am about to discuss the disease called "sacred." It is not, in my opinion, any more divine or more sacred than other diseases, but has a natural cause, and its supposed divine origin is due to men's inexperience, and to their wonder at its peculiar character. Now while men continue to believe in its divine origin because they are at a loss to understand it, they really disprove its divinity by the facile method of healing which they adopt, consisting as it does of purifications and incantations. But if it is to be considered divine just because it is wonderful, there will be not one sacred disease but many, for I will show that other diseases are no less wonderful and portentous, and yet nobody considers them sacred. For instance, quotidian fevers, tertians and quartans seem to me to be no less sacred and god-sent than this disease,* but nobody wonders at them. . . .

II. My own view is that those who first attributed a sacred character to this malady were like the magicians, purifiers, charlatans and quacks of our own day, men who claim great piety and superior knowledge. Being at a loss, and having no treatment which would help, they

concealed and sheltered themselves behind superstition, and called this illness sacred, in order that their utter ignorance might not be manifest. They added a plausible story, and established a method of treatment that secured their own position. They used purifications and incantations; they forbade the use of baths, and of many foods that are unsuitable for sick folk. . . .

But if to eat or apply these things engenders and increases the disease, while to refrain works a cure, then neither is godhead to blame nor are the purifications beneficial; it is the foods that cure or hurt, and the power of godhead disappears.

III. Accordingly I hold that those who attempt in this manner to cure these diseases cannot consider them either sacred or divine; for when they are removed by such purifications and by such treatment as this, there is nothing to prevent the production of attacks in men by devices that are similar. If so, something human is to blame, and not godhead. He who by purifications and magic can take away such an affliction can also by similar means bring it on, so that by this argument the action of godhead is disproved. By these sayings and devices they claim superior knowledge, and deceive men by prescribing for them purifications and cleansings, most of their talk turning on the intervention of gods and spirits.

---

*Because of the regularity of the attacks of fever, which occur every day (quotidians), every other day (tertians), or with intermission of two whole days (quartans).

Thucydides
METHOD OF HISTORICAL INQUIRY

Thucydides' history was another expression of the movement from myth to reason that pervaded every aspect of Greek culture. Mesopotamians and Egyptians kept annals purporting to narrate the deeds of gods and their human agents. The Greeks carefully investigated events—the first people to examine the past with a critical eye. Thucydides examined men's actions and their motives, explicitly rejected divine explanations for human occurrences, searched for natural causes, and based his conclusions on evidence. In this approach, he was influenced by the empiricism of the Hippocratic physicians. For Thucydides, a work of history, as distinguished from poetry, was a creation of the rational mind and not an expression of the poetic imagination. Thus, in Thucydides' *History of the Peloponnesian War* there was no place for legend, for myth, for the fabulous—all hindrances to historical truth. In the following passage, Thucydides describes his method of inquiry.

I began my history at the very outbreak of the war, in the belief that it was going to be a great war and more worth writing about than any of those which had taken place in the past. My belief was based on the fact that the two sides were at the very height of their power and preparedness, and I saw, too, that the rest of the Hellenic [Greek] world was committed to one side or the other; even those who were not immediately engaged were deliberating on the courses which they were to take later. This was the greatest disturbance in the history of the Hellenes, affecting also a large part of the non-Hellenic world, and indeed, I might almost say, the whole of mankind. For though I have found it impossible, because of its remoteness in time, to acquire a really precise knowledge of the distant past or even of the history preceding our own period, yet, after looking back into it as far as I can, all the evidence leads me to conclude that these periods were not great periods either in warfare or in anything else. . . .

In investigating past history, and in forming the conclusions which I have formed, it must be admitted that one cannot rely on every detail which has come down to us by way of tradition. People are inclined to accept all stories of ancient times in an uncritical way—even when these stories concern their own native countries. . . .

. . . Most people, in fact, will not take trouble in finding out the truth, but are much more inclined to accept the first story they hear.

However, I do not think that one will be far wrong in accepting the conclusions I have reached from the evidence which I have put forward. It is better evidence than that of the poets, who exaggerate the importance of their themes, or of the prose chroniclers, who are less interested in telling the truth than in catching the attention of their public, whose authorities cannot be checked, and whose subject-matter, owing to the passage of time, is mostly lost in the unreliable streams of mythology. We may claim instead to have used only the plainest evidence and to have reached conclusions which are reasonably accurate, considering that we have been dealing with ancient history. As for this present war, even though people are apt to think that the war in which they are fighting is the greatest of all wars and, when it is over, to relapse again into their admiration of the past, nevertheless, if one looks at the facts themselves, one will see that this was the greatest war of all.

In this history I have made use of set speeches some of which were delivered just before and others during the war. I have found it difficult to remember the precise words used in the speeches which I listened to myself and my various informants have experienced the same difficulty; so my method has been, while keeping as closely as possible to the general sense of the words that were actually used, to make the speakers say what, in my opinion, was called for by each situation.

And with regard to my factual reporting of the events of the war I have made it a principle not to write down the first story that came my way, and not even to be guided by my own general impressions; either I was present myself at the events which I have described or else I heard of them from eye-witnesses whose reports I have checked with as much thoroughness as possible. Not that even so the truth was easy to discover: different eye-witnesses give different accounts of the same events, speaking out of partiality for one side or the other or else from imperfect memories. And it may well be that my history will seem less easy to read because of the absence in it of a romantic element. It will be enough for me, however, if these words of mine are judged useful by those who want to understand clearly the events which happened in the past and which (human nature being what it is) will, at some time or other and in much the same ways, be repeated in the future. My work is not a piece of writing designed to meet the taste of an immediate public, but was done to last for ever.

Critias
RELIGION AS A HUMAN INVENTION

After the Greek philosophers of Asia Minor began to employ natural, rather than supernatural, explanations for nature, Greek thinkers on the mainland applied reason to human affairs. Exemplifying this trend were the Sophists, who wandered from city to city teaching rhetoric, grammar, poetry, mathematics, music, and gymnastics. The Sophists sought to develop their students' minds, and they created a secular curriculum—for these reasons they enriched the humanist tradition of the West.

The Sophist Critias (c. 480–403 B.C.) was a poet, philosopher, orator, and historian; also he was originally an eager follower of Socrates. Later, Critias became the most bloodthirsty of the so-called Thirty Tyrants, oligarchs who seized control of Athens in 404 B.C. and massacred their democratic opponents. The following passage, a surviving fragment of a play by Critias, demonstrates the Sophists' use of critical thought.

There was a time when the life of men was unordered, bestial and the slave of force, when there was no reward for the virtuous and no punishment for the wicked. Then, I think, men devised retributory laws, in order that Justice might be dictator and have arrogance as its slave, and if anyone sinned, he was punished. Then, when the laws forbade them to commit open crimes of violence, and they began to do them in secret, a wise and clever man invented fear (of the gods) for mortals, that there might be some means of frightening the wicked, even if they do anything or say or think it in secret. Hence he introduced the Divine (religion), saying that there is a God flourishing with immortal life, hearing and seeing with his mind, and thinking of everything and caring about these things, and having divine nature, who will hear everything said among mortals, and will be able to see all that is done. And even if you plan anything evil in secret, you will not escape the gods in this; for they have surpassing intelligence. In saying these words, he introduced the pleasantest of teachings, covering up the truth with a false theory; and he said that the gods dwelt there where he could most frighten men by saying it, whence he knew that fears exist for mortals and rewards for the hard life: in the upper periphery, where they saw lightnings and heard the dread rumblings of thunder, and the starry-faced body of heaven, the beautiful embroidery of Time the skilled craftsman, whence come forth the bright mass of the sun, and the wet shower upon the earth. With such fears did he surround mankind, through which he well established the deity with his argument, and in a fitting place, and quenched lawlessness among men. . . . Thus, I think, for the first time did someone persuade mortals to believe in a race of deities.

REVIEW QUESTIONS

1. Hippocrates distinguishes between magic and medicine. Discuss this statement.
2. What were some of the methods that Thucydides promised to use to make his history more accurate and credible?
3. What was revolutionary about Critias' approach to religion?

3 Greek Drama

The Greek dramatist portrayed the sufferings, weaknesses, and triumphs of individuals. Just as a Greek sculptor shaped a clear visual image of the human form, so a Greek dramatist brought the inner life of human beings, their fears and hopes, into sharp focus and tried to find the deeper meaning of human experience. Thus, both art and drama evidenced the growing self-awareness of the individual.

Because of the grandeur of the dramatists' themes, the eminence of their heroes, and the loftiness of their language, Greek spectators felt intensely involved in the tragedies of the lives portrayed. What they were witnessing went beyond anything in their ordinary lives, and they experienced the full range of human emotions.

The essence of Greek tragedy lies in the tragic hero's struggle against cosmic forces and insurmountable obstacles, which eventually crush him. But what impressed the Greek spectators (and impresses today's readers and viewers of Greek drama) was not the vulnerability or weaknesses of human beings, but their courage and determination in the face of these forces.

Sophocles
ANTIGONE

In *Antigone,* the dramatist Sophocles expresses the Greeks' high esteem for humanity and its potential. He also deals with a theme that recurs in Western thought over the centuries: the conflict between individual morality and the requirements of the state, between personal conscience and the state's laws. Creon, king of Thebes, forbids the burial of Polyneikes, Antigone's brother, because he rebelled against the state. The body, decrees Creon, shall remain unburied, food for dogs and vultures, despite the fact that Antigone is his niece and betrothed to his son. Antigone believes that a higher law compels her to bury her brother, even though this means certain death for her and for her sister Ismene, if the latter helps Antigone.

SCENE II

CREON (*to* ANTIGONE)
You there. You, looking at the ground. Tell me.
Do you admit this or deny it? Which?

ANTIGONE
Yes, I admit it. I do not deny it.

CREON (*to* GUARD)
Go. You are free. The charge is dropped.

Exit GUARD

Now you,
Answer this question. Make your answer brief.
You knew there was a law forbidding this?

ANTIGONE
Of course I knew it. Why not? It was public.

CREON
And you have dared to disobey the law?

ANTIGONE
Yes. For this law was not proclaimed by Zeus,
Or by the gods who rule the world below.
I do not think your edicts have such power
That they can override the laws of heaven,
Unwritten and unfailing, laws whose life
Belongs not to today or yesterday
But to time everlasting; and no man
Knows the first moment that they had
    their being.
If I transgressed these laws because I feared
The arrogance of man, how to the gods
Could I make satisfaction? Well I know,
Being a mortal, that I have to die,
Even without your proclamations. Yet
If I must die before my time is come,
That is a blessing. Because to one who lives,
As I live, in the midst of sorrows, death
Is of necessity desirable.
For me, to face death is a trifling pain
That does not trouble me. But to have left
The body of my brother, my own brother,
Lying unburied would be bitter grief.
And if these acts of mine seem foolish to you,
Perhaps a fool accuses me of folly.

CHORUS
The violent daughter of a violent father,
She cannot bend before a storm of evils.

CREON (*to* ANTIGONE)
Stubborn? Self-willed? People like that, I tell
    you,
Are the first to come to grief. The hardest iron,
Baked in the fire, most quickly flies to pieces.
An unruly horse is taught obedience
By a touch of the curb. How can you be so
    proud?
You, a mere slave? (*to* CHORUS) She was well
    schooled already
In insolence, when she defied the law.
And now look at her! Boasting, insolent,
Exulting in what she did. And if she triumphs
And goes unpunished, I am no man—she is.
If she were more than niece, if she were closer

Than anyone who worships at my altar,
She would not even then escape her doom,
A dreadful death. Nor would her sister. Yes,
Her sister had a share in burying him.
(*to* ATTENDANT) Go bring her here. I have just
    seen her, raving,
Beside herself. Even before they act,
Traitors who plot their treason in the dark
Betray themselves like that. Detestable!
(*to* ANTIGONE) But hateful also is an evil-doer
Who, caught red-handed, glorifies the crime.

ANTIGONE
Now you have caught me, will you do more
    than kill me?

CREON
No, only that. With that I am satisfied.

ANTIGONE
Then why do you delay? You have said
    nothing
I do not hate. I pray you never will.
And you hate what I say. Yet how could I
Have won more splendid honor than by giving
Due burial to my brother? All men here
Would grant me their approval, if their lips
Were not sealed up in fear. But you, a king,
Blessed by good fortune in much else besides,
Can speak and act with perfect liberty.

CREON
All of these Thebans disagree with you.

ANTIGONE
No. They agree, but they control their tongues.

CREON
You feel no shame in acting without their
    help?

ANTIGONE
I feel no shame in honoring a brother.

CREON
Another brother died who fought against him.

ANTIGONE
Two brothers. The two sons of the same
    parents.

CREON
Honor to one is outrage to the other.

ANTIGONE
Eteocles will not feel himself dishonored.

CREON
What! When his rites are offered to a traitor?

ANTIGONE
It was his brother, not his slave, who died.

CREON
One who attacked the land that he defended.

ANTIGONE
The gods still wish those rites to be performed.

CREON
Are the just pleased with the unjust as their
    equals?

ANTIGONE
That may be virtuous in the world below.

CREON
No. Even there a foe is never a friend.

ANTIGONE
I am not made for hatred but for love.

CREON
Then go down to the dead. If you must love,
Love them. While I yet live, no woman
    rules me.

CHORUS
Look there. Ismene, weeping as sisters weep,
The shadow of a cloud of grief lies deep.
On her face, darkly flushed; and in her pain
Her tears are falling like a flood of rain.

Enter ISMENE *and* ATTENDANTS

CREON
You viper! Lying hidden in my house,
Sucking my blood in secret, while I reared,
Unknowingly, two subverters of my throne.
Do you confess that you have taken part
In this man's burial, or deny it? Speak.

ISMENE
If she will recognize my right to say so,
I shared the action and I share the blame.

ANTIGONE
No. That would not be just. I never let you
Take any part in what you disapproved of.

ISMENE
In your calamity, I am not ashamed
To stand beside you, beaten by this tempest.

ANTIGONE
The dead are witnesses of what I did,
To love in words alone is not enough.

ISMENE
Do not reject me, Sister! Let me die
Beside you, and do honor to the dead.

ANTIGONE
No. You will neither share my death nor claim
What I have done. My death will be sufficient.

ISMENE
What happiness can I have when you are gone?

ANTIGONE
Ask Creon that. He is the one you value.

ISMENE
Do you gain anything by taunting me?

ANTIGONE
Ah, no! By taunting you, I hurt myself.

ISMENE
How can I help you? Tell me what I can do.

ANTIGONE
Protect yourself. I do not grudge your safety.

ISMENE
Antigone! Shall I not share your fate?

ANTIGONE
We both have made our choices life, and death.

ISMENE
At least I tried to stop you. I protested.

ANTIGONE
Some have approved your way; and others,
    mine.

ISMENE
Yet now I share your guilt. I too am ruined.

ANTIGONE

Take courage. Live your life. But I long since
Gave myself up to death to help the dead. . . .

Haemon, grief-stricken at the condemnation
of his fiancée Antigone, approaches his father Creon, and tries to resolve the crisis.
Creon is suspicious about Haemon's loyalty.

CREON

We soon shall know better than seers could tell
us.
My son, Antigone is condemned to death.
Nothing can change my sentence. Have you
learned
Her fate and come here in a storm of anger,
Or do you love me and support my acts?

HAEMON

Father, I am your son. Your greater knowledge
Will trace the pathway that I mean to follow.
My marriage cannot be of more importance
Than to be guided always by your wisdom.

CREON

Yes, Haemon, this should be the law you
live by!
In all things to obey your father's will.
Men pray for children round them in their
homes
Only to see them dutiful and quick
With hatred to require [for] their father's foe,
With honor to repay their father's friend.
But what is there to say of one whose children
Prove to be valueless? That he has fathered
Grief for himself and laughter for his foes.
Then, Haemon, do not, at the lure of pleasure,
Unseat your reason for a woman's sake.
This comfort soon grows cold in your embrace:
A wicked wife to share your bed and home.
Is there a deeper wound than to find worthless
The one you love? Turn from this girl with
loathing,
As from an enemy, and let her go
To get a husband in the world below.

For I have found her openly rebellious,
Her only out of all the city. Therefore,
I will not break the oath that I have sworn.
I will have her killed. Vainly she will invoke
The bond of kindred blood the gods make
sacred.
If I permit disloyalty to breed
In my own house, I nurture it in strangers.
He who is righteous with his kin is righteous
In the state also. Therefore, I cannot pardon
One who does violence to the laws or thinks
To dictate to his rulers; for whoever
May be the man appointed by the city,
That man must be obeyed in everything,
Little or great, just or unjust. And surely
He who was thus obedient would be found
As good a ruler as he was a subject;
And in a storm of spears he would stand fast
With loyal courage at his comrade's side.
But disobedience is the worst of evils.
For it is this that ruins cities; this
Makes our homes desolate; armies of allies
Through this break up in rout. But most men
find
Their happiness and safety in obedience.
Therefore we must support the law, and never
Be beaten by a woman. It is better
To fall by a man's hand, if we must fall,
Than to be known as weaker than a girl.

CHORUS

We may in our old age have lost our judgment,
And yet to us you seem to have spoken wisely.

HAEMON

The gods have given men the gift of reason,
Greatest of all things that we call our own.
I have no skill, nor do I wish to have it,
To show where you have spoken wrongly. Yet
Some other's thought, beside your own, might
prove
To be of value. Therefore it is my duty,
My natural duty as your son, to notice,
On your behalf, all that men say, or do,
Or find to blame. For your frown frightens
them,

So that the citizen dares not say a word
That would offend you. I can hear, however,
Murmurs in darkness and laments for her.
They say: "No woman ever less deserved
Her doom, no woman ever was to die
So shamefully for deeds so glorious.
For when her brother fell in bloody battle,
She would not let his body lie unburied
To be devoured by carrion dogs or birds.
Does such a woman not deserve reward,
Rewards of golden honor?" This I hear,
A rumor spread in secrecy and darkness.
Father, I prize nothing in life so highly
As your well-being. How can children have
A nobler honor than their father's fame
Or father than his son's? Then do not think
Your mood must never alter; do not feel
Your word, and yours alone, must be correct.
For if a man believes that he is right
And only he, that no one equals him
In what he says or thinks, he will be found
Empty when searched and rested. Because
   a man
Even if he be wise, feels no disgrace
In learning many things, in taking care
Not to be over-rigid. You have seen
Trees on the margin of a stream in winter:
Those yielding to the flood save every twig,
And those resisting perish root and branch.
So, too, the mariner who never slackens
His taut sheet overturns his craft and spends
Keel uppermost the last part of his voyage.
Let your resentment die. Let yourself change.
For I believe—if I, a younger man,
May have a sound opinion—it is best
That men by nature should be wise in all
   things.
But most men find they cannot reach that goal;
And when this happens, it is also good
To learn to listen to wise counselors.

CHORUS

Sir, when his words are timely, you should heed
   them.
And Haemon, you should profit by his words.
Each one of you has spoken reasonably.

CREON

Are men as old as I am to be taught
How to behave by men as young as he?

HAEMON

Not to do wrong. If I am young, ignore
My youth. Consider only what I do.

CREON

Have you done well in honoring the rebellious?

HAEMON

Those who do wrong should not command
   respect.

CREON

Then that disease has not infected her?

HAEMON

All of our city with one voice denies it.

CREON

Does Thebes give orders for the way I rule?

HAEMON

How young you are! How young in saying
   that!

CREON

Am I to govern by another's judgment?

HAEMON

A city that is one man's is no city.

CREON

A city is the king's. That much is sure.

HAEMON

You would rule well in a deserted country.

REVIEW QUESTIONS

1. What was Antigone's justification for disobeying the command of the king?
   Provide examples of historical figures who have employed a similar justification
   for their actions.

2. Why did Creon react so violently to Antigone's action?
3. Which lines best reveal Antigone's position? Creon's position?

---

4 Athenian Greatness

The Persian Wars were decisive in the history of the West. Had the Greeks been defeated, it is very likely that their cultural and political vitality would have been aborted. The confidence and pride that came with victory, however, propelled Athens into a golden age.

Thucydides
THE FUNERAL ORATION OF PERICLES

The central figure in Athenian political life for much of the period after the Persian Wars was Pericles (c. 495–429 B.C.), a gifted statesman and military commander. In the opening stage of the Peloponnesian War between Athens and Sparta (431–404 B.C.), Pericles delivered an oration in honor of the Athenian war dead. In this speech, as reconstructed by the historian Thucydides, Pericles brilliantly described Athenian greatness.

Pericles contrasted Sparta's narrow conception of excellence with the Athenian ideal of the self-sufficiency of the human spirit. The Spartans subordinated all personal goals and interests to the demands of the Spartan state. As such, Sparta—a totally militarized society—was as close as the ancient Greeks came to a modern totalitarian society. The Athenians, said Pericles, did not require grinding military discipline in order to fight bravely for their city. Their cultivation of the mind and love of beauty did not make them less courageous.

To be sure, Pericles' "Funeral Oration," intended to bolster the morale of a people locked in a brutal war, idealized Athenian society. Athenians did not always behave in accordance with Pericles' high principles. Nevertheless, as both Pericles and Thucydides knew, Athenian democracy was an extraordinary achievement.

"Let me say that our system of government does not copy the institutions of our neighbours. It is more the case of our being a model to others, than of our imitating anyone else. Our constitution is called a democracy because power is in the hands not of a minority but of the whole people. When it is a question of settling private disputes, everyone is equal before the law; when it is a question of putting one person before another in positions of public responsibility, what counts is not membership of a particular class, but the actual ability which the man possesses. No one, so long as he has it in him to be of service to the state, is kept in political obscurity because of poverty. And, just as our political life is free and open, so is our day-to-day life in our relations with each other. We do not get into a state with our next-door neighbour if he enjoys himself in his own way, nor do we give him the kind of black looks which, though they do no real harm, still do hurt people's feelings. We are free and tolerant in our private lives; but in public affairs we keep to the law. This is because it commands our deep respect.

"We give our obedience to those whom we put in positions of authority, and we obey the laws themselves, especially those which are for the protection of the oppressed, and those unwritten laws which it is an acknowledged shame to break.

"And here is another point. When our work is over, we are in a position to enjoy all kinds of recreation for our spirits. There are various kinds of contests [in poetry, drama, music, and athletics] and sacrifices regularly throughout the year; in our own homes we find a beauty and a good taste which delight us every day and which drive away our cares. Then the greatness of our city brings it about that all the good things from all over the world flow in to us, so that to us it seems just as natural to enjoy foreign goods as our own local products.

"Then there is a great difference between us and our opponents, in our attitude towards military security. Here are some examples: Our city is open to the world, and we have no periodical deportations in order to prevent people observing or finding out secrets which might be of military advantage to the enemy. This is because we rely, not on secret weapons, but on our own real courage and loyalty. There is a difference, too, in our educational systems. The Spartans, from their earliest boyhood, are submitted to the most laborious training in courage; we pass our lives without all these restrictions, and yet are just as ready to face the same dangers as they are. Here is a proof of this: When the Spartans invade our land, they do not come by themselves, but bring all their allies with them; whereas we, when we launch an attack abroad, do the job by ourselves, and, though fighting on foreign soil, do not often fail to defeat opponents who are fighting for their own hearths and homes. As a matter of fact none of our enemies has ever yet been confronted with our total strength, because we have to divide our attention between our navy and the many missions on which our troops are sent on land. Yet, if our enemies engage a detachment of our forces and defeat it, they give themselves credit for having thrown back our entire army; or, if they lose, they claim that they were beaten by us in full strength. There are certain advantages, I think, in our way of meeting danger voluntarily, with an easy mind, instead of with a laborious training, with natural rather than with state-induced courage. We do not have to spend our time practising to meet sufferings which are still in the future; and when they are actually upon us we show ourselves just as brave as these others who are always in strict training. This is one point in which, I think, our city deserves to be admired. There are also others:

"Our love of what is beautiful does not lead to extravagance; our love of the things of the mind does not make us soft. We regard wealth as something to be properly used, rather than as something to boast about. As for poverty, no one need be ashamed to admit it: the real shame is in not taking practical measures to escape from it. Here each individual is interested not only in his own affairs but in the affairs of the state as well: even those who are mostly occupied with their own business are extremely well-informed on general politics—this is a peculiarity of ours: we do not say that a man who takes no interest in politics is a man who minds his own business; we say that he has no business here at all. We Athenians, in our own persons, take our decisions on policy or submit them to proper discussions: for we do not think that there is an incompatibility between words and deeds; the worst thing is to rush into action before the consequences have been properly debated. And this is another point where we differ from other people. We are capable at the same time of taking risks and of estimating them beforehand. Others are brave out of ignorance; and, when they stop to think, they begin to fear. But the man who can most truly be accounted brave is he who best knows the meaning of what is sweet in life and of what is terrible, and then goes out undeterred to meet what is to come.

"Again, in questions of general good feeling there is a great contrast between us and most other people. We make friends by doing good to others, not by receiving good from them. This makes our friendship all the more reliable, since we want to keep alive the gratitude of those who are in our debt by showing continued goodwill to them: whereas the feelings of one who owes us something lack the same enthusiasm, since he knows that, when he repays our kindness, it will be more like paying back a debt than giving something spontaneously. We are unique in this. When we do kindnesses to others, we do not do them out of any calculations of profit or loss: we do them without afterthought, relying on our free liberality. Taking everything together then, I declare that our city is an education to Greece, and I declare that in my opinion each single one of our citizens, in all the manifold aspects of life, is able to show himself the rightful lord and owner of his own person, and do this, moreover, with exceptional grace and exceptional versatility. And to show that this is no empty boasting for the present occasion, but real tangible fact, you have only to consider the power which our city possesses and which has been won by those very qualities which I have mentioned. Athens, alone of the states we know, comes to her testing time in a greatness that surpasses what was imagined of her. In her case, and in her case alone, no invading enemy is ashamed at being defeated, and no subject can complain of being governed by people unfit for their responsibilities. Mighty indeed are the marks and monuments of our empire which we have left. Future ages will wonder at us, as the present age wonders at us now."

REVIEW QUESTIONS

1. According to Pericles, what are the chief characteristics of a democratic society?
2. What were the attitudes of the Athenians to such things as wealth, learning, and public affairs?
3. How did the Athenians differ from the Spartans in their views on education and military training?

5 The Status of Women in Classical Greek Society

Women occupied a subordinate position in Greek society. A woman's chief functions were to bear male heirs for her husband and to manage his household. In Athens, respectable women were secluded in their homes; they did not go into the marketplace or eat at the same table as their husbands and guests. Nor did women have political rights; they could not vote or hold office. In order to exercise her property rights, a woman was represented by a male guardian—usually a father, husband, brother, or son.

Parents usually arranged the marriage of their daughters. A father who discovered that his daughter had been unchaste could sell her into slavery. Adultery was a crime. A husband was compelled by law to divorce his adulterous wife and could have her lover executed.

Euripides
MEDEA

The Greek dramatist Euripides (c. 485–406 B.C.) applied a keen critical spirit to the great question of individual life versus the demands of society. His play *Medea* focuses on a strong-willed woman whose despair at being cast off by her husband leads her to exact a terrible revenge. But in the following passage, Medea might speak for the deepest feelings of any Greek woman.

It was everything to me to think well of one
  man,
And he, my own husband, has turned out
  wholly vile.
Of all things which are living and can form a
  judgement
We women are the most unfortunate creatures.
Firstly, with an excess of wealth it is required
For us to buy a husband and take for our bodies
A master; for not to take one is even worse.
And now the question is serious whether we
  take
A good or bad one; for there is no easy escape
For a woman, nor can she say no to her marriage.
She arrives among new modes of behaviour
  and manners,
And needs prophetic power, unless she has
  learnt at home,
How best to manage him who shares the bed
  with her.

And if we work out all this well and carefully,
And the husband lives with us and lightly
  bears his yoke,
Then life is enviable. If not, I'd rather die.
A man, when he's tired of the company in his
  home,
Goes out of the house and puts an end to his
  boredom
And turns to a friend or companion of his own
  age.
But we are forced to keep our eyes on one
  alone.
What they say of us is that we have a peaceful
  time
Living at home, while they do the fighting in
  war.
How wrong they are! I would very much
  rather stand
Three times in the front of battle than bear
  one child.

Aristophanes
LYSISTRATA

Aristophanes (c. 448–c. 380 B.C.), the greatest Athenian comic playwright, wrote *Lysistrata* in 412 B.C. to convey his revulsion for the Peloponnesian War that was destroying Greece. In the play, the women of Athens, led by Lysistrata, resolve to refrain from sexual relations with their husbands until the men make peace. When the women seize the Acropolis—the rocky hill in the center of Athens—the men resort to force but are doused with water. At this point a commissioner, accompanied by four constables, enters and complains about the disturbance; Koryphaios, one of the doused men, vents his anger. The ensuing dialogue between the commissioner and Lysistrata reflects some attitudes of Greek men and women toward each other.

COMMISSIONER . . . That's what women are good for: a complete disaster.

MAN I Save your breath for actual crimes, Commissioner. Look what's happened to us. Insolence, insults, insufferable effrontery, and apart from that, they've soaked us. It looks as though we pissed in our tunics.

COMMISSIONER By Poseidon, that liquid deity, you got what you deserved. It's all our own fault. We taught them all they know. We are the forgers of fornication. We sowed in them sexual license and now we reap rebellion. . . . (*shrugs*) What do you expect? This is what happens. . . . (*indicates doors of Acropolis*) Take my own case.

I'm the Commissioner for Public Safety. I've got men to pay. I need the money and look what happens. The women have shut me out of the public treasury. (*taking command*) All right, men. On your feet. Take up that log over there. Form a line. Get a move on. You can get drunk later. I'll give you a hand. (*They ram the gates without success. After three tries, as they are stepping back, Lysistrata opens the door. Calonike and Myrrhine accompany her.*)

LYSISTRATA Put that thing down! I'm coming out of my own free will. What we want here is not bolts and bars and locks, but common sense.

COMMISSIONER Sense? Common sense? You . . . you . . . you . . . Where's a policeman? Arrest her! Tie her hands behind her back.

LYSISTRATA (*who is carrying wool on a spindle or a knitting needle*) By Artemis, goddess of the hunt, if he touches me, you'll be dropping one man from your payroll. (*Lysistrata jabs him*)

COMMISSIONER What's this? Retreat? Get back in there. Grab her, the two of you.

MYRRHINE (*holding a large chamber pot*) By Artemis, goddess of the dew, if you lay a hand on her, I'll kick the shit out of you.

COMMISSIONER Shit? Disgusting. Arrest her for using obscene language.

CALONIKE (*carrying a lamp*) By Artemis, goddess of light, if you lay a finger on her, you'll need a doctor.

COMMISSIONER Apprehend that woman. Get her, NOW!

BOEOTIAN (*from the roof, with a broom*) By Artemis, goddess of witchcraft, if you go near her, I'll break your head open.

COMMISSIONER Good God, what a mess. Athens' finest disgraced! Defeated by a gaggle of girls. Close ranks, men! On your marks, get set, CHARGE!

LYSISTRATA (*holds her hands up and they stop*) Hold it! We've got four battalions of fully equipped infantry women back there.

COMMISSIONER Go inside and disarm them.

LYSISTRATA (*gives a loud whistle and women crowd the bottlenecks and the doorway with brooms, pots and pans, etc.*) Attack! Destroy them, you sifters of flour and beaters of eggs, you pressers of garlic, you dough girls, you bar maids, you market militia. Scratch them and tear them, bite and kick. Fall back, don't strip the enemy—the day is ours. (*the policemen are overpowered*)

COMMISSIONER (*in tears*) Another glorious military victory for Athens!

LYSISTRATA What did you think we were? There's not an ounce of servility in us. A woman scorned is something to be reckoned with. You underestimated the capacity of freeborn women.

COMMISSIONER Capacity? I sure as hell did. You'd cause a drought in the saloons if they let you in.

MAN I Your honor, there's no use talking to animals. I know you're a civil servant, but don't overdo it.

MAN II Didn't we tell you? They gave us a public bath, fully dressed, without any soap.

WOMAN I What did you expect, sonny? You made the first move—we made the second. Try it again and you'll get another black eye. *(flute)* We are really sweet little stay-at-homes by nature, all sweetness and light, good little virgins, perfect dolls *(they all rock to and fro coyly)*. But if you stick your finger in a hornet's nest, you're going to get stung.

MEN ALL *(and drums—they beat their feet rhythmically on the ground)*
Oh Zeus, Oh Zeus.
Of all the beasts that thou has wrought,
What monster's worse than woman?
Who shall encompass with his thought
Their endless crimes? Let me tell you . . . no
    man!

They've seized the heights, the rock, the shrine.
But to what end I know not.
There must be *reasons* for the crime *(to audience)*
Do you know why? (pause) I thought not.

MAN I Scrutinize those women. Assess their rebuttals.

MAN II 'Twould be culpable negligence not to probe this affair to the bottom.

COMMISSIONER *(as if before a jury)* My first question is this, gentlemen of the . . . What possible motive could you have had in seizing the Treasury?

LYSISTRATA We wanted to keep the money. *No money, no war.*

COMMISSIONER You think that money is the cause of the war?

LYSISTRATA Money is the cause of all our problems. . . . They'll not get another penny.

COMMISSIONER Then what do you propose to do?

LYSISTRATA Control the Treasury.

COMMISSIONER Control the Treasury?

LYSISTRATA Control the Treasury. National economics and home economics—they're one and the same.

COMMISSIONER No, they're not.

LYSISTRATA Why do you say so?

COMMISSIONER The national economy is for the war effort.

LYSISTRATA Who needs the war effort?

COMMISSIONER How can we protect the city?

LYSISTRATA Leave that to us.

ALL MEN You?

ALL WOMEN Us.

COMMISSIONER God save us.

LYSISTRATA Leave that to us.

COMMISSIONER Subversive nonsense!

LYSISTRATA Why get so upset? There's no stopping us now.

COMMISSIONER It's a downright crime.

LYSISTRATA We *must* save you.

COMMISSIONER *(pouting)* What if I don't want to be saved?

LYSISTRATA All the more reason to.

COMMISSIONER Might I ask where you got these ideas of war and peace?

LYSISTRATA If you'll allow me, I'll tell you.

COMMISSIONER Out with it then, or I'll . . .

LYSISTRATA Relax and put your hands down.

COMMISSIONER I can't help myself. You make me so damned angry.

CALONIKE Watch it.

COMMISSIONER Watch it yourself, you old wind bag.

LYSISTRATA Because of our natural self-restraint, we women have tolerated you men ever since this war began. We tolerated you and kept our thoughts to ourselves. (You never let us utter a peep, anyway.) But that does not mean that we were happy with you. We knew you all too well. Very often, in the evening, at suppertime, we would listen to you talk of some enormously important decision you had made. Deep down inside all we felt was pain, but we would force a smile and ask, "How was the assembly today, dear? Did you get to talk about peace?" And my husband would answer, "None of your business. Shut up!" And I would shut up.

CALONIKE I wouldn't have.

COMMISSIONER I'd have shut your mouth for you.

LYSISTRATA But then we would find out that you had passed a more disgusting resolution, and I would ask you, "Darling, how did you manage to do something so absolutely stupid?" And my husband would glare at me and threaten to slap my face if I did not attend to the distaff side of things. And then he'd always quote Homer: "The men must see to the fighting."

COMMISSIONER Well done. Well done.

LYSISTRATA What do you mean? Not to let us advise against your idiocy was bad enough, but then again we'd actually hear you out in public saying things like, "Who can we draft? There's not a man left in the country." Someone else would say, "Quite right, not a man left. Pity." And so we women got together and decided to save Greece. There was no time to lose. Therefore, you keep quiet for a change and listen to us. For we have valuable advice to give this country. If you'll listen, we'll put you back on your feet again.

COMMISSIONER You'll do what? I'm not going to put up with this. I'm not going . . .

LYSISTRATA SILENCE!

COMMISSIONER I categorically decline to be silent for a woman. Women wear hats.

LYSISTRATA If that's what is bothering you, try one on and shut up! *(puts one on him)*

CALONIKE Here's a spindle.

MYRRHINE And a basket of wool.

CALONIKE Go on home. There's a sweetheart. Put on your girdle, wind your wool, and mind the beans don't boil over.

LYSISTRATA "THE WOMEN MUST SEE TO THE FIGHTING."

COMMISSIONER Beside the point, beside the point. Things are in a tangle. How can you set them straight?

LYSISTRATA Simple.

COMMISSIONER Explain.

LYSISTRATA Do you know anything about weaving? Say the wool gets tangled. We lift it up, like this, and work out the knots by winding it this way and that, up and down, on the spindles. That's how we'll unravel the war. We'll send our envoys this way and that, up and down, all over Greece.

COMMISSIONER Wool? Spindles? Are you out of your mind? War is a serious business.

LYSISTRATA If you had any sense, you'd learn a lesson from women's work.

COMMISSIONER Prove it.

LYSISTRATA The first thing we have to do is give the wool a good wash, get the dirt out of the fleece. We beat out the [worthless] musk and pick out the hickies. Do the same for the city. Lambaste the loafers and discard the dodgers. Then our spoiled wool—that's like your [office-seeking parasites]—sack the spongers, decapitate the dabblers. But toss together into the wool basket the good [resident] aliens, the allies, the strangers, and begin spinning them into a ball. The colonies are loose threads; pick up the ends and gather them in. Wind them all into one, make a great bobbin of yarn, and weave, without bias or seam, a garment of government fit for the people.

COMMISSIONER It's all very well this weaving and bobbing—when you have absolutely no earthly idea what a war means.

LYSISTRATA You disgusting excuse for a man! The pain of giving birth was only our first pain. You took our boys and sent *them to their deaths in Sicily* [site of a recent disastrous Athenian defeat].

COMMISSIONER Quiet! I beg you, let that memory lie still.

LYSISTRATA And now, when youth and beauty are still with us and our blood is hot, you take our husbands away, and we sleep alone. That's bad enough for us married women. But I pity the virgins growing old, alone in their beds.

COMMISSIONER Well, men grow old too, you know.

LYSISTRATA But it's not the same. A soldier's discharged, bald as a coot he may be, and . . . zap! he marries a nymphette. But a woman only has one summer, and when that has slipped by, she can spend her days and her years consulting oracles and fortune tellers, but they'll never send her a husband.

———

MEN ALL There's something rotten in the state of Athens.
An ominous aroma of constitutional rot.
My nose can smell a radical dissenter,
An anarchist, tyrannous, feminist plot.

The Spartans are behind it.
They must have masterminded
This anarchist, tyrannous, feminist plot.

REVIEW QUESTIONS

1. List several reasons Medea gives to support her claim that "we women are the most unfortunate creatures."
2. What were the grievances of Greek women as listed by Aristophanes?
3. What attitudes of ancient Greek males toward females are reflected in the contemporary world?

---

6 The Peloponnesian War

After the defeat of the Persian invaders in 479 B.C., the Athenians organized a mutual defense pact, called the Delian League, among the smaller Greek states. With the largest population and greatest wealth and naval forces, Athens became the dominant power within the league. In the course of time, Athens converted the alliance from an organization of equal sovereign states to an empire under Athenian control. This outcome aroused suspicion among the other Greek states in the Peloponnese, particularly Sparta, that an imperialistic Athens was a threat to their own independence and freedom. That fear precipitated the Peloponnesian War (431–404 B.C.), which devastated the Greek world during the late fifth century B.C.

Elected general during the war, Thucydides was banished from Athens for failing to rescue Amphipolis, a town under attack by Sparta. During his twenty-year exile, Thucydides gathered information about the war, which he correctly viewed as an event of world-historical importance. He was also right to regard his account as a unique documentary achievement that would serve as a model for future historians.

Above all, Thucydides studied politics, the lifeblood of Athenian society. For him, history was essentially the study of political behavior. Consistent with the Greek character, Thucydides sought underlying patterns and general truths pertaining to statesmanship and political power. His chronicle contains rich insights into human nature, the techniques of demagogues, the ruinous consequences of mob behavior, and the spiritual deterioration of men under the stress of war.

Thucydides
THE MELIAN DIALOGUE

The Athenians, who saw no conflict between imperialism and democracy, considered it natural for strong states to dominate weaker ones. This view coincided with the position of those Sophists (see page 49) who argued that might makes right. The classic expression of this view is found in Thucydides' history.

During the war, Athens decided to invade the island of Melos, which resisted this unprovoked act of aggression. Thucydides reconstructed a dialogue based on a meeting between Athenian envoys and Melian officials, who tried unsuccessfully to persuade the Athenians not to launch an unjust war. Subsequently, Athens attacked. After capturing the town, the Athenians slaughtered the men, enslaved the women and children, and colonized the territory. Following is the famous Melian Dialogue.

MELIANS No one can object to each of us putting forward our own views in a calm atmosphere. That is perfectly reasonable. What is scarcely consistent with such a proposal is the present threat, indeed the certainty, of your making war on us. We see that you have come prepared to judge the argument yourselves, and that the likely end of it all will be either war, if we prove that we are in the right, and so refuse to surrender, or else slavery.

ATHENIANS If you are going to spend the time in enumerating your suspicions about the future, or if you have met here for any other reason except to look the facts in the face and on the basis of these facts to consider how you can save your city from destruction, there is no point in our going on with this discussion. If, however, you will do as we suggest, then we will speak on.

MELIANS It is natural and understandable that people who are placed as we are should have recourse to all kinds of arguments and different points of view. However, you are right in saying that we are met together here to discuss the safety of our country and, if you will have it so, the discussion shall proceed on the lines that you have laid down.

ATHENIANS Then we on our side will use no fine phrases saying, for example, that we have a right to our empire because we defeated the Persians, or that we have come against you now because of the injuries you have done us—a great mass of words that nobody would believe. And we ask you on your side not to imagine that you will influence us by saying that you, though a colony of Sparta, have not joined Sparta in the war, or that you have never done us any harm. Instead we recommend that you should try to get what it is possible for you to get, taking into consideration what we both really do think; since you know as well as we do that when these matters are discussed by practical people, the standard of justice depends on the equality of power to compel and that in fact the strong do what they have the power to do and the weak accept what they have to accept.

MELIANS Then in our view (since you force us to leave justice out of account and to confine ourselves to self-interest)—in our view it is at any rate useful that you should not destroy a principle that is to the general good of all men—namely, that in the case of all who fall into danger there should be such a thing as fair play and just dealing, and that such people should be allowed to use and to profit by arguments that fall short of a mathematical accuracy. And this is a principle which affects you as much as anybody, since your own fall would be visited by the most terrible vengeance and would be an example to the world.

ATHENIANS . . . What we shall do now is to show you that it is for the good of our own empire that we are here and that it is for the preservation of your city that we shall say what we are going to say. We do not want any trouble in bringing you into our empire, and we want you to be spared for the good both of yourselves and of ourselves.

MELIANS And how could it be just as good for us to be the slaves as for you to be the masters?

ATHENIANS You, by giving in, would save yourselves from disaster; we, by not destroying you, would be able to profit from you.

MELIANS So you would not agree to our being neutral, friends instead of enemies, but allies of neither side?

ATHENIANS No, because it is not so much your hostility that injures us; it is rather the case that, if we were on friendly terms with you, our subjects would regard that as a sign of weakness in us, whereas your hatred is evidence of our power. . . . [Our subjects think] that those who still preserve their independence do so because they are strong, and that if we fail to attack them it is because we are afraid. So that by conquering you we shall increase not only the size but the security of our empire. We rule the sea and you are islanders, and weaker islanders too than the others; it is therefore particularly important that you should not escape. . . .

MELIANS Then surely, if such hazards are taken by you to keep your empire . . . we who are still free would show ourselves great cowards and weaklings if we failed to face everything that comes rather than submit to slavery.

ATHENIANS No, not if you are sensible. This is no fair fight, with honour on one side and shame on the other. It is rather a question of saving your lives and not resisting those who are far too strong for you.

MELIANS Yet we know that in war fortune sometimes makes the odds more level than could be expected from the difference in numbers of the two sides. And if we surrender, then all our hope is lost at once, whereas, so long as we remain in action, there is still a hope that we may yet stand upright.

ATHENIANS Hope, that comforter in danger! If one already has solid advantages to fall back upon, one can indulge in hope. . . . [D]o not be like those people who, as so commonly happens, miss the chance of saving themselves in a human and practical way, and, when every clear and distinct hope has left them in their adversity, turn to what is blind and vague, to prophecies and oracles and such things which by encouraging hope lead men to ruin.

MELIANS It is difficult, and you may be sure that we know it, for us to oppose your power. . . . Nevertheless we trust that the gods will give us fortune as good as yours, because we are standing for what is right against what is wrong; and as for what we lack in power, we trust that it will be made up for by our alliance with the Spartans, who are bound, if for no other reason, then for honour's sake, and because we are their kinsmen, to come to our help. Our confidence, therefore, is not so entirely irrational as you think.

ATHENIANS . . . Our opinion of the gods and our knowledge of men lead us to conclude that it is a general and necessary law of nature to rule wherever one can. . . . [W]ith regard to your views about Sparta and your confidence that she, out of a sense of honour, will come to your aid, we must say that we congratulate you on your simplicity but do not envy you your folly. . . .

. . . You, if you take the right view . . . will see that there is nothing disgraceful in giving way to the greatest city in Hellas when she is offering you such reasonable terms—alliance on a tribute-paying basis and liberty to enjoy your own property. And, when you are allowed to choose between war and safety, you will not be so insensitively arrogant as to make the wrong choice. This is the safe rule—to stand up to one's equals, to behave with deference towards one's superiors, and to treat one's inferiors with moderation. Think it over again, then, when we have withdrawn from the meeting, and let this be a point that constantly recurs to your minds—that you are discussing the fate of your country, that you have only one country, and that its future for good or ill depends on this one single decision which you are going to make.

The Athenians then withdrew from the discussion. The Melians, left to themselves, reached a conclusion which was much the same as they had indicated in their previous replies. Their answer was as follows:

MELIANS Our decision, Athenians, is just the same as it was at first. We are not prepared to give up in a short moment the liberty which our city has enjoyed from its foundation for 700 years. We put our trust in the fortune that the gods will send and which has saved us up to now, and in the help of men—that is, of the Spartans; and so we shall try to save ourselves. But we invite you to allow us to be friends of yours and enemies to neither side, to make a treaty which shall be agreeable to both you and us, and so to leave our country.

REVIEW QUESTIONS

1. In what way did the debate between the Athenians and Melians reflect the new rationalist spirit in Greek society?
2. Evaluate the performance of the Melian negotiators.

---

7 Socrates: The Rational Individual

Socrates (469–399 B.C.) marked a decisive turning point in Greek philosophy and in the history of Western thought. The Socratic conception of the rational individual became an essential component of the tradition of classical humanism. Socrates agreed with the Sophists that the study of physical nature was less important than the study of man. But whereas the Sophists concentrated on teaching specific skills—how to excel in debates, for example—Socrates was concerned with comprehending and improving human character. Although ethical concerns lay at the center of Socrates' thought, he never provided a list of ethical commands; in Socratic philosophy, there is nothing comparable to the Ten Commandments. What he did provide was a method—the dialectic or dialogue—of arriving at knowledge, including moral values.

For Socrates, the dialogue (the asking and answering of questions between two or more individuals) was the sole avenue to moral insights and self-knowledge. The interchange implied that a human mind was not a passive vessel into which a teacher poured knowledge. Participants in a dialogue were obliged to play an active role and to think critically about human values. The use of the dialogue implied further that relations between people should involve rational discussion through which people learn from each other and improve themselves.

When Socrates was seventy, he was accused by his enemies of corrupting the youth of Athens and of not believing in the city's gods but in other, new divinities, and he went on trial for his life.

Plato
THE APOLOGY

Knowledge of Socrates' trial comes principally from *The Apology* written by Plato (see page 53), Socrates' most illustrious student. (The original meaning of *apology* was a defense or explanation.) In the first passage from *The Apology*, presented below, Socrates tells the court that the Delphic Oracle, the prophetess of Apollo at Delphi, had said that there was no one wiser than Socrates. Not considering himself wise, Socrates resolved to discover what the oracle meant, by conversing with people reputed to be wise.

I went to a man who seemed wise: thinking that there, if anywhere, I should prove the answer wrong, and be able to say to the oracle, "You said that I am the wisest of men; but this man is wiser than I am." So I examined him—I need not tell you his name, he was a public man, but this was the result, Athenians. When I conversed with him, I came to see that, though many persons, and chiefly he himself, thought that he was wise, yet he was not wise. And then I tried to show him that he was not wise, though he fancied that he was; and by that I gained his hatred, and the hatred of many of the bystanders. So when I went away, I thought to myself, "I am wiser than this man: neither of us probably knows anything that is really good, but he thinks that he has knowledge, when he has it not, while I, seeing that I have no knowledge, do not think that I have." In this point, at least, I seem to be a little wiser than he is; I do not think that I know what I do not know. Next I went to another man, who seemed to be still wiser, with just the same result. And there again I gained his hatred. . . . After the public men I went to the poets, tragic, dithyrambic [frenzied], and others, thinking there to find myself manifestly more ignorant than they. So I took up the poems on which I thought that they had spent most pains, and asked them what they meant wishing also for instruction. I am ashamed to tell you the truth, my friends, but I must say it. In short, almost any of the bystanders would have spoken better about the works of these poets than the poets themselves. So I soon found that it is not by wisdom that the poets create their works, but by a certain natural power, and by inspiration, like soothsayers and prophets: for though such persons say many fine things, they know nothing of what they say. And the poets seemed to me to be in a like case. And at the same time I perceived that, because of their poetry, they thought that they were the wisest of men in other matters too, which they were not. So I went away again, thinking that I had the same advantage over them as over the public men.

Finally I went to the artisans: for I was conscious, in a word, that I had no knowledge at all, and I was sure that I should find that they knew many fine things. And in that I was not mistaken. They knew what I did not know, and so far they were wiser than I. But, Athenians, it seemed to me that the skilled craftsmen made the same mistake as the poets. Each of them claimed to have great wisdom in the highest matters because he was skilful in his own art; and this fault of theirs threw their real wisdom into the shade. So I asked myself on behalf of the oracle whether I would choose to remain as I was, neither wise in their wisdom nor ignorant in their ignorance, or to have both, as they had them. And I made answer to myself and to the oracle that it were better for me to remain as I was.

This search, Athenians, has gained me much hatred of a very fierce and bitter kind, which has caused many false accusations against me; and I am called by the name of wise. For the bystanders always think that I am wise myself in any matter wherein I convict another man of ignorance. But in truth, my friends, perhaps it is God who is wise: and by this oracle he may have meant that man's wisdom is worth little or nothing. He did not mean, I think, that Socrates is wise: he only took me as an example, and made use of my name, as though he would say to men: "He among you is wisest, who, like Socrates, is convinced that for wisdom he is verily worthless." And therefore I still go about searching and testing every man whom I think wise, whether he be a citizen or a stranger, according to the word of the God [Apollo]; and whenever I find that he is not wise, I point that out to him in the service of the God. And I am so busy in this pursuit that I have never had leisure to take any part worth mentioning in public matters, or to look after my private affairs. I am in very great poverty by my service to the God.

And besides this, the young men who follow me about, who are the sons of wealthy persons and with much leisure, by nature delight in hearing men cross-questioned: and they often imitate me among themselves: then they try their hand at cross-questioning other people. And, I imagine, they find a great abundance of men who think that they know a great deal, when in truth they know little or nothing. And then the persons who are cross-questioned are angry with me instead of with themselves: and say that Socrates is an abominable fellow who corrupts the young. And when they are asked, Why, what does he do? what does he teach? they have nothing to say; but, not to seem at a loss, they repeat the stock charges against all philosophers, and say that he investigates things in the air and under the earth, and that he teaches people to disbelieve in the gods, and "to make the worst appear the better reason." For I fancy they would not like to confess the truth, that they are shown up as mere ignorant pretenders to knowledge. And so they have filled your ears with their fierce slanders for a long time, for they are zealous and fierce, and numerous: they are well-disciplined too, and plausible in speech. . . .

Had Socrates been willing to compromise and to stop teaching his philosophy, it is likely that he would not have received the death penalty. However, for Socrates the pursuit of truth was the highest human activity; it involved the person's whole being. It transformed the individual, enabling him to live in accordance with moral values that had been arrived at through thought and that could be defended rationally.

. . . But I know well that it is evil and base to do wrong and to disobey my better, whether he be man or god. And I will never choose what I know to be evil, and fear and fly from what may possibly be a good. And so, even if you acquit me now, and do not listen to Anytus' [his prosecutor's] argument that I ought never to have been brought to trial, if I was to be acquitted; and that as it is, you are bound to put me to death, because if I were to escape, all your children would forthwith be utterly corrupted by practising what Socrates teaches: if you were therefore to say to me, "Socrates, this time we will not listen to Anytus: we will let you go: but on this condition, that you cease from carrying on this search, and from philosophy: if you are found doing that again, you shall die:" I say, if you offered to let me go on these terms, I should reply:—"Athenians, I hold you in the highest regard and love; but I will obey the God rather than you: and as long as I have breath and power I will not cease from philosophy, and from exhorting you and setting forth the truth to any of you whom I meet, saying as I am wont, 'My excellent friend, you are a citizen of Athens, a city very great and very famous for wisdom and power of mind: are you not ashamed of caring so much for the making of money, and for reputation and honour? Will you not spend thought or care on wisdom and truth and the perfecting of your soul?' " And if he dispute my words, and say that he does care for these things, I shall not forthwith release him and go away: I shall question him and cross-examine him: and if I think that he has not virtue, though he says that he has, I shall reproach him for setting the least value on the most important things; and the greater value on the more worthless. This shall I do to every one whom I meet, old or young, citizen or stranger; but especially to the citizens, for they are more nearly akin to me. For know well, the God commands me so to do. And I think that nothing better has ever happened to you in your city than my service to the God. For I spend my whole life in going about persuading you all, both young and old, to give your first and chiefest care to the perfection of your souls: and not till you have done that to care for your bodies or your wealth. I tell you, that virtue does not come from wealth, but that wealth and every other good, whether public or private, which men have, come from virtue. If then I corrupt the youth by this teaching, the mischief is great; but if any man says that I teach anything else, he speaks falsely. And therefore, Athenians, I say, either listen to Anytus, or do not listen to him: either acquit me, or do not acquit me: but be sure that I shall not alter my life; no, not if I have to die for it many times.

Do not interrupt me, Athenians. Remember the request which I made to you, and listen to my words. I think that it will do you good to hear them. I have something more to say to you, at which perhaps you will cry out: but do not do that. Be sure that if you kill me, a man such as I say I am, you will harm yourselves more than you will harm me. Meletus [another prosecutor] and Anytus can do me no harm; that is impossible, for I do not think that God will allow a good man to be harmed by a bad one. They may indeed kill me, or drive me into exile, or deprive me of my civil rights; and perhaps Meletus and others think these things great evils. But I do not think so: I think that to do as he is doing, and to try to kill a man unjustly, is a much greater evil. And now, Athenians, I am not going to argue for my own sake at all, as you might think, but for yours, that you may not sin

against the God and reject his gift to you, by condemning me. If you put me to death, you will hardly find another man to fill my place. The God has sent me to attack the city, if I may use a ludicrous simile, just as if it were a great and noble horse, which was rather sluggish from its size and needed a gadfly to rouse it: and I think that I am the gadfly that the God has set upon the city: for I never cease settling on you as it were at every point, and rousing, and exhorting, and reproaching each man of you all day long. You will hardly find any one else, my friends, to fill my place: and, if you take my advice, you will spare my life. You are indignant, as drowsy persons are when they are awakened, and, of course, if you are persuaded by Anytus, you could easily kill me with a single blow, and then sleep on undisturbed for the rest of your lives. . . .

Perhaps someone will say, "Why cannot you withdraw from Athens, Socrates, and hold your peace?" It is the most difficult thing in the world to make you understand why I cannot do that. If I say that I cannot hold my peace because that would be to disobey the God, you will think that I am not in earnest and will not believe me. And if I tell you that no greater good can happen to a man than to discuss human excellence every day and the other matters about which you have heard me arguing and examining myself and others, and that an unexamined life is not worth living, then you will believe me still less. But that is so, my friends, though it is not easy to persuade you. . . .

Socrates is convicted and sentenced to death.

. . . Perhaps, my friends, you think that I have been convicted because I was wanting in the arguments by which I could have persuaded you to acquit me, if I had thought it right to do or to say anything to escape punishment. It is not so. I have been convicted because I was wanting, not in arguments, but in impudence and shamelessness—because I would not plead before you as you would have liked to hear me plead, or appeal to you with weeping and wailing, or say and do many other things which I maintain are unworthy of me, but which you have been accustomed to from other men. But when I was defending myself, I thought that I ought not to do anything unworthy of a free man because of the danger which I ran, and I have not changed my mind now. I would very much rather defend myself as I did, and die, than as you would have had me do, and live. . . .

And now I wish to prophesy to you, Athenians, who have condemned me. For I am going to die, and that is the time when men have most prophetic power. And I prophesy to you who have sentenced me to death that a far more severe punishment than you have inflicted on me will surely overtake you as soon as I am dead. You have done this thing, thinking that you will be relieved from having to give an account of your lives. But I say that the result will be very different. There will be more men who will call you to account, whom I have held back, though you did not recognize it. And they will be harsher toward you than I have been, for they will be younger, and you will be more indignant with them. For if you think that you will restrain men from reproaching you for not living as you should, by putting them to death, you are very much mistaken. That way of escape is neither possible nor honorable. It is much more honorable and much easier not to suppress others, but to make yourselves as good as you can. This is my parting prophecy to you who have condemned me.

REVIEW QUESTIONS

1. What is the nature of Socrates' wisdom?
2. Was Socrates a subversive force in Athenian society? Explain your answer.
3. According to Socrates, what is the true vocation of a philosopher? What price may the philosopher pay for his effort?
4. Compare and contrast the vocation of Socrates as a philosopher to that of the Hebrew prophets.
5. Why did some Athenians believe that Socrates corrupted the young?
6. What did Socrates say would be his reaction if he were offered an acquittal on the condition that he give up teaching his philosophy? What were his reasons?

8 Plato: The Philosopher-King

Plato (c. 429–347 B.C.), an Athenian aristocrat and disciple of Socrates, based his philosophy on Socrates' teachings. Plato was greatly affected by the deterioration of Athenian politics during and immediately after the Peloponnesian War. The rise of demagogues, the violent conflicts between oligarchs and democrats, and the execution of Socrates convinced Plato that Athenian democracy was a failure. His hostility toward democracy also stemmed from his upper-class background and temperament.

Socratic philosophy held promise of reforming the individual through the critical use of reason. Plato felt that the individual could not undergo a moral transformation while living in a wicked and corrupt society. For the individual to be able to achieve virtue, the state must be reformed.

Plato
THE REPUBLIC

In *The Republic,* Plato proposed organizing government in harmony with the needs of human nature. Those people who are driven by a desire for food, possessions, and sexual gratification, Plato said, should be farmers, tradesmen, or artisans. Those who are naturally courageous and assertive should be soldiers. And the few who have the capacity for wisdom—the philosophers—should be entrusted with political power.

In the ideal state, Plato asserted, the many would be ruled by the few who have a natural endowment for leadership. These philosopher-kings, the finest product of the state's carefully designed educational program, would wield absolute power: the people would lose their right to participate in political affairs, and the state would manufacture propaganda and strictly control education in order to keep the masses obedient. In exchange, the citizens would gain leaders distinguished by their rationality, wisdom, and virtue. In the form of a dialogue between Socrates and a man called Glaucon, Plato in the following reading presents his views on the character of the philosopher.

[SOCRATES] Unless either philosophers become kings in their countries or those who are now called kings and rulers come to be sufficiently inspired with a genuine desire for wisdom; unless that is to say, political power and philosophy meet together . . . there can be no rest from troubles, my dear Glaucon, for states, nor yet, as I believe, for all mankind. . . . There is no other way of happiness either for the state or for the individual. . . .

Now . . . we must, I think, define . . . whom we mean by these lovers of wisdom who, we have dared to assert, ought to be our rulers. Once we have a clear view of their character, we shall be able to defend our position by pointing to some who are naturally fitted to combine philosophic study with political leadership, while the rest of the world should accept their guidance and let philosophy alone.

[GLAUCON] Yes, this is the moment for a definition. . . .

[S] . . . One trait of the philosophic nature we may take as already granted: a constant passion for any knowledge that will reveal to them something of that reality which endures for ever and is not always passing into and out of existence. And, we may add, their desire is to know the whole of that reality; they will not willingly renounce any part of it as relatively small and insignificant, as we said before when we compared them to the lover and to the man who covets honour.

[G] True.

[S] Is there not another trait which the nature we are seeking cannot fail to possess—truthfulness, a love of truth and a hatred for falsehood that will not tolerate untruth in any form?

[G] Yes, it is natural to expect that.

[S] It is not merely natural, but entirely necessary that an instinctive passion for any object should extend to all that is closely akin to it; and there is nothing more closely akin to wisdom than truth. So the same nature cannot love wisdom and falsehood; the genuine lover of knowledge cannot fail, from his youth up, to strive after the whole of truth.

[G] I perfectly agree.

[S] Now we surely know that when a man's desires set strongly in one direction, in every other channel they flow more feebly, like a stream diverted into another bed. So when the current has set towards knowledge and all that goes with it, desire will abandon those pleasures of which the body is the instrument and be concerned only with the pleasure which the soul enjoys independently—if, that is to say, the love of wisdom is more than a mere pretence. Accordingly, such a one will be temperate and no lover of money; for he will be the last person to care about the things for the sake of which money is eagerly sought and lavishly spent.

{G} That is true.

{S} Again, in seeking to distinguish the philosophic nature, you must not overlook the least touch of meanness. Nothing could be more contrary than pettiness to a mind constantly bent on grasping the whole of things, both divine and human.

{G} Quite true.

{S} And do you suppose that one who is so high-minded and whose thought can contemplate all time and all existence will count this life of man a matter of much concern?

{G} No, he could not.

{S} So for such a man death will have no terrors.

{G} None.

{S} A mean and cowardly nature, then, can have no part in the genuine pursuit of wisdom.

{G} I think not.

{S} And if a man is temperate and free from the love of money, meanness, pretentiousness, and cowardice, he will not be hard to deal with or dishonest. So, as another indication of the philosophic temper, you will observe whether, from youth up, he is fair-minded, gentle, and sociable.

{G} Certainly.

{S} Also you will not fail to notice whether he is quick or slow to learn. No one can be expected to take a reasonable delight in a task in which much painful effort makes little headway. And if he cannot retain what he learns, his forgetfulness will leave no room in his head for knowledge; and so, having all his toil for nothing, he can only end by hating himself as well as his fruitless occupation. We must not, then, count a forgetful mind as competent to pursue wisdom; we must require a good memory.

{G} By all means.

{S} Further, there is in some natures a crudity and awkwardness that can only tend to a lack of measure and proportion; and there is a close affinity between proportion and truth. Hence, besides our other requirements, we shall look for a mind endowed with measure and grace, which will be instinctively drawn to see every reality in its true light.

{G} Yes.

{S} Well then, now that we have enumerated the qualities of a mind destined to take its full part in the apprehension of reality, have you any doubt about their being indispensable and all necessarily going together?

{G} None whatever.

{S} Then have you any fault to find with a pursuit which none can worthily follow who is not by nature quick to learn and to remember, magnanimous and gracious, the friend and kinsman of truth, justice, courage, temperance?

Plato said that genuine philosophers are "those whose passion it is to see the truth." For Plato, unlike the Sophists, standards of beauty, justice, and goodness exist that are universally valid—that apply to all peoples at all times. Plato held that these standards are in a higher world, the realm of Forms or Ideas. This world of Forms is known only through the mind, not the senses. For example, a sculptor observes many bodies but they all possess flaws; in his mind's eye he perceives the world of Ideas and tries to reproduce with his art the perfect human form. Plato says that the ordinary person, basing opinion on everyday experience, has an imperfect understanding of beauty, goodness, and justice, whereas the philosopher, through reason, reaches beyond sense perception to the realm of Forms and discovers truth. Such people are the natural rulers of the state; only they are capable of a correct understanding of justice; only they have the wisdom to reform the state in the best interests of all its citizens.

The distinction between a higher world of truth and a lower world of imperfection, deception, and illusion is illustrated in Plato's famous Allegory of the Cave. Plato, through the dialogue of Socrates and Glaucon, compares those persons without a knowledge of the Forms to prisoners in a dark cave.

[S] Next, said I, here is a parable to illustrate the degrees in which our nature may be enlightened or unenlightened. Imagine the condition of men living in a sort of cavernous chamber underground, with an entrance open to the light and a long passage all down the cave. Here they have been from childhood, chained by the leg and also by the neck, so that they cannot move and can see only what is in front of them, because the chains will not let them turn their heads. At some distance higher up is the light of a fire burning behind them; and between the prisoners and the fire is a track with a parapet built along it, like the screen at a puppet-show, which hides the performers while they show their puppets over the top.

[G] I see, said he.

[S] Now behind this parapet imagine persons carrying along various artificial objects, including figures of men and animals in wood or stone or other materials, which project above the parapet. Naturally, some of these persons will be talking, others silent.

[G] It is a strange picture, he said, and a strange sort of prisoners.

[S] Like ourselves, I replied; for in the first place prisoners so confined would have seen nothing of themselves or of one another, except the shadows thrown by the firelight on the wall of the Cave facing them, would they?

[G] Not if all their lives they had been prevented from moving their heads.

[S] And they would have seen as little of the objects carried past.

[G] Of course.

[S] Now, if they could talk to one another, would they not suppose that their words referred only to those passing shadows which they saw?

[G] Necessarily.

[S] And suppose their prison had an echo from the wall facing them? When one of the people crossing behind them spoke, they could only suppose that the sound came from the shadow passing before their eyes.

[G] No doubt.

[S] In every way, then, such prisoners would recognize as reality nothing but the shadows of those artificial objects.

[G] Inevitably. . . .

To the prisoners chained in the cave, the shadows of the artificial objects constitute reality. When a freed prisoner ascends from the cave to the sunlight, he sees a totally different world. Returning to the cave, he tries to tell the prisoners that the shadows are only poor imitations of reality, but they laugh at him, for their opinions have been shaped by the only world they know. The meaning of the parable is clear: the philosophers who ascend to the higher world of Forms possess true knowledge; everyone else possesses mere opinions, deceptive beliefs, and illusions. The philosophers have a duty to guide the ignorant.

[S] Now consider what would happen if their release from the chains and the healing of their unwisdom should come about in this way. Suppose one of them were set free and forced suddenly to stand up, turn his head, and walk with eyes lifted to the light; all these movements would be painful, and he would be too dazzled to make out the objects whose shadows he had been used to see. What do you think he would say, if someone told him that what he had formerly seen was meaningless illusion, but now, being somewhat nearer to reality and turned towards more real objects, he was getting a truer view? Suppose further that he were shown the various objects being carried by and were made to say, in reply to questions, what each of them was. Would he not be perplexed and believe the objects now shown him to be not so real as what he formerly saw?

[G] Yes, not nearly so real.

[S] And if he were forced to look at the firelight itself, would not his eyes ache, so that he would try to escape and turn back to the things which he could see distinctly, convinced that they really were clearer than these other objects now being shown to him?

[G] Yes.

[S] And suppose someone were to drag him away forcibly up the steep and rugged ascent and not let him go until he had hauled him out into the sunlight, would he not suffer pain and vexation at such treatment, and, when he had come out into the light, find his eyes so full of its radiance that he could not see a single one of the things that he was now told were real?

[G] Certainly he would not see them all at once.

[S] He would need, then, to grow accustomed before he could see things in that upper world. At first it would be easiest to make out shadows, and then the images of men and things reflected in water, and later on the things themselves. After that, it would be easier to watch the heavenly bodies and the sky itself by night, looking at the light of the moon and stars rather than the Sun and the Sun's light in the day-time.

[G] Yes, surely.

[S] Last of all, he would be able to look at the Sun and contemplate its nature, not as it appears when reflected in water or any alien medium, but as it is in itself in its own domain.

[G] No doubt.

[S] And now he would begin to draw the conclusion that it is the Sun that produces the seasons and the course of the year and controls everything in the visible world, and moreover is in a way the cause of all that he and his companions used to see.

[G] Clearly he would come at last to that conclusion.

[S] Then if he called to mind his fellow prisoners and what passed for wisdom in his former dwelling place, he would surely think himself happy in the change and be sorry for them. They may have had a practice of honouring and commending one another, with prizes for the man who had the keenest eye for the passing shadows and the best memory for the order in which they followed or accompanied one another, so that he could make a good guess as to which was going to come next. Would our released prisoner be likely to covet those prizes or to envy the men exalted to honour and power in the Cave? Would he not feel like Homer's Achilles, that he would far sooner "be on earth as a hired servant in the house of a landless man" or endure anything rather than go back to his old beliefs and live in the old way?

[G] Yes, he would prefer any fate to such a life.

[S] Now imagine what would happen if he went down again to take his former seat in the Cave. Coming suddenly out of the sunlight, his eyes would be filled with darkness. He might be required once more to deliver his opinion on those shadows, in competition with the prisoners who had never been released, while his eyesight was still dim and unsteady; and it might take some time to become used to the darkness. They would laugh at him and say that he had gone up only to come back with his sight ruined; it was worth no one's while even to attempt the ascent. If they could lay hands on the man who was trying to set them free and lead them up, they would kill him.

[G] Yes, they would.

[S] Every feature in this parable, my dear Glaucon, is meant to fit our earlier analysis. The prison dwelling corresponds to the region revealed to us through the sense of sight, and the firelight within it to the power of the Sun. The ascent to see the things in the upper world you may take as standing for the upward journey of the soul into the region of the intelligible; then you will be in possession of what I surmise, since that is what you wish to be told. Heaven knows whether it is true; but this, at any rate, is how it appears to me. In the world of knowledge, the last thing to be perceived and only with great difficulty is the essential Form of Goodness. Once it is perceived, the conclusion must follow that, for all things, this is the cause of whatever is right and good; in the visible world it gives birth to light and to the lord of light, while it is itself sovereign in the intelligible world and the parent of intelligence and truth. Without having had a vision of this Form no one can act with wisdom, either in his own life or in matters of state. . . .

For Plato, the perfect state, like the well-formed soul, is one governed by reason. By contrast, in the imperfect state, as in the imperfect soul, greed, selfishness, desire, and disorder predominate. Democracy is flawed, said Plato, because most people lack the ability to deal intelligently with matters of state. In the end, said Plato, the democratic state degenerates into anarchy, and the way is prepared for a tyrant. Plato viewed the tyrant as the most despicable of persons. A slave to his own passions, said Plato, the tyrant is like a lunatic who "dreams that he can lord it over all mankind and heaven besides." The character of the philosopher is the very opposite of the sick soul of the tyrant. In the following passage, Plato discusses what he regards as democracy's weaknesses.

[S] And when the poor win, the result is a democracy. They kill some of the opposite party, banish others, and grant the rest an equal share in civil rights and government, officials being usually appointed by lot.

[G] Yes, that is how a democracy comes to be established, whether by force of arms or because the other party is terrorized into giving way.

[S] Now what is the character of this new régime? Obviously the way they govern themselves will throw light on the democratic type of man.

[G] No doubt.

[S] First of all, they are free. Liberty and free speech are rife everywhere; anyone is allowed to do what he likes.

[G] Yes, so we are told.

[S] That being so, every man will arrange his own manner of life to suit his pleasure. The result will be a greater variety of individuals than under any other constitution. So it may be the finest of all, with its variegated pattern of all sorts of characters. Many people may think it the best, just as women and children might admire a mixture of colours of every shade in the pattern of a dress. At any rate if we are in search of a constitution, here is a good place to look for one. A democracy is so free that it contains a sample of every kind; and perhaps anyone who intends to found a state, as we have been doing,

ought first to visit this emporium of constitutions and choose the model he likes best.

[G] He will find plenty to choose from.

[S] Here, too, you are not obliged to be in authority, however competent you may be, or to submit to authority, if you do not like it; you need not fight when your fellow citizens are at war, nor remain at peace when they do, unless you want peace; and though you may have no legal right to hold office or sit on juries, you will do so all the same if the fancy takes you. . . .

. . . When he [the democrat] is told that some pleasures should be sought and valued as arising from desires of a higher order, others chastised and enslaved because the desires are base, he will shut the gates of the citadel against the messengers of truth, shaking his head and declaring that one appetite is as good as another and all must have their equal rights. So he spends his days indulging the pleasure of the moment, now intoxicated with wine and music, and then taking to a spare diet and drinking nothing but water; one day in hard training, the next doing nothing at all, the third apparently immersed in study. Every now and then he takes a part in politics, leaping to his feet to say or do whatever comes into his head. . . . His life is subject to no order or restraint, and he has no wish to change an existence which he calls pleasant, free, and happy.

That well describes the life of one whose motto is liberty and equality. . . .

In a democratic country you will be told that liberty is its noblest possession, which makes it the only fit place for a free spirit to live in.

[G] True; that is often said.

[S] Well then, as I was saying, perhaps the insatiable desire for this good to the neglect of everything else may transform a democracy and lead to a demand for despotism. A democratic state may fall under the influence of unprincipled leaders, ready to minister to its thirst for liberty with too deep draughts of this heady wine; and then, if its rulers are not complaisant enough to give it unstinted freedom, they will be arraigned as accursed oligarchs and punished. Law-abiding citizens will be insulted as nonentities who hug their chains; and all praise and honour will be bestowed, both publicly and in private, on rulers who behave like subjects and subjects who behave like rulers. In such a state the spirit of liberty is bound to go to all lengths. . . .

. . . The parent falls into the habit of behaving like the child, and the child like the parent: the father is afraid of his sons, and they show no fear or respect for their parents, in order to assert their freedom. . . . To descend to smaller matters, the schoolmaster timidly flatters his pupils, and the pupils make light of their masters as well as of their attendants. Generally speaking, the young copy their elders, argue with them,

and will not do as they are told; while the old, anxious not to be thought disagreeable tyrants, imitate the young and condescend to enter into their jokes and amusements. . . .

Putting all these items together, you can see the result: the citizens become so sensitive that they resent the slightest application of control as intolerable tyranny, and in their resolve to have no master they end by disregarding even the law, written or unwritten.

[G] Yes, I know that only too well.

[S] Such then, I should say, is the seed, so full of fair promise, from which springs despotism.

REVIEW QUESTIONS

1. According to Plato, what were the character traits a philosopher should possess? What traits should he avoid?
2. In terms of the Allegory of the Cave, what is real and what is illusion?
3. Why did Plato believe that philosophers would make the best rulers?
4. In Plato's view, what were the principal arguments against democracy? What is your assessment of his critique?

9 Aristotle: Science, Politics, and Ethics

Aristotle (384–322 B.C.) was born at Stagira, a Greek city-state on the Macedonian coast. About 367 B.C., he came to Athens to study with Plato, and he remained a member of Plato's Academy for twenty years. In 342 B.C., Philip II, king of Macedonia, invited Aristotle to tutor his son Alexander, who was then fourteen years old. When Alexander succeeded Philip and set out to conquer the Persian Empire, Aristotle left Macedonia for Athens, where he opened a school of philosophy called the Lyceum, named for a nearby temple to Apollo Lyceus. Aristotle synthesized the thought of earlier philosophers, including his teacher Plato, and was the leading authority of his day in virtually every field of knowledge.

Aristotle
HISTORY OF ANIMALS, POLITICS, AND NICOMACHEAN ETHICS

Scientific thinking encompasses both rationalism and empiricism. Rationalism—pursuit of truth through thought alone, independent of experience with the natural world—was advocated by Plato. This approach points in the direction of theoretical mathematics. Like Plato, Aristotle valued reason, but unlike his teacher he also had great respect for the concrete details of nature obtained through sense experience. In *History of Animals,* Aristotle demonstrated his empirical approach: observing nature and collecting, classifying, and analyzing data. Aristotle's empiricism is the foundation of such sciences as geology, botany, and biology. The first excerpt, a careful observation of the development of a chick embryo, illustrates Aristotle's empiricism.

When he turned to the study of politics, Aristotle also followed an empirical methodology. He undertook a series of historical studies of the constitutions of 158 Greek states. The most significant and complete study that has survived describes the constitution of Athens. On the basis of these extensive surveys, Aristotle proceeded to write *Politics,* his masterwork of political philosophy, excerpted in the second reading.

Like Socrates and Plato, Aristotle based his ethics on reason. People could achieve moral well-being, said Aristotle, when they avoided extremes of behavior and rationally chose the way of moderation. In his *Nicomachean Ethics,* dedicated to his son Nicomachus, Aristotle described the "proud man." This passage, excerpted in the third reading, sketches characteristics that make up the Greek ideal of excellence.

HISTORY OF ANIMALS

. . . With the common hen after three days and three nights there is the first indication of the embryo; with larger birds the interval being longer, with smaller birds shorter. Meanwhile the yolk comes into being, rising towards the sharp end, where the primal element of the egg is situated, and where the egg gets hatched; and the heart appears, like a speck of blood, in the white of the egg. This point beats and moves as though endowed with life, . . . and a membrane carrying bloody fibres now envelops the yolk. . . . A little afterwards the body is differentiated, at first very small and white. The head is clearly distinguished, and in it the eyes, swollen out to a great extent. This condition of the eyes lasts on for a good while, as it is only by degrees that they diminish in size and collapse. At the outset the under portion of the body appears insignificant in comparison with the upper portion. . . . The life-element of the chick is in the white of the egg, and the nutriment comes through the navel-string out of the yolk.

When the egg is now ten days old the chick and all its parts are distinctly visible. The head is still larger than the rest of its body, and the eyes larger than the head, but still devoid of vision. The eyes, if removed about this time, are found to be larger than beans, and black; if the cuticle be peeled off them there is a white and cold liquid inside, quite glittering in the sunlight, but there is no hard substance whatsoever. Such is the condition of the head and eyes. At this time also the larger internal organs are visible. . . .

About the twentieth day, if you open the egg and touch the chick, it moves inside and chirps; and it is already coming to be covered with down, when, after the twentieth day is past, the chick begins to break the shell. The head is situated over the right leg close to the flank, and the wing is placed over the head. . . .

In the following selection from *Politics,* Aristotle begins by defining the nature of a state and its purpose.

POLITICS

It is clear therefore that the state cannot be defined merely as a community dwelling in the same place and preventing its members from wrong-doing and promoting the exchange of goods and services. Certainly all these must be present if there is to be a state, but even the presence of every one of them does not *ipso facto* [by that fact] make a state. The state is intended to enable all, in their households and their kinships, to live *well,* meaning by that a full and satisfying life. . . .

He then addresses the problem of where the sovereign power of the state ought to reside.

. . . "Where ought the sovereign power of the state to reside?" With the people? With the propertied classes? With the good? With one man, the best of all the good? With one man, the tyrant? There are objections to all these. Thus suppose we say the people is the supreme authority, then if they use their numerical superiority to make a distribution of the property of the rich, is not that unjust? It has been done by a valid decision of the sovereign power, yet what can we call it save the very height of injustice? Again, if the majority, having laid their hands on everything, distribute the possessions of the few, they are obviously destroying the state. But that cannot be goodness which destroys its possessor and justice cannot be destructive of the state. So it is clear that this process, though it may be the law, cannot be just. Or, if that is just, the actions taken by a tyrant must be just; his superior power enables him to use force, just as the masses force their will on the rich. Thirdly, if it is just for the few and wealthy to rule, and if they too rob and plunder and help themselves to the goods of the many, is that just? If it is, then it is just in the former case also. The answer clearly is that all these three are bad and unjust. The fourth alternative, that the good should rule and have the supreme authority, is also not free from objection; it means that all the rest must be without official standing, debarred from holding office under the constitution. The fifth alternative, that one man, the best, should

rule, is no better; by making the number of rulers fewer we leave still larger numbers without official standing. It might be objected too that it is a bad thing for any human being, subject to all possible disorders and affections of the human mind, to be the sovereign authority, which ought to be reserved for the law itself. . . .

. . . [A]t the moment it would seem that the most defensible, perhaps even the truest, answer to the question would be to say that the majority ought to be sovereign. . . . For where there are many people, each has some share of goodness and intelligence, and when these are brought together, they become as it were one multiple man with many pairs of feet and hands and many minds. So too in regard to character and powers of perception. That is why the general public is a better judge of works of music and poetry; some judge some parts, some others, but their joint pronouncement is a verdict upon the whole. . . .

Aristotle seeks to determine what is the best constitution. His conclusion reflects the premise developed in his *Ethics* that moderation, or the middle way, is the path to virtue in all things. So, Aristotle says that in forming a constitution for the state, power should reside in the hands of the middle class rather than the aristocracy or the poor.

If we were right when in our *Ethics* we stated that Virtue is a Mean and that the happy life is life free and unhindered and according to virtue, then the best life must be the middle way, [or the mean] . . . between two extremes which it is open to those at either end to attain. And the same principle must be applicable to the goodness or badness of cities and states. For the constitution of a city is really the way it lives.

In all states there are three sections of the community—the very well-off, the very badly-off, and those in between. Seeing therefore that it is agreed that moderation and a middle position are best, it is clear that in the matter of possessions to own a middling amount is best of all.

This condition is most obedient to reason, and following reason is just what is difficult both for the exceedingly rich, handsome, strong, and well-born, and for the opposite, the extremely poor, the weak, and the downtrodden. The former commit deeds of violence on a large scale, the latter are delinquent and wicked in petty ways. The misdeeds of the one class are due to *hubris* [overweening pride, arrogance], the misdeeds of the other to rascality. . . . There are other drawbacks about the two extremes. Those who have a super-abundance of all that makes for success, strength, riches, friends, and so forth, neither wish to hold office nor understand the work; and this is ingrained in them from childhood on; even at school they are so full of their superiority that they have never learned to do what they are told. Those on the other hand who are greatly deficient in these qualities are too subservient. So they cannot command and can only obey in a servile régime, while the others cannot obey in any régime and can command only in a master-slave relationship. The result is a state not of free men but of slaves and masters, the one full of envy, the other of contempt. Nothing could be farther removed from friendship or from the whole idea of a shared partnership in a state. . . . The state aims to consist as far as possible of those who are like and equal, a condition found chiefly among the middle section. . . . The middle class is also the steadiest element, the least eager for change. They neither covet, like the poor, the possessions of others, nor do others covet theirs, as the poor covet those of the rich. . . .

It is clear then both that the political partnership which operates through the middle class is best, and also that those cities have every chance of being well-governed in which the middle class is large, stronger if possible than the other two together, or at any rate stronger than one of them. . . . For this reason it is a happy state of affairs when those who take part in the life of the state have a moderate but adequate amount of property. . . . Tyranny often emerges from an over-enthusiastic democracy or from an oligarchy, but much more rarely from middle-class constitutions or from those very near to them.

The superiority of the middle type of constitution is clear also from the fact that it alone is free from fighting among factions. Where the middle element is large, there least of all arise faction and counter-faction among citizens. . . .

The following selection from *Ethics* shows how Aristotle's ethical theory rests on the principles of moderation and balance. Aristotle notes that some people become "angry at the wrong things, more than is right, and longer, and cannot be appeased until they inflict vengeance or punishment." On the other extreme, foolish and slavish people endure every insult without defending themselves. Between these extremes is the proud man, "who is angry at the right thing and with the right people, and, further, as he ought, when he ought, and as long as he ought." Even-tempered and moderate in all things, such a man "tends to be unperturbed and not to be led by passion."

ETHICS

. . . In the first place, then, as has been said, the proud man is concerned with honours; yet he will also bear himself with moderation towards wealth and power and all good or evil fortune, whatever may befall him, and will be neither over-joyed by good fortune nor over-pained by evil. For not even towards honour does he bear himself as if it were a very great thing. . . .

He does not run into trifling dangers, nor is he fond of danger, because he honours few things; but he will face great dangers, and when he is in danger he is unsparing of his life, knowing that there are conditions on which life is not worth having. And he is the sort of man to confer benefits, but he is ashamed of receiving them; for the one is the mark of a superior, the other of an inferior. And he is apt to confer greater benefits in return; for thus the original benefactor besides being paid will incur a debt to him, and will be the gainer by the transaction. They seem also to remember any service they have done, but not those they have received (for he who receives a service is inferior to him who has done it, but the proud man wishes to be superior), and to hear of the former with pleasure, of the latter with displeasure. . . . It is a mark of the proud man also to ask for nothing or scarcely anything, but to give help readily, and to be dignified towards people who enjoy high position and good fortune, but unassuming towards those of the middle class; for it is a difficult and lofty thing to be superior to the former, but easy to be so to the latter, and a lofty bearing over the former is no mark of ill-breeding, but among humble people it is as vulgar as a display of strength against the weak. Again, it is characteristic of the proud man not to aim at the things commonly held in honour, or the things in which others excel; to be sluggish and to hold back except where great honour or a great work is at stake, and to be a man of few deeds, but of great and notable ones. He must also be open in his hate and in his love (for to conceal one's feelings, i.e. to care less for truth than for what people will think, is a coward's part), and must speak and act openly; for he is free of speech because he is contemptuous, and he is given to telling the truth, except when he speaks in irony to the vulgar. He must be unable to make his life revolve round another, unless it be a friend; for this is slavish, and for this reason all flatterers are servile and people lacking in self-respect are flatterers. Nor is he given to admiration; for nothing to him is great. Nor is he mindful of wrongs; for it is not the part of a proud man to have a long memory, especially for wrongs, but rather to overlook them. Nor is he a gossip; for he will speak neither about himself nor about another, since he cares not to be praised nor for others to be blamed; nor again is he given to praise; and for the same reason he is not an evil-speaker, even about his enemies, except from haughtiness. With regard to necessary or small matters he is least of all men given to lamentation or the asking of favours; for it is the part of one who takes such matters seriously to behave so with respect to them. He is one who will possess beautiful and profitless things rather than profitable and useful ones; for this is more proper to a character that suffices to itself.

Further, a slow step is thought proper to the proud man, a deep voice, and a level utterance; for the man who takes few things seriously is not likely to be hurried, nor the man who thinks nothing great to be excited, while a shrill voice and a rapid gait are the results of hurry and excitement.

Such, then, is the proud man; the man who falls short of him is unduly humble, and the man who goes beyond him is vain.

REVIEW QUESTIONS

1. What evidence in Aristotle's description of chick embryo development illustrates his use of empirical methods of scientific inquiry?
2. Why did Aristotle believe that state power was best left in the hands of the middle classes? Why did he fear government by the poor, the tyrant, the few, the good, or the rich?
3. According to Aristotle, how did the "proud man," a man of excellence, relate to others? To worldly success and riches?
4. What kind of moral values did the proud man cultivate?
5. Aristotle urged both self-sufficiency and moderation as guiding principles in human life. In what specific ways would the proud man demonstrate these virtues?

10 Hellenistic Culture: Universalism and Individualism

During the Hellenistic Age, Greek civilization spread to the Near East in the wake of Alexander's conquests, and Mesopotamian, Egyptian, Persian, and Jewish traditions—particularly religious beliefs—moved westward. Thousands of Greeks settled in newly established cities throughout the ancient Near East, carrying with them Greek urban institutions and culture—laws, cults, educational methods, artistic and architectural styles, customs, and dress. The new Hellenistic cities were dominated by a Greek upper class, which recruited native non-Greeks to its ranks to the degree that they became *Hellenized,* that is, adopted the Greek language and lifestyle. Through intermarriage, education in Greek schools, and the prospect of political and economic advantage, non-Greeks came to participate in and contribute to a common Greek civilization that spread from the western Mediterranean to the Indus River.

Cultural exchange permeated all phases of cultural life. Sculpture showed the influence of many lands. Historians wrote world histories, not just local ones. Greek astronomers worked with data collected over the centuries by the Babylonians. Greeks increasingly demonstrated a fascination with Near Eastern religious cults. Philosophers helped to break down the barriers between peoples by asserting that all inhabit a single fatherland. As the philosopher Crates said, "My fatherland has no single tower, no single roof. The whole earth is my citadel, a home ready for us all to live in."

Plutarch
CULTURAL FUSION

The Greek biographer Plutarch (c. A.D. 46–120) provides a glowing account of Alexander the Great in the following passage. Plutarch saw Alexander as a philosopher in action and an apostle of universalism and human brotherhood. Many modern historians reject this assessment of Alexander's intentions, but the scope of his conquests and their significance in reducing the distinctions between Near Easterners and Greeks remain impressive.

[W]hen Alexander was civilizing Asia, Homer was commonly read, and the children of the Persians, of the Susianians, and of the Gedrosians[1] learned to chant the tragedies of Sophocles and Euripides. . . . [y]et through Alexander Bactria[2] and the Caucasus learned to revere the gods of the Greeks. Plato wrote a book on the One Ideal Constitution, but because of its forbidding character he could not persuade anyone to adopt it; but Alexander established more than seventy cities

---

[1]The Susianians lived in and near the city of Susa, the capital of the Persian Empire; the Gedrosians lived just north of the Arabian Sea, in what is now southeastern Iran and western Pakistan.

[2]Bactria, a northeastern province of the ancient Persian Empire, was located in the area of modern Afghanistan and Central Asia.

among savage tribes, and sowed all Asia[3] with Grecian magistracies, and thus overcame its uncivilized and brutish manner of living. Although few of us read Plato's *Laws,* yet hundreds of thousands have made use of Alexander's laws, and continue to use them. Those who were vanquished by Alexander are happier than those who escaped his hand; for these had no one to put an end to the wretchedness of their existence, while the victor compelled those others to lead a happy life.... Thus Alexander's new subjects would not have been civilized, had they not been vanquished; Egypt would not have its Alexandria, nor Mesopotamia its Seleuceia, nor Sogdiana its Prophthasia, nor India its Bucephalia,[4] nor the Caucasus a Greek city hard by; for by the founding of cities in these places savagery was extinguished and the worse element, gaining familiarity with the better, changed under its influence. If, then, philosophers take the greatest pride in civilizing and rendering adaptable the intractable and untutored elements in human character, and if Alexander has been shown to have changed the savage natures of countless tribes, it is with good reason that he should be regarded as a very great philosopher.

Moreover, the much-admired *Republic* of Zeno, the founder of the Stoic sect, may be summed up in this one main principle: that all the inhabitants of this world of ours should not live differentiated by their respective rules of justice into separate cities and communities, but that we should consider men to be of one community and one polity, and that we should have a common life and an order common to us all, even as a herd that feeds together and shares the pasturage of a common field. This Zeno wrote, giving shape to a dream or, as it were, shadowy picture of a well-ordered and philosophic commonwealth; but it was Alexander who gave effect to the idea. For Alexander did not follow Aristotle's advice to treat the Greeks as if he were their leader, and other peoples as if he were their master; to have regard for the Greeks as for friends and kindred, but to conduct himself toward other peoples as though they were plants or animals; for to do so would have been to cumber his leadership with numerous battles and banishments and festering seditions. But, as he believed that he came as a heaven-sent governor to all, and as a mediator for the whole world, those whom he could not persuade to unite with him, he conquered by force of arms, and he brought together into one body all men everywhere, uniting and mixing in one great loving-cup, as it were, men's lives, their characters, their marriages, their very habits of life. He bade them all consider as their fatherland the whole inhabited earth, as their stronghold and protection his camp, as akin to them all good men, and as foreigners only the wicked; they should not distinguish between Grecian and foreigner by Grecian cloak and targe [shield], or scimitar [curved sword] and jacket; but the distinguishing mark of the Grecian should be seen in virtue, and that of the foreigner in iniquity; clothing and food, marriage and manner of life they should regard as common to all, being blended into one by ties of blood and children....

... For he did not overrun Asia like a robber nor was he minded to tear and rend it, as if it were booty and plunder bestowed by unexpected good fortune, after the manner in which Hannibal later descended upon Italy.... But Alexander desired to render all upon earth subject to one law of reason and one form of government and to reveal all men as one people, and to this purpose he made himself conform. But if the deity that sent down Alexander's soul into this world of ours had not recalled him quickly, one law would govern all mankind, and they all would look toward one rule of justice as though toward a common source of light. But as it is, that part of the world which has not looked upon Alexander has remained without sunlight.

---

[3]"All Asia" referred to western Asia Minor at first, then, as Alexander's conquests spread further, the term was broadened to include the other territory to the east, extending to what is now India and Central Asia.

[4]Seleuceia (named for one of Alexander's generals) was near modern Baghdad. Prophthasia, a city founded by Alexander, was in Sogdiana, north of modern Afghanistan. Bucephalia, on a northern branch of the Indus River, was named for Alexander's horse Bucephalus.

Epicurus
SELF-SUFFICIENCY

Hellenistic philosophy marks a second stage in the evolution of Greek thought. In the Hellenic Age, philosophers dealt primarily with the individual's relationship to the city-state. In the Hellenistic Age, philosophers were concerned with defining the individual's relationship to a wider, often competitive and hostile community that consisted of a plurality of peoples and a variety of cultures. In particular, the later philosophers sought to help people become emotionally self-sufficient so that they could attain peace of mind in such an environment. Among the most significant schools of philosophy that emerged during the Hellenistic Age were Stoicism (see page 74) and Epicureanism.

Epicureanism was named for its founder, Epicurus (341–270 B.C.), who established a school at Athens in 307 or 306 B.C. To achieve peace of mind, taught Epicurus, one should refrain from worrying about death or pleasing the gods, avoid intense involvements in public affairs, cultivate friendships, and pursue pleasure prudently. The following excerpts from Epicurus' works reveal his prescription for achieving emotional well-being. The passages have been grouped according to particular subjects.

THE GODS

. . . We must grasp this point, that the principal disturbance in the minds of men arises because they think that these celestial bodies are blessed and immortal, and yet have wills and actions and motives inconsistent with these attributes; and because they are always expecting or imagining some everlasting misery [inflicted on them by the gods], such as is depicted in legends, or even fear the loss of feeling in death . . . and, again, because they are brought to this pass not by reasoned opinion, but rather by some irrational presentiment . . . and, by learning the true causes of celestial phenomena and all other occurrences that come to pass from time to time, we shall free ourselves from all which produces the utmost fear in other men.

————

It is vain to ask of the gods what a man is capable of supplying for himself.

DEATH

. . . So death, the most terrifying of ills, is nothing to us, since so long as we exist, death is not with us; but when death comes, then we do not exist. It does not then concern either the living or the dead, since for the former it is not, and the latter are no more.

But the many at one moment shun death as the greatest of evils, at another yearn for it as a respite from the evils in life. But the wise man neither seeks to escape life nor fears the cessation of life, for neither does life offend him nor does the absence of life seem to be any evil. And just as with food he does not seek simply the larger share and nothing else, but rather the most pleasant, so he seeks to enjoy not the longest period of time, but the most pleasant.

REASON AND PHILOSOPHY

Let no one when young delay to study philosophy, nor when he is old grow weary of his study. For no one can come too early or too late to secure the health of his soul. And the man who says that the age for philosophy has either not yet come or has gone by is like the man who says that the age for happiness is not yet come to him, or has passed away. Wherefore both when young and old a man must study philosophy, that as he grows old he may be young in blessings through the grateful recollection of what has been and that in youth he may be old as well, since he will know no fear of what is to come. We must then meditate on the things that make our happiness, seeing that when that is with us we have all, but when it is absent we do all to win it.

———

A man cannot dispel his fear about the most important matters if he does not know what is the nature of the universe but suspects the truth of some mythical story. So that without natural science it is not possible to attain our pleasures unalloyed.

———

We must not pretend to study philosophy, but study it in reality: for it is not the appearance of health that we need, but real health.

LIVING WELL

When, therefore, we maintain that pleasure is the end, we do not mean the pleasures of profligates and those that consist in sensuality, as is supposed by some who are either ignorant or disagree with us or do not understand, but freedom from pain in the body and from trouble in the mind. For it is not continuous drinkings and revellings, nor the satisfaction of lusts, nor the enjoyment of fish and other luxuries of the wealthy table, which produce a pleasant life, but sober reasoning, searching out the motives for all choice and avoidance, and banishing mere opinions, to which are due the greatest disturbance of the spirit.

Of all this the beginning and the greatest good is prudence. Wherefore prudence is a more precious thing even than philosophy; for from prudence are sprung all the other virtues, and it teaches us that it is not possible to live pleasantly without living prudently and honourably and justly. . . .

———

Of all the things which wisdom acquires to produce the blessedness of the complete life, far the greatest is the possession of friendship.

———

We must release ourselves from the prison of affairs and politics.

———

A free life cannot acquire many possessions, because this is not easy to do without servility to mobs or monarchs. . . .

———

The noble soul occupies itself with wisdom and friendship. . . .

———

The first measure of security is to watch over one's youth and to guard against what makes havoc of all by means of pestering desires.

REVIEW QUESTIONS

1. According to Plutarch, what benefits did Alexander confer on the peoples he conquered?
2. In Plutarch's view, how did Alexander's policies reflect Stoic philosophic ideals?
3. What did Epicurus believe were the chief causes of emotional distress among human beings?
4. What advice did he offer for achieving inner peace and happiness?
5. How did Epicurean teachings both continue and break with traditional Greek values?

CHAPTER 3

The Romans

FORUM IN ROME. The forum, a large rectangular space that served as a marketplace, was the center of a Roman city. In Rome itself, the forum evolved into a political center surrounded by large public buildings. *(©Adam Woolfitt/Woodfin Camp.)*

Roman history falls into two broad periods—the Republic and the Empire. The Roman Republic began in 509 B.C. with the overthrow of the Etruscan monarchy and lasted until 27 B.C., when Octavian (Augustus) became in effect the first Roman emperor, ending almost five hundred years of republican self-government. For the next five hundred years, Rome would be governed by emperors. In 264 B.C., the Roman Republic had established dominion over the Italian peninsula. By 146 B.C., Rome had emerged victorious over the Mediterranean world.

The Roman Republic, which had conquered a vast empire, was destroyed not by foreign armies but by internal weaknesses. In the century after 133 B.C., the senate, which had governed Rome well during its march to empire, degenerated into a self-seeking oligarchy; it failed to resolve critical domestic problems and fought to preserve its own power and prestige. When Rome had been threatened by foreign enemies, all classes united in a spirit of patriotism. This social harmony broke down when the threat from outside diminished, and the Republic was torn by internal dissension and civil war.

In the chaotic years following Julius Caesar's assassination in 44 B.C., Octavian (Augustus) emerged victorious over his rivals, becoming the unchallenged ruler of Rome. His long reign, from 27 B.C. to A.D. 14, marks the beginning of the *Pax Romana,* the Roman Peace, which endured until A.D. 180.

The period of the Pax Romana was one of the finest in the ancient world. Revolts against Roman rule were few, and Roman legions ably defended the Empire's borders. The Mediterranean world had never enjoyed so many years of peace, effective government, and economic well-being. Stretching from Britain to the Arabian Desert and from the Danube River to the sands of the Sahara, the Roman Empire united some fifty to sixty million people. In many ways the Roman Empire was the fulfillment of the universalism and cosmopolitanism of the Hellenistic Age. The same law bound together Italians, Spaniards, North Africans, Greeks, Syrians, and other peoples. Although dissatisfaction was sometimes violently expressed and separatist tendencies persisted, notably in Judea and Gaul, people from diverse backgrounds viewed themselves as Romans even though they had never set foot in the capital city.

During the third century the Roman Empire suffered hard times, and the ordered civilization of the Pax Romana was destroyed. The Empire was plunged into anarchy as generals vied for the throne. Taking advantage of the weakened border defenses, the barbarians (Germanic tribesmen) crossed the Danube frontier and pillaged Roman cities. At the end of the fourth and the opening of the fifth century, several barbarian tribes poured into the Empire in great numbers. In succeeding decades Germanic tribes overran Roman provinces and set up kingdoms on lands that had been Roman. The Roman Empire in the west fell; the eastern provinces, however, survived as the Byzantine Empire.

The history of the Roman Empire influenced Western civilization in many ways. From Latin, the language of Rome, came the Romance languages: French, Italian, Spanish, Portuguese, and Romanian. Roman law became the basis of the legal codes of most modern European states. Rome preserved Greek culture, the foundation of Western learning and aesthetics, and spread it to other lands. And Christianity, the religion of the West, was born in the Roman Empire.

1 Rome's March to World Empire

By 146 B.C., Rome had become the dominant state in the Mediterranean world. Roman expansion had occurred in three main stages: the uniting of the Italian peninsula, which gave Rome the manpower that transformed it from a city-state into a great power; the collision with Carthage, from which Rome emerged as ruler of the western Mediterranean; and the subjugation of the Hellenistic states, which brought Romans in close contact with Greek civilization. As Rome expanded territorially, its leaders enlarged their vision. Instead of restricting citizenship to people having ethnic kinship, Rome assimilated other peoples into its political community. Just as law had grown to cope with the earlier grievances of the plebeians, so it adjusted to the new situations resulting from the creation of a multinational empire. The city of Rome was evolving into the city of humanity—the cosmopolis envisioned by the Stoics.

Polybius
THE ROMAN ARMY

The discipline and dedication of the citizen-soldiers help explain Rome's success in conquering a world empire. In the following account, Polybius (c. 200–c. 118 B.C.) tells how the commanders enforced obedience and fostered heroism.

A court-martial composed of the tribunes immediately sits to try him [a soldier], and if he is found guilty, he is punished by beating *(fustuarium)*. This is carried out as follows. The tribune takes a cudgel and lightly touches the condemned man with it, whereupon all the soldiers fall upon him with clubs and stones, and usually kill him in the camp itself. But even those who contrive to escape are no better off. How indeed could they be? They are not allowed to return to their homes, and none of their family would dare to receive such a man into the house. Those who have once fallen into this misfortune are completely and finally ruined. The *optio* [lieutenant] and the *decurio* [sergeant] of the squadron are liable to the same punishment if they fail to pass on the proper orders at the proper moment to the patrols and the *decurio* of the next squadron. The consequence of the extreme severity of this penalty and of the absolute impossibility of avoiding it is that the night watches of the Roman army are faultlessly kept.

The ordinary soldiers are answerable to the tribunes [elected military administrators] and the tribunes to the consuls [commanders]. A tribune, and in the case of the allies a prefect [commander of a large unit], has power to inflict fines, distrain on [confiscate] goods, and to order a flogging. The punishment of beating to death is also inflicted upon those who steal from the camp, those who give false evidence, those who in full manhood commit homosexual offences, and finally upon anyone who has been punished three times for the same offence. The above are the offences which are punished as crimes. The following actions are regarded as unmanly and dishonourable in a soldier: to make a false report to the tribune of your courage in the field in order to earn distinction; to leave the post to which you have been assigned in a covering force because of fear; and similarly to throw away out of fear any of your weapons on the field of battle. For this reason the men who have been posted to a covering force are often doomed to certain death. This is because they will remain at their posts even when they are overwhelmingly outnumbered on account of their dread of the punishment that awaits them. Again, those who have lost a shield or a sword or any other weapon on the battlefield often hurl themselves upon the enemy hoping that they will either recover the weapon they have lost, or else escape by death from the inevitable disgrace and the humiliations they would suffer at home.

If it ever happens that a large body of men break and run in this way and whole maniples [units of 120 to 300 men] desert their posts under extreme pressure, the officers reject the idea of beating to death or executing all who are guilty, but the solution they adopt is as effective as it is terrifying. The tribune calls the legion [large military unit] on parade and brings to the front those who are guilty of having left the ranks. He then reprimands them sharply, and finally chooses by lot some five or eight or twenty of the offenders, the number being calculated so that it represents about a tenth[1] of those who have shown themselves guilty of cowardice. Those on whom the lot has

fallen are mercilessly clubbed to death in the manner I have already described. The rest are put on rations of barley instead of wheat, and are ordered to quarter themselves outside the camp in a place which has no defences. The danger and the fear of drawing the fatal lot threatens every man equally, and since there is no certainty on whom it may fall, and the public disgrace of receiving rations of barley is shared by all alike, the Romans have adopted the best possible practice both to inspire terror and to repair the harm done by any weakening of their warlike spirit.

The Romans also have an excellent method of encouraging young soldiers to face danger. Whenever any have especially distinguished themselves in a battle, the general assembles the troops and calls forward those he considers to have shown exceptional courage. He praises them first for their gallantry in action and for anything in their previous conduct which is particularly worthy of mention, and then he distributes gifts such as the following: to a man who has wounded one of the enemy, a spear; to one who has killed and stripped an enemy, a cup if he is in the infantry, or horse-trappings if in the cavalry—originally the gift was simply a lance. These presentations are not made to men who have wounded or stripped an enemy in the course of a pitched battle, or at the storming of a city, but to those who during a skirmish or some similar situation in which there is no necessity to engage in single combat, have voluntarily and deliberately exposed themselves to danger.

At the storming of a city the first man to scale the wall is awarded a crown of gold. In the same way those who have shielded and saved one of their fellow-citizens or of the allies are honoured with gifts from the consul, and the men whose lives they have preserved present them of their own free will with a crown; if not, they are compelled to do so by the tribunes who judge the case. Moreover, a man who has been saved in this way reveres his rescuer as a father for the rest of his life and must treat him as if he were a parent. And so by means of such incentives even those who

---

[1]This custom is the origin of the word *decimate,* from the Latin *decem,* ten.

stay at home feel the impulse to emulate such achievements in the field no less than those who are present and see and hear what takes place. For the men who receive these trophies not only enjoy great prestige in the army and soon afterwards in their homes, but they are also singled out for precedence in religious processions when they return. On these occasions nobody is allowed to wear decorations save those who have been honoured for their bravery by the consuls, and it is the custom to hang up the trophies they have won in the most conspicuous places in their houses, and to regard them as proofs and visible symbols of their valour. So when we consider this people's almost obsessive concern with military rewards and punishments, and the immense importance which they attach to both, it is not surprising that they emerge with brilliant success from every war in which they engage.

REVIEW QUESTIONS

1. How did the Romans ensure good discipline among their soldiers?
2. What factors mentioned by Polybius help explain Rome's emergence as a great power?

Livy
THE SECOND PUNIC WAR: THE THREAT FROM HANNIBAL

In 264 B.C., Rome, which had just completed its conquest of Italy, went to war with Carthage, the dominant power in the western Mediterranean. A threat to the north Sicilian city of Messana (now Messina) was the immediate cause of the war. Rome feared that Carthage might use Messana as a springboard from which to attack the cities of southern Italy, which were allied to Rome, or to interfere with their trade. The First Punic War (264–241 B.C.) was a grueling conflict; drawing manpower from its loyal allies, Rome finally prevailed. Carthage surrendered Sicily to Rome, and three years later Rome seized the large islands of Corsica and Sardinia, west of Italy, from a weakened Carthage.

Carthaginian expansion in Spain led to the Second Punic War (218–201 B.C.). The Carthaginian army was led by Hannibal (247–183 B.C.), whose military genius impressed and frightened Rome. Hannibal brought the battle to Rome by leading his seasoned army, including war elephants, across the Alps into Italy.

Hannibal demonstrated his superb generalship at the battle of Cannae in 216 B.C., where the Carthaginians destroyed a Roman army of sixty thousand. Hannibal removed some of his soldiers in the center and commanded the thin line to retreat as the Romans charged. Believing that the enemy was on the run, the Romans continued their headlong thrust into the Carthaginian center. Then, according to plan, Carthaginian troops stationed on the wings attacked the Roman flanks and the cavalry closed in on the Roman rear, completely encircling the Roman troops. News of the disaster, one of the worst in the Republic's history, brought anguish to the Romans, who feared that Hannibal would march on the capital itself. Adding to Rome's distress was the desertion of some of its Italian allies to Hannibal. In the following passage, the Roman historian Livy (59 B.C.–A.D. 17) describes the mood in Rome after Cannae.

. . . Never, without an enemy actually within the gates, had there been such terror and confusion in the city [Rome]. To write of it is beyond my strength, so I shall not attempt to describe what any words of mine would only make less than the truth. In the previous year a consul and his army had been lost at Trasimene [location of an overwhelming defeat for Rome], and now there was news not merely of another similar blow, but of a multiple calamity—two consular armies annihilated, both consuls[1] dead, Rome left without a force in the field, without a commander, without a single soldier, Apulia and Samnium [two provinces in southern Italy] in Hannibal's hands, and now nearly the whole of Italy overrun. No other nation in the world could have suffered so tremendous a series of disasters, and not been overwhelmed. It was unparalleled in history: the naval defeat off the Aegates islands,* a defeat which forced the Carthaginians to abandon Sicily and Sardinia and suffer themselves to pay taxes and tribute to Rome; the final defeat in Africa to which Hannibal himself afterwards succumbed—neither the one nor the other was in any way comparable to what Rome had now to face, except in the fact that they were not borne with so high a courage.

The praetors[2] Philus and Pomponius summoned the Senate[3] to meet . . . to consider the defence of the City, as nobody doubted that Hannibal, now that the armies were destroyed, would attack Rome—the final operation to crown his victory. It was not easy to work out

a plan: their troubles, already great enough, were made worse by the lack of firm news; the streets were loud with the wailing and weeping of women, and nothing yet being clearly known, living and dead alike were being mourned in nearly every house in the city. In these circumstances, Quintus Fabius Maximus[4] put forward some proposals: riders, he suggested, lightly equipped, should be sent out along the Appian and Latin Ways[5] to question any survivors they might meet roaming the countryside, and report any tidings they could get from them of what had happened to the consuls and the armies. If the gods, in pity for the empire, had suffered any of the Roman name to survive, [the investigators] should inquire where they were, where Hannibal went after the battle, what his plans were, what he was doing, and what he was likely to do next. The task of collecting this information should be entrusted to vigorous and active men. There was also a task, Fabius suggested, for the Senate itself to perform, as there was a lack of public officers: this was, to get rid of the general confusion in the city and restore some sort of order. Women must be forbidden to appear out of doors, and compelled to stay in their homes; family mourning should be checked, and silence imposed everywhere; anyone with news to report should be taken to the praetors, and all individuals should await in their homes the news which personally concerned them. Furthermore, guards should be

---

[1]The consuls served dual offices as elected magistrates of Rome in peacetime and commanders-in-chief of the Roman army.
*The end of the First Punic war in 241 B.C.
[2]Praetors were magistrates who governed the city of Rome when the consuls were absent.
[3]The senate, originally drawn from the patrician caste, was the true ruler of Rome. It advised the magistrates on all matters of public policy.

[4]Fabius (Quintus Fabius Maximus Verrucosus, nicknamed "the Delayer," d. 203 B.C.) was elected consul several times, but his tactics in trying to avoid pitched battles displeased the Romans. However, Fabius' successors were totally defeated at Cannae, and Fabius, elected consul for the fifth time, recaptured Tarentum in 209.
[5]The Appian Way, parts of which exist today, was the main highway from Rome southward to Campania. The Latin Way (Via Latina), a parallel route, passed through hill towns before rejoining the Appian Way.

posted at the gates to prevent anyone from leaving the city, and every man and woman should be made to believe that there was no hope of safety except within the walls of Rome. Once, he ended, the present noise and disorder were under control, then would be the proper time to recall the Senate and debate measures for defence.

The proposals of Fabius won unanimous support. The city magistrates cleared the crowds out of the forum and the senators went off to restore some sort of order in the streets. . . .

How much more serious was the defeat at Cannae than those which had preceded it can be seen by the behaviour of Rome's allies: before that fatal day their loyalty had remained unshaken; now it began to waver, for the simple reason that they despaired of the survival of Roman power. The following peoples went over to the Carthaginian cause: the Atellani, Calatini, Hirpini, some of the Apulians, all the Samnites except the Pentri, the Bruttii, the Lucanians, the Uzentini, and nearly all the Greek settlements on the coast, namely Tarentum, Metapontum, Croton, and Locri, and all the Gauls on the Italian side of the Alps.

But neither the defeats they had suffered nor the subsequent defection of all these allied peoples moved the Romans ever to breathe a word about peace.

---

2   The Spread of Greek Philosophy to Rome

One of the chief consequences of Roman expansion was growing contact with Greek culture. During the third century B.C., Greek civilization started to exercise an increasing and fruitful influence on the Roman mind. Greek teachers, both slave and free, came to Rome and introduced Romans to Hellenic cultural achievements. As they conquered the eastern Mediterranean, Roman generals began to ship libraries and works of art from Greek cities to Rome. Roman sculpture and painting imitated Greek prototypes. In time, Romans acquired from Greece knowledge of scientific thought, medicine, and geography. Roman writers and orators used Greek history, poetry, and oratory as models. Roman philosophers borrowed the ideas of Greek philosophical schools and adapted them to Roman culture.

Cicero
ADVOCATE OF STOICISM

Marcus Tullius Cicero, a leading Roman statesman, was also a distinguished orator, an unsurpassed Latin stylist, and a student of Greek philosophy. His letters, more than eight hundred of which have survived, provide modern historians with valuable insights into late republican politics. His orations before the Senate and law courts have been models of eloquence and rhetorical technique for students of Latin and later European languages.

Like many other Romans, Cicero was influenced by the Greek philosophy of Stoicism. Cicero adopted the Stoic belief that natural law governs the universe and applies to all and that all belong to a common humanity. The gift of reason, which is common to all people, enables us to comprehend this natural law and to order our lives in accordance with its principles, which are unchangeable and eternal. Natural law as understood by right reason commands people to do what is right and deters them from doing what is wrong. Thus there is a unity of knowledge and virtue. For Cicero, the laws of the state should accord with the natural law underlying the universe. Adherence to such rationally formulated laws creates a moral bond among citizens and the peoples of all nations and states. In the following passage from his philosophic treatise *The Laws,* Cicero explored the implications of the Stoic concept of natural law.

. . . Now let us investigate the origins of Justice.

Well then, the most learned men have determined to begin with Law, and it would seem that they are right, if, according to their definition, Law is the highest reason, implanted in Nature, which commands what ought to be done and forbids the opposite. This reason, when firmly fixed and fully developed in the human mind, is Law. And so they believe that Law is intelligence whose natural function it is to command right conduct and forbid wrongdoing. They think that this quality has derived its name in Greek from the idea of granting to every man his own, and in our language I believe it has been named from the idea of choosing. For as they have attributed the idea of fairness to the word law, so we have given it that of selection, though both ideas properly belong to Law. Now if this is correct, as I think it to be in general, then the origin of Justice is to be found in Law, for Law is a natural force; it is the mind and reason of the intelligent man, the standard by which Justice and Injustice are measured. But since our whole discussion has to do with the reasoning of the populace, it will sometimes be necessary to speak in the popular manner, and give the name of law to that which in written form decrees whatever it wishes, either by command or prohibition. For such is the crowd's definition of law. But in determining what Justice is, let us begin with that supreme Law which had its origin ages before any written law existed or any State had been established.

. . . I shall seek the root of Justice in Nature, under whose guidance our whole discussion must be conducted.

. . . [T]hat animal which we call man, endowed with foresight and quick intelligence, complex, keen, possessing memory, full of reason and prudence, has been given a certain distinguished status by the supreme God who created him; for he is the only one among so many different kinds and varieties of living beings who has a share in reason and thought, while all the rest are deprived of it. But what is more divine, I will not say in man only, but in all heaven and earth, than reason? And reason, when it is full grown and perfected, is rightly called wisdom. Therefore, since there is nothing better than reason, and since it exists both in man and God, the first common possession of man and God is reason. But those who have reason in common must also have right reason in common. And since right reason is Law, we must believe that men have Law also in common with the gods. Further, those who share Law must also share Justice; and those who share these are to be regarded as members of the same commonwealth. If indeed they obey the same authorities and powers, this is true in a far greater degree; but as a matter of fact they do obey this celestial system, the divine mind, and the God of transcendent power. Hence we must now conceive of this whole universe as one commonwealth of which both gods and men are members.

Moreover, virtue exists in man and God alike, but in no other creature besides; virtue, however, is nothing else than Nature perfected and developed to its highest point; therefore there is a likeness between man and God. As this is true, what relationship could be closer or clearer than this one? For this reason, Nature has lavishly yielded such a wealth of things adapted to man's convenience and use that what she produces seems intended as a gift to us, and not brought forth by chance; and this is true, not only of what the fertile earth bountifully bestows in the form of grain and fruit, but also of the animals; for it is clear that some of them have been created to be man's slaves, some to supply him with their products, and others to serve as his food. Moreover innumerable arts have been discovered through the teachings of Nature; for it is by a skilful imitation of her that reason has acquired the necessities of life. . . .

. . . [O]ut of all the material of the philosophers' discussions, surely there comes nothing more valuable than the full realization that we are born for Justice, and that right is based, not upon men's opinions, but upon Nature. This fact will immediately be plain if you once get a clear conception of man's fellowship and union with his fellow-men. For no single thing is so like another, so exactly its counterpart, as all of us are to one another. Nay, if bad habits and false beliefs did not twist the weaker minds and turn them in whatever direction they are inclined, no one would be so like his own self as all men would be

like all others. And so, however we may define man, a single definition will apply to all. This is a sufficient proof that there is no difference in kind between man and man; for if there were, one definition could not be applicable to all men; and indeed reason, which alone raises us above the level of the beasts and enables us to draw inferences, to prove and disprove, to discuss and solve problems, and to come to conclusions, is certainly common to us all, and, though varying in what it learns, at least in the capacity to learn it is invariable. For the same things are invariably perceived by the senses, and those things which stimulate the senses, stimulate them in the same way in all men; and those rudimentary beginnings of intelligence to which I have referred, which are imprinted on our minds, are imprinted on all minds alike; and speech, the mind's interpreter, though differing in the choice of words, agrees in the sentiments expressed. In fact, there is no human being of any race who, if he finds a guide, cannot attain to virtue.

Cato the Elder
HOSTILITY TO GREEK PHILOSOPHY

Some conservative Romans were hostile to the Greek influence, which they felt threatened traditional Roman values. Cato the Elder (also the Censor; 234–149 B.C.) denounced Socrates for undermining respect for Athenian law and warned that Greek philosophy might lure Roman youth into similar subversive behavior. The following passage from Plutarch's *Lives* (see page 64) shows Cato's hostility to Greek philosophy.

He was now grown old, when Carneades the Academic, and Diogenes the Stoic, came as deputies from Athens to Rome, praying for release from a penalty of five hundred talents laid on the Athenians, in a suit, to which they did not appear, in which the Oropians were plaintiffs and Sicyonians[1] judges. All the most studious youth immedi-

ately waited on these philosophers, and frequently, with admiration, heard them speak. But the gracefulness of Carneades's oratory, whose ability was really greatest, and his reputation equal to it, gathered large and favourable audiences, and ere long filled, like a wind, all the city with the sound of it. So that it soon began to be told that a Greek, famous even to admiration, winning and carrying all before him, had impressed so strange a love upon the young men, that quitting all their pleasures and pastimes, they ran mad, as it were, after

---

[1]The Oropians came from the town of Oropus in east central Greece. Sicyonians came from the city of Sicyon in southern Greece.

philosophy; which indeed much pleased the Romans in general; nor could they but with much pleasure see the youth receive so welcomely the Greek literature, and frequent the company of learned men. But Cato, on the other side, seeing the passion for words flowing into the city, from the beginning took it ill, fearing lest the youth should be diverted that way, and so should prefer the glory of speaking well before that of arms and doing well. And when the fame of the philosophers increased in the city, and Caius Acilius, a person of distinction, at his own request, became their interpreter to the senate at their first audience, Cato resolved, under some specious pretence, to have all philosophers cleared out of the city; and, coming into the senate, blamed the magistrates for letting these deputies stay so long a time without being despatched, though they were persons that could easily persuade the people to what they pleased; that therefore in all haste something should be determined about their petition, that so they might go home again to their own schools, and declaim to the Greek children, and leave the Roman youth to be obedient, as hitherto, to their own laws and governors.

Yet he did this not out of any anger, as some think, to Carneades; but because he wholly despised philosophy, and out of a kind of pride scoffed at the Greek studies and literature; as, for example, he would say, that Socrates was a prat-

ing, seditious fellow, who did his best to tyrannise over his country, to undermine the ancient customs, and to entice and withdraw the citizens to opinions contrary to the laws. Ridiculing the school of Isocrates,[2] he would add, that his scholars grew old men before they had done learning with him, as if they were to use their art and plead causes in the court of Minos in the next world. And to frighten his son from anything that was Greek, in a more vehement tone than became one of his age, he pronounced, as it were, with the voice of an oracle, that the Romans would certainly be destroyed when they began once to be infected with Greek literature; though time indeed has shown the vanity of this his prophecy; as, in truth, the city of Rome has risen to its highest fortune while entertaining Grecian learning. Nor had he an aversion only against the Greek philosophers, but the physicians also; for having, it seems, heard how Hippocrates, when the king of Persia sent for him, with offers of a fee of several talents, said, that he would never assist barbarians who were enemies of the Greeks; he affirmed, that this was now become a common oath taken by all physicians, and enjoined his son to have a care and avoid them.

---

[2]Isocrates (436–338 B.C.) was an Athenian orator whose students distinguished themselves as orators, historians, and statesmen.

REVIEW QUESTIONS

1. What is Cicero's view on the nature of law and what conclusions does he derive from it?
2. Why does Cicero conclude that the sense of justice is common to all humans? What implication does he draw from this conclusion?
3. Why did Cato fear Carneades in particular and Greek thought in general?

3 Roman Slavery

Slavery was practiced in ancient times, in many lands and among most peoples. Although conditions might vary in detail from place to place, essentially a slave was considered legally to be a piece of property, not a person with normal citizen's rights. Age, sex, skills, ethnic origin, demeanor, appearance, and personal character determined a slave's value in the marketplace. The status of slave was usually hereditary, but a person might be enslaved for debt or as a penalty for crime. Pirates would kidnap and sell their captives as slaves. But the most common source of slaves was defeated people captured during wars. They were assigned to all kinds of work, and their labors were vital in sustaining the luxury and leisure of the Roman upper classes. Even families of modest fortunes could usually afford a slave to do domestic chores, to help farm, or to assist in the family's business or craft.

Diodorus Siculus
SLAVES: TORMENT AND REVOLT

The Roman war machine created hundreds of thousands of slaves during the last centuries of the Republic and the early centuries of the imperial age. Under the Republic, the Romans were notably harsh toward slaves; until the full influence of Greek Stoic philosophy penetrated the governing class, little was done to protect them from the absolute power of their Roman masters. Diodorus Siculus, a Greek historian, describes the condition of Roman slaves toiling in silver and gold mines in Iberia (present-day Spain) and then tells of an uprising of slaves that lasted from 135 to 132 B.C.

THE ORDEAL OF SLAVES IN THE MINES

... After the Romans had made themselves masters of Iberia, a multitude of Italians have swarmed to the mines and taken great wealth away with them, such was their greed. For they purchase a multitude of slaves whom they turn over to the overseers of the working of the mines; and these men, opening shafts in a number of places and digging deep into the ground, seek out the seams of earth which are rich in silver and gold; and not only do they go into the ground a great distance, but they also push their diggings many stades [measure equalling about 607 feet] in depth and run galleries off at every angle, turning this way and that, in this manner bringing up from the depths the ore which gives them the profit they are seeking. . . .

But to continue with the mines, the slaves who are engaged in the working of them produce for their masters revenues in sums defying belief, but they themselves wear out their bodies both by day and by night in the diggings under the earth, dying in large numbers because of the exceptional hardships they endure. For no respite or pause is granted them in their labours, but compelled beneath blows of the overseers to endure the severity of their plight, they throw away their lives in this wretched manner, although certain of them who can endure it, by virtue of their bodily strength and their persevering souls, suffer such hardships over a long period; indeed death in their eyes is more to be desired than life, because of the magnitude of the hardships they must bear.

A SLAVE REVOLT IN SICILY

There was never a sedition of slaves so great as that which occurred in Sicily, whereby many cities met with grave calamities, innumerable men and women, together with their children, experienced the greatest misfortunes, and all the island was in danger of falling into the power of fugitive slaves. . . .

... The Servile [slave] War broke out for the following reason. The Sicilians, having shot up in prosperity and acquired great wealth, began to purchase a vast number of slaves, to whose bodies, as they were brought in droves from the slave markets, they at once applied marks and brands. The young men they used as cowherds, the others in such ways as they happened to be useful. But they treated them with a heavy hand in their service, and granted them the most meagre care, the bare minimum for food and clothing. ...

The slaves, distressed by their hardships, and frequently outraged and beaten beyond all reason, could not endure their treatment. Getting together as opportunity offered, they discussed the possibility of revolt, until at last they put their plans into action. ... The beginning of the whole revolt took place as follows.

There was a certain Damophilus of Enna [a city in central Sicily], a man of great wealth but insolent of manner; he had abused his slaves to excess, and his wife Megallis vied even with her husband in punishing the slaves and in her general inhumanity towards them. The slaves, reduced by this degrading treatment to the level of brutes, conspired to revolt and to murder their masters. Going to Eunus [a Syrian slave believed to be a seer and magician] they asked him whether their resolve had the favour of the gods. He, resorting to his usual mummery, promised them the favour of the gods, and soon persuaded them to act at once. Immediately, therefore, they brought together four hundred of their fellow slaves and, having armed themselves in such ways as opportunity permitted, they fell upon the city of Enna, with Eunus at their head and working his miracle of the flames of fire for their benefit. When they found their way into the houses they shed much blood, sparing not even suckling babes. Rather they tore them from the breast and dashed them to the ground, while as for the women—and under their husbands' very eyes—but words cannot tell the extent of their outrages and acts of lewdness! By now a great multitude of slaves from the city had joined them, who, after first demonstrating against their own masters their utter ruthlessness, then turned to the slaughter of others. When Eunus and his men learned that Damophilus and his wife were in the garden that lay near the city, they sent some of their band and dragged them off, both the man and his wife, fettered and with hands bound behind their backs, subjecting them to many outrages along the way. Only in the case of the couple's daughter were the slaves seen to show consideration throughout, and this was because of her kindly nature, in that to the extent of her power she was always compassionate and ready to succour the slaves. Thereby it was demonstrated that the others were treated as they were, not because of some "natural savagery of slaves," but rather in revenge for wrongs previously received. The men appointed to the task, having dragged Damophilus and Megallis into the city, as we said, brought them to the theatre, where the crowd of rebels had assembled. But when Damophilus attempted to devise a plea to get them off safe and was winning over many of the crowd with his words, Hermeias and Zeuxis, men bitterly disposed towards him, denounced him as a cheat, and without waiting for a formal trial by the assembly the one ran him through the chest with a sword, the other chopped off his head with an axe. Thereupon Eunus was chosen king, not for his manly courage or his ability as a military leader, but solely for his marvels and his setting of the revolt in motion. ...

Established as the rebels' supreme commander, he called an assembly and put to death all the citizenry of Enna except for those who were skilled in the manufacture of arms: these he put in chains and assigned them to this task. He gave Megallis to the maidservants to deal with as they might wish; they subjected her to torture and threw her over a precipice. He himself murdered his own masters, Antigenes and Pytho. Having set a diadem upon his head, and arrayed himself in full royal style, he proclaimed his wife queen (she was a fellow Syrian and of the same city), and appointed to the royal council such men as seemed to be gifted with superior intelligence. ...

. . . In three days Eunus had armed, as best he could, more than six thousand men, besides others in his train who had only axes and hatchets, or slings, or sickles, or fire-hardened stakes, or even kitchen spits; and he went about ravaging the countryside. Then, since he kept recruiting untold numbers of slaves, he ventured even to do battle with Roman generals, and on joining combat repeatedly overcame them with his superior numbers, for he now had more than ten thousand soldiers.

Soon after, engaging in battle with a general arrived from Rome, Lucius Hypsaeus [the Roman governor], who had eight thousand Sicilian troops, the rebels were victorious, since they now numbered twenty thousand. Before long their band reached a total of two hundred thousand,[1] and in numerous battles with the Romans they acquitted themselves well, and failed but seldom. As word of this was bruited about, a revolt of one hundred and fifty slaves, banded together, flared up in Rome, of more than a thousand in Attica, and of yet others in Delos [an island off the southeastern Greek coast] and many other places. But thanks to the speed with which forces were brought up and to the severity of their punitive measures, the magistrates of

these communities at once disposed of the rebels and brought to their senses any who were wavering on the verge of revolt. In Sicily, however, the trouble grew. Cities were captured with all their inhabitants, and many armies were cut to pieces by the rebels, until Rupilius, the Roman commander, recovered Tauromenium [Taormina] for the Romans by placing it under strict siege and confining the rebels under conditions of unspeakable duress and famine: conditions such that, beginning by eating the children, they progressed to the women, and did not altogether abstain even from eating one another. . . .

Finally, after Sarapion, a Syrian, had betrayed the citadel, the general laid hands on all the runaway slaves in the city, whom, after torture, he threw over a cliff. From there he advanced to Enna, which he put under siege in much the same manner, bringing the rebels into extreme straits and frustrating their hopes. . . . Rupilius captured this city also by betrayal, since its strength was impregnable to force of arms. Eunus, taking with him his bodyguards, a thousand strong, fled in unmanly fashion. . . .

. . . He met such an end as befitted his knavery, and died at Morgantina [in central Sicily]. Thereupon Rupilius, traversing the whole of Sicily with a few picked troops, sooner than had been expected rid it of every nest of robbers.

---

[1]The ancients often exaggerated numbers; the slaves probably raised an army of some 70,000.

REVIEW QUESTIONS

1. What was the character of slavery under the early Romans?
2. According to Diodorus Siculus, what was the impact of slavery on the moral character of both masters and slaves?

4 Women in Republican Society

The status of women in late republican Roman society was considerably better than that of Greek women during the classical age. Like Greek law, Roman law had originally placed each female under the jurisdiction of a male, the *paterfamilias* (literally, "family father"), but Roman women obtained some freedom from male control during the times of the late Republic and the early Empire. Although women never achieved full civil equality and they could not formally participate in the political institutions of Rome, they did eventually exercise much practical control over their own property and indirectly exercised political influence through their husbands, sons, and fathers.

Quintus Lucretius Vespillo
A FUNERAL EULOGY FOR A ROMAN WIFE

Documenting intimate relationships between Roman men and women is difficult because ordinary people were unlikely to write about such things. Although personal records are scant or now lost, glimpses have survived in the writings of historians and poets or as inscriptions on tombstones.

In the late Republic, it became more common for distinguished men to pronounce funeral eulogies for distinguished female as well as male members of their families. One such eulogy was composed by the ex-Consul Quintus Lucretius Vespillo for his wife Turia, who died about 8 B.C. Though marriages among persons of the higher social ranks were usually undertaken for political and economic considerations, clearly this couple had gone beyond such a formal alliance to achieve a most touching love.

Before the day fixed for our marriage, you were suddenly left an orphan, by the murder of your parents in the solitude of the country. . . .

Through your efforts chiefly, their death did not remain unavenged. . . .

In our day, marriages of such long duration, not dissolved by divorce, but terminated by death alone, are indeed rare. For our union was prolonged in unclouded happiness for forty-one years. Would that it had been my lot to put an end to this our good fortune and that I as the older—which was more just—had yielded to fate [death].

Why recall your inestimable qualities, your modesty, deference, affability, your amiable disposition, your faithful attendance to the household duties, your enlightened religion, your unassuming elegance, the modest simplicity and refinement of your manners? Need I speak of your attachment to your kindred, your affection for your family—when you respected my mother as you did your own parents and cared for her tomb as you did for that of your own mother and fa-

ther,—you who share countless other virtues with Roman ladies most jealous of their fair name? These qualities which I claim for you are your own, equalled or excelled by but few; for the experience of men teaches us how rare they are.

With common prudence we have preserved all the patrimony which you received from your parents. Intrusting it all to me, you were not troubled with the care of increasing it; thus did we share the task of administering it, that I undertook to protect your fortune, and you to guard mine. . . .

You gave proof of your generosity not only towards several of your kin, but especially in your filial devotion. . . . You brought up in your own home, in the enjoyment of mutual benefits, some young girls of your kinship. And that these might attain to a station in life worthy of our family, you provided them with dowries. . . .

I owe you no less a debt than Cæsar Augustus [27 B.C.–A.D. 14, emperor of Rome] himself, for this my return from exile to my native land. For unless you had prepared the way for my safety, even Cæsar's promises of assistance had been of no avail. So I owe no less a debt to your loyal devotion than to the clemency of Cæsar.

Why shall I now conjure up the memory of our domestic counsels and plans stored away in the hidden recesses of the heart?—That, aroused by the sudden arrival of messages from you to a realization of the present and imminent perils, I was saved by your counsel? That you suffered me not to be recklessly carried away by a foolish rashness, or that, when bent on more temperate plans, you provided for me a safe retreat, having as sharers in your plans for my safety, when an exile,—fraught with danger as they were for you all,—your sister and her husband. . . .

Vespillo then relates what happened to his wife when she begged his enemy M. Lepidus to honor her husband's writ of pardon from Octavian Caesar.

. . . Then prostrating yourself at his feet, he not only did not raise you up,—but, dragged along and abused as though a common slave, your body all covered with bruises, yet with unflinching steadfastness of purpose, you recalled to him Cæsar's edict (of pardon) and the letter of felicitation on my return, that accompanied it. Braving his taunts and suffering the most brutal treatment, you denounced these cruelties publicly so that he (Lepidus) was branded as the author of all my perils and misfortunes. And his punishment was not long delayed.

Could such courage remain without effect? Your unexampled patience furnished the occasion for Cæsar's clemency, and, by guarding my life, he branded the infamous and savage cruelty (of the tyrant Lepidus). . . .

When all the world was again at peace and the Republic reestablished, peaceful and happy days followed. We longed for children, which an envious fate denied us. Had Fortune smiled on us in this, what had been lacking to complete our happiness? But an adverse destiny put an end to our hopes. . . . Disconsolate to see me without children . . . you wished to put an end to my chagrin by proposing to me a divorce, offering to yield the place to another spouse more fertile, with the only intention of searching for and providing for me a spouse worthy of our mutual affection, whose children you assured me you would have treated as your own. . . .

I will admit that I was so irritated and shocked by such a proposition that I had difficulty in restraining my anger and remaining master of myself. You spoke of divorce before the decree of fate [death] had forced us to separate, and I could not comprehend how you could conceive of any reason why you, still living, should not be my wife, you who during my exile had always remained most faithful and loyal. . . .

Would that our time of life had permitted our union to have endured until I, the older, had passed away—which was more just— and that you might perform for me the last sad rites and that I might have departed, leaving you behind, with a daughter to replace me at your side.

By fate's decree your course was run before mine. You left me the grief, the heart-ache, the longing for you, the sad fate to live alone. . . .

The conclusion of this discourse will be that you have deserved all, and that I remain with the chagrin of not being able to give you all. Your wishes have always been my supreme law; and whatever it will be permitted me to accord them still, in this I shall not fail.

May the gods, the Manes [spirits of dead ancestors, considered godlike], assure and protect your repose!

REVIEW QUESTIONS

1. What does Vespillo's eulogy reveal about the virtues a Roman husband might expect in his wife? What duties were expected of a wife?
2. In your opinion, what was Turia's most commendable quality?

5 The Decline of the Republic

In 133 B.C. the Romans effectively controlled all the lands that touched the Mediterranean Sea. The old enemies of Rome, Carthage and Macedonia, had become Roman provinces; the Hellenistic kingdoms of Syria and Egypt were clients of Rome without effective power to challenge Roman hegemony. The Mediterranean Sea had become a "Roman lake."

Yet, at the very moment of its imperial supremacy, the internal order and institutions of the Roman Republic began to break down. The senatorial leaders, who had served Rome responsibly in its march to empire, no longer governed effectively. The ruling class engaged in shameless corruption in administering the provinces, resorted to bribery and force to maintain control over public offices, and failed to solve the deeply rooted problems that afflicted the state.

Triggering the Republic's downhill slide was an agricultural crisis that destroyed the small independent peasant.

Plutarch
TIBERIUS GRACCHUS

The wars of expansion had a disastrous effect on Roman agriculture. Hannibal's ravaging of Italian farmlands and the obligatory military service that kept peasants away from their fields for long periods left many small farms in near ruins. The importation of thousands of prisoners of war to work as slaves on large plantations also squeezed small farmers out of business. Sinking ever deeper into debt and poverty, many lost their lands and went to Rome, where lack of jobs condemned them to permanent poverty. The once sturdy and independent Roman farmer, who had done all that his country had asked of him, became part of a vast urban underclass—poor, embittered, and alienated.

Tiberius Gracchus (163–133 B.C.), a scion of one of Rome's most honored families, was distressed by this injustice. Moreover, he realized that small landowners were the backbone of the Roman army. Elected tribune (an office created in 493 B.C. to protect plebeian rights), Tiberius Gracchus in 133 B.C. proposed land reforms that the senatorial nobility regarded as a potential menace to their property. They also viewed Tiberius Gracchus as a threat to their political authority. The Roman nobility feared that this popular reformer was building a following among the commoners in order to undermine senatorial rule and that his real ambition was to subvert republican institutions and to become a tyrant, a one-man ruler. This fear was strengthened when Tiberius, in violation of constitutional custom, announced that he would seek reelection as tribune. Senatorial extremists killed Tiberius Gracchus and some three hundred of his followers. The Republic had entered an age of political violence that would eventually destroy it. (Tiberius' younger brother, Gaius, became tribune in 123 B.C. and suffered a fate similar to his brother's.) The following account of Tiberius Gracchus is by Plutarch, the second-century Greek biographer.

Of the territory which the Romans won in war from their neighbours, a part they sold, and a part they made common land, and assigned it for occupation to the poor and indigent among the citizens, on payment of a small rent into the public treasury. And when the rich began to offer larger rents and drove out the poor, a law was enacted forbidding the holding by one person of more than five hundred acres of land. For a short time this enactment gave a check to the rapacity of the rich, and was of assistance to the poor, who remained in their places on the land which they had rented and occupied the allotment which each had held from the outset. But later on the neighbouring rich men, by means of fictitious personages, transferred these rentals to themselves, and finally held most of the land openly in their own names. Then the poor, who had been ejected from their land, no longer showed themselves eager for military service, and neglected the bringing up of children, so that soon all Italy was conscious of a dearth of freemen, and was filled with gangs of foreign slaves, by whose aid the rich cultivated their estates, from which they had driven away the free citizens. An attempt was therefore made to rectify this evil, and by Caius Laelius[1] the comrade of Scipio; but the men of influence opposed his measures, and he, fearing the disturbance which might ensue, desisted, and received the surname of *Wise* or *Prudent* [for the Latin word "sapiens" would seem to have either meaning]. Tiberius, however, on being elected tribune of the people, took the matter directly in hand. . . .

He did not, however, draw up his law by himself, but took counsel with the citizens who were foremost in virtue and reputation. . . .

. . . And it is thought that a law dealing with injustice and rapacity so great was never drawn up in milder and gentler terms. For men who ought to have been punished for their disobedience and to have surrendered with payment of a fine the land which they were illegally enjoying, these men it merely ordered to abandon their injust acquisitions upon being paid their value, and to admit into ownership of them such citizens as needed assistance. But although the rectification of the wrong was so considerate, the people were satisfied to let bygones be bygones if they could be secure from such wrong in the future; the men of wealth and substance, however, were led by their greed to hate the law, and by their wrath and contentiousness to hate the lawgiver, and tried to dissuade the people by alleging that Tiberius was introducing a re-distribution of land for the confusion of the body politic, and was stirring up a general revolution.

But they accomplished nothing; for Tiberius, striving to support a measure which was honourable and just with an eloquence that would have adorned even a meaner cause, was formidable and invincible, whenever, with the people crowding around the rostra [speaker's platforms], he took his stand there and pleaded for the poor. "The wild beasts that roam over Italy," he would say, "have every one of them a cave or lair to lurk in; but the men who fight and die for Italy enjoy the common air and light, indeed, but nothing else; houseless and homeless they wander about with their wives and children. And it is with lying lips that their imperators[2] exhort the soldiers in their battles to defend sepulchres and shrines from the enemy; for not a man of them has an hereditary altar, not one of all these many Romans an ancestral tomb, but they fight and die to support others in wealth and luxury, and though they are styled masters of the world, they have not a single clod of earth that is their own."

Such words as these, the product of a lofty spirit and genuine feeling, and falling upon the ears of a people profoundly moved and fully aroused to the speaker's support, no adversary of Tiberius could successfully withstand.

---

[1]Caius Laelius Sapiens, a leading military hero in the Third Punic War and a close friend of Scipio Aemilianus, the conqueror of Carthage, attempted unsuccessfully to resettle the poor on public land.

[2]First, a commander, general, or captain in the army, later *imperator* meant "emperor."

Cicero
JUSTIFYING CAESAR'S ASSASSINATION

In the century following the assassination of Tiberius Gracchus in 133 B.C., the Republic was torn by conspiracies to seize the state, civil wars, assassinations, mob violence, and confiscations of property by political opponents.

In 49 B.C., Julius Caesar (100–44 B.C.), a talented and ambitious commander, marched on Rome. After defeating the senate's forces, he was appointed dictator for ten years. A creative statesman, Caesar introduced reforms to resolve the grievances of Romans and provincials. Some senators feared that Caesar aimed to establish a typical Hellenistic monarchy over Rome with himself as absolute king. The very word *king* was abhorrent to patriotic Romans, who gloried in their status as free citizens of a five-centuries-old republic. Finally, on the Ides (the fifteenth) of March, 44 B.C., Julius Caesar was slain by some sixty senators, who acted, they said, to restore the liberty of the Roman people. Their leaders were Marcus Junius Brutus (82–42 B.C.) and Gaius Cassius (d. 42 B.C.), both of whom Caesar had previously pardoned.

In the following reading from *On Duties,* Cicero, who was not one of the assassins, justifies the killing of Caesar.

Our tyrant deserved his death for having made an exception of the one thing that was the blackest crime of all. Why do we gather instances of petty crime—legacies criminally obtained and fraudulent buying and selling? Behold, here you have a man who was ambitious to be king of the Roman People and master of the whole world; and he achieved it! The man who maintains that such an ambition is morally right is a madman; for he justifies the destruction of law and liberty and thinks their hideous and detestable suppression glorious. But if anyone agrees that it is not morally right to be king in a state that once was free and that ought to be free now, and yet imagines that it is advantageous for him who can reach that position, with what remonstrance or rather with what appeal should I try to tear him away from so strange a delusion? For, oh ye immortal gods! can the most horrible and hideous of all murders—that of fatherland—bring advantage to anybody, even though he who has committed such a crime receives from his enslaved fellow-citizens the title of "Father of his Country"?

Sallust
MORAL DETERIORATION

In the dark days of the Republic after the assassination of Julius Caesar in 44 B.C., the Roman politician and historian Sallust (Gaius Sallustius Crispus, 86–35 B.C.) reflected on the causes of the Republic's collapse. In his account of a failed coup d'état that occurred in 63 B.C., Sallust contrasted the virtues of the early Republic with the moral decline that set in after the destruction of Carthage. Having failed to be elected consul in 63 B.C., Catiline, a Roman noble, organized a conspiracy to seize the state. The coup d'état was thwarted by the vigorous action of the consul Cicero, who arrested the known conspirators and had them executed. Catiline, who led an army against the forces loyal to the government, was defeated and killed.

In peace and war [in the early Republic], as I have said, virtue was held in high esteem. The closest unity prevailed, and avarice was a thing almost unknown. Justice and righteousness were upheld not so much by law as by natural instinct. They quarrelled and fought with their country's foes; between themselves the citizens contended only for honour. In making offerings to the gods they spared no expense; at home they lived frugally and never betrayed a friend. By combining boldness in war with fair dealing when peace was restored, they protected themselves and the state. There are convincing proofs of this. In time of war, soldiers were often punished for attacking against orders or for being slow to obey a signal of recall from battle, whereas few ever ventured to desert their standards or to give ground when hard pressed. In peace, they governed by conferring benefits on their subjects, not by intimidation; and when wronged they would rather pardon than seek vengeance.

Thus by hard work and just dealing the power of the state increased. Mighty kings were vanquished, savage tribes and huge nations were brought to their knees; and when Carthage, Rome's rival in her quest for empire, had been annihilated [in 146 B.C.], every land and sea lay open to her. It was then that fortune turned unkind and confounded all her enterprises. To the men who had so easily endured toil and peril, anxiety and adversity, the leisure and riches which are generally regarded as so desirable proved a burden and a curse. Growing love of money, and the lust for power which followed it, engendered every kind of evil. Avarice destroyed honour, integrity, and every other virtue, and instead taught men to be proud and cruel, to neglect religion, and to hold nothing too sacred to sell. Ambition tempted many to be false, to have one thought hidden in their hearts, another ready on their tongues, to become a man's friend or enemy not because they judged him worthy or unworthy but because they thought it

would pay them, and to put on the semblance of virtues that they had not. At first these vices grew slowly and sometimes met with punishment; later on, when the disease had spread like a plague, Rome changed: her government, once so just and admirable, became harsh and unendurable.

Reflecting on the last stages of the Republic's decline, Sallust believed that men had learned a most dangerous lesson: that they could gain power and wealth through violence and corruption rather than through virtue and self-restraint.

Never in its history—it seems to me—had the empire of Rome been in such a miserable plight. From east to west all the world had been vanquished by her armies and obeyed her will; at home there was profound peace and abundance of wealth, which mortal men esteem the chiefest of blessings. Yet there were Roman citizens obstinately determined to destroy both themselves and their country. In spite of two senatorial decrees, not one man among all the conspirators was induced by the promise of reward to betray their plans, and not one deserted from Catiline's camp. A deadly moral contagion had infected all their minds. And this madness was not confined to those actually implicated in the plot. The whole of the lower orders, impatient for a new régime, looked with favour on Catiline's enterprise.* In this they only did what might have been expected of them. In every country paupers envy respectable citizens and make heroes of unprincipled characters, hating the established order of things and hankering after innovation; discontented with their own lot, they are bent

---

*This surely cannot have been true. Sallust must be exaggerating the popular support for the conspiracy.

on general upheaval. Turmoil and rebellion bring them carefree profit, since poverty has nothing to lose.

The city populace were especially eager to fling themselves into a revolutionary adventure. There were several reasons for this. To begin with, those who had made themselves conspicuous anywhere by vice and shameless audacity, those who had wasted their substance by disgraceful excesses, and those whom scandalous or criminal conduct had exiled from their homes—all these had poured into Rome till it was like a sewer. Many, remembering Sulla's victory,[1] and seeing men who had served under him as common soldiers now risen to be senators, or so rich that they lived as luxuriously as kings, began to hope that they too, if they took up arms, might find victory a source of profit. Young men from the country, whose labour on the farms had barely kept them from starvation, had been attracted by the private and public doles available at Rome, and preferred an idle city life to such thankless toil. These, like all the rest, stood to gain by public calamities. It is no wonder, therefore, that these paupers, devoid of moral scruple and incited by ambitious hopes, should have held their country as cheap as they held themselves. Those also to whom Sulla's victory had brought disaster by the proscription of their parents, the confiscation of their property, and the curtailment of their civil rights, looked forward with no less sanguine expectations to what might result from the coming struggle. Moreover, all the factions opposed to the Senate would rather see the state embroiled than accept their own exclusion from political power.

Such was the evil condition by which, after an interval of some years, Rome was once more afflicted. After the restoration of the power of the tribunes in the consulship of Pompey and Crassus,*[2] this very important office was obtained by certain men whose youth intensified their natural aggressiveness. These tribunes began to rouse the mob by inveighing against the Senate, and then inflamed popular passion still further by handing out bribes and promises, whereby they won renown and influence for themselves. They were strenuously opposed by most of the nobility, who posed as defenders of the Senate but were really concerned to maintain their own privileged position. The whole truth—to put it in a word—is that although all disturbers of the peace in this period put forward specious pretexts, claiming either to be protecting the rights of the people or to be strengthening the authority of the Senate, this was mere pretence: in reality, every one of them was fighting for his personal aggrandizement. Lacking all self-restraint, they [stopped] at nothing to gain their ends, and both sides made ruthless use of any successes they won.

---

[1]Lucius Cornelius Sulla (c. 138–78 B.C.) was a successful politician and general, whose rivalry with another politician and general, Gaius Marius (c. 155–86 B.C.), led to civil war. After seizing Rome and massacring his opponents, Sulla made himself dictator and increased the power of the aristocratic senate, suppressing the office of tribune of the people. The latter had been used by Tiberius and Gaius Gracchus, among others (see page 83), to better the condition of the poorer classes.

*In 70 B.C.
[2]Pompey (Gnaeus Pompeius, 106–48 B.C.) and Crassus (Marcus Licinius Crassus, c. 115–53 B.C.) held the office of consul in 55 B.C. In 59 B.C., together with Julius Caesar, they had formed a political alliance called a triumvirate (meaning "group of three men"), which dominated Roman government for the next decade.

REVIEW QUESTIONS

1. What factors created a socioeconomic class struggle in the late Roman Republic?
2. According to Plutarch, what was the reaction of the senatorial order to the reforms proposed by Tiberius Gracchus?
3. Why did Cicero consider Caesar guilty of "the blackest crime of all"?
4. To what virtues did Sallust attribute the greatness of Rome?
5. What vices did Sallust believe could ruin a great state? Does his analysis have any contemporary significance?

6 The Roman Peace

The two-hundred-year period from Augustus' assumption of sole power in 27 B.C. to the death of Emperor Marcus Aurelius in A.D. 180 marks the Pax Romana, the Roman Peace. Roman poets and officials extolled the Roman achievement—the creation of a well-run world-state that brought order and stability to the different nations of the Mediterranean world.

Aelius Aristides
THE ROMAN ORATION
THE BLESSINGS OF THE PAX ROMANA

In the following reading, Aelius Aristides (A.D. 117–187), a Greek intellectual, glowingly praises the Pax Romana in an oration that was probably delivered in Rome. In the tradition of Roman orators, Aristides used hyperbole and exaggeration. Nevertheless, the oration does capture the universalism and cosmopolitanism that characterized the Roman Empire.

"If one considers the vast extent of your empire he must be amazed that so small a fraction of it rules the world, but when he beholds the city and its spaciousness it is not astonishing that all the habitable world is ruled by such a capital. . . . Your possessions equal the sun's course. . . . You do not rule within fixed boundaries, nor can anyone dictate the limits of your sway. . . . Whatever any people produces can be found here, at all times and in abundance. . . . Egypt, Sicily, and the civilized part of Africa are your farms; ships are continually coming and going. . . .

"Vast as it is, your empire is more remarkable for its thoroughness than its scope: there are no dissident or rebellious enclaves. . . . The whole world prays in unison that your empire may endure forever.

"Governors sent out to cities and peoples each rule their charges, but in their relations to each other they are equally subjects. The principal difference between governors and their charges is this—they demonstrate the proper way to be a subject. So great is their reverence for the great Ruler [the emperor], who administers all things. Him they believe to know their business better than they themselves do, and hence they respect and heed him more than one would a master overseeing a task and giving orders. No one is so self-assured that he can remain unmoved upon hearing the emperor's name; he rises in prayer and adoration and utters a twofold prayer—to the gods for the Ruler, and to the Ruler for himself. And if the governors are in the least doubt concerning the justice of claims or suits of the governed, public or private, they send to the Ruler for instructions at once and await his reply, as a chorus awaits its trainer's directions. Hence the Ruler need not exhaust himself by traveling to various parts to settle matters in person. It is easy for him to abide in his place and manage the world through letters; these arrive almost as soon as written, as if borne on wings.

"But the most marvelous and admirable achievement of all, and the one deserving our fullest gratitude, is this. . . . You alone of the imperial powers of history rule over men who are free. You have not assigned this or that region to this nabob or that mogul; no people has been turned over as a domestic and bound holding—to a man not himself free. But just as citizens in an individual city might designate magistrates, so you, whose city is the whole world, appoint governors to protect and provide for the governed, as if they were elective, not to lord it over their charges. As a result, so far from disputing the office as if it were their own, governors make way for their successors readily when their term is up, and may not even await their coming. Appeals to a higher jurisdiction are as easy as appeals from parish to county. . . .

"But the most notable and praiseworthy feature of all, a thing unparalleled, is your magnanimous conception of citizenship. All of your subjects (and this implies the whole world) you have divided into two parts: the better endowed and more virile, wherever they may be, you have granted citizenship and even kinship; the rest you govern as obedient subjects. Neither the seas nor expanse of land bars citizenship; Asia and Europe are not differentiated. Careers are open to talent. . . . Rich and poor find contentment and profit in your system; there is no other way of life. Your polity is a single and all-embracing harmony. . . .

"You have not put walls around your city, as if you were hiding it or avoiding your subjects; to do so you considered ignoble and inconsistent with your principles, as if a master should show fear of his slaves. You did not overlook walls, however, but placed them round the empire, not the city. The splendid and distant walls you erected are worthy of you; to men within their circuit they are visible, but it requires a journey of months and years from the city to see them. Beyond the outermost ring of the civilized world you drew a second circle, larger in radius and easier to defend, like the outer fortifications of a city. Here you built walls and established cities in diverse parts. The cities you filled with colonists; you introduced arts and crafts and established an orderly culture. . . . Your military organization makes all others childish. Your soldiers and officers you train to prevail not only over the enemy but over themselves. The soldier lives under discipline daily, and none ever deserts the post assigned him.

"You alone are, so to speak, natural rulers. Your predecessors were masters and slaves in turn; as rulers they were counterfeits, and reversed their positions like players in a ball game. . . . You have measured out the world, bridged rivers, cut roads through mountains, filled the wastes with posting stations, introduced orderly and refined modes of life. . . .

"Be all gods and their offspring invoked to grant that this empire and this city flourish forever and never cease until stones float upon the sea and trees forbear to sprout in the springtide. May the great Ruler and his sons be preserved to administer all things well."

Tacitus
THE OTHER SIDE OF THE PAX ROMANA

Not all peoples in the Roman Empire welcomed Roman rule. Some nations, particularly Jews, Gauls, Britons, and Egyptians, saw themselves as victims of brutal domination and rose in revolt against their Roman governors. Our knowledge of their motives and grievances is usually secondhand, being found in the records of their enemies—the Romans and their collaborators.

Cornelius Tacitus, Roman historian and orator, wrote a biography of his father-in-law, Agricola (A.D. 40–93), a general who completed the conquest of northern Britain. In this work, Tacitus describes the character and motives

of Roman imperialism from a Briton's viewpoint. The speech that follows is ut-
tered by Calgacus, a leader of the northern, or Caledonian, tribes during the Roman campaign in the years A.D. 77–83. The ideas expressed, however, are those
that Tacitus, a well-informed Roman of high social rank, believed the victims of
Roman military conquest held about their situation.

"Whenever I consider why we are fighting and how we have reached this crisis, I have a strong sense that this day of your splendid rally may mean the dawn of liberty for the whole of Britain. You have mustered to a man, and to a man you are free. There are no lands behind us, and even the sea is menaced by the Roman fleet. The clash of battle—the hero's glory—has become the safest refuge for the coward. Battles against Rome have been lost and won before—but never without hope; we were always there in reserve. We, the choice flower of Britain, were treasured in her most secret places. Out of sight of subject shores, we kept even our eyes free from the defilement of tyranny. We, the last men on earth, the last of the free, have been shielded till to-day by the very remoteness and the seclusion for which we are famed. We have enjoyed the impressiveness of the unknown. But today the boundary of Britain is exposed; beyond us lies no nation, nothing but waves and rocks and the Romans, more deadly still than they, for you find in them an arrogance which no reasonable submission can elude. Brigands of the world, they have exhausted the land by their indiscriminate plunder, and now they ransack the sea. The wealth of an enemy excites their [greed], his poverty their lust of power. East and West have failed to glut their maw [stomach]. They are unique in being as violently tempted to attack the poor as the wealthy. Robbery, butchery, rapine, the liars call Empire; they create a desolation and call it peace.

"We instinctively love our children and our kinsmen above all else. These are torn from us by conscription to slave in other lands. Our wives and sisters, even if they are not raped by Roman enemies, are seduced by them in the guise of guests and friends. Our goods and fortunes are ground down to pay tribute, our land and its harvest to supply corn, our bodies and hands to build roads through woods and swamps—all under blows and insults. Slaves, born into slavery, once sold, get their keep from their masters. But as for Britain, never a day passes but she pays and feeds her enslavers. In a private household it is the latest arrival who is always the butt of his fellow-slaves; so, in this establishment, where all the world have long been slaves, it is we, the cheap new acquisitions, who are picked out for extirpation. You see, we have no fertile lands, no mines, no harbours, which we might be spared to work. Courage and martial spirit we have, but the master does not relish them in the subject. Even our remoteness and seclusion, while they protect, expose us to suspicion. Abandon, then, all hope of mercy and at last take courage, whether it is life or honour that you hold most dear. . . . Let us, then, uncorrupted, unconquered as we are, ready to fight for freedom but never to repent failure, prove at the first clash of arms what heroes Caledonia[1] has been holding in reserve. . . . Or can you seriously think that those Gauls or Germans[2]—and, to our bitter shame, many Britons too!—are bound to Rome by genuine loyalty or love? They may be lending their life-blood to foreign tyrants, but they were enemies of Rome much longer than they have been her slaves. Apprehension and terror are weak bonds of affection; once break them, and, where fear ends, hatred will begin. All that can goad men to victory is on our side. . . . In the ranks of our very enemies we shall find hands to help us. . . . They [the Romans] have nothing in reserve that need alarm

---

[1]Caledonia was the name given by the Romans to the section of Scotland north of what is now the Firth of Forth.
[2]The Gauls consisted of several groups of tribes in modern Belgium, the Netherlands, France, and Switzerland. The Germans (Germani) who had been conquered by Rome lived north of the Gauls, just south of the Rhine; the rest of the Germani occupied a large territory north and east of the Rhine.

us—only forts without garrisons, colonies of grey-beards, towns sick and distracted between rebel subjects and tyrant masters. Here before us is their general, here his army; behind are the tribute, the mines and all the other whips to scourge slaves. Whether you are to endure these for ever or take summary vengeance, this field must decide. On, then, into action and, as you go, think of those that went before you and of those that shall come after."

REVIEW QUESTIONS

1. According to Aelius Aristides, how did Roman rule benefit the peoples of the Roman Empire?
2. What views about Rome do you think Tacitus wishes to express through the speech he attributes to Calgacus the Briton?

7 Imperial Culture

The reign of Augustus marks the golden age of Latin literature. This outpouring of literary works stemmed in part from the patronage of authors by Augustus and other prominent Romans. Roman poets and dramatists used Greek models, just as Roman philosophers, mathematicians, scientists, doctors, and geographers did. Not surprisingly, writers of the Augustan Age often expressed strong patriotic sentiments and were extravagant in their praise of Augustus.

Virgil
THE AENEID

The poet Virgil (Publius Vergilius Maro, 70–19 B.C.) admired Augustus, who was his patron, for ending the civil wars and bringing order to the Roman world. Augustus urged Virgil to compose a grand opus that would glorify Rome's imperial achievement—the emperor knew that he would find an honored place in such a work. It took Virgil ten years to produce the *Aeneid,* which was not fully completed when he died. Augustus disobeyed Virgil's deathbed request that the manuscript be destroyed, and the patriotic poem became Rome's national epic.

The *Aeneid* was greatly influenced by Homer's *Iliad* and *Odyssey* (see page 27). In *The Iliad,* Homer dealt with the conflict between the early Greeks and the Trojans. Roman legend held that a Trojan remnant led by Prince Aeneas, son of Venus (the goddess of love) and a mortal father, Anchises, escaped the sacking of Troy. (Caesar Augustus claimed descent from the goddess Venus through Aeneas.) In book six, Aeneas, escorted by the Sybil, prophetess and priestess of Apollo, descends to the underworld in order to reach his father. There his father's soul describes the illustrious future that will be Rome's.

. . . Turn your two eyes
This way and see this people, your own Ro-
    mans.
Here is Caesar, and all the line of Iulus
    [founder of the Julian family],
All who shall one day pass under the dome
Of the great sky: this is the man, this one,
Of whom so often you have heard the promise,
Caesar Augustus, son of the deified [Julius
    Caesar],
Who shall bring once again an Age of Gold
To Latium,[1] to the land where Saturn [Roman
    god] reigned
In early times. He will extend his power

Beyond the Garamants[2] and Indians,
Over far territories north and south.

. . .

Others will cast more tenderly in bronze
Their breathing figures, I can well believe,
And bring more lifelike portraits out of
    marble;
Argue more eloquently, use the pointer
To trace the paths of heaven accurately
And accurately foretell the rising stars.
Roman, remember by your strength to rule
Earth's peoples—for your arts are to be these:
To pacify, to impose the rule of law,
To spare the conquered, battle down the
    proud.

---

[1]Latium was the ancient country in which stood the towns of Lavinium and Alba Longa; Rome was established in that region and became its most significant city.

[2]The Garamants (Garamantes) were a warlike nomadic people living in the northwestern Sahara.

Juvenal
THE SATIRES

Juvenal (Decimus Junius Juvenalis, c. A.D. 60–c. 131), Rome's greatest satirical poet, found much fault with the Rome of his day. The streets were crowded, noisy, and unsafe; bullies itched to fight; criminals stole and murdered; the poor suffered even more than other Romans. The following excerpt from *The Satires* is Juvenal's account of the underside of life in Rome.

. . . A man's word
Is believed just to the extent of the
    wealth in his coffers stored.
Though he swear on all the altars from
    here to Samothrace,[1]
A poor man isn't believed. . . .

Anyway, a poor man's the butt of jokes if
    his cloak has a rip
Or is dirty, if his toga is slightly soiled, if
    a strip

Of leather is split in his shoes and gapes,
    if coarse thread shows
New stitches patching not one but many
    holes. Of the woes
Of unhappy poverty, none is more
    difficult to bear
Than that it heaps men with ridicule.
    Says an usher, "How dare
You sit there? Get out of the rows
    reserved for knights to share. . . ."

. . . What poor man ever inherits
A fortune or gets appointed as clerk to a
    magistrate?

---

[1]Samothrace, an island in the northern Aegean Sea, is best known today as the place where the famous statue of the Winged Victory (Nike) was found.

Long ago the penniless Romans ought to
    have staged a great
Mass walkout. It's no easy job for a man
    to advance
When his talents are balked by his
    impoverished circumstance,
But in Rome it's harder than
    elsewhere. . . .
Here most of the sick die off because
    they get no sleep
(But the sickness is brought on by the
    undigested heap
Of sour food in their burning stomachs),
    for what rented flat
Allows you to sleep? Only rich men in
    this city have that.
There lies the root of the illness—carts
    rumbling in narrow streets
And cursing drivers stalled in a traffic
    jam—it defeats
All hope of rest. . . .

. . . Though we hurry, we merely crawl;
We're blocked by a surging mass ahead,
    a pushing wall
Of people behind. A man jabs me,
    elbowing through, one socks
A chair pole against me, one cracks my
    skull with a beam, one knocks
A wine cask against my ear. My legs are
    caked with splashing
Mud, from all sides the weight of
    enormous feet comes smashing
On mine, and a soldier stamps his
    hobnails through to my sole. . . .

. . . a piece of a pot
Falls down on my head, how often a
    broken vessel is shot
From the upper windows, with what a
    force it strikes and dints
The cobblestones! . . .

The besotted bully, denied his chance in
    the shabby bars
Of killing somebody, suffers torments,
    itching to fight.

Like Achilles[2] bemoaning his friend, he
    tosses about all night,
Now flat on his face, now on his back—
    there's no way at all
He can rest, for some men can't sleep till
    after a bloody brawl.
But however rash and hot with youth
    and flushed with wine,
He avoids the noble whose crimson cloak
    and long double line
Of guards with brass lamps and torches
    show they're too much to handle.
But for me, whom the moon escorts, or
    the feeble light of a candle
Whose wick I husband and trim—he
    has no respect for me.
Now hear how the pitiful fight begins—
    if a fight it be,

When he delivers the punches and I am
    beaten to pulp.
He blocks my way and tells me to stop. I
    stop, with a gulp—
What else can you do when a madman
    stronger than you attacks? . . .

This is the poor man's freedom: having
    been soundly mauled
And cut to pieces by fists, he begs and
    prays, half dead,
To be allowed to go home with a few
    teeth still in his head.

But these aren't your only terrors. For
    you can never restrain
The criminal element. Lock up your
    house, put bolt and chain
On your shop, but when all's quiet,
    someone will rob you or he'll
Be a cutthroat perhaps and do you in
    quickly with cold steel. . . .

---

[2]Achilles, the Greeks' most formidable warrior in Homer's *Iliad*, was torn by grief when his best friend Patroclus was killed by the Trojans.

Juvenal gives us an unflattering picture of women and marriage.

You once had your wits about you,
    Postumus; but now you think
Of taking a wife? What Fury, what
    serpents, are driving you mad?

Can you let a termagant [shrewish woman]
    boss you when rope is so easily had
And so many windows open on dizzy
    leaps and the height
Of the Aemilian bridge so handy?
    If none of these modes of flight
Is to your taste, don't you think it
    might be better to take
Some boy as bedmate, who'd never
    quarrel all night, or make
You promise gifts as you twine, or
    complain if you resist
His pleas and sleep, instead of panting,
    and leave him unkissed? . . .

And who is so deeply in love he never
    shrinks at all
From the very woman he praises to the
    skies—what's more,
Hates her at least sixteen hours out
    of the twenty-four? . . .

If you don't intend to love the woman
    you embrace
And marry in legal form, there seems
    no reason for you
To marry, no reason why you should
    waste the supper and new
Wedding cakes that must be given to
    well-stuffed guests who leave
When the party's over, or waste the
    gift of the bridal eve,
The rich tray gleaming with coins
    engraved with victories
In Dacia and Germany. If you simply
    must appease

Yourself with a wife and are devoted
    to one, incline
Your head, submit your neck to the
    marriage yoke. You'll find
No woman who spares the man who loves
    her. Though she glow
With passion, she loves to torment
    and plunder her lover. So,
The more he's good and desirable as
    a husband, the less
Beneficial by far will be his wife.
    You'll never address
A gift if she says no, never sell
    things if she objects,
Never buy anything unless she consents.
    And she will select
Your friends for you and turn your now
    aged friend from the door. . . .

You'll have to despair of knowing
    any peace at home
If your mother-in-law's alive. She
    teaches your wife to delight
In stripping you of wealth. . . .

There's hardly a case in court that
    a woman's fuss didn't start.

The bed where a wife lies never is free
    of complaints and a host
Of quarrels back and forth. There'll
    be little sleep in that bed.
There she assails her husband, worse
    than a tigress is said
To be at the loss of her cubs. Aware
    of her own secret deeds,
She pretends to grieve, denounces
    the boys he's known, and weeps
At some feigned mistress, always with
    floods of tears at hand
Ever ready at their station, waiting
    for her command
On how they should flow. You think,
    poor worm, it's love they show. . . .

1. Why are some poems a valuable source for historians?
2. According to Virgil, what was Rome's destiny and the basis of its greatness?
3. According to Juvenal, what were some of the hazards of urban life in ancient Rome?
4. Why did Juvenal expect men to be unhappy in marriage?

---

8 Roman Law

One of the most significant legacies of Rome to Western civilization is the system of law developed by the Romans over many centuries. Roman law evolved into three distinct types: the civil law (*ius civile*), which was peculiar to the Roman state and applicable only to its citizens; the law of nature (*ius naturale*), an unchanging, everlasting, universal law that was binding on all persons by reason of their common humanity; the law of nations (*ius gentium*), an international law governing the relationship between Romans and other peoples. The law of nations was fashioned by Roman jurists as Rome came into contact with and conquered other cultures; it incorporated elements from Roman civil law and the legal traditions of the other peoples, particularly the Greeks. Roman jurists held that the law of nations accorded with natural law: that is, it rested upon principles of reason that were common to all humans.

Justinian
CORPUS IURIS CIVILIS

The principles of Roman law are drawn from many sources, from the statutes of emperors, edicts of magistrates, and commentaries of learned jurists, such as Ulpian (Domitius Ulpianus, d. A.D. 228), Gaius (c. A.D. 130–180), and Julius Paulus (second–third century A.D.). These past laws and judicial commentaries were culled and selectively incorporated in the *Corpus Iuris Civilis,* the imperial code drawn up by order of Emperor Justinian (A.D. 527–565) and promulgated in A.D. 534. It has been said that next to the Bible, no book has had a deeper impact on Western civilization than Justinian's code. It became the official body of laws of the eastern Roman (or Byzantine) Empire through the Middle Ages and was gradually reintroduced into western Europe in the twelfth century. Roman law continued in the postmedieval world and formed the basis of common law in all Western lands except England and its dependencies, where its influence was less marked. Some principles of Roman law are readily recognizable in today's legal systems, as the following excerpts indicate.

- The Divine Trajan stated in a Rescript addressed to Julius Frontonus that anyone who is absent should not be convicted of crime.

Likewise, no one should be convicted on suspicion; for the Divine Trajan stated in a Rescript to Assiduus Severus: "It is better to permit the crime of a guilty person to go unpunished than to condemn one who is innocent."

- No one suffers a penalty for merely thinking.

- Proof is incumbent upon the party who affirms a fact, not upon him who denies it.

- In inflicting penalties, the age and inexperience of the guilty party must always be taken into account.

- Nothing is so opposed to consent, which is the basis of *bona fide* contracts, as force and fear; and to approve anything of this kind is contrary to good morals.

- The crime or the punishment of a father can place no stigma upon his son; for each one is subjected to fate in accordance with his conduct, and no one is appointed the successor of the crime of another.

- Women are excluded from all civil or public employments; therefore they cannot be judges, or perform the duties of magistrates, or bring suits in court, or become sureties for others, or act as attorneys.

- A minor, also, must abstain from all civil employments.

- Every person should support his own offspring, and anyone who thinks that he can abandon his child shall be subjected to the penalty prescribed by law. We do not give any right to masters or to patrons to recover children who have been abandoned, when children exposed by them, as it were, to death, have been rescued through motives of pity, for no one can say that a child whom he has left to perish belongs to him.

- The authority and observance of long-established custom should not be treated with contempt, but it should not prevail to the extent of overcoming either reason or law.

Not all principles of Roman law have been incorporated into the legal codes of modern societies. One example is the use of torture to test the testimony of witnesses, particularly those of low social status. In those lands where Roman law remained in effect, torture was legal until the eighteenth century, when it was purged from European judicial systems.

- Torture is employed in the detection of crime, but a beginning should not be made with its application; and, therefore, in the first place, evidence should be resorted to, and if the party is liable to suspicion, he shall be compelled by torture to reveal his accomplices and crimes.

- Where several culprits are implicated in the same offence, they should be examined in such a way as to begin with the one who appears to be more timid than the others, and of tender age.

- Torture is not applied in pecuniary [financial] matters, unless when an investigation is made with reference to property belonging to an estate; other things, however, are established by oath, or by the evidence of witnesses.

- Torture should not be inflicted upon a minor under fourteen years of age, as the Divine Pius stated in a Rescript addressed to Caecilius Jubentinus.

- All persons, however, without exception, shall be tortured in a case of high treason which has reference to princes, if their testimony is necessary, and circumstances demand it.

- Torture should not be applied to the extent that the accuser demands, but as reason and moderation may dictate.

- In questions where freedom is involved it is not necessary to seek for the truth by the torture of those whose status is in dispute.

- It was declared by the Imperial Constitutions that while confidence should not always be reposed in torture, it ought not to be rejected as absolutely unworthy of it, as the evidence obtained is weak and dangerous, and inimical to the truth; for most persons, either through their power of endurance, or through the severity of the torment, so despise suffering that the truth can in no way be extorted from them. Others are so little able to suffer that they prefer to lie rather than to endure the question, and hence it happens that they make confessions of different kinds, and they not only implicate themselves, but others as well.

• The Edict of the Divine Augustus, which he published during the Consulate of Vivius Avitus and Lucius Apronianus, is as follows: "I do not think that torture should be inflicted in every instance, and upon every person; but when capital and atrocious crimes cannot be detected and proved except by means of the torture of slaves, I hold that it is most effective for ascertaining the truth, and should be employed."

REVIEW QUESTIONS

1. What is the *ius naturale* and what are its implications when applied to particular legal cases?
2. What is the *ius gentium* and what were its origins?
3. What provisions of Justinian's code are reflected in present-day legal systems in Europe and America?
4. Why are both torture and slavery in the modern world seen as incompatible with the basic premises of natural law?

9 The Demise of Rome

The conquest of the western provinces of the Roman Empire by various Germanic tribes in the fifth century A.D. was made easier by the apathy and frequent collaboration of Roman citizens themselves. Many Romans had grown to hate the bureaucratic oppressors who crushed them with constant demands for excessive and unfair taxes, forced labor on government projects, extortion, and all the evils of a police state. In some areas of Gaul and Spain, peasants had revolted and successfully defended their homes and farms against the Roman authorities. When such barbarians as the Visigoths, Vandals, and Ostrogoths entered the region, many Romans welcomed them as liberators and cooperated with them in establishing their new kingdoms.

Salvian
POLITICAL AND SOCIAL INJUSTICE

The growing hatred of citizens for the Roman state is well delineated in a book called *The Governance of God,* by Salvian (Salvianus) of Marseilles (c. A.D. 400–470). A Christian priest, Salvian was an eyewitness to the end of Roman rule in Gaul. He describes the political and moral causes of the collapse of the Roman state in the west in the following reading.

What towns, as well as what municipalities and villages are there in which there are not as many tyrants as *curiales*.[1] Perhaps they glory in this name of tyrant because it seems to be considered powerful and honored. For, almost all robbers rejoice and boast, if they are said to be more fierce than they really are. What place is there, as I have said, where the bowels of widows and orphans are not devoured by the leading men of the cities, and with them those of almost all holy men? . . . Not one of them [widows and orphans], therefore, is safe. In a manner, except for the very powerful, neither is anyone safe from the devastation of general brigandage, unless they are like the robbers themselves. To this state of affairs, indeed, to this crime has the world come that, unless one is bad, he cannot be safe. . . .

All the while, the poor are despoiled, the widows groan, the orphans are tread underfoot, so much so that many of them, and they are not of obscure birth and have received a liberal education, flee to the enemy lest they die from the pain of public persecution. They seek among the barbarians the dignity of the Roman because they cannot bear barbarous indignity among the Romans. Although these Romans differ in religion and language from the barbarians to whom they flee, and differ from them in respect to filthiness of body and clothing, nevertheless, as I have said, they prefer to bear among the barbarians a worship unlike their own rather than rampant injustice among the Romans.

Salvian tells how Roman citizens are deserting Rome to live under the rule of the Goths and other barbarian invaders. Moreover, in many parts of Spain and Gaul (France), peasants called *Bagaudae* have rebelled and established zones free from Roman authority.

Thus, far and wide, they migrate either to the Goths[2] or to the Bagaudae, or to other barbarians everywhere in power; yet they do not repent having migrated. They prefer to live as freemen under an outward form of captivity than as captives under an appearance of liberty. Therefore, the name of Roman citizens, at one time not only greatly valued but dearly bought, is now repudiated and fled from, and it is almost considered not only base but even deserving of abhorrence.

And what can be a greater testimony of Roman wickedness than that many men, upright and noble and to whom the position of being a Roman citizen should be considered as of the highest splendor and dignity, have been driven by the cruelty of Roman wickedness to such a state of mind that they do not wish to be Romans? . . .

I am now about to speak of the Bagaudae who were despoiled, oppressed and murdered by evil and cruel judges. After they had lost the right of Roman citizenship, they also lost the honor of bearing the Roman name. We blame their misfortunes on themselves. We ascribe to them a name which signifies their downfall. We give to them a name of which we ourselves are the cause. We call them rebels. We call those outlaws whom we compelled to be criminal.

For, by what other ways did they become Bagaudae, except by our wickedness, except by the wicked ways of judges, except by the proscription and pillage of those who have turned the assessments of public taxes into the benefit of their own gain and have made the tax levies their own booty? Like wild beasts, they did not rule but devoured their subjects, and feasted not only on the spoils of men, as most robbers are wont to do, but even on their torn flesh and, as I may say, on their blood.

---

[1] The *curiales* were members of the municipal councils. In the late years of the Roman Empire, they were forced to act as tax collectors for the central government and to pay from their own pockets whatever sums they could not collect from the overtaxed inhabitants.

[2] The Goths were Germanic tribes that invaded Rome. The Visigoths invaded Italy in the early fifth century and seized Rome for a few days. This was the first time in eight centuries that a foreign enemy had entered the capital. Later the Visigoths occupied large areas of Spain and Gaul. In the late fifth century, the Ostrogoths invaded and conquered Italy, establishing a kingdom there.

Thus it happened that men, strangled and killed by the robberies of judges, began to live as barbarians because they were not permitted to be Romans. They became satisfied to be what they were not, because they were not permitted to be what they were. They were compelled to defend their lives at least, because they saw that they had already completely lost their liberty. . . .

But what else can these wretched people wish for, they who suffer the incessant and even continuous destruction of public tax levies. To them there is always imminent a heavy and relentless proscription. They desert their homes, lest they be tortured in their very homes. They seek exile, lest they suffer torture. The enemy is more lenient to them than the tax collectors. This is proved by this very fact, that they flee to the enemy in order to avoid the full force of the heavy tax levy. This very tax levying, although hard and inhuman, would nevertheless be less heavy and harsh if all would bear it equally and in common. Taxation is made more shameful and burdensome because all do not bear the burden of all. They extort tribute from the poor man for the taxes of the rich, and the weaker carry the load for the stronger. There is no other reason that they cannot bear all the taxation except that the burden imposed on the wretched is greater than their resources. . . .

Therefore, in the districts taken over by the barbarians, there is one desire among all the Romans, that they should never again find it necessary to pass under Roman jurisdiction. In those regions, it is the one and general prayer of the Roman people that they be allowed to carry on the life they lead with the barbarians. And we wonder why the Goths are not conquered by our portion of the population, when the Romans prefer to live among them rather than with us. Our brothers, therefore, are not only altogether unwilling to flee to us from them, but they even cast us aside in order to flee to them.

Jerome
THE FATE OF ROME

Saint Jerome (Hieronymus, c. A.D. 340–420) was one of the major theologians and scriptural scholars of the late Roman period. He left Rome itself to join a monastery in Bethlehem in Judea, where he studied Hebrew and began work on a monumental new translation of the Hebrew and Christian Scriptures into Latin. This new edition, called the Vulgate (written in the Latin of the common people), became the standard text of the Bible in the Western church for more than a thousand years. In the following letter to Agenuchia, a highborn lady of Gaul, Saint Jerome bemoans the fate of Rome, once so proud and powerful. The letter, dated A.D. 409, was written at a critical moment: the Visigoths had accepted a huge ransom to end their siege of Rome.

Nations innumerable and most savage have invaded all Gaul. The whole region between the Alps and the Pyrenees, the ocean and the Rhine, has been devastated by the Quadi, the Vandals, the Sarmati, the Alani, the Gepidae, the hostile Heruli, the Saxons, the Burgundians, the Alemanni, and the Pannonians [all barbarian tribes]. O wretched Empire! Mayence [Mainz], formerly so noble a city, has been taken and ruined, and in the church many thousands of men have been massacred. Worms has been destroyed after a long siege. Rheims, that powerful city, Amiens, Arras, Speyer, Strasburg,*—all have seen their citizens led away captive into Germany.

---

*The names of modern cities here used are not in all cases exact equivalents for the names of the regions mentioned by Jerome.

Aquitaine and the provinces of Lyons and Narbonne, all save a few towns, have been depopulated; and these the sword threatens without, while hunger ravages within. I cannot speak without tears of Toulouse, which the merits of the holy Bishop Exuperius have prevailed so far to save from destruction. Spain, even, is in daily terror lest it perish, remembering the invasion of the Cimbri;[1] and whatsoever the other provinces have suffered once, they continue to suffer in their fear.

I will keep silence concerning the rest, lest I seem to despair of the mercy of God. For a long time, from the Black Sea to the Julian Alps,[2] those things which are ours have not been ours; and for thirty years, since the Danube boundary was broken, war has been waged in the very midst of the Roman Empire. Our tears are dried by old age. Except a few old men, all were born in captivity and siege, and do not desire the liberty they never knew. . . .

When the Visigoths led by Alaric sacked Rome in 410, Jerome lamented in another passage.

Who could believe that Rome, built upon the conquest of the whole world, would fall to the ground? that the mother herself would become the tomb of her peoples?

---

[1]The Cimbri, originally from what is now Denmark, spread southward to invade Spain, Gaul, and Italy in the late part of the second century B.C. They were defeated by the Roman general Marius (c. 157–86 B.C.).

[2]The mountains called the Julian Alps are in northwest Slovenia.

Pope Gregory I
THE END OF ROMAN GLORY

In the late sixth century, the Lombards, the last Germanic tribe to invade those lands that had once been Roman, swept down the Tiber valley and in 593 were at the gates of Rome. At that time, Pope Gregory I, the Great (590–604), descendant of a prominent and wealthy Roman senatorial family, reflected on Rome, once the mistress of the world.

We see on all sides sorrows; we hear on all sides groans. Cities are destroyed, fortifications razed to the ground, fields devastated, the land reduced to solitude. No husbandman is left in the field, few inhabitants remain in the cities, and yet these scanty remnants of the human race are still each day smitten without ceasing. . . . Some men are led away captive, others are mutilated, others slain before our eyes. What is there, then, my brethren to please us in this world?

What Rome herself, once deemed the Mistress of the World, has now become, we see—wasted away with afflictions, grievous and many, with the loss of citizens, the assaults of enemies, the frequent fall of ruined buildings. . . . For where is the Senate? Where is the People [the State]? The bones are dissolved, the flesh is consumed, all the pomp of the dignities of this world is gone. . . .

Yet even we who remain few as we are, still are daily smitten with the sword, still are daily crushed by innumerable afflictions. . . . For the Senate is no more, and the People has perished, yet sorrow and sighing are multiplied daily among the few that are left. Rome is, as it were, already empty and burning. . . . But where are they who once rejoiced in her glory? Where is their pomp? Where their pride? Where their constant and immediate joy? . . .

. . . The Sons of men of the world, when they wished for worldly advancement came together from all parts of the earth to this city. But now behold! she is desolate. Behold! she is wasted away. No one hastens to her for worldly advancement.

REVIEW QUESTIONS

1. What conditions in late Roman society undermined the social and political bonds between the rulers and the ruled?
2. What were the consequences of the Germanic invasions as depicted by Saint Jerome and Pope Gregory I?

CHAPTER 4
Early Christianity

FOURTEENTH-CENTURY FRENCH PSALTER depicting monks singing. *(Ms. 124, fol. 98. Bibliothèque Municipal, Amiens, France. Giraudon/Art Resource, N.Y.)*

Christianity, the core religion of Western civilization, emerged during the first century of the Roman Empire. The first Christians were followers of Jesus Christ, a Jew, who, in the tradition of the Hebrew prophets, called for a moral reformation of the individual. Jesus' life, teachings, crucifixion, and the belief that he had risen from the dead convinced his followers that Jesus had shown humanity the way to salvation. Dedicated disciples spread this message throughout the Mediterranean world.

Surviving persecution and gaining in numbers, Christians influenced all classes from slave to aristocrat, and Christianity had become the state religion of Rome by the end of the fourth century. The reasons for the spread and triumph of Christianity are diverse. The poor and oppressed of the Roman world were drawn to Jesus' message of love and compassion, his concern for humanity; the promise of eternal life had an immense attraction to people who were burdened with misfortune and fearful of death. Jesus' call for a moral transformation of the individual addressed itself to the inner conscience of men and women of all social classes.

The Judeo-Christian and Greco-Roman (classical humanist) traditions constitute the foundations of Western civilization. Nevertheless, they represent two contrasting views of the world. For classical humanists, the ultimate aim of life was the achievement of excellence in this world, the maximum cultivation of human talent; Christians subordinated this world to a higher reality. For Christians, the principal purpose of life was the attainment of salvation—entrance into a heavenly kingdom after death.

In the Greco-Roman tradition, reason was autonomous: that is, the intellect depended on its own powers and neither required nor accepted guidance from a supernatural authority. For example, Socrates held that ethical standards were arrived at through rational thought alone; they were not divine commandments revealed to human beings by a heavenly lawmaker. Conservative Christian churchmen, believing that Greek intellectualism posed a threat to Christian teachings, wanted nothing to do with Greek philosophy. But other Christians, recognizing the value of Greek philosophy, sought to integrate Greek learning into the Christian framework. Greek philosophy, they said, could help Christians clarify, organize, and explain their teachings. Those who advocated studying and utilizing Greek philosophy prevailed; thus Christianity preserved rational thought, the priceless achievement of the Greek mind. In the process, however, philosophy lost its autonomy, for early Christian thinkers insisted that to reason properly one must first believe in God and his revelation, with the Bible as the ultimate authority. Without these prior conditions, the Christians argued, reason would lead to error. Thus, for early Christian thinkers, unlike their Greek predecessors, reason was not autonomous: it was subject to divine authority as interpreted by the church.

In the late Roman Empire, when Roman institutions were breaking down and classical values were being discarded, Christianity was a dynamic movement. Surviving the barbarian invasions, the Christian church gave form and direction to the European culture that emerged in the Middle Ages.

1   The Teachings of Jesus

During the reign (A.D. 14–37) of the Emperor Tiberius, the Roman governor in Judea, Pontius Pilate, executed on charges of sedition an obscure Jewish religious teacher, Jesus of Nazareth. While performing healings and exorcisms, Jesus expounded a message of hope and salvation for sinners who repented. To the Jews who were attracted to Jesus' person and teachings, Jesus appeared to be a new prophet or even the long-awaited Messiah, the divinely promised leader who would restore Israel to freedom and usher in a new age.

Jesus made enemies among those powerful Jewish leaders who believed that the popular preacher was undermining their authority and weakening respect for their teachings on the requirements of Jewish law. The Romans viewed Jesus as a political agitator who might lead the Jews in a revolt against Roman rule. Some Jewish leaders denounced Jesus to the Roman authorities, who executed him.

After the death of Jesus, his loyal followers, who believed in his resurrection, continued to preach his teachings, forming small congregations of those faithful to his mission and words. They soon spread out as missionaries to Jewish and Gentile communities throughout the Roman Empire. These followers of Jesus, the Messiah, or in Greek, *Christos* (the Anointed One), were the founders of the Christian church.

Like Socrates, Jesus himself never wrote a book; all we know of his life and teachings are the recollections of his disciples, passed down orally until put in written form some thirty to seventy years after his death. These primary sources include the gospels ("good news") attributed to the Saints Mark, Matthew, Luke, and John; the letters of Saint Paul and others; the Acts of the Apostles, a historical account of their missionary work; and the book of Revelation, a prophetic portrayal of the coming messianic kingdom of Jesus and God's destruction of the powers of evil. These works, written several decades after Jesus' death and collected together definitively in the fourth century, comprise the New Testament, the Christian sacred scriptures. They reflect the ways in which the early Christians remembered Jesus' teachings and the meaning of his life and ministry.

THE GOSPEL ACCORDING TO SAINT MARK

In this reading from Saint Mark's gospel, Jesus stated in a few words the core of his ethical teaching.

28 And one of the scribes* came up and heard them disputing with one another, and seeing that he answered them well, asked him, "Which commandment is the first of all?" 29Jesus answered, "The first is, 'Hear, O Israel: The Lord our God, the Lord is one;† 30and you shall love the Lord your God with all your heart, and with all your soul, and with all your mind, and with all your strength.' 31The second is this, 'You shall love your neighbor as yourself.' There is no other commandment greater than these." 32And the scribe said to him, "You are right, Teacher; you have truly said that he is one, and there is no other but he; 33and to love him with all the heart, and with all the understanding, and with all the strength, and to love one's neighbor as oneself, is much more than all whole burnt offerings and sacrifices." 34And when Jesus saw that he answered wisely, he said to him, "You are not far from the kingdom of God." And after that no one dared to ask him any question. (Mark 12)

---

*Scribes were not only copyists of the scrolls that contained Jewish law, but they were also students of that law. Editors' footnotes for Bible readings in this chapter are not numbered, to eliminate confusion with verse numbers.—Eds.
†"Hear, O Israel" occurs in the Book of Deuteronomy in the Hebrew Scriptures as the "first law," that of monotheism (one God). Here, as a Jew, Jesus was reminding his followers of this fact.—Eds.

THE GOSPEL ACCORDING TO SAINT MATTHEW

In the gospel of Saint Matthew, Jesus outlined to his disciples the attitudes pleasing to God; this is the famous Sermon on the Mount.

1 Seeing the crowds, he went up on the mountain, and when he sat down his disciples came to him. 2And he opened his mouth and taught them, saying:

3 "Blessed are the poor in spirit, for theirs is the kingdom of heaven.

4 "Blessed are those who mourn, for they shall be comforted.

5 "Blessed are the meek, for they shall inherit the earth.

6 "Blessed are those who hunger and thirst for righteousness, for they shall be satisfied.

7 "Blessed are the merciful, for they shall obtain mercy.

8 "Blessed are the pure in heart, for they shall see God.

9 "Blessed are the peacemakers, for they shall be called sons of God.

10 "Blessed are those who are persecuted for righteousness' sake, for theirs is the kingdom of heaven.

11 "Blessed are you when men revile you and persecute you and utter all kinds of evil against you falsely on my account. 12Rejoice and be glad, for your reward is great in heaven, for so men persecuted the prophets who were before you. . . ."

A characteristic feature of Jesus' teaching—one that angered the Jewish leaders—was a demand that his followers go beyond the letter of the Jewish law. In the tradition of the Hebrew prophets, Jesus stressed the ethical demands that underlie this law and urged a moral transformation of human character, based on a love of God and neighbor. In the next reading from Saint Matthew, Jesus reinterpreted the Hebrew commandments on killing, adultery, divorce, vengeance, the definition of a neighbor, and almsgiving.

---

17 "Think not that I have come to abolish the law and the prophets; I have come not to abolish them but to fulfil them. . . .

21 "You have heard that it was said to the men of old, 'You shall not kill; and whoever kills shall be liable to judgment.' 22But I say to

you that every one who is angry with his brother shall be liable to judgment; whoever insults his brother shall be liable to the council, and whoever says, 'You fool!' shall be liable to the hell of fire. ²³So if you are offering your gift at the altar, and there remember that your brother has something against you, ²⁴leave your gift there before the altar and go; first be reconciled to your brother, and then come and offer your gift. ²⁵Make friends quickly with your accuser. . . .

27 "You have heard that it was said, 'You shall not commit adultery.' ²⁸But I say to you that every one who looks at a woman lustfully has already committed adultery with her in his heart. ²⁹If your right eye causes you to sin, pluck it out and throw it away; it is better that you lose one of your members than that your whole body be thrown into hell. ³⁰And if your right hand causes you to sin, cut it off and throw it away; it is better that you lose one of your members than that your whole body go into hell.

31 "It was also said, 'Whoever divorces his wife, let him give her a certificate of divorce.' ³²But I say to you that every one who divorces his wife, except on the ground of unchastity, makes her an adulteress; and whoever marries a divorced woman commits adultery. . . .

38 "You have heard that it was said, 'An eye for an eye and a tooth for a tooth.' ³⁹But I say to you, Do not resist one who is evil. But if any one

strikes you on the right cheek, turn to him the other also; ⁴⁰and if any one would sue you and take your coat, let him have your cloak as well; ⁴¹and if any one forces you to go one mile, go with him two miles. ⁴²Give to him who begs from you, and do not refuse him who would borrow from you.

43 "You have heard that it was said, 'You shall love your neighbor and hate your enemy.' ⁴⁴But I say to you, Love your enemies and pray for those who persecute you, ⁴⁵so that you may be sons of your Father who is in heaven. . . . (Matthew 5)

1 "Beware of practicing your piety before men in order to be seen by them; for then you will have no reward from your Father who is in heaven.

2 "Thus, when you give alms, sound no trumpet before you, as the hypocrites do in the synagogues‡ and in the streets, that they may be praised by men. Truly, I say to you, they have their reward. ³But when you give alms, do not let your left hand know what your right hand is doing, ⁴so that your alms may be in secret; and your Father who sees in secret will reward you. . . ." (Matthew 6)

---

‡Synagogues, originally a name given to substitutes outside Judea for the Temple in Jerusalem, coexisted with the Temple; they were places for public prayer and study of the Hebrew Scriptures.—Eds.

REVIEW QUESTIONS

1. What did Jesus believe to be the basic tenets of his teachings?
2. Why might his message appeal to many people?

---

2 Christianity and Greco-Roman Learning

Should the cultural inheritance of the Greco-Roman world be retained or discarded? This was a formidable problem for early Christian thinkers. Those who urged abandoning Greco-Roman learning argued that such knowledge would corrupt the morality of the young and would lead Christians to doubt Scripture. On the other hand, several Christian intellectuals, particularly those educated in the Greco-Roman classics, defended the study of pagan works. Their view ultimately prevailed.

Christians preserved the intellectual tradition of Greece. However, philosophy underwent a crucial change: philosophic thought among Christians had to be directed in accordance with the requirements of their faith. The intellect was not fully autonomous; it could not question or challenge Christian teachings but had to accept the church's dictums regarding God's existence, the creation of the universe, the mission of Jesus, and the purpose of life and death.

Tertullian
WHAT HAS JERUSALEM TO DO WITH ATHENS?

A native of Carthage, Tertullian (Quintus Septimus Florens Tertullianus, c. A.D. 160–c. 240) became a Christian about A.D. 190 and thereafter was a defender of Christian morals against both pagans and less rigorous Christians. He emphasized the sacredness of life and the Christian abhorrence of violence. His *Prescriptions Against Heretics* reveals hostility toward Greco-Roman learning, an attitude shared by some other early Christian thinkers.

. . . Worldly wisdom culminates in philosophy with its rash interpretation of God's nature and purpose. It is philosophy that supplies the heresies[1] with their equipment. . . . The idea of a mortal soul was picked up from the Epicureans,[2] and the denial of the restitution of the flesh was taken from the common tradition of the philosophical schools. . . . Heretics and philosophers [ponder] the same themes and are caught up in the same discussions. What is the origin of evil and why? The origin of man, and how? . . . A plague on Aristotle, who taught them dialectic [logical argumentation], the art which destroys as much as it builds, which changes its opinions like a coat, forces its conjectures, is stubborn in argument, works hard at being contentious and is a burden even to itself. For it reconsiders every point to make sure it never finishes a discussion.

From philosophy come those fables and . . . fruitless questionings, those "words that creep like as doth a canker." To hold us back from such things, the Apostle [Paul] testifies expressly in his letter to the Colossians [Colossians 2:8] that we should beware of philosophy. "Take heed lest any man [beguile] you through philosophy or vain deceit, after the tradition of men," against the providence of the Holy Ghost. He had been at Athens where he had come to grips with the human wisdom which attacks and perverts truth, being itself divided up into its own swarm of heresies by the variety of its mutually antagonistic sects. What has Jerusalem to do with Athens, the Church with [Plato's] Academy, the Christian with the heretic? Our principles come from the Porch of Solomon,[3] who had himself taught that the Lord is to be sought in simplicity of heart. I have no use for a Stoic or a Platonic or a dialectic Christianity. After Jesus Christ we have no need of speculation, after the Gospel no need of research. When we come to believe, we have no desire to believe anything else; for we begin by believing that there is nothing else which we have to believe.

---

[1]A heresy is any belief that differs from official or standard doctrine.

[2]Chapter 2, page 66.

[3]The Stoic philosophers took their name from the Greek word *stoa*, porch, the place where Zeno, their founder, used to teach. *Porch of Solomon* is used to designate the teachings of King Solomon, who built the great Temple in Jerusalem. Tertullian makes it clear he follows Solomon's wisdom.

Clement of Alexandria
IN DEFENSE OF GREEK LEARNING

In the following passage, Clement of Alexandria (c. A.D. 150–c. 220) expresses his admiration for Greek learning. A Greek Christian theologian, Clement combined Christianity with Platonism.

The Greeks should not be condemned by those who have merely glanced at their writings, for comprehension of these works requires careful investigation. Philosophy is not the originator of false practices and base deeds as some have calumniated it; nor does it beguile us and lead us away from faith.

Rather philosophy is a clear image of truth, a divine gift to the Greeks. Before the advent of the Lord, philosophy helped the Greeks to attain righteousness, and it is now conducive to piety; it supplies a preparatory teaching for those who will later embrace the faith. God is the cause of all good things: some given primarily in the form of the Old and the New Testament; others are the consequence of philosophy. Perchance too philosophy was given to the Greeks primarily till the Lord should call the Greeks to serve him. Thus philosophy acted as a schoolmaster to the Greeks, preparing them for Christ, as the laws of the Jews prepared them for Christ.

The way of truth is one. But into it, as into a perennial river, streams flow from all sides. We assert that philosophy, which is characterized by investigation into the form and nature of things, is the truth of which the Lord Himself said, "I am the truth." Thus Greek preparatory culture, including philosophy itself, is shown to have come down from God to men.

Some do not wish to touch either philosophy or logic or to learn natural science. They demand bare faith alone, as if they wished, without bestowing any care on the vine, straightway to gather clusters from the first. I call him truly learned who brings everything to bear on the truth; so that from geometry, music, grammar, and philosophy itself, he culls what is useful and guards the faith against assault. And he who brings everything to bear on a right life, learning from Greeks and non-Greeks, this man is an experienced searcher after truth. And how necessary it is for him who desires to be partaker of the power of God to treat of intellectual subjects by philosophising.

According to some, Greek philosophy apprehended the truth accidentally, dimly, partially. Others will have it that Greek philosophy was instituted by the devil. Several hold that certain powers descending from heaven inspired the whole of philosophy. But if Greek philosophy does not comprehend the whole of truth and does not encompass God's commandments, yet it prepares the way for God's teachings; training in some way or other, molding character, and fitting him who believes in Providence for the reception of truth.

REVIEW QUESTIONS

1. Why did Tertullian oppose the study of pagan literature on the part of Christians?
2. Why did Clement of Alexandria favor the study of pagan learning?
3. What might have been the consequences if the Christian church had followed the advice of Tertullian rather than that of Clement?

3 Monastic Life

In the late third century A.D., inspired by Jesus' example of self-denial and seeking to escape from the distractions of worldly concerns, some zealous Christians withdrew to the deserts of Roman Egypt in search of peace and isolation. They turned their minds wholly to prayer, contemplation, and ascetic practices. These hermits were the earliest Christian monks. In time, some hermits banded together to form monastic communities, living under written rules that established a form of monastic government and way of life.

The hermit or monk "took up the Cross"—that is, emulated the way of Christ through a life of prayer, introspective self-examination, hard work, and ascetic practices like fasting, sexual abstinence, physical deprivation, and poverty. The hermitage and the monastery were schools for sanctity; thus the hermits and monks have been the spiritual models for many male and female Christians from late Roman times down to the present age.

The many early Christians who were drawn to the austerity of the African desert sought to escape the distractions of the world, to find religious insight and come closer to God. These hermits and mystics produced a vast body of literature describing their lives and experiences. Written first in Greek by the participants themselves, these accounts were translated into Latin in the fourth, fifth, and sixth centuries, and finally collected into a comprehensive work, *Vitae Patrum* (Lives of the Fathers), in the seventeenth century.

Saint Jerome
THE AGONY OF SOLITUDE IN THE DESERT

The Christian's vision of the world was honed in the isolation of the desert. The price of such insight was the agony that came with self-denial and solitude. Saint Jerome (A.D. 374–419), who lived in the desert during the fourth century, vividly described this suffering in a letter written to his female pupil Eustochium. He recounts the effects of the desert's austerity, which debilitated his body and disoriented his mind with delirious memories of earlier years and "enchantments" in Rome.

"Oh, how many times did I, set in the desert, in that vast solitude parched with the fires of the sun that offers a dread abiding to the monk, how often did I think myself back in the old Roman enchantments. There I sat solitary, full of bitterness; my disfigured limbs shuddered away from the sackcloth, my dirty skin was taking on the hue of the Ethiopian's flesh: every day tears, every day sighing: and if in spite of my struggles sleep would tower over and sink upon me, my battered body ached on the naked earth. Of food and drink I say nothing, since even a sick monk uses only cold water, and to take anything cooked is wanton luxury. Yet that same I, who for fear of hell condemned myself to such a prison, I, the comrade of scorpions and wild beasts, was there, watching the maidens in their dances: my face haggard with fasting, my mind burnt with desire in my frigid body, and the fires of lust alone leaped before a man prematurely dead. So, destitute of all aid, I used to lie at the feet of Christ, watering them with my tears, wiping them with my hair, struggling to subdue my rebellious flesh with seven days' fasting. I do not blush to confess the misery of my hapless days: rather could I weep that I am not what I was once. I remember crying out till day became one with night, nor ceasing to beat my breast until my Lord would chide and tranquillity return. I grew to dread even my cell, with its knowledge of my imaginings; and grim and angry with myself, would set out solitary to explore the desert: and wherever I would spy the depth of a valley or a mountainside or a precipitous rock, there was my place of prayer, there the torture-house of my unhappy flesh: and, the Lord Himself is witness, after many tears, and eyes that clung to heaven, I would sometimes seem to myself to be one with the angelic hosts."

Saint Benedict of Nursia
THE BENEDICTINE RULE

The monastic way of life soon spread from Egypt to Palestine and Syria and eventually throughout the Christian Roman Empire. In Italy, Benedict of Nursia (c. 480–547), scion of a wealthy Roman family, founded twelve monasteries, the best known being at Monte Cassino in the mountains of southern Italy. Benedict wrote a set of rules for the governance of his monks; the Benedictine Rule became the model for many monasteries throughout Latin Christendom. In the following extract, Benedict summarizes the purpose and principles of monastic life.

WHAT THE ABBOT SHOULD BE LIKE

The abbot who is worthy to rule a monastery ought to remember by what name they are called, and to justify by their deeds the name of a superior. For he is believed to take the place of Christ in the monastery, since he is called by his name, as the apostle says: "Ye have received the spirit of adoption of sons, whereby we call, Abba, Father."

And so the abbot ought not (God forbid) to teach or decree or order anything apart from the precept of the Lord; but his rules and his teaching ought always to be leavened with the leaven of divine justice in the minds of his disciples; and let the abbot be always mindful that in the great judgment of God, both his teaching and the obedience of his disciples will be weighed in the balance. And let the abbot know that whatever the master finds lacking in the sheep will be charged to the fault of the shepherd. Only in case the pastor has shown the greatest diligence in his management of an unruly and disobedient flock, and has given his whole care to the correction of their evil doings, will that pastor be cleared at the judgment of God. . . .

Therefore when anyone takes on himself the name of abbot, he should govern his disciples by a twofold teaching, that is, let him show forth all the good and holy things by his deeds rather than by his words; to ready disciples he ought to set forth the commands of God in words, but to the hard of heart, and to the simple-minded he ought to illustrate the divine precepts in his deeds. And all things which he has taught his disciples to be wrong, let him demonstrate in his action that they should not be done. . . .

ABOUT CALLING THE BROTHERS TO COUNCIL

Whenever anything especial is to be done in the monastery, the abbot shall convoke the whole body and himself set forth the matter at issue. And after listening to the advice of the brothers, he shall consider it by himself, and shall do what he shall have judged most useful. Now we say all should be called to the council, because the Lord often reveals to the younger brother what is best to be done.

But let the brothers give advice with all subjection of humility and not presume to defend boldly what seemed good to them, but rather rely on the judgment of the abbot, and all obey him in what he has judged to be for their welfare. But just as it is fitting that the disciples obey the master, so is it incumbent on him to dispose everything wisely and justly.

Therefore, let all follow the rule of the master in all things, and let no one depart from it rashly; let no one in the monastery follow the desire of his own heart. And let no one strive with his abbot shamelessly either within or without the monastery; and if he shall have presumed to do so, let him be subjected to the regular discipline. And let the abbot himself do all things in the fear of God and in the observance of the rule, knowing that he must without doubt render account unto God, the most just judge, for all his judgments.

CONCERNING THOSE WHO, BEING OFTEN REBUKED, DO NOT AMEND

If any brother, having frequently been rebuked for any fault, do not amend even after he has been excommunicated [cut off from the church's sacraments], a more severe rebuke shall fall upon him;—that is, the punishment of the lash shall be inflicted upon him. But if he do not even then amend; or, if perchance—which God forbid,—swelled with pride he try even to defend his works: then the abbot shall act as a wise physician. If he have applied . . . the ointments of exhortation, the medicaments [medicines] of the Divine Scriptures; if he have proceeded to the last blasting of excommunication, or to blows with rods, and if he sees that his efforts avail nothing: let him also—what is greater—call in the prayer of himself and all the brothers for him: that God who can do all things may work a cure upon an infirm brother. But if he be not healed even in this way, then at last the abbot may use the pruning knife, as the apostle says: "Remove evil from you," etc.: lest one diseased sheep contaminate the whole flock.

WHETHER BROTHERS WHO LEAVE THE MONASTERY OUGHT AGAIN TO BE RECEIVED

A brother who goes out, or is cast out, of the monastery for his own fault, if he wish to return, shall first promise every amends for the fault on account of which he departed; and thus he shall be received into the lowest degree—so that thereby his humility may be proved. But if he again depart, up to the third time he shall be received. Knowing that after this every opportunity of return is denied to him.

CONCERNING BOYS UNDER AGE, HOW THEY SHALL BE CORRECTED

Every age or intelligence ought to have its proper bounds. Therefore as often as boys or youths, or those who are less able to understand how great is the punishment of excommunication: as often as such persons offend, they shall either be afflicted with excessive fasts, or coerced with severe blows, that they may be healed.

CONCERNING THE RECEPTION OF GUESTS

All guests who come shall be received as though they were Christ; for He Himself said: "I was a stranger and ye took Me in." And to all, fitting honour shall be shown; but, most of all, to servants of the faith and to pilgrims. When, therefore, a guest is announced, the prior or the brothers shall run to meet him, with every office of love. And first they shall pray together; and thus they shall be joined together in peace. . . .

The monks gathered together for prayer seven times in the course of the day. Prayers were chanted from set texts.

CONCERNING REVERENCE FOR PRAYER

If when to powerful men we wish to suggest anything, we do not presume to do it unless with reverence and humility: how much more should we supplicate with all humility, and devotion of purity, God who is the Lord of all. And let us know that we are heard, not for much speaking, but for purity of heart and compunction of tears. And, therefore, prayer ought to be brief and pure; unless perchance it be prolonged by the influence of the inspiration of the divine grace. When assembled together, then, let the prayer be altogether brief; and, the sign being given by the prior, let us rise together.

CONCERNING THE DAILY MANUAL LABOUR

Idleness is the enemy of the soul. And therefore, at fixed times, the brothers ought to be occupied in manual labour; and again, at fixed times, in sacred reading.

CONCERNING HUMILITY

. . . Now the first grade of humility is this: keeping the fear of God before his eyes, let him

avoid forgetfulness and ever remember all the precepts of the Lord; and continually consider in his heart that eternal life which is prepared for those who fear God, just as the mockers of God fall into hell. . . .

The fifth grade of humility is this, if one reveals to the abbot in humble confession all the vain imaginings that come into his heart, and all the evil he has done in secret. . . .

This is the eighth grade of humility; if a monk do nothing except what the common rule of the monastery or the examples of his superior urges him to do.

. . . The tenth grade of humility is this, that he be not easily moved nor prompt to laughter, since it is written: "The fool raiseth his voice in laughter."

The eleventh grade of humility is this: if, when the monk speaks, he says few words and those to the point, slowly and without laughter, humbly and gravely; and be not loud of voice, as it is written: "A wise man is known by his few words."

The twelfth grade of humility is this: that a monk conduct himself with humility not only in his heart but also in his bearing, in the sight of all; that is, in the service of God, in the oratory [chapel], in the monastery, in the garden, on the road, in the field; and everywhere, sitting or walking or standing, let him always have his head bowed, and his eyes fixed on the ground. Always mindful of his sins, let him think of himself as being already tried in the great judgment, saying in his heart what that publican, spoken of in the gospel, said with his eyes fixed on the earth: "Lord, I a sinner am not worthy to lift mine eyes to the heavens;" and again with the prophet: "I am bowed down and humbled wheresoever I go." . . .

REVIEW QUESTIONS

1. Why did the desert fathers feel that solitude and self-mortification were the best ways to serve Christ?
2. What would you recommend for a Christian today as the best way to serve God?
3. Describe the government of a Benedictine monastery.
4. How did monasticism help to shape Western cultural values?

4   Christian Way of Life

Although the principal concern of Jesus' followers was the attainment of salvation, Christians still had to deal with the world and its ways. In the process of doing so, they developed attitudes and customs that have had an enduring influence on Western culture.

Saint Benedict of Nursia
THE VIRTUOUS CHRISTIAN

In the following selection from his monastic book of rules, Saint Benedict of Nursia (see page 110) advises his monks on the attitudes and conduct necessary to live a virtuous Christian life.

WHAT ARE THE INSTRUMENTS OF GOOD WORKS?

In the first place, to love the Lord God with the whole heart, whole soul, whole strength, then his neighbor as himself.

Then not to kill, not to commit adultery, not to steal, not to covet, not to bear false witness, to honor all men, and what anyone would not have done to him, let him not do to another. To deny himself, that he may follow Christ, to chasten the body, to renounce luxuries, to love fasting. To relieve the poor, to clothe the naked, to visit the sick, to bury the dead, to help in tribulation, to console the afflicted.

To make himself a stranger to the affairs of the world, to prefer nothing before the love of Christ, not to give way to anger, not to bear any grudge, not to harbour deceit in the heart, not to forsake charity. Not to swear, lest haply he perjure himself, to utter truth from his heart and his mouth. Not to return evil for evil, not to do injuries, but rather to bear them patiently, to love his enemies, not to curse again those who curse him, but rather to bless them, to endure persecution for righteousness' sake. Not to be proud, not given to wine, not gluttonous, not addicted to sleep, not slothful, not given to murmur, not a slanderer. To commit his hope to God; when he sees anything good in himself to attribute it to God, and not to himself, but let him always know that which is evil is his own doing, and impute it to himself. To fear the day of judgment, to dread hell, to desire eternal life with all spiritual longing, to have the expectation of death every day before his eyes. To watch over his actions at all times, to know certainly that in all places the eye of God is upon him; those evil thoughts which come into his heart to dash to pieces on Christ, and to make them known to his spiritual senior. To keep his lips from evil and wicked discourse, not to be fond of much talking, not to speak vain words or such as provoke laughter, not to love much or violent laughter. To give willing attention to the sacred readings, to pray frequently every day, to confess his past sins to God, in prayer, with tears and groanings; from thence forward to reform as to those sins.

Not to fulfill the desires of the flesh, to hate his own will, in all things to obey the commands of the abbot, even though he himself (which God forbid) should do otherwise, remembering our Lord's commands: "What they say, do; but what they do, do ye not." Not to desire to be called a saint before he is one, but first to be one that he may be truly called one; every day to fulfill the commands of God in his deeds, to love chastity, to hate no one, not to have jealousy or envy, not to love contention, to avoid self-conceit; to reverence seniors, to love juniors, to pray for enemies in the love of Christ, to be reconciled with his adversary, before the going down of the sun, and never to despair of the mercy of God. . . .

REVIEW QUESTION

1. Why would Benedict's message appeal to many people?

5 Christian Demonization of Jews

Numerous links connect early Christianity and Judaism. Jesus himself and his earliest followers, including the Twelve Apostles, were Jews who were faithful to Jewish law. Jesus' message was first spread in synagogues throughout the Roman Empire. Early Christianity's affirmation of the preciousness of the human being, created in God's image, its belief that God rules history, its awareness of human sinfulness, its call for repentance, and its appeal to God for forgiveness are rooted in Judaism. The Christian reference to God as a "merciful Father" derives from Jewish prayer. Also rooted in Judaism are the moral norms proclaimed by Jesus in the Sermon on the Mount and on other occasions. For example, "Thou shalt love thy neighbor as thyself" was the motto of the Jewish sage Hillel, a contemporary of Jesus, who founded a school. The great value that the Torah gives to charity was inherited by Christianity. Jesus' use of parables to convey his teachings, the concept of the Messiah, respect for the Sabbath, and congregational worship also stem from Judaism. And, of course, Christians viewed the Hebrew Scriptures as God's word.

Over the years, however, Christians forgot or devalued this relationship to Judaism, and some thinkers began to show hostility toward Judaism and Jews that had tragic consequences in later centuries. Several factors fueled this anti-Judaism: resentment against Jews for their refusal to embrace Jesus; the polemics of the Jewish establishment against the followers of Jesus; the role in Jesus' death ascribed to Jews by the New Testament; resentment against those Christians who Judaized: that is, continued to observe Jewish festivals and the Jewish Sabbath, regard the synagogue as holy, and practice circumcision; and anger that Judaism remained a vital religion, for this undermined the conviction that Christianity was the fulfillment of Judaism and the one true faith.

What made Christian anti-Judaism particularly ominous was the effort of some theologians to demonize the Jewish people. The myth emerged that the Jews, murderers of the incarnate God who embodied all that was good, were a cursed people, children of the Devil, whose suffering was intended by God.

The diabolization of the Jew, which bore no relationship to the actual behavior of Jews or to their highly ethical religion, and the "theology of victimization," which held that the Jews were collectively and eternally cursed for denying Christ, became powerful myths, which, over the centuries, poisoned Christians' hearts and minds against Jews, spurring innumerable humiliations, persecutions, and massacres.

Saint John Chrysostom
DISCOURSES AGAINST JUDAIZING CHRISTIANS

A particularly fierce attack on Jews was made by John Chrysostom (A.D. 347–407), a prominent church father. John sought to discourage Christians from participating in Jewish festivals, which still maintained their attraction for converts. In a series of sermons, he repeatedly castigated the Jews as demons and deicides. Since Jews are hated by God, he told the congregation, it is also a Christian's duty to hate these pitiable and miserable people.

What is this disease? The festivals of the pitiful and miserable Jews are soon to march upon us one after the other and in quick succession: the feast of Trumpets,* the feast of Tabernacles,† the fasts.‡ There are many in our ranks who say they think as we do. Yet some of these are going to watch the festivals and others will join the Jews in keeping their feasts and observing their fasts. I wish to drive this perverse custom from the Church right now. . . . But now that the Jewish festivals are close by and at the very door, if I should fail to cure those who are sick with the Judaizing disease, I am afraid that, because of their ill-suited association and deep ignorance, some Christians may partake in the Jews' transgressions; once they have done so, I fear my discourses on these transgressions will be in vain. For if they hear no word from me today, they will then join the Jews in their fasts; once they have committed this sin, it will be useless for me to apply the remedy.

And so it is that I hasten to anticipate this danger and prevent it. . . .

But do not be surprised that I called the Jews pitiable. They really are pitiable and miserable. When so many blessings from heaven came into their hands, they thrust them aside and were at great pains to reject them. . . . From their childhood they read the prophets, but they crucified him whom the prophets had foretold. We did not hear the divine prophecies but we did worship him of whom they prophesied. And so they are pitiful because they rejected the blessings which were sent to them, while others seized hold of these blessings and drew them to themselves. . . .

Many, I know, respect the Jews and think that their present way of life is a venerable one. This is why I hasten to uproot and tear out this deadly opinion. . . . [T]he synagogue is not only a brothel and a theater; it also is a den of robbers and a lodging for wild beasts. . . . [W]hen God forsakes a people, what hope of salvation is left? When God forsakes a place, that place becomes the dwelling of demons.

But at any rate the Jews say that they, too, adore God. God forbid that I say that. No Jew adores God! Who says so? The Son of God says so. For he said: "If you were to know my Father, you would also know me. But you neither know me nor do you know my Father."§ Could I produce a witness more trustworthy than the Son of God?

If, then, the Jews fail to know the Father, if they crucified the Son, if they thrust off the help of the Spirit, who should not make bold to declare plainly that the synagogue is a dwelling of demons? God is not worshipped there. Heaven forbid! From now on it remains a place of idolatry. But still some people pay it honor as a holy place. . . .

---

*This is the New Year or Rosh Ha-Shanah, which falls on the first of Tishri (Sept.–Oct.).

†This falls on the fifteenth of Tishri and lasts a week, during which the Jews danced and "made merry before the Lord" (cf. Lv 23.33–43).

‡The fasts here referred to would seem to be the Ten Days of Penitence between Rosh Ha-Shanah and Yom Kippur (the Day of Atonement).

§John 8:19.

. . . In our churches we hear countless discourses on eternal punishments, on rivers of fire, on the venomous worm, on bonds that cannot be burst, on exterior darkness. But the Jews neither know nor dream of these things. They live for their bellies, they gape for the things of this world, their condition is no better than that of pigs or goats because of their wanton ways and excessive gluttony. They know but one thing: to fill their bellies and be drunk, to get all cut and bruised, to be hurt and wounded while fighting for their favorite charioteers. . . .

. . . Indeed the synagogue is less deserving of honor than any inn. It is not merely a lodging place for robbers and cheats but also for demons. This is true not only of the synagogues but also of the souls of the Jews, as I shall try to prove at the end of my discourse. . . .

But I must get back again to those who are sick. Consider, then, with whom they are sharing their fasts. It is with those who shouted: "Crucify him, Crucify him,"‖ with those who said: "His blood be upon us and upon our children."# . . . Is it not strange that those who worship the Crucified keep common festival with those who crucified him? Is it not a sign of folly and the worst madness?

Since there are some who think of the synagogue as a holy place, I must say a few words to them. Why do you reverence that place? Must you not despise it, hold it in abomination, run away from it? They answer that the Law and the books of the prophets are kept there. What is this? Will any place where these books be a holy place? By no means! This is the reason

above all others why I hate the synagogue and abhor it. They have the prophets but do not believe them; they read the sacred writings but reject their witness—and this is a mark of men guilty of the greatest outrage.

Tell me this. If you were to see a venerable man, illustrious and renowned, dragged off into a tavern or den of robbers: if you were to see him outraged, beaten, and subjected there to the worst violence, would you have held that tavern or den in high esteem because that great and esteemed man had been inside it while undergoing that violent treatment? I think not. Rather, for this very reason you would have hated and abhorred the place.

Let that be your judgment about the synagogue, too. For they brought the books of Moses and the prophets along with them into the synagogue, not to honor them but to outrage them with dishonor. When they say that Moses and the prophets knew not Christ and said nothing about his coming, what greater outrage could they do to those holy men than to accuse them of failing to recognize their Master, than to say that those saintly prophets are partners of their impiety? And so it is that we must hate both them and their synagogue all the more because of their offensive treatment of those holy men. . . .

Therefore, flee the gatherings and holy places of the Jews. Let no man venerate the synagogue because of the holy books; let him hate and avoid it because the Jews outrage and maltreat the holy ones, because they refuse to believe their words, because they accuse them of the ultimate impiety. . . .

Certainly it is the time for me to show that demons dwell in the synagogue, not only in the place itself but also in the souls of the Jews. . . . Do you see that demons dwell in their souls and that these demons are more dangerous than the ones of old? And this is very reasonable. In the old days the Jews acted impiously toward the prophets; now they outrage the Master of the prophets. Tell me this. Do you not shudder to come into the same place with men possessed, who have so many unclean spirits, who have been reared amid slaughter and bloodshed? Must you

---

‖Lk 23.21.
#Mt 27.25. Chrysostom obviously holds the position, which was common for centuries, that all Jews are responsible for Christ's passion and death. Vatican II's "Declaration on the Relationship of the Church to Non-Christian Religions" states that these "cannot be blamed on all the Jews then living, without distinction, nor upon the Jews of today. Although the Church is the new people of God, the Jews should not be presented as repudiated or cursed by God, as if such views followed from the holy Scriptures." A footnote at this point says that Cardinal Bea and others explained Mt 27.25 as the cry of a Jerusalem crowd that had no right to speak for the whole Jewish people.

share a greeting with them and exchange a bare word? Must you not turn away from them since they are the common disgrace and infection of the whole world? Have they not come to every form of wickedness? Have not all the prophets spent themselves making many and long speeches of accusation against them?**. . .

Tell me this. If a man were to have slain your son, would you endure to look upon him, or to accept his greeting? Would you not shun him as a wicked demon, as the devil himself? They slew the Son of your Lord; do you have the boldness to enter with them under the same roof? After he was slain he heaped such honor upon you that he made you his brother and coheir. But you dishonor him so much that you pay honor to those

---

**Chrysostom argues from the guilt of their forebears to the guilt of contemporary Jews.

who slew him on the cross, that you observe with them the fellowship of the festivals, that you go to their profane places, enter their unclean doors, and share in the tables of demons. For I am persuaded to call the fasting of the Jews a table of demons because they slew God. If the Jews are acting against God, must they not be serving the demons? . . .

Meanwhile, I ask you to rescue your brothers, to set them free from their error, and to bring them back to the truth. . . . I want them to learn these facts from you and to free themselves from their wicked association with the Jews. I want them then to show themselves sincere and genuine Christians. I want them to shun the evil gatherings of the Jews and their synagogues, both in the city and in the suburbs, because these are robbers' dens and dwellings of demons.

REVIEW QUESTIONS

1. In what ways did John Chrysostom demonize the Jews?
2. What is the historical significance of this form of anti-Judaism?

---

6 The Christian World-View

Building on the life and teachings of Jesus as reported in the Gospels and apostolic letters collected in the New Testament, the early Christian thinkers formulated a comprehensive world-view. The Christian view stressed the sinful nature of human beings—their almost unlimited capacity for evildoing. The church taught that only through the gift of God's grace could individuals overcome the consequences of sin and obtain salvation. Christian leaders drew a sharp distinction between a spiritual realm (called the City of God by Saint Augustine) and the secular world (the City of Man), where Christians had to live out their earthly, material existence. Christians were urged to live in the world, but not to live by its values. Rather, they were to imitate the ways of Jesus in thought, word, and deed, as interpreted by the authorities of the church.

The task of living a Christian life in a secular world was not easy. Not the least of the problems was how Christians could relate to the political power structure of earthly societies. The task of finding a Christian basis for relations between church and state has been a continuous process since early Christian times. It has had wide repercussions in creating a distinctive Christian view of the legitimate powers of the state.

Saint Augustine
THE CITY OF GOD

Augustine (Aurelius Augustinus, A.D. 354–430), bishop of Hippo (now Souk-Ahras in modern Algeria), was one of the great theologians of the early Christian church. He formulated a view of life and of the individual that became definitive for Western Christians until it was partially superseded by the writings of Thomas Aquinas in the thirteenth century. Although Augustine admired the achievements of Socrates and Plato, he could not accept their central premise: that in the search for truth the individual relied on reason alone.

The sacking of Rome by the Visigoths in A.D. 410 shocked the entire Roman world. Pagans blamed the catastrophe on the Christians; by abandoning the old gods, said pagans, Christians had brought down the wrath of heaven on Rome. In reply to these charges, Saint Augustine wrote the *City of God,* setting forth the Christian view of the world and humanity.

The theme of the first group of passages from Augustine's *City of God* is a crucial element in the Christian outlook: that when human beings turn away from God to follow their own desires as Adam and Eve did—the original sin—they fall into evil and become afflicted with many miseries, which can be relieved only through God's grace.

I have already said, in previous Books, that God had two purposes in deriving all men from one man. His first purpose was to give unity to the human race by the likeness of nature. His second purpose was to bind mankind by the bond of peace, through blood relationship, into one harmonious whole. I have said further that no member of this race would ever have died had not the first two [Adam and Eve]—one created from nothing and the second from the first—merited this death by disobedience. The sin which they committed was so great that it impaired all human nature—in this sense, that the nature has been transmitted to posterity with a propensity to sin and a necessity to die. . . .

When a man lives "according to man" and not "according to God" he is like the Devil. . . .

When man lives according to himself, that is to say, according to human ways and not according to God's will, then surely he lives according to falsehood. Man himself, of course, is not a lie, since God who is his Author and Creator could not be the Author and Creator of a lie. Rather, man has been so constituted in truth that he was meant to live not according to himself but to Him who made him—that is, he was meant to

do the will of God rather than his own. It is a lie not to live as a man was created to live.

Man indeed desires happiness even when he does so live as to make happiness impossible. . . . The happiness of man can come not from himself but only from God, and that to live according to oneself is to sin, and to sin is to lose God. . . .

Moreover, our first parents [Adam and Eve] only fell openly into the sin of disobedience because, secretly, they had begun to be guilty. Actually, their bad deed could not have been done had not bad will preceded it; what is more, the root of their bad will was nothing else than pride. For, "pride is the beginning of all sin." And what is pride but an appetite for inordinate exaltation? Now, exaltation is inordinate when the soul cuts itself off from the very Source [God] to which it should keep close and somehow makes itself and becomes an end to itself. This takes place when the soul becomes inordinately pleased with itself, and such self-pleasing occurs when the soul falls away from the unchangeable Good which ought to please the soul far more than the soul can please itself. Now, this falling away is the soul's own doing, for, if the will had merely remained firm in the love of that higher immutable Good which lighted its mind into knowledge and warmed its will into love, it would not have turned away in search of satisfaction in itself and, by so doing, have lost that light and warmth. And thus Eve would not have believed that the serpent's lie was true, nor would Adam have preferred the will of his wife to the will of God. . . .

This life of ours—if a life so full of such great ills can properly be called a life—bears witness to the fact that, from its very start, the race of mortal men has been a race condemned. Think, first, of that dreadful abyss of ignorance from which all error flows and so engulfs the sons of Adam in a darksome pool that no one can escape without the toll of toils and tears and fears. Then, take our very love for all those things that prove so vain and poisonous and breed so many heartaches, troubles, griefs, and fears; such insane joys in discord, strife, and war; such wrath and plots of enemies, deceivers, sycophants; such fraud and theft and robbery; such perfidy and pride, envy and ambition, homicide and murder, cruelty and savagery, lawlessness and lust; all the shameless passions of the impure—fornication and adultery, incest and unnatural sins, rape and countless other uncleannesses too nasty to be mentioned; the sins against religion—sacrilege and heresy, blasphemy and perjury; the iniquities against our neighbors—calumnies and cheating, lies and false witness, violence to persons and property; the injustices of the courts and the innumerable other miseries and maladies that fill the world, yet escape attention.

It is true that it is wicked men who do such things, but the source of all such sins is that radical canker [sinfulness] in the mind and will that is innate in every son of Adam. . . .

Yet, for all this blight of ignorance and folly, fallen man has not been left without some ministries of Providence, nor has God, in His anger, shut up His mercies. There are still within the reach of man himself, if only he will pay the price of toil and trouble, the twin resources of law and education. With the one, he can make war on human passion; with the other, he can

keep the light of learning lit even in the darkness of our native ignorance. . . .

From this all but hell of unhappiness here on earth, nothing can save us but the grace of Jesus Christ, who is our Saviour, Lord and God. In fact, the very meaning of the name, Jesus, is Saviour, and when we say "save" we mean, especially, that He saves us from passing from the misery of this mortal life to a still more miserable condition, which is not so much a life as death. . . .

Augustine saw a conflict between the earthly city, visible, temporal, and corrupt, and the City of God, invisible, eternal, and perfect. Those Christians favored with God's grace lived in this earthly city as strangers and pilgrims passing through on their journey to their true homeland, the heavenly kingdom. The fate of the earthly city was of no ultimate concern to these Christians. For Augustine, this earthly world represented the forces of evil that would finally be destroyed at the end of time, when Christ would come again.

What we see, then, is that two societies have issued from two kinds of love. Worldly society has flowered from a selfish love which dared to despise even God, whereas the communion of saints is rooted in a love of God that is ready to trample on self. In a word, this latter relies on the Lord, whereas the other boasts that it can get along by itself. The city of man seeks the praise of men, whereas the height of glory for the other is to hear God in the witness of conscience. The one lifts up its head in its own boasting; the other says to God: "Thou art my glory, thou liftest up my head."

In the city of the world both the rulers themselves and the people they dominate are dominated by the lust for domination; whereas in the City of God all citizens serve one another in charity, whether they serve by the responsibilities of office or by the duties of obedience. The one city loves its leaders as symbols of its own strength; the other says to its God: "I love thee, O Lord, my strength." Hence, even the wise men in the city of man live according to man, and their only goal has been the goods of their bodies or of the mind or of both; though some of them have reached a knowledge of God, "they did not glorify him as God or give thanks but became vain in their reasonings, and their senseless minds have been darkened. For while professing to be wise" (that is to say, while glorying in their own wisdom, under the domination of pride), "they have become fools, and they have changed the glory of the incorruptible God for an image made like to corruptible man and to birds and four-footed beasts and creeping things" (meaning that they either led their people, or imitated them, in adoring idols shaped like these things), "and they worshiped and served the creature rather than the Creator who is blessed forever." In the City of God, on the contrary, there is no merely human wisdom, but there is a piety which worships the true God as He should be worshiped and has as its goal that reward of all holiness whether in the society of saints on earth or in that of angels of heaven, which is "that God may be all in all." . . .

Augustine says that history reveals the intermingling of the City of God and the City of Man in time and space, and the incessant combat between the partisans of these two cities. This struggle will continue until time itself is annulled by God when Christ returns—and the saints are separated from sinners at the Last Judgment. Then the saints will join Jesus and be with him for eternity, and the sinners will be separated from God and confined to hell, also for eternity.

—————

. . . In the eternal City of God, each and all of the citizens are personally immortal with an immortality which the holy angels never lost and which even human beings can come to share. This is to be achieved by the supreme omnipotence of the Creator, the Founder of the City. . . .

Who can measure the happiness of heaven, where no evil at all can touch us, no good will be out of reach; where life is to be one long laud extolling God, who will be all in all; where there will be no weariness to call for rest, no need to call for toil, no place for any energy but praise. . . .

. . . There will be such poise, such grace, such beauty as become a place where nothing unbecoming can be found. Wherever the spirit wills, there, in a flash, will the body be. Nor will the spirit ever will anything unbecoming either to itself or to the body.

In heaven, all glory will be true glory, since no one could ever err in praising too little or too much. True honor will never be denied where due, never be given where undeserved, and, since none but the worthy are permitted there, no one will unworthily [pursue] glory. Perfect peace will reign, since nothing in ourselves or in any others could disturb this peace.

REVIEW QUESTIONS

1. According to Saint Augustine, what was the origin of the unity of the human race? What was the origin of human sinfulness?
2. Describe Augustine's conception of the two cities—the City of God and the City of Man—and the radical implications of this teaching in shaping Christian culture.

CHAPTER 5

The Early Middle Ages

HISTOIRE DE CHARLEMAGNE (detail). This fifteenth-century tapestry shows Charlemagne wearing the heraldic insignia of France and the Holy Roman Empire. His courtiers surround him. *(Wool, 2.55 × 1.45 m. Musée des Beaux-Arts, Dijon.)*

The establishment of Germanic kingdoms in the fifth and sixth centuries on Roman lands marked the end of the ancient world and the start of the Middle Ages, a period that spanned a thousand years. During the Middle Ages the center of Western civilization shifted northward from the lands bordering the Mediterranean Sea to parts of Europe that Greco-Roman civilization had barely penetrated.

The Early Middle Ages (500–1050) marked an age of transition. The humanist culture that characterized the Greco-Roman past had disintegrated, and a new civilization was emerging in Latin Christendom, which covered western and central Europe. Medieval civilization consisted of a blending of the remnants of Greco-Roman culture with Germanic customs and Christian principles. The central element was Christianity; the Christian view of a transcendent God and the quest for salvation pervaded the medieval outlook, and the church was the dominant institution.

During the Early Middle Ages, Latin Christendom was a pioneer society struggling to overcome invasions, a breakdown of central authority, a decline in trade and town life, and a deterioration of highly refined culture. The Latin Christian church, centered in Rome and headed by the pope, progressively gave form and unity to the new civilization. Christian clergy preserved some of the learning of the ancient world, which they incorporated into the Christian outlook. Dedicated missionaries converted various Germanic, Celtic, and Slavic peoples to Latin Christianity. From Italy to the North Sea and from Ireland to Poland, an emerging Christian tradition was providing unity to people with differing cultural traditions.

The center of emerging medieval civilization was the kingdom of the Franks, located in Gaul (France) and western Germany. Migrating westward from their homeland in the valley of the Rhine River, the Germanic Franks conquered Roman Gaul in the fifth and sixth centuries. Charlemagne (768–814), the greatest of the Frankish rulers, added large areas of Germany and Italy to his kingdom. On Christmas Day in the year 800, Pope Leo III crowned Charlemagne emperor of the Romans, a sign that the memory of Imperial Rome still persisted. Without Roman law, a professional civil service, and great cities serving as centers of trade, however, Charlemagne's empire was only a pale shadow of the Roman Empire. Rather, the crowning of a German king as emperor of the Romans by the pope signified something new: the intermingling of Germanic, Christian, and Roman elements that came to characterize medieval Latin Christendom.

Charlemagne's empire rested more on the strength of the emperor's personality than it did on viable institutions. Charlemagne's heirs were unable to hold the empire together; power passed gradually into the hands of large landholders, who exercised governmental authority in their own regions. Also contributing to this decline in centralized authority were devastating raids by Muslims from Spain, North Africa, and Mediterranean islands; Northmen from Scandinavia; and Magyars from western Asia. Europe had entered an age of feudalism, in which public authority was dispersed among lords and held as if it were private inheritable property.

Feudalism rested on an economic base known as manorialism. Although family farms owned by free peasants still existed, the essential agricultural arrangement in medieval society was the village community (manor), headed by a lord or his steward and farmed by serfs, who were bound to the land. A lord controlled at least one manorial village; great lords might possess scores. Much land was held by various clerical institutions; the church's manors were similar to those run by nonclerics.

Feudalism was an improvised response to the challenge posed by ineffectual central authority, and it provided some order and law during a period of breakdown. Medieval feudal practices were not uniform but differed from region to region. In later centuries, when kings reasserted their authority and fashioned strong central governments, the power of lords declined.

Latin Christendom was only one of three new civilizations based on religion that emerged after the decline of the Roman Empire; Byzantium and Islam were the other two. During the Early Middle Ages both of these eastern civilizations were far more advanced than Latin Christendom. And yet it was Latin Christendom, not Byzantine or Islamic civilizations, that eventually produced the modern world.

---

1 The Byzantine Cultural Achievement

During the Early Middle Ages, when learning was in retreat in Latin Christendom, Byzantine civilization preserved the intellectual tradition of ancient Greece. Although the Roman Empire in the West fell to the German tribes, the eastern provinces of the Empire survived. They did so because they were richer, more urbanized, and more populous and because the main thrust of the Germanic and Hunnish invaders had been directed at the western regions. In the eastern parts, Byzantine civilization took shape. Its religion was Christianity, its culture Greek, and its machinery of administration Roman. Contacts with Byzantine learning during the High Middle Ages stimulated learning in the Latin West.

Theophylact Simocattes
THE VALUE OF REASON AND HISTORY

In the following selection Theophylact Simocattes, a seventh-century Byzantine historian, shows respect for the tradition of reason that was inherited from the classical world and familiarity with Homer, the wellspring of Greek literature. Like Thucydides, he values history, considering it a far better avenue to knowledge than the myths and fables created or embellished by poets.

Man is adorned not only by the endowments of nature but also by the fruits of his own efforts. For reason, which he possesses, is an admirable and divine trait by which he renders to God his adoration and homage. Through reason he enters into knowledge of himself and does not remain ignorant of the ordering of his creation. Accordingly, through reason men come together with each other and, turning away from external considerations, they direct their thoughts toward the mystery of their own nature.

Reason has given many good things to men and is an excellent helpmate of nature. The things which nature has withheld from man, reason provides in the most effective manner, embellishing those things which are seen, adding spice to those that are tasted, roughening or softening things to the touch, composing poetry and music for the ear, soothing the soul by lessening discord, and bringing sounds into concord. Is not reason also the most persuasive master of the crafts?—reason which has made a well-woven tunic from wool, which from wood has constructed carts for farmers, oars for sailors, and small wicker shields for soldiers as protection against the dangers of the battlefield.

Most important of all, reason provides the hearer with that pleasure which reflects the greatest amount of experience, the study of history, which is the instructor of the spirit. Nothing can be more seductive than history for the minds of those who desire to learn. It is sufficient to cite an example from Homer to demonstrate this: Soon after he had been thrown on the beach by violent waves of the sea, the son of Laertes, Odysseus, almost naked and with his body emaciated from the mishap of the shipwreck, was graciously received at the court of Alcinous. There he was clothed in a bright robe and given a place at the table of the king. Although only just arrived, he was granted permission to speak and an opportunity to relate his adventures. His recital pleased the Phocaeans so much that the banquet seemed to have changed into a theater. Indeed, they lent him an attention altogether remarkable, nor did they feel during his long narration any tedium, although he described the many misfortunes he had suffered. For listening brings an overwhelming desire (to hear more) and thus easily accepts a strange tale.

It is for this reason that in learning the poets are considered most estimable, for they realize that the spirits of men are fond of stories, always yearning to acquire knowledge and thirsty for strange narrations. Thus the poets create myths for men and clothe their phrases with adornments, fleshing out the fables with method, and embellishing their nonsense with meter as if with enchanted spells. This artifice has succeeded so well that poets are considered to be theologians, intimately associated with the gods. It is believed that through the poets' mouths the gods reveal their own personal affairs and also whether a felicitous or a calamitous event will happen to men in their lifetime.

This being so, one may term history the common teacher of all men: it shows which course to follow and which to avoid as profitless. The most competent generals are those who have been instructed by history, for history reveals how to draw up troops and by what means to outmaneuver the enemy through ambush. History renders these generals more prudent because they know about the misfortunes of others, and it directs them through observation of the mistakes of others. Similarly, it has shown that men become happier through good conduct, pushing men to higher peaks of virtue through gradual advances. For the old man history is his support and staff, while for the young, it is the fairest and wisest instructor, applying (the fruit of) great experience to new situations and thus anticipating somewhat the lessons of time. I now dedicate my own zeal and efforts to history, although I know that I am undertaking a greater task than I am able to fulfill effectively, since I lack elegance of expression, profundity of thought, purity of syntax, and skill in composition. If any parts of my work should prove pleasing in any way, let this be ascribed rather to the result of chance than to my own skill.

REVIEW QUESTION

1. Why did Theophylact value reason? History? What is his debt to ancient Greece?

---

2 Islam

The vital new religion of Islam emerged in the seventh century among the Arabs of Arabia. Its founder was Muhammad (c. 570–632), a prosperous merchant in Mecca, a trading city near the Red Sea. When Muhammad was about forty, he believed that he was visited by the angel Gabriel, who ordered him to "recite in the name of the Lord!" Transformed by this vision, Muhammad was convinced that he had been chosen to serve as a prophet.

Although most desert Arabs worshiped tribal gods, in the towns and trading centers many Arabs were familiar with Judaism and Christianity, and some had accepted the idea of one God. Rejecting the many deities of the tribal religions, Muhammad offered the Arabs a new monotheistic faith, Islam, which means "surrender to Allah" (God).

Muhammad
THE KORAN

Islamic standards of morality and rules governing daily life are set by the Koran, the book that Muslims believe contains the words of Allah as revealed to Muhammad. Muslims see their religion as the completion and perfection of Judaism and Christianity. They regard the ancient Hebrew prophets as sent from God and value their messages about compassion and the oneness of humanity. Muslims also regard Jesus as a great prophet but do not consider him divine. They see Muhammad as the last and greatest of the prophets and believe that he was entirely human, not divine. Muslims worship only Allah, the creator and ruler of heaven and earth, a single, all-powerful God who is merciful, compassionate, and just. Following are excerpts from the Koran grouped by topics.

GOD

God: there is no god but Him, the Living, the Eternal One. Neither slumber nor sleep overtakes Him. His is what the heavens and the earth contain. Who can intercede with Him except by His permission? He knows what is before and behind men. They can grasp only that part of His knowledge which He wills. His throne is as vast as the heavens and the earth, and the preservation of both does not weary

Him. He is the Exalted, the Immense One. (2:255–257)

———

In the Name of God, the Compassionate, the Merciful

It is the Merciful who has taught the Koran.

He created man and taught him articulate speech. The sun and the moon pursue their ordered course. The plants and the trees bow down in adoration.

He raised the heaven on high and set the balance of all things, that you might not transgress that balance. Give just weight and full measure.

He laid the earth for His creatures, with all its fruits and blossom-bearing palm, chaff-covered grain and scented herbs. Which of your Lord's blessings would you deny?

He created man from potter's clay, and the jinn [spirits] from smokeless fire. Which of your Lord's blessings would you deny? (55:1–18)

———

All that is in the heavens and the earth gives glory to God. He is the Mighty, the Wise One.

It is He that has sovereignty over the heavens and the earth. He ordains life and death, and has power over all things.

He is the First and the Last, the Visible and the Unseen. He has knowledge of all things.

It was He who created the heavens and the earth in six days, and then mounted the throne. He knows all that goes into the earth and all that emerges from it, all that comes down from heaven and all that ascends to it. He is with you wherever you are. God is cognizant of all your actions.

He has sovereignty over the heavens and the earth. To God shall all things return. He causes the night to pass into the day, and causes the day to pass into the night. He has knowledge of the inmost thoughts of men. (57:1–7)

RIGHTEOUSNESS AND MERCY

Righteousness does not consist in whether you face towards the East or the West. The righteous man is he who believes in God and the Last Day, in the angels and the Book and the prophets; who, though he loves it dearly, gives away his wealth to kinsfolk, to orphans, to the destitute, to the traveller in need and to beggars, and for the redemption of captives; who attends to his prayers and renders the alms levy; who is true to his promises and steadfast in trial and adversity and in times of war. Such are the true believers; such are the God-fearing. (2:176–178)

———

Serve God and associate none with Him. Show kindness to parents and kindred, to orphans and to the destitute, to near and distant neighbours, to those that keep company with you, to the traveller in need, and to the slaves you own. God does not love arrogant and boastful men, who are themselves niggardly and enjoin others to be niggardly; who conceal the riches which God of His bounty has bestowed upon them (We have prepared a shameful punishment for the unbelievers); and who spend their wealth for the sake of ostentation, believing neither in God nor in the Last Day. He that chooses Satan for his friend, an evil friend has he. (4:36–39)

CHRISTIANITY

And remember the angels' words to Mary. They said:* "God has chosen you. He has made you pure and exalted you above womankind. Mary, be obedient to your Lord; bow down and worship with the worshippers."

This is an account of a divine secret. We reveal it to you.† You were not present when they cast lots to see which of them should have charge of Mary; nor were you present when they argued about her.

The angels said to Mary: "God bids you rejoice in a word from Him. His name is the Messiah, Jesus the son of Mary. He shall be noble in

———

*Cf. Luke i, 26–38.
†Muhammad.

this world and in the hereafter, and shall be one of those who are favoured. He shall preach to men in his cradle and in the prime of manhood, and shall lead a righteous life."

"Lord," she said, "how can I bear a child when no man has touched me?"

He replied: "Even thus. God creates whom He will. When He decrees a thing He need only say: 'Be,' and it is. He will instruct him in the Scriptures and in wisdom, in the Torah and in the Gospel, and send him forth as an apostle to the Israelites. He will say: 'I bring you a sign from your Lord. From clay I will make for you the likeness of a bird. I shall breathe into it and, by God's leave, it shall become a living bird. By God's leave I shall heal the blind man and the leper, and raise the dead to life. I shall tell you what to eat and what to store up in your houses. Surely that will be a sign for you, if you are true believers. I come to confirm the Torah which preceded me and to make lawful to you some of the things you are forbidden. I bring you a sign from your Lord: therefore fear God and obey me. God is my Lord and your Lord: therefore serve Him. That is a straight path.'" (3:42–51)

———

People of the Book,‡ do not transgress the bounds of your religion. Speak nothing but the truth about God. The Messiah, Jesus the son of Mary, was no more than God's apostle and His Word which He cast to Mary: a spirit from Him. So believe in God and His apostles and do not say: "Three."§ Forbear, and it shall be better for you. God is but one God. God forbid that He should have a son! His is all that the heavens and the earth contain. God is the all-sufficient protector. The Messiah does not disdain to be a servant of God, nor do the angels who are nearest to Him. Those who through arrogance disdain His service shall all be brought before Him. (4:171–172)

HEAVEN AND HELL

THAT WHICH IS COMING

In the Name of God, the Compassionate, the Merciful

When that which is coming comes—and no soul shall then deny its coming—some shall be abased and others exalted.

When the earth shakes and quivers, and the mountains crumble away and scatter abroad into fine dust, you shall be divided into three multitudes: those on the right (blessed shall be those on the right); those on the left (damned shall be those on the left); and those to the fore (foremost shall be those). Such are they that shall be brought near to their Lord in the gardens of delight: a whole multitude from the men of old, but only a few from the latter generations.

They shall recline on jewelled couches face to face, and there shall wait on them immortal youths with bowls and ewers and a cup of purest wine (that will neither pain their heads nor take away their reason); with fruits of their own choice and flesh of fowls that they relish. And theirs shall be the dark-eyed houris [beautiful virgins], chaste as hidden pearls: a guerdon [reward] for their deeds.

There they shall hear no idle talk, no sinful speech, but only the greeting, "Peace! Peace!" Those on the right hand—happy shall be those on the right hand! They shall recline on couches raised on high in the shade of thornless sidrs and clusters of talh;‖ amidst gushing waters and abundant fruits, unforbidden, neverending.

We created the houris and made them virgins, loving companions for those on the right hand: a multitude from the men of old, and a multitude from the latter generations.

As for those on the left hand (wretched shall be those on the left hand!) they shall dwell amidst scorching winds and seething water: in the shade of pitch-black smoke, neither cool nor

———

‡Christians.
§Muslims regard the Trinity—God, Jesus, and the Holy Spirit—as a form of polytheism (see footnote on page 150).

———

‖Probably the banana fruit.

refreshing. For they have lived in comfort and persisted in the heinous sin,** saying: "When we are once dead and turned to dust and bones, shall we be raised to life? And our forefathers, too?"

Say: "Those of old, and those of the present age, shall be brought together on an appointed day. As for you sinners who deny the truth, you shall eat the fruit of the Zaqqūm tree and fill your bellies with it. You shall drink scalding water: yet you shall drink it as the thirsty camel drinks."

Such shall be their fare on the Day of Reckoning. (56:1–56)

———
**Idolatry.

WOMEN

Men have authority over women because God has made the one superior to the other, and because they spend their wealth to maintain them. Good women are obedient. They guard their unseen parts because God has guarded them. As for those from whom you fear disobedience, admonish them and send them to beds apart and beat them. Then if they obey you, take no further action against them. Surely God is high, supreme.

If you fear a breach between a man and his wife, appoint an arbiter from his people and another from hers. If they wish to be reconciled God will bring them together again. Surely God is all-knowing and wise. (4:34–35)

REVIEW QUESTIONS

1. Compare and contrast the views of God and morality described in the Koran with those found in the Hebrew Scriptures and the New Testament.
2. What advice does the Koran give to Christians?

---

3   Islam and Greek Learning

In the eighth and ninth centuries, Muslim civilization, which creatively integrated Arabic, Byzantine, Persian, and Indian cultural traditions, entered its golden age. Muslim science, philosophy, and mathematics, based largely on the achievements of the ancient Greeks, made brilliant contributions to the sum of knowledge at a time when Latin Christendom had lost much of Greco-Roman thought and culture. The Muslims had acquired Greek learning from the older Persian and Byzantine civilizations, which had kept alive the Greek inheritance. By translating Greek works into Arabic and commenting on them, Muslim scholars performed the great historical task of preserving the philosophical and scientific heritage of ancient Greece. Along with this heritage, the original contributions of Muslim scholars and scientists were also passed on to Christian Europe.

Avicenna
LOVE OF LEARNING

The most eminent Muslim thinker, Ibn-Sina, known to the West as Avicenna (980–1037), was a poet, doctor, scientist, and philosopher who wrote on every field of knowledge. His philosophical works, which relied heavily on Aristotle, had an important influence on medieval Christian thinkers. In his autobiography, excerpted below, Avicenna describes his love for learning and his debt to ancient Greece.

[In] Bukhara [in present-day Uzbekistan] I was put under teachers of the Koran and of letters. By the time I was ten I had mastered the Koran and a great deal of literature, so that I was marvelled at for my aptitude. . . . Then there came to Bukhara a man called Abū ʿAbd Allāh al-Nātilī who claimed to be a philosopher; my father invited him to stay in our house, hoping that I would learn from him also. Before his advent I had already occupied myself with Muslim jurisprudence, attending Ismāʿīl the Ascetic; so I was an excellent enquirer, having become familiar with the methods of postulation and the techniques of rebuttal according to the usages of the canon lawyers. I now commenced reading the *Isagoge* (of Porphyry)[1] with al-Nātilī: when he mentioned to me the definition of *genus* as a term applied to a number of things of different species in answer to the question "What is it?" I set about verifying this definition in a manner such as he had never heard. He marvelled at me exceedingly, and warned my father that I should not engage in any other occupation but learning; whatever problem he stated to me, I showed a better mental conception of it than he. So I continued until I had read all the straightforward parts of Logic with him; as for the subtler points, he had no acquaintance with them.

From then onward I took to reading texts by myself; I studied the commentaries, until I had completely mastered the science of Logic. Similarly with Euclid[2] I read the first five or six figures with him, and thereafter undertook on my own account to solve the entire remainder of the book. Next I moved on to the *Almagest* (of Ptolemy)[3]; when I had finished the prolegomena

[introductory essay] and reached the geometrical figures, al-Nātilī told me to go on reading and to solve the problems by myself; I should merely revise what I read with him, so that he might indicate to me what was right and what was wrong. The truth is that he did not really teach this book; I began to solve the work, and many were the complicated figures of which he had no knowledge until I presented them to him, and made him understand them. Then al-Nātilī took leave of me, setting out for Gurganj.

I now occupied myself with mastering the various texts and commentaries on natural science and metaphysics, until all the gates of knowledge were open to me. Next I desired to study medicine, and proceeded to read all the books that have been written on this subject. Medicine is not a difficult science, and naturally I excelled in it in a very short time, so that qualified physicians began to read medicine with me. I also undertook to treat the sick, and methods of treatment derived from practical experience revealed themselves to me such as baffle description. At the same time I continued between whiles to study and dispute on law, being now sixteen years of age.

The next eighteen months I devoted entirely to reading; I studied Logic once again, and all the parts of philosophy. During all this time I did not sleep one night through, nor devoted my attention to any other matter by day. I prepared a set of files; with each proof I examined, I set down the syllogistic premises and put them in order in the files, then I examined what deductions might be drawn from them. I observed methodically the conditions of the premises, and proceeded until the truth of each particular problem was confirmed for me. Whenever I

[1]Porphyry (A.D. 233–c. 305) wrote a history of philosophy and edited the lectures of Plotinus, the Neoplatonist. The *Isagoge* was Porphyry's introduction to the categories of Aristotle.
[2]Euclid, an Alexandrian mathematician who lived around 300 B.C. He creatively synthesized earlier developments in geometry.

[3]Ptolemy, a mathematician, geographer, and astronomer who worked at Alexandria in the second century A.D. His *Almagest,* a Greek-Arabic term meaning "the greatest," summed up antiquity's knowledge of astronomy and became the authoritative text during the Middle Ages.

found myself perplexed by a problem, or could not find the middle term in any syllogism, I would repair to the mosque and pray, adoring the All-Creator, until my puzzle was resolved and my difficulty made easy. At night I would return home, set the lamp before me, and busy myself with reading and writing; whenever sleep overcame me or I was conscious of some weakness, I turned aside to drink a glass of wine until my strength returned to me; then I went back to my reading. If ever the least slumber overtook me, I would dream of the precise problem which I was considering as I fell asleep; in that way many problems revealed themselves to me while sleeping. So I continued until I had made myself master of all the sciences; I now comprehended them to the limits of human possibility. All that I learned during that time is exactly as I know it now; I have added nothing more to my knowledge to this day.

I was now a master of Logic, natural sciences and mathematics. I therefore returned to metaphysics; I read the *Metaphysica* (of Aristotle), but did not understand its contents and was baffled by the author's intention; I read it over forty times, until I had the text by heart. Even then I did not understand it or what the author meant, and I despaired within myself, saying, "This is a book which there is no way of understanding." But one day at noon I chanced to be in the booksellers' quarter, and a broker was there with a volume in his hand which he was calling for sale. He offered it to me, but I returned it to him impatiently, believing that there was no use in this particular science. However he said to me, "Buy this book from me: it is cheap, and I will sell it to you for four dirhams. The owner is in need of the money." So I bought it, and found that it was a book by Abū

Naṣr al-Fārābī *On the Objects of the Metaphysica.* I returned home and hastened to read it; and at once the objects of that book became clear to me, for I had it all by heart. I rejoiced at this, and upon the next day distributed much in alms to the poor in gratitude to Almighty God.

Now the Sultan of Bukhara at that time was Nūḥ ibn Manṣūr, and it happened that he fell sick of a malady which baffled all the physicians. My name was famous among them because of the breadth of my reading; they therefore mentioned me in his presence, and begged him to summon me. I attended the sick-room, and collaborated with them in treating the royal patient. So I came to be enrolled in his service. One day I asked his leave to enter their library, to examine the contents and read the books on medicine; he granted my request, and I entered a mansion with many chambers, each chamber having chests of books piled one upon another. In one apartment were books on language and poetry, in another law, and so on; each apartment was set aside for books on a single science. I glanced through the catalogue of the works of the ancient Greeks, and asked for those which I required; and I saw books whose very names are as yet unknown to many—works which I had never seen before and have not seen since. I read these books, taking notes of their contents; I came to realize the place each man occupied in his particular science.

So by the time I reached my eighteenth year I had exhausted all these sciences. My memory for learning was at that period of my life better than it is now, but to-day I am more mature; apart from this my knowledge is exactly the same, nothing further having been added to my store since then.

REVIEW QUESTIONS

1. Provide examples of Avicenna's familiarity with Greek learning.
2. Show how Avicenna combined Greek learning with Islamic teachings.

4 Converting the Germanic Peoples to Christianity

From its beginnings, Christianity sought to carry to all peoples its offer of salvation through faith in Jesus. After Christianity had become the religion of the Roman state, pagan cults were suppressed. When the western Roman provinces fell under the power of invading Germanic tribes, Christian Romans faced the task of converting their new rulers to their religion.

The ability of the Christian religion to penetrate and absorb alien cultures while preserving its own core beliefs was continually to be tested in the Early Middle Ages. Roman Britain had been invaded in the fifth century by various tribes from northwestern Germany, Denmark, and the Netherlands. Among these tribes were the Angles (from which the word *English* is derived), the Saxons, and the Jutes. The Romano-Britons, who were Christians, were forced to retreat westward to occupy what became the Celtic-speaking Christian principalities of Cornwall, Wales, and Cumberland. Pagan Germans ruled the rest of England.

Bede
HISTORY OF THE ENGLISH CHURCH AND PEOPLE

The English monk called the Venerable Bede (673–735), in his *History of the English Church and People,* cites a letter from Pope Gregory I (the Great) written in 601. In the letter, the pope forwarded instructions for Augustine of Canterbury, whom he had appointed leader of a mission to convert the English to Christianity. He wrote his emissary to tell Augustine to win the favor of the pagan English by accommodating the requirements of Christian beliefs to the existing non-Christian cultural practices, as the excerpt shows.

When these [missionaries] had left, the holy father Gregory sent after them letters worthy of our notice, which show most clearly his unwearying interest in the salvation of our nation. The letter runs as follows:

"To our well loved son Abbot[1] Mellitus: Gregory, servant of the servants of God.

"Since the departure of yourself and your companions, we have been somewhat anxious, because we have received no news of the success of your journey. Therefore, when by God's help you reach our most reverend brother, Bishop Augustine,[2] we wish you to inform him that we have been giving careful thought to the affairs of the English, and have come to the conclusion that the temples of the idols in that country should on no account be destroyed. He is to destroy the idols, but the temples themselves are

---

[1]The elected head of a monastic community, the abbot was supposed to rule justly and paternally following the constitution (rule) of the community.

[2]Augustine (not to be confused with Augustine of Hippo) was an Italian monk who was sent in 597 to convert the English to Christianity. He established his see (bishopric) at Canterbury and founded others at Rochester and London, successfully directing missionary activity in the southern part of what is now England.

to be aspersed [sprinkled] with holy water, altars set up, and relics enclosed in them. For if these temples are well built, they are to be purified from devil-worship,[3] and dedicated to the service of the true God. In this way, we hope that the people, seeing that its temples are not destroyed, may abandon idolatry and resort to these places as before, and may come to know and adore the true God. And since they have a custom of sacrificing many oxen to devils, let some other solemnity be substituted in its place, such as a day of Dedication[4] or the Festivals of the holy martyrs [saints' days] whose relics are enshrined there. On such occasions they might well construct shelters of boughs for themselves around the churches that were once temples, and celebrate the solemnity with devout feasting. They are no longer to sacrifice beasts to the Devil, but they may kill them for food to the praise of God, and give thanks to the Giver of all gifts for His bounty. If the people are allowed some worldly pleasures in this way, they will more readily come to desire the joys of the spirit. For it is certainly impossible to eradicate all errors from obstinate minds at one stroke, and whoever wishes to climb to a mountain top climbs gradually step by step, and not in one leap. It was in this way that God revealed Himself to the Israelite people in Egypt, permitting the sacrifices formerly offered to the Devil to be offered thenceforward to Himself instead. So He bade them sacrifice beasts to Him, so that, once they became enlightened, they might abandon a wrong conception of sacrifice, and adopt the right. For, while they were to continue to offer beasts as before, they were to offer them to God instead of to idols, thus transforming the idea of sacrifice. Of your kindness, you are to inform our brother Augustine of this policy, so that he may consider how he may best implement it on the spot. God keep you safe, my very dear son." . . .

---

[3]As Christianity was monotheistic, it denied the validity of any other gods. Therefore, Christians customarily designated the pagan deities as "devils," or evil spirits.

[4]The anniversary of the dedication or consecration of a church was celebrated as a holiday.

Einhard
FORCIBLE CONVERSION UNDER CHARLEMAGNE

Although most conversions were based on peaceful persuasion or a voluntary act of consent, occasionally Christianity was imposed by force. Thus, after his long wars against the pagan Saxons, Charlemagne required the Saxons to adopt Christianity and be assimilated into the Frankish kingdom. In his biography of Charlemagne, the Frankish historian Einhard (770–840) described this event.

No war ever undertaken by the Frank nation was carried on with such persistence and bitterness, or cost so much labor, because the Saxons,[1] like almost all the tribes of Germany, were a fierce people, given to the worship of devils, and hostile to our religion, and did not consider it dishonorable to transgress and violate all law, human and divine. Then there were peculiar circumstances that tended to cause a breach of peace every day. Except in a few places, where large forests or mountain ridges intervened and made the bounds certain, the line between ourselves and the Saxons passed almost in its whole extent through an open country, so that there was no end to the murders, thefts, and arsons on

---

[1]The Saxons were members of a Germanic tribe living between the Rhine and Elbe rivers.

both sides. In this way the Franks became so embittered that they at last resolved to make reprisals no longer, but to come to open war with the Saxons [in 772]. Accordingly war was begun against them, and was waged for thirty-three successive years with great fury; more, however, to the disadvantage of the Saxons than of the Franks. It could doubtless have been brought to an end sooner, had it not been for the faithlessness of the Saxons. It is hard to say how often they were conquered, and humbly submitting to the King, promised to do what was enjoined upon them, gave without hesitation the required hostages, and received the officers sent them from the King. They were sometimes so much weakened and reduced that they promised to renounce the worship of devils, and to adopt Christianity, but they were no less ready to violate these terms than prompt to accept them, so that it is impossible to tell which came easier to them to do; scarcely a year passed from the beginning of the war without such changes on their part. But the King did not suffer his high purpose and steadfastness—firm alike in good and evil fortune—to be wearied by any fickleness on their part, or to be turned from the task that he had undertaken; on the contrary, he never allowed their faithless behavior to go unpunished, but either took the field against them in person, or sent his counts[2] with an army to wreak vengeance and exact righteous satisfaction. At last, after conquering and subduing all who had offered resistance, he took ten thousand of those that lived on the banks of the Elbe,[3] and settled them, with their wives and children, in many different bodies here and there in Gaul and Germany. The war that had lasted so many years was at length ended by their acceding to the terms offered by the King; which were renunciation of their national religious customs and the worship of devils, acceptance of the sacraments of the Christian faith and religion, and union with the Franks to form one people.

---

[2]Counts were royal officials exercising the king's authority in districts called counties.
[3]The Elbe River, in central Germany, flows northwestward into the North Sea.

REVIEW QUESTIONS

1. Give examples of the methods Pope Gregory I suggested for introducing Christianity in pagan England.
2. Compare the methods Charlemagne used to convert the Saxons with the instruction given by Pope Gregory I to Augustine of Canterbury.

---

5 The Carolingian Renaissance

The Early Middle Ages witnessed a marked decline in learning and the arts. Patronage of both the liberal and the visual arts by the old Roman aristocracy was not widely copied by the Germanic ruling class that replaced the Romans. Support for learning and the arts shifted from secular to ecclesiastical patrons. Monasteries became the new centers for intellectual and artistic activities, and Christian themes and values almost entirely displaced the worldly values of Greco-Roman culture.

Under the patronage of Charlemagne (742–814), the great Frankish emperor, a conscious revival of classical Greek and Roman learning and the visual arts occurred. Charlemagne realized that his great empire could not be effectively governed without a cadre of literate clergy and administrators. To educate the leaders of the Frankish empire, Charlemagne sponsored a number of reforms designed to improve the educational institutions and the quality of literacy and learning in his realm. At court, he completely reformed the school conducted for the children of his family and his courtiers and recruited the best scholars in western Europe to staff it. Among these scholars was the English deacon Alcuin of York (735–804), who became his chief advisor on educational and religious affairs. They aimed at restoring classical learning to serve the needs of the new Christian culture.

Einhard
CHARLEMAGNE'S APPRECIATION OF LEARNING

The revival of classical learning and the visual arts under Charlemagne is called the Carolingian Renaissance, a cultural awakening that helped shape medieval civilization. One of Charlemagne's most significant decisions was ordering the making of copies of old manuscripts dating back to Roman times. Much of today's knowledge of Roman learning and literature comes from surviving Carolingian copies of older Latin texts that no longer exist. In the first reading, Charlemagne's biographer Einhard describes western Europe's greatest royal patron of the liberal arts since the fall of the western Roman Empire.

Charles [Charlemagne] had the gift of ready and fluent speech, and could express whatever he had to say with the utmost clearness. He was not satisfied with command of his native language merely, but gave attention to the study of foreign ones, and in particular was such a master of Latin that he could speak it as well as his native tongue; but he could understand Greek better than he could speak it. He was so eloquent, indeed, that he might have passed for a teacher of eloquence. He most zealously cultivated the liberal arts, held those who taught them in great esteem, and conferred great honors upon them. He took lessons in grammar of the deacon Peter of Pisa,[1] at that time an aged man. Another deacon, Albin of Britain, surnamed Alcuin, a man

of Saxon extraction, who was the greatest scholar of the day, was his teacher in other branches of learning. The King spent much time and labor with him studying rhetoric, dialectics, and especially astronomy; he learned to reckon, and used to investigate the motions of the heavenly bodies most curiously, with an intelligent scrutiny. He also tried to write, and used to keep tablets and blanks in bed under his pillow, that at leisure hours he might accustom his hand to form the letters; however, as he did not begin his efforts in due season, but late in life, they met with ill success.

He cherished with the greatest fervor and devotion the principles of the Christian religion, which had been instilled into him from infancy. Hence it was that he built the beautiful basilica[2] at Aix-la-

---

[1]Peter of Pisa, a famous grammarian (in Latin, the international language of the Middle Ages), was brought from Italy to teach at the school in Charlemagne's palace. He encouraged interest in pre-Christian classical writing, which influenced the court poets of that era.

[2]A basilica is usually a rectangular-shaped church, whose main chamber is divided by columns into a central nave and side aisles. There was usually a semicircular apse at the narrow end facing the east, which was the visual focal point and the location of the main altar.

Chapelle,[3] which he adorned with gold and silver and lamps, and with rails and doors of solid brass. He had the columns and marbles for this structure brought from Rome and Ravenna,[4] for he could not find such as were suitable elsewhere. He was a constant worshipper at this church as long as his health permitted, going morning and evening, even after nightfall, besides attending mass; and he took care that all the services there conducted should be administered with the utmost possible propriety, very often warning the sextons not to let any improper or unclean thing be brought into the building or

remain in it. He provided it with a great number of sacred vessels of gold and silver and with such a quantity of clerical robes that not even the doorkeepers who fill the humblest office in the church were obliged to wear their everyday clothes when in the exercise of their duties. He was at great pains to improve the church reading and psalmody [singing], for he was well skilled in both, although he neither read in public nor sang, except in a low tone and with others.

He was very forward in succoring the poor, and in that gratuitous generosity which the Greeks call alms, so much so that he not only made a point of giving in his own country and his own kingdom, but when he discovered that there were Christians living in poverty in Syria, Egypt, and Africa, at Jerusalem, Alexandria, and Carthage, he had compassion on their wants, and used to send money over the seas to them. . . .

---

[3]Aix-la-Chapelle, now Aachen, was Charlemagne's capital. It was located in what is now western Germany, near the Netherlands–Belgium frontier.

[4]Ravenna, in northeastern Italy, was the final capital of the western Roman Empire, in the fifth century; in the sixth and seventh centuries it was the capital of the Byzantine governors of Italy. Ravenna is famous for its magnificent sixth-century churches and mosaic art.

Charlemagne
AN INJUNCTION TO MONASTERIES TO CULTIVATE LETTERS

In a letter to the Abbot Baugulf of Fulda (in Germany), Charlemagne announced his decision to use monasteries as schools for training future clergymen in grammar, writing, and rhetoric.

Charles, by the grace of God, King of the Franks and Lombards and Patrician of the Romans, to Abbot Baugulf and to all the congregation, also to the faithful committed to you, we have directed a loving greeting by our ambassadors in the name of omnipotent God.

Be it known, therefore, to your devotion pleasing to God, that we, together with our faithful, have considered it to be useful that the bishoprics and monasteries entrusted by the favor of Christ to our control, in addition to the [rule] of monastic life and the intercourse of holy religion, . . . also ought to be zeal-

ous in [the cultivation of letters], teaching those who by the gift of God are able to learn, according to the capacity of each individual, so that just as the observance of the rule imparts order and grace to honesty of morals, so also zeal in teaching and learning may do the same for sentences, so that those who desire to please God by living rightly should not neglect to please him also by speaking correctly. For it is written: "Either from thy words thou shalt be justified or from thy words thou shalt be condemned."*

---

*Matthew, xii. 37.

For although correct conduct may be better than knowledge, nevertheless knowledge precedes conduct. Therefore, each one ought to study what he desires to accomplish, so that . . . the mind may know more fully what ought to be done, as the tongue hastens in the praises of omnipotent God without the hindrances of errors. For since errors should be shunned by all men, . . . the more they ought to be avoided as far as possible by those who are chosen for this very purpose alone, so that they ought to be the especial servants of truth. For when in the years . . . [past], letters were often written to us from several monasteries in which it was stated that the brethren who dwelt there offered up in our behalf sacred and pious prayers, we have recognized in most of these letters both correct thoughts and uncouth expressions; because what pious devotion dictated faithfully to the mind, the tongue, uneducated on account of the neglect of study, was not able to express in the letter without error. . . . We began to fear lest perchance, as the skill in writing was less, so also the wisdom for understanding the Holy Scriptures might be much less than it rightly ought to be. And we all know well that, although errors of speech are dangerous, far more dangerous are errors of the understanding. Therefore, we exhort you not only not to neglect the study of letters, but also with most humble mind, pleasing to God, to study earnestly in order that you may be able more easily and more correctly to penetrate the mysteries of the divine Scriptures. Since, moreover, images . . . and similar figures are found in the sacred pages, no one doubts that each one in reading these will understand the spiritual sense more quickly if previously he shall have been fully instructed in the mastery of letters. Such men truly are to be chosen for this work as have both the will and the ability to learn and a desire to instruct others. And may this be done with a zeal as great as the earnestness with which we command it.

REVIEW QUESTION

1. Why was Charlemagne so anxious to raise the educational standards of both the clergy and laity of his empire? How did he go about doing it?

---

6 The Feudal Lord: Vassal and Warrior

In societies in which the state's role in regulating human relationships is minimal, law and order are maintained through custom and contract. This condition prevailed in the Early Middle Ages, particularly among the Germanic peoples. Laws were based on the community's assumptions about what was right and wrong, enforced by public opinion and community-approved use of force. To enforce law and to protect oneself and one's family, a person formed contractual ties with others and sought security and justice in mutual aid. A principal form of such a contract was called vassalage. By its terms, two free men of different means bound themselves to assistance and loyal support. The socially and economically superior man was called the lord; the man of inferior social status was called the vassal. The vassal pledged to be loyal and fight on behalf of his lord when called upon, in return for the lord's loyalty and protection when they were needed. The contract was lifelong and had deep emotional meaning in addition to the obvious self-interest of both parties.

Vassalage was a dynamic relationship, ever changing in content and meaning according to time, place, and circumstances. In the Carolingian Empire, vassalage was practiced by all members of the free class wealthy enough to afford weapons. Charlemagne and his successors tried to use vassalage as a means of controlling their warlike subjects and organizing them to serve more effectively for the defense of their realms. Eventually, the kings' vassals used their military skills, their own landed wealth, and their political power to diminish royal power. The royal vassals then became the true center of authority within medieval society.

An important part of the lord–vassal relationship was the lord's grant of a fief to his vassal. The fief might be any object of value that reflected the vassal's social status and the lord's respect for his services. A fief could be a warhorse, sword, and suit of armor; a public office; a right to collect a tax or toll; or authority to hold a court of justice in a specified district. The most sought-after fief was a land grant—one or more manors from which to draw income. Fiefs were held for the duration of the bond of vassalage. If the bond was broken by death or disloyalty, the fief was forfeited to its grantor. By the late ninth century, however, fiefs had become hereditary, as had the right to be a vassal to a specific lord.

Galbert of Bruges
COMMENDATION AND THE OATH OF FEALTY

This reading contains an eyewitness account of the ceremony of commendation or investiture in which vassals swore an oath of fealty (loyalty) to their new lord, William Clito, the count of Flanders, in 1127, and were then invested with their fiefs. The account comes from an early-twelfth-century chronicle written by a Flemish notary, Galbert of Bruges (a major medieval commercial city in Flanders, now part of Belgium).

Through the whole remaining part of the day those who had been previously enfeoffed [given fiefs] by the most pious count Charles,[1] did homage to the count, taking up now again their fiefs and offices and whatever they had before rightfully and legitimately obtained. On Thursday the seventh of April, homages were again made to the count being completed in the following order of faith and security.

First they did their homage thus: The count asked if he was willing to become completely his man, and the other replied, "I am willing;" and with clasped hands, surrounded by the hands of the count, they were bound together by a kiss. Secondly, he who had done homage gave his fealty to the representative of the count in these words, "I promise on my faith that I will in future be faithful to count William, and will observe my homage to him completely against all persons in good faith and without deceit," and thirdly, he took his oath to this upon the relics of the saints. Afterward, with a little rod which the count held in his hand, he gave investitures to all who by this agreement had given their security and homage and accompanying oath.

---

[1]Charles, count of Flanders, was murdered on March 2, 1127.

Fulbert, Bishop of Chartres
OBLIGATIONS OF LORDS AND VASSALS

In a letter written in 1020 to William, Duke of Aquitaine, Bishop Fulbert (c. 960–1028) of Chartres summarizes the obligations of the lord and the vassal.

To William most glorious duke of the Aquitanians,[1] bishop Fulbert [asks] the favor of his prayers.

Asked to write something concerning the form of fealty, I have noted briefly for you on the authority of the books the things which follow. He who swears fealty to his lord ought always to have these six things in memory; what is harmless, safe, honorable, useful, easy, practicable. Harmless, that is to say that he should not be injurious to his lord in his body; safe, that he should not be injurious to him in his secrets or in the defences through which he is able to be secure; honorable, that he should not be injurious to him in his justice or in other matters that pertain to his honor; useful, that he should not be injurious to him in his possessions; easy or practicable, that that good which his lord is able to do easily, he make not difficult, nor that which is practicable he make impossible to him.

However, that the faithful vassal should avoid these injuries is proper, but not for this does he deserve his holding; for it is not sufficient to abstain from evil, unless what is good is done also. It remains, therefore, that in the same six things mentioned above he should faithfully counsel and aid his lord, if he wishes to be looked upon as worthy of his benefice and to be safe concerning the fealty which he has sworn.

The lord also ought to act toward his faithful vassal reciprocally in all these things. And if he does not do this he will be justly considered guilty of bad faith, just as the former, if he should be detected in the avoidance of or the doing of or the consenting to them, would be perfidious and perjured.

---

[1]The Aquitanians inhabited the kingdom of Aquitaine in southwestern France—later a province of France.

REVIEW QUESTIONS

1. In the Middle Ages, contracts were symbolized and publicly noted by the use of various ritual acts or gestures. Explain how the contract of vassalage was signified by specific rituals or actions.
2. What were some of the ethical and emotive dimensions of vassalage? Describe the mutual obligations of lords and vassals.

CHAPTER 6

The High and Late Middle Ages

THE ILLUSTRATION on this page depicts Christine de Pisan presenting her manuscript to Isabel of Bavaria. *(Historical Picture Archive/Corbis)*

The High Middle Ages (1050–1300) were an era of growth and vitality in Latin Christendom. Improvements in technology and cultivation of new lands led to an increase in agricultural production; the growing food supply, in turn, reduced the number of deaths from starvation and malnutrition, and better cultivation methods freed more people to engage in nonagricultural pursuits, particularly commerce.

The revival of trade and the improved production of food led to the rebirth of towns in the eleventh century. During the Early Middle Ages, urban life had largely disappeared in Latin Christendom except in Italy, and even Italian towns had declined since Roman times both in population and as centers of trade and culture. During the twelfth century, towns throughout Latin Christendom became active centers of commerce and intellectual life. The rebirth of town life made possible the rise of a new social class: the middle class, consisting of merchants and artisans. These townspeople differed significantly from the clergy, the nobles, and the serfs—the other social strata in medieval society. The world of the townspeople was the marketplace rather than the church, the castle, or the manorial village. These merchants and artisans resisted efforts by lords to impose obligations upon them, as their livelihood required freedom from such constraints. The middle class became a dynamic force for change.

The High Middle Ages were also characterized by political and religious vitality. Strong kings extended their authority over more and more territory, often at the expense of feudal lords; in the process, they laid the foundation of the modern European state system. The church tried to maintain high standards of discipline among the clergy and to resist domination by powerful lords and kings.

Economic, political, and religious vitality was complemented by a cultural and intellectual awakening. The twelfth and thirteenth centuries marked the high point of medieval civilization. The Christian outlook, with its otherworldly emphasis, shaped and inspired this awakening. Christian scholars rediscovered the writings of ancient Greek thinkers, which they tried to harmonize with Christian teachings. In the process, they constructed an impressive philosophical system that integrated Greek rationalism into the Christian worldview. The study of Roman law was revived, and some of its elements were incorporated into church law. A varied literature expressed both secular and religious themes, and a distinctive form of architecture, the Gothic, conveyed the overriding Christian concern with things spiritual.

During the Late Middle Ages, roughly the fourteenth and early fifteenth centuries, medieval civilization declined. In contrast to the vigor of the twelfth and thirteenth centuries, the fourteenth century was burdened by crop failures, famine, plagues, and reduced population. The church also came under attack from reformers who challenged clerical authority and questioned church teachings; from powerful kings who resisted papal interference in the political life of their kingdoms; and from political theorists who asserted that the pope had no authority to intervene in matters of state. In the city-states of Italy, a growing secularism signified a break with medieval otherworldliness and heralded the emergence of the modern outlook. Known as the Renaissance, this development is discussed in Chapter 7.

---

1 The Revival of Trade and the Growth of Towns

Several factors contributed to economic vitality in the High Middle Ages: the end of the Viking raids in northwestern Europe, greater political stability provided by kings and powerful lords, and increased agricultural productivity, which freed some people to work at other pursuits and facilitated a population increase. The prime movers in trade were the merchant adventurers, a new class of entrepreneurs. Neither bound to the soil nor obligated to lifelong military service, merchants traveled the sea lanes and land roads to distant places in search of goods that could profitably be traded in other markets.

HOW TO SUCCEED IN BUSINESS

In the following reading from *The King's Mirror,* an anonymous thirteenth-century Norseman outlined the characteristics and skills a merchant needed and described the hazards of the job. In typical medieval fashion, he emphasized the moral dimensions of commercial transactions.

The man who is to be a trader will have to brave many perils, sometimes at sea and sometimes in heathen lands, but nearly always among alien peoples; and it must be his constant purpose to act discreetly wherever he happens to be. On the sea he must be alert and fearless.

When you are in a market town, or wherever you are, be polite and agreeable; then you will secure the friendship of all good men. Make it a habit to rise early in the morning, and go first and immediately to church. . . .

. . . When the services are over, go out to look after your business affairs. If you are unacquainted with the traffic of the town, observe carefully how those who are reputed the best and most prominent merchants conduct their business. You must also be careful to examine the wares that you buy before the purchase is finally made to make sure that they are sound and flawless. And whenever you make a purchase, call in a few trusty men to serve as witnesses as to how the bargain was made.

You should keep occupied with your business till breakfast or, if necessity demands it, till midday; after that you should eat your meal. Keep your table well provided and set with a white cloth, clean victuals, and good drinks. Serve enjoyable meals, if you can afford it. After the meal you may either take a nap or stroll about a little while for pastime and to see what other good merchants are employed with, or whether any new wares have come to the borough which you ought to buy. On returning to your lodgings examine your wares, lest they suffer damage after coming into your hands. If they are found to be injured and you are about to dispose of them, do not conceal the flaws from the purchaser: show him what the defects are and make such a bargain as you can; then you cannot be called a deceiver. Also put a good price on your wares, though not too high, and yet very near what you see can be obtained; then you cannot be called a foister [trickster].

Finally, remember this, that whenever you have an hour to spare you should give thought to your studies, especially to the law books; for it is clear that those who gain knowledge from books have keener wits than others, since those who are the most learned have the best proofs for their knowledge. Make a study of all the laws. . . . If you are acquainted with the law, you will not be annoyed by quibbles when you have suits to bring against men of your own class, but will be able to plead according to law in every case.

But although I have most to say about laws, I regard no man perfect in knowledge unless he has thoroughly learned and mastered the customs of the place where he is sojourning. And if you wish to become perfect in knowledge, you must learn all the languages, first of all Latin and French, for these idioms are most widely used; and yet, do not neglect your native tongue or speech.

. . . Train yourself to be as active as possible, though not so as to injure your health. Strive never to be downcast, for a downcast mind is always morbid; try rather to be friendly and genial at all times, of an even temper and never moody. Be upright and teach the right to

every man who wishes to learn from you; and always associate with the best men. Guard your tongue carefully; this is good counsel, for your tongue may honor you, but it may also condemn you. Though you be angry speak few words and never in passion; for unless one is careful, he may utter words in wrath that he would later give gold to have unspoken. On the whole, I know of no revenge, though many employ it, that profits a man less than to bandy heated words with another, even though he has a quarrel to settle with him. You shall know of a truth that no virtue is higher or stronger than the power to keep one's tongue from foul or profane speech, tattling, or slanderous talk in any form. If children be given to you, let them not grow up without learning a trade; for we may expect a man to keep closer to knowledge and business when he comes of age, if he is trained in youth while under control.

And further, there are certain things which you must beware of and shun like the devil himself: these are drinking, chess, harlots, quarreling, and throwing dice for stakes. For upon such foundations the greatest calamities are built; and unless they strive to avoid these things, few only are able to live long without blame or sin.

Observe carefully how the sky is lighted, the course of the heavenly bodies, the grouping of the hours, and the points of the horizon. Learn also how to mark the movements of the ocean and to discern how its turmoil ebbs and swells; for that is knowledge which all must possess who wish to trade abroad. Learn arithmetic thoroughly, for merchants have great need of that.

If you come to a place where the king or some other chief who is in authority has his officials, seek to win their friendship; and if they demand any necessary fees on the ruler's behalf, be prompt to render all such payments, lest by holding too tightly to little things you lose the greater. . . . If you can dispose of your wares at suitable prices, do not hold them long; for it is the wont of merchants to buy constantly and to sell rapidly. . . .

. . . If you attend carefully to all these things, with God's mercy you may hope for success.

This, too, you must keep constantly in mind, if you wish to be counted a wise man, that you ought never to let a day pass without learning something that will profit you. Be not like those who think it beneath their dignity to hear or learn from others such things even as might avail them much if they knew them. For a man must regard it as great an honor to learn as to teach, if he wishes to be considered thoroughly informed. . . .

. . . Always buy good clothes and eat good fare if your means permit; and never keep unruly or quarrelsome men as attendants or messmates. Keep your temper calm though not to the point of suffering abuse or bringing upon yourself the reproach of cowardice. Though necessity may force you into strife, be not in a hurry to take revenge; first make sure that your effort will succeed and strike where it ought. Never display a heated temper when you see that you are likely to fail, but be sure to maintain your honor at some later time, unless your opponent should offer a satisfactory atonement.

If your wealth takes on rapid growth, divide it and invest it in a partnership trade in fields where you do not yourself travel; but be cautious in selecting partners. Always let Almighty God, the holy Virgin Mary, and the saint whom you have most frequently called upon to intercede for you be counted among your partners. Watch with care over the property which the saints are to share with you and always bring it faithfully to the place to which it was originally promised.

REVIEW QUESTIONS

1. What attitudes were merchants encouraged to cultivate when dealing with customers and fellow merchants? How did their outlook differ from that of medieval clergy and nobility?
2. What business practices were recommended to merchants?

2 Theological Basis for Papal Power

The authority of the papacy was weakened by lords who dominated churches and monasteries by appointing bishops and abbots and by collecting the income from church taxes. These bishops and abbots, appointed for political reasons, lacked the spiritual devotion to maintain high standards of discipline among priests and monks. Church reformers were determined to end this subordination of the church to lay authority.

The practice of lay investiture led to a conflict between the papacy and the German monarchy. It began when the German king and future Holy Roman Emperor Henry IV (1056–1108) invested the new archbishop of Milan with his pastoral staff and ring, symbols of the episcopal office. Henry was immediately challenged and threatened with excommunication by Pope Gregory VII (1073–1085), a most ardent champion of reform. Gregory's action sparked a struggle between the papacy and the Holy Roman Empire that lasted for half a century. Later, after he was actually excommunicated for a second time, Henry invaded Italy, and Pope Gregory fled from Rome to the monastery of Monte Cassino, where he died in 1085. Civil war broke out in the imperial territories between partisans of the pope and those of the empire, and widespread death and destruction ensued. Although a compromise was effected at a synod (council of bishops) at Worms, Germany, in 1122, the ideological principles raised in the dispute were never wholly resolved.

Pope Gregory VII
THE SECOND LETTER TO BISHOP HERMAN OF METZ AND THE *DICTATUS PAPAE*

Like no other pope before him, Gregory VII had asserted the preeminence of the papacy over secular rulers. He declared that princes should "not seek to subdue or subject holy Church to themselves as a handmaiden; but indeed let them fittingly strive to honor her eyes, namely the priests of the Lord, by acknowledging them as masters and fathers." His exaltation of the spiritual authority of the church encouraged future popes to challenge the state whenever it threatened the supremacy of Christian moral teachings or the church's freedom to carry out its mission. The first reading is a letter written by Pope Gregory VII to a German bishop, Herman of Metz, at the height of the lay investiture struggle. The pope outlined the theological basis for the authority and powers he claimed. The exalted conception of the papacy as the central authority in the Christian church was expressed in its most extreme and detailed form in a series of propositions called the *Dictatus papae* (Rules of the Pope), which appear as numbered paragraphs in the second excerpt.

You ask us to fortify you against the madness of those who babble with accursed tongues about the authority of the Holy Apostolic See [the bishopric of Rome] not being able to excommunicate King Henry as one who despises the law of Christ, a destroyer of churches and of the empire, a promoter and partner of heresies, nor to release anyone from his oath of fidelity to him; but it has not seemed necessary to reply to this request, seeing that so many and such convincing proofs are to be found in Holy Scripture. . . .

To cite but a few out of the multitude of proofs: Who does not remember the words of our Lord and Savior Jesus Christ: "Thou art Peter and on this rock I will build my Church, and the gates of hell shall not prevail against it. And I will give thee the keys of the kingdom of heaven and whatsoever thou shalt bind

on earth shall be bound in heaven and whatsoever thou shalt loose on earth shall be loosed in heaven." Are kings excepted here? Or are they not of the sheep which the Son of God committed to St. Peter? Who, I ask, thinks himself excluded from this universal grant of the power of binding and loosing to St. Peter unless, perchance, that unhappy man who, being unwilling to bear the yoke of the Lord, subjects himself to the burden of the Devil and refuses to be numbered in the flock of Christ? His wretched liberty shall profit him nothing; for if he shakes off from his proud neck the power divinely granted to Peter, so much the heavier shall it be for him in the day of judgment.

This institution of the divine will, this foundation of the rule of the Church, this privilege granted and sealed especially by a heavenly decree to St. Peter, chief of the Apostles, has been accepted and maintained with great reverence by the holy fathers, and they have given to the Holy Roman Church, as well in general councils as in their other acts and writings, the name of "universal mother." They have not only accepted her expositions of doctrine and her instructions in (our) holy religion, but they have also recognized her judicial decisions. They have agreed as with one spirit and one voice that all major cases, all especially important affairs and the judgments of all churches ought to be referred to her as to their head and mother, that from her there shall be no appeal, that her judgments may not and cannot be reviewed or reversed by anyone.

Thus Pope Gelasius [492–496], writing to the [Byzantine] emperor Anastasius, gave him these instructions as to the right theory of the principate of the Holy and Apostolic See, based upon divine authority:

Although it is fitting that all the faithful should submit themselves to all priests who perform their sacred functions properly, how much the more should they accept the judgment of that prelate who has been appointed by the supreme divine ruler to be superior to all priests and whom the loyalty of the whole later Church has recognized as such. Your Wisdom sees plainly that no human capacity *(concilium)* whatsoever can equal that of him [Saint Peter] whom the word of Christ raised above all others and whom the reverend Church has always confessed and still devotedly holds as its Head.

Pope Gregory then comments on the origins of the authority of civil rulers and their motives when they seek to govern the clergy. Gregory argues that church and state are separate spheres of governing authority and that the responsibility of clergymen is greater than that of civil rulers.

Who does not know that kings and princes derive their origin from men ignorant of God who raised themselves above their fellows by pride, plunder, treachery, murder—in short, by every kind of crime—at the instigation of the Devil, the prince of this world, men blind with greed and intolerable in their audacity? If, then, they strive to bend the priests of God to their will, to whom may they more properly be compared than to him who is chief over all the sons of pride? For he, tempting our High Priest [Jesus], head of all priests, son of the Most High, offering him all the kingdoms of this world, said: "All these will I give thee if thou wilt fall down and worship me."

Does anyone doubt that the priests of Christ are to be considered as fathers and masters of kings and princes and of all believers? Would it not be regarded as pitiable madness if a son should try to rule his father or a pupil his master and to bind with unjust obligations the one through whom he expects to be bound or loosed, not only on earth but also in heaven? Evidently recognizing this the emperor Constantine the Great, lord over all kings and princes throughout almost the entire earth, as St. Gregory [pope, 590–604] relates in his letter to the emperor Mauritius [Maurice, Byzantine ruler, 582–602], at the holy synod of 'Nicaea'[1] took his place below all the bishops and did not venture to pass any judgment upon them but, even addressing them as gods, felt that they ought not to be subject to his judgment but that he ought to be bound by their decisions.

Pope Gelasius, urging upon the emperor Anastasius not to feel himself wronged by the truth that was called to his attention said: "There are two powers, O august Emperor, by which the world is governed, the sacred authority of the priesthood and the power of kings. Of these the priestly is by so much the greater as they will have to answer for kings themselves in the day of divine judgment";

[1]The council of Nicaea in Asia Minor mentioned here took place in 325; it was the first ecumenical council of the church—all bishops were invited to participate.

and a little further: "Know that you are subject to their judgment, not that they are to be subjected to your will."

In reliance upon such declarations and such authorities, many prelates [popes or other powerful church officials] have excommunicated kings or emperors.

Drawn up by the papal government during the pontificate of Gregory VII, the *Dictatus papae* represents claims and ambitions that would inspire many popes and theologians throughout the Middle Ages.

RULES OF THE POPE

1. That the Roman church was established by God alone.

2. That the Roman pontiff [bishop] alone is rightly called universal.

3. That he alone has the power to depose and reinstate bishops.

4. That his legate [emissary], even if he be of lower ecclesiastical rank, presides over bishops in council, and has the power to give sentence of deposition against them.

5. That the pope has the power to depose those who are absent (*i.e.,* without giving them a hearing).

6. That, among other things, we ought not to remain in the same house with those whom he has excommunicated.

7. That he alone has the right, according to the necessity of the occasion, to make new laws, to create new bishoprics, to make a monastery of a chapter of canons,[2] and *vice versa,* and either to divide a rich bishopric or to unite several poor ones.

8. That he alone may use the imperial insignia.

9. That all princes shall kiss the foot of the pope alone.

10. That his name alone is to be recited in the churches.

11. That the name applied to him belongs to him alone.

12. That he has the power to depose emperors.

13. That he has the right to transfer bishops from one see to another when it becomes necessary.

14. That he has the right to ordain as a cleric anyone from any part of the church whatsoever.

15. That anyone ordained by him may rule (as bishop) over another church, but cannot serve (as priest) in it, and that such a cleric may not receive a higher rank from any other bishop.

16. That no general synod may be called without his order.

17. That no action of a synod and no book shall be regarded as canonical [official] without his authority.

18. That his decree can be annulled by no one, and that he can annul the decrees of anyone.

19. That he can be judged by no one.

20. That no one shall dare to condemn a person who has appealed to the apostolic seat.

21. That the important cases of any church whatsoever shall be referred to the Roman church (that is, to the pope).

22. That the Roman church has never erred and will never err to all eternity, according to the testimony of the holy scriptures.

23. That the Roman pontiff who has been canonically ordained is made holy by the merits of St. Peter, according to the testimony of St. Ennodius, bishop of Pavia, which is confirmed by many of the holy fathers, as is shown by the decrees of the blessed pope Symmachus [498–513].

24. That by his command or permission subjects may accuse their rulers.

25. That he can depose and reinstate bishops without the calling of a synod.

26. That no one can be regarded as catholic who does not agree with the Roman church.

27. That he has the power to absolve subjects from their oath of fidelity to wicked rulers.

---

[2]A chapter of canons is a corporate ecclesiastical body composed of priests who administer cathedrals or monastic communities.

REVIEW QUESTIONS

1. What was the scriptural basis claimed by Pope Gregory VII for his authority as head of the church?
2. What were Gregory VII's views on the origin and limits of royal authority?
3. What powers did Gregory VII claim over secular princes? Over the bishops of the church?
4. In what sense did Gregory VII revolutionize earlier views on the proper relationship between church and state?

---

3 The First Crusade

In the eleventh century the Seljuk Turks, recent converts to Islam, conquered vast regions of the Near East including most of Asia Minor, the heartland of the Byzantine Empire. When the Seljuk empire crumbled, Byzantine emperor Alexius I Comnenus (1081–1118), seeing an opportunity to regain lost lands, appealed to Latin princes and the pope for assistance, an appeal answered by Urban II (1088–1099).

In 1095 at the Council of Clermont, Pope Urban II in a dramatic speech urged Frankish lords to take up the sword against the Muslims, an event that marked the beginning of the Crusades—the struggle to regain the Holy Land from Islam. A Christian army mobilized by the papacy to defend the Christian faith accorded with the papal concept of a just war. Moreover, Urban hoped that such a venture might bring the Byzantine church under papal authority. Nobles viewed Urban's appeal as a great adventure that held the promise of glory, wealth, and new lands; they were also motivated by religious reasons: recovery of Christian holy places and a church-approved way of doing penance for their sins.

The Crusades demonstrated the growing strength and confidence of Latin Christendom, which previously had been on the defensive against Islam; it was also part of a wider movement of expansion on the part of Latin Christians. In the eleventh century, Italians had already driven the Muslims from Sardinia; Normans had taken Sicily from the Muslims and southern Italy from Byzantium; and Christian knights, supported by the papacy, were engaged in a long struggle to expel the Muslim Moors from Spain.

The First Crusade demonstrated Christian fanaticism as well as idealism and growing power, as contingents of crusaders robbed and massacred thousands of Jews in the Rhineland (see page 154). The First Crusade was climaxed by the storming of Jerusalem in June 1099 and the slaughter of the city's Muslim and Jewish inhabitants.

Robert the Monk
APPEAL OF URBAN II TO THE FRANKS

Pope Urban's speech, as reported by Robert the Monk, shows how skillfully the pope appealed to the Frankish lords.

"O race of the Franks, O people who live beyond the mountains, O people loved and chosen of God, as is clear from your many deeds, distinguished over all other nations by the situation of your land, your catholic faith, and your regard for the holy church, we have a special message and exhortation for you. For we wish you to know what a grave matter has brought us to your country. The sad news has come from Jerusalem and Constantinople that the people of Persia, an accursed and foreign race [the Turks], enemies of God, 'a generation that set not their heart aright, and whose spirit was not steadfast with God' (Ps. 78:8), have invaded the lands of those Christians and devastated them with the sword, rapine, and fire. Some of the Christians they have carried away as slaves, others they have put to death. The churches they have either destroyed or turned into mosques. They desecrate and overthrow the altars. . . . They have taken from the Greek empire a tract of land so large that it takes more than two months to walk through it. Whose duty is it to avenge this and recover that land, if not yours? For to you more than to other nations the Lord has given the military spirit, courage, agile bodies, and the bravery to strike down those who resist you. Let your minds be stirred to bravery by the deeds of your forefathers, and by the efficiency and greatness of . . . [Charlemagne], and of . . . his son [Louis the Pious], and of the other kings who have destroyed [Muslim] kingdoms, and established Christianity in their lands. You should be moved especially by the holy grave of our Lord and Saviour which is now held by unclean peoples, and by the holy places which are treated with dishonor and irreverently befouled with their uncleanness.

"O bravest of knights, descendants of unconquered ancestors, do not be weaker than they, but remember their courage. . . . Let no possessions keep you back, no solicitude for your property. Your land [France] is shut in on all sides by the sea and mountains, and is too thickly populated. There is not much wealth here, and the soil scarcely yields enough to support you. On this account you kill and devour each other, and carry on war and mutually destroy each other. Let your hatred and quarrels cease, your civil wars come to an end, and all your dissensions stop. Set out on the road to the holy sepulchre [site of Jesus' burial], take the land from that wicked people, and make it your own. That land which, as the Scripture says, is flowing with milk and honey, God gave to the children of Israel. Jerusalem is the best of all lands, more fruitful than all others, as it were a second Paradise of delights. This land our Saviour [Jesus] made illustrious by his birth, beautiful with his life, and sacred with his suffering; he redeemed it with his death and glorified it with his tomb. This royal city is now held captive by her enemies, and made pagan by those who know not God. She asks and longs to be liberated and does not cease to beg you to come to her aid. She asks aid especially from you because, as I have said, God has given more of the military spirit to you than to other nations. Set out on this journey and you will obtain the remission of your sins and be sure of the incorruptible glory of the kingdom of heaven."

When Pope Urban had said this and much more of the same sort, all who were present were moved to cry out with one accord, "It is the will of God, it is the will of God." When the pope heard this he raised his eyes to heaven and gave thanks to God, and, commanding silence with a gesture of his hand, he said: "My dear brethren. . . . [L]et these words be your battle cry, because God caused you to speak them. Whenever you meet the enemy in battle, you shall all cry out, 'It is the will of God, it is the will of God.' . . . Whoever therefore shall determine to make this journey and shall make a vow to God and shall offer himself as a living sacrifice, holy, acceptable to God (Rom. 12:1), shall wear a cross on his brow or on his breast. And when he returns after having fulfilled his vow he shall wear the cross on his back. In this way he will obey the command of the Lord, 'Whosoever doth not bear his cross and come after me is not worthy of me'" (Luke 14:27).

REVIEW QUESTIONS

1. Modern political propaganda frequently uses popular fears, prejudices, moral idealism, and patriotic fervor to shape public opinion. Discuss the techniques used by Pope Urban II to create public support for the Crusade.
2. What types of people did Urban II address and what were his motives?

---

4 Religious Dissent

Like many groups held together by common ideology, the medieval church wanted to protect its doctrines from novel, dissident, or erroneous interpretations. To ensure orthodoxy and competency, therefore, all preachers were licensed by the bishop; unlicensed preaching, especially by unschooled laymen, was forbidden. In the western church, heresy had not been a serious problem in the post-Roman period. But in the twelfth century, heretical movements attracted significant numbers of supporters among both the clergy and laity and cut across frontiers and social classes.

One major heretical movement was that of the Cathari, more commonly called the Albigensians. The Albigensian heresy apparently entered western Europe from the Balkans, where similar religious ideas could be traced back to non-Christian sects of the early Roman Empire. The Albigensians were not Christians in any orthodox sense: they rejected the Old Testament and claimed the God of Israel to be the Evil One, who created the material world in which souls were trapped, separating them from the Good God. Although the Albigensians accepted the New Testament with their own emendations, they rejected the Christian doctrine of Jesus as both God and Man; they believed that Jesus was a disembodied spirit, and that all flesh was evil, marriage was evil, and the begetting of children was evil. Rejecting the medieval church, they constituted an alternative religion in the midst of Christian southern France and Italy.

Emperor Frederick II
HERETICS: ENEMIES OF GOD AND HUMANITY

The new religious movements threatened to undermine the existing religious, social, and political order. Pope Gregory IX in 1231 decided to create special courts of inquisition to seek out the dissenters, or heretics. Those who repented could be sent to prison for life; those who remained unrepentant were excommunicated from the church and turned over to the secular authorities, who executed them. The property of the guilty was confiscated and divided equally among the local bishop, the inquisitors, and the local civil ruler. The ordinary procedural standards of European penal law were abandoned in the courts of inquisition. The inquiry was secret, witnesses were not identified to the accused, guilt was presumed, legal counsel was denied, and torture was applied to verify statements given under oath.

The papal inquisitors were not permitted to function everywhere. The rulers of the northern and eastern European kingdoms forbade them entry, as did England, Portugal, and Castile. In the next reading, from the first section of the Constitutions of Melfi, promulgated for the kingdom of Sicily by the Emperor Frederick II (1220–1250) in 1231, the typical attitude of medieval Christians toward heretics (or those who gave them aid or comfort) and the savage penalties imposed are graphically depicted. Ironically, in 1245, Frederick II himself was accused of heresy and deposed by Pope Innocent IV (1243–1254), leading to a war between the emperor and the papacy.

Heretics try to tear the seamless robe of our God. As slaves to the vice of a word that means division [sect], they strive to introduce division into the unity of the indivisible faith and to separate the flock from the care of Peter [the Pope], the shepherd to whom the Good Shepherd [Christ] entrusted it. Inside they are violent wolves, but they pretend the tameness of sheep until they can get inside the sheepfold of the Lord. They are the most evil angels. They are sons of depravity from the father of wickedness and the author of evil, who are resolved to deceive simple souls. They are snakes who deceive doves. They are serpents who seem to creep in secretly and, under the sweetness of honey, spew out poison. While they pretend to administer the food of life, they strike from their tails. They mix up a potion of death as a certain very deadly poison.

. . . Indeed, these miserable Patarines [Patarenes, one group of heretics], who do not possess the holy faith of the Eternal Trinity,[1] offend at the same time three persons under one cover of wickedness: God, their neighbors, and themselves. They offend God because they do not know the faith of God, and they do not know his son. They deceive their neighbors insofar as they administer the delights of heretical wickedness to them under the guise of spiritual nourishment. They rage against themselves even more cruelly insofar as, besides risking their souls,

these sectaries, lavish of life and improvident with death, also expose their bodies to the enticements of cruel death which they could avoid by true knowledge and the steadfastness of true faith. What is even worse, the survivors are not frightened by the example. We cannot contain our emotions against such men so hostile to God, to themselves, and to mankind. Therefore, we draw the sword of righteous vengeance against them, and we pursue them more urgently insofar as they are known to practice the crimes of their superstition within the Roman Church herself, which is considered the head of all the other churches, to the more evident injury of the Christian faith. . . . Because we consider this so repulsive, we have decided in the first place that the crime of heresy and these condemned sects should be numbered among the public crimes as it was promulgated in the ancient laws. . . . In order to expose the wickedness of those who, because they do not follow God, walk in darkness, even if no one reports it, we desire that the perpetrators of these crimes should be investigated diligently and should be sought after by our officials like other criminals. We order that those who become known by an inquisition [trial], even if they are touched by the evidence of a slight suspicion, should be examined by ecclesiastics and prelates. If they should be found by them to deviate from the Catholic faith in the least wise, and if, after they have been admonished by them in a pastoral way, they should be unwilling to relinquish the insidious darkness of the Devil and to recognize the God of Light, but they persist in the con-

---

[1]The central Christian doctrine that teaches that there are three divine persons in one God: Father, Son, and Holy Spirit, who are coequal, coeternal, and consubstantial.

stancy of conceived error, we order by the promulgation of our present law that these Patarines should be condemned to suffer the death for which they strive. Committed to the judgment of the flames, they should be burned alive in the sight of the people. We do not grieve that in this we satisfy their desire, from which they obtain punishment alone and no other fruit of their error. No one should presume to intervene with us

in behalf of such persons. But if anyone does, we shall turn against him the deserved stings of our indignation. . . .

. . . We order that the shelterers, believers, accomplices of Patarines, and those who support them in any way at all, who give no heed to fear for themselves so that they can protect others from punishment, should be sent into perpetual exile and all their goods confiscated.

REVIEW QUESTION

1. How did Frederick II view heretics and what methods did he determine to use to eliminate them?

---

5 Medieval Learning: Synthesis of Reason and Christian Faith

The twelfth century witnessed a revived interest in classical learning and the founding of universities. Traditional theology was broadened by the application of a new system of critical analysis, called scholasticism. Scholastic thinkers assumed that some teachings of Christianity, which they accepted as true by faith, could also be demonstrated to be true by reason. They sought to explain and clarify theological doctrines by subjecting them to logical analysis.

Saint Thomas Aquinas
SUMMA THEOLOGICA

For most of the Middle Ages, religious thought was dominated by the influence of Saint Augustine (d. 430), the greatest of the Latin church fathers (see page 118). Augustine placed little value on the study of nature; for him, the City of Man (the world) was a sinful place from which people tried to escape in order to enter the City of God (heaven). Regarding God as the source of knowing, he held that reason by itself was an inadequate guide to knowledge: without faith in revealed truth, there could be no understanding. An alternative approach to that of Augustine was provided by Thomas Aquinas (1225–1274), a friar of the Order of Preachers (Dominicans), who taught theology at Paris and later in Italy. Both Augustine and Aquinas believed that God was the source of all truth, that human nature was corrupted by the imprint of the original sin of Adam and Eve, and that God revealed himself through the Bible and in the person of Jesus Christ. But, in contrast to Augustine, Aquinas expressed great confidence in the power of reason and favored applying it to investigate the natural world.

Aquinas held that as both faith and reason came from God, they were not in opposition to each other; properly understood, they supported each other. Because reason was no enemy of faith, it should not be feared. In addition to showing renewed respect for reason, Aquinas—influenced by Aristotelian empiricism (the acquisition of knowledge of nature through experience)—valued knowledge of the natural world. He saw the natural and supernatural worlds not as irreconcilable and hostile to each other, but as a continuous ascending hierarchy of divinely created orders of being moving progressively toward the Supreme Being. In constructing a synthesis of Christianity and Aristotelianism, Aquinas gave renewed importance to the natural world, human reason, and the creative human spirit. Nevertheless, by holding that reason was subordinate to faith, he remained a typically medieval thinker.

In the opening reading from his most ambitious work, the *Summa Theologica*, Thomas Aquinas asserts that reason by itself is insufficient to lead human beings to salvation.

Whether, Besides the Philosophical Sciences, Any Further Doctrine Is Required?

It was necessary for man's salvation that there should be a knowledge revealed by God, besides the philosophical sciences investigated by human reason. First, because man is directed to God as to an end that surpasses the grasp of his reason. . . . But the end must first be known by men who are to direct their thoughts and actions to the end. Hence it was necessary for the salvation of man that certain truths which exceed human reason should be made known to him by divine revelation. Even as regards those truths about God which human reason can investigate, it was necessary that man be taught by a divine revelation. For the truth about God, such as reason can know it, would only be known by a few, and that after a long time, and with the admixture of many errors; whereas man's whole salvation, which is in God, depends upon the knowledge of this truth. Therefore, in order that the salvation of men might be brought about more fitly and more surely, it was necessary that they be taught divine truths by divine revelation. It was therefore necessary that, besides the philosophical sciences investigated by reason, there should be a sacred science by way of revelation.

In the next selection, Aquinas uses the categories of Aristotelian philosophy to demonstrate through natural reason God's existence.

Whether God Exists?

The existence of God can be proved in five ways.

The first and more manifest way is the argument from motion. It is certain, and evident to our senses, that in the world some things are in motion. Now whatever is moved is moved by another, for nothing can be moved except it is in potentiality to that towards which it is moved; whereas a thing moves inasmuch as it is in actuality. For motion is nothing else than the reduction of something from potentiality to actuality. But nothing can be reduced from potentiality to actuality, except by something in a state of actuality. Thus that which is actually hot, as fire, makes wood, which is potentially hot, to be actually hot, and thereby moves and changes it. Now it is not possible that the same thing should be at once in actuality and potentiality in the same respect, but only in different respects. For what is actually hot cannot simultaneously be potentially hot; but it is simultaneously potentially cold. It is therefore impossible that in the same respect and in the same way a thing should be both mover and moved, *i.e.,* that it should move itself. Therefore, whatever is moved must be moved by another. If that by which it is moved be itself moved, then this also must needs be moved by another, and that by another again. But this cannot go on to infinity, because then there would be no first mover, and, consequently, no other mover, seeing that subsequent movers move only inasmuch as they are moved by the first mover; as the staff moves only because it is moved by the hand. Therefore it is necessary to arrive at a first mover, moved by no other; and this everyone understands to be God.

The second way is from the nature of efficient cause. In the world of sensible things we find there is an order of efficient causes. There is no case known (neither is it, indeed, possible) in which a thing is found to be the efficient cause of itself; for so it would be prior to itself, which is impossible. Now in efficient causes it is not possible to go on to infinity, because in all efficient causes following in order, the first is the cause of the intermediate cause, and the intermediate is the cause of the ultimate cause, whether the intermediate cause be several, or one only. Now to take away the cause is to take away the effect. Therefore, if there be no first cause among efficient causes, there will be no ultimate, nor any intermediate, cause. But if in efficient causes it is possible to go on to infinity, there will be no first efficient cause, neither will there be an ultimate effect, nor any intermediate efficient causes; all of which is plainly false. Therefore it is necessary to admit a first efficient cause, to which everyone gives the name of God.

The third way is taken from possibility and necessity, and runs thus. We find in nature things that are possible to be and not to be, since they are found to be generated, and to be corrupted, and consequently, it is possible for them to be and not to be. But it is impossible for these always to exist, for that which can not-be at some time is not. Therefore, if everything can not-be, then at one time there was nothing in existence. Now if this were true, even now there would be nothing in existence, because that which does not exist begins to exist only through something already existing. Therefore, if at one time nothing was in existence, it would have been impossible for anything to have begun to exist; and thus even now nothing would be in existence—which is absurd. Therefore, not all beings are merely possible, but there must exist something the existence of which is necessary. But every necessary thing either has its necessity caused by another, or not. Now it is impossible to go on to infinity in necessary things which have their necessity caused by another, as has been already proved in regard to efficient causes. Therefore we cannot but admit the existence of some being having of itself its own necessity, and not receiving it from another, but rather causing in others their necessity. This all men speak of as God.

The fourth way is taken from the graduation to be found in things. Among beings there are some more and some less good, true, noble, and the like. But *more* and *less* are predicated of different things according as they resemble in their different ways something which is the maximum, as a thing is said to be hotter according as it more nearly resembles that which is hottest; so that there is something which is truest, something best, something noblest, and, consequently, something which is most being, for those things that are greatest in truth are greatest in being. . . . Now the maximum in any genus is the cause of all in that genus, as fire, which is the maximum of heat, is the cause of all hot things. . . . Therefore there must also be something which is to all beings the cause of their being, goodness, and every other perfection; and this we call God.

The fifth way is taken from the governance of the world. We see that things which lack knowledge, such as natural bodies, act for an end, and this is evident from their acting always, or nearly always, in the same way, so as to obtain the best result. Hence it is plain that they achieve their end, not fortuitously, but designedly. Now whatever lacks knowledge cannot move towards an end, unless it be directed by some being endowed with knowledge and intelligence; as the arrow is directed by the archer. Therefore some intelligent being exists by whom all natural things are directed to their end; and this being we call God.

REVIEW QUESTIONS

1. According to Thomas Aquinas, when does a person require more than reason to arrive at truth?
2. Show how Aquinas used both logic and an empirical method to prove the existence of God.

---

6 The Jews in the Middle Ages

Toward the end of the eleventh century, small communities of Jews were living in many of the larger towns of Christian Europe. Most of these Jews were descended from Jewish inhabitants of the Roman Empire. Under the protection of the Roman law or of individual Germanic kings, they had managed to survive amid a sometimes hostile Christian population. But religious fanaticism unleashed by the call for the First Crusade undermined Christian–Jewish relations gravely. Bands of Crusaders began systematically to attack and massacre the Jewish inhabitants of Rhineland towns. Thousands were killed—many because they refused to become converts to Christianity; their houses were looted and burned. Efforts by the bishops and civil authorities to protect their Jewish subjects were largely ineffective. Anti-Semitism became endemic in Latin Christendom.

Albert of Aix-la-Chapelle
MASSACRE OF THE JEWS OF MAINZ

In this reading, Albert, a twelfth-century priest of the city of Aix-la-Chapelle, describes the massacre of Jews (1096) at the beginning of the First Crusade.

At the beginning of summer in the same year in which Peter [the Hermit] and Gottschalk,[1] after collecting an army, had set out, there assembled in like fashion a large and innumerable host of Christians from diverse kingdoms and lands; namely, from the realms of France, England, Flanders, and Lorraine. . . . I know not whether by a judgment of the Lord, or by some error of mind, they rose in a spirit of cruelty against the Jewish people scattered throughout these cities and slaughtered them without mercy, especially in the Kingdom of

---

[1]A brilliant propagandist, Peter the Hermit raised a large army of poor and sparsely armed Frenchmen, who marched to Cologne to begin a Crusade to the Holy Land. Most of them were killed by Turkish forces after crossing into Asia Minor. Gottschalk was a German priest who gathered a band of undisciplined soldiers to join the First Crusade. His forces were killed by Hungarians defending their families and property from these Crusaders.

Lorraine,[2] asserting it to be the beginning of their expedition and their duty against the enemies of the Christian faith. This slaughter of Jews was done first by citizens of Cologne.[3] These suddenly fell upon a small band of Jews and severely wounded and killed many; they destroyed the houses and synagogues of the Jews and divided among themselves a very large amount of money. When the Jews saw this cruelty, about two hundred in the silence of the night began flight by boat to Neuss. The pilgrims and crusaders discovered them, and after taking away all their possessions, inflicted on them similar slaughter, leaving not even one alive.

Not long after this, they started upon their journey, as they had vowed, and arrived in a great multitude at the city of Mainz. There Count Emico, a nobleman, a very mighty man in this region, was awaiting, with a large band of Teutons [German soldiers], the arrival of the pilgrims who were coming thither from diverse lands by the King's highway.

The Jews of this city, knowing of the slaughter of their brethren, and that they themselves could not escape the hands of so many, fled in hope of safety to Bishop Rothard. They put an infinite treasure in his guard and trust, hav-

ing much faith in his protection, because he was Bishop of the city. Then that excellent Bishop of the city cautiously set aside the incredible amount of money received from them. He placed the Jews in the very spacious hall of his own house, away from the sight of Count Emico and his followers, that they might remain safe and sound in a very secure and strong place.

But Emico and the rest of his band held a council and, after sunrise, attacked the Jews in the hall with arrows and lances. Breaking the bolts and doors, they killed the Jews, about seven hundred in number, who in vain resisted the force and attack of so many thousands. They killed the women, also, and with their swords pierced tender children of whatever age and sex. The Jews, seeing that their Christian enemies were attacking them and their children, and that they were sparing no age, likewise fell upon one another, brother, children, wives, and sisters, and thus they perished at each other's hands. Horrible to say, mothers cut the throats of nursing children with knives and stabbed others, preferring them to perish thus by their own hands rather than to be killed by the weapons of the uncircumcised.

From this cruel slaughter of the Jews a few escaped; and a few because of fear, rather than because of love of the Christian faith, were baptized. With very great spoils taken from these people, Count Emico, Clarebold, Thomas, and all that intolerable company of men and women then continued on their way to Jerusalem.

---

[2]Lorraine, a duchy in the western part of the Holy Roman Empire, is now part of France.
[3]Cologne (Köln), founded by the Romans in the first century A.D., was the largest city in the Rhine Valley, a center of commerce, industry, and learning. Its politically powerful archbishop was a prince of the Holy Roman Empire.

THE LIBEL OF RITUAL MURDER

Despite efforts by some popes to protect Jews, outbreaks of violence toward them persisted and bizarre myths about them emerged, often fomented by the clergy. Jews were seen as agents of Satan conspiring to destroy Christendom and as sorcerers employing black magic against Christians. Perhaps the most absurd (and dangerous) charge against the Jewish people was the accusation of ritual murder—that the Jews, requiring Christian blood for the Passover service, sacrificed a Christian child. Despite the vehement denials of Jews and the protests of some enlightened Christian leaders, hundreds of such libelous accusations were made, resulting in the torture, trials, murder, and expulsion of many Jews. Allegations of ritual murder and accompanying trials persisted into the twentieth century, to the consternation and anger of enlightened people who regarded the charge as so much nonsense, a lingering medieval fabrication and superstition.

In the next passage, an English chronicler reports on the death of one young Harold of Gloucester purported to be murdered by Jews in 1168.

. . . [The eight-year-old] boy Harold, who is buried in the Church of St. Peter the Apostle, at Gloucester . . . , is said to have been carried away secretly by Jews, in the opinion of many,* on Feb. 21, and by them hidden till March 16. On that night, on the sixth of the preceding feast, the Jews of all England coming together as if to circumcise a certain boy, pretend deceitfully that they are about to celebrate the feast [Passover] appointed by law in such case, and deceiving the citizens of Gloucester with that fraud, they tortured the lad placed before them with immense tortures. It is true no Christian was present, or saw or heard the deed, nor have we found that anything was betrayed by any Jew. But a little while after when the whole convent of monks of Gloucester and almost all the citizens of that city, and innumerable persons coming to the spectacle, saw the wounds of the dead body, scars of fire, the thorns fixed on his head, and liquid wax poured into the eyes and face, and touched it with the diligent examination of their hands, those tortures were believed or guessed to have been inflicted on him in that manner. It was clear that they had made him a glorious martyr to Christ, being slain without sin, and having bound his feet with his own girdle, threw him into the river Severn. (The body is taken to St. Peter's Church, and there performs miracles.)

_____
*Even the chronicler puts it doubly doubtfully.

Maimonides
JEWISH LEARNING

Medieval Jews, despite frequent persecution, carried on a rich cultural and intellectual life based on their ancestral religion. The foremost Jewish scholar of the Middle Ages was Moses ben Maimon, also called by the Greek name Maimonides (1135–1204), who was born in Córdoba, Spain, then under Muslim rule. After his family emigrated from Spain, Maimonides went to Egypt, where he became physician to the sultan. During his lifetime, Maimonides achieved fame as a philosopher, theologian, mathematician, and physician; he was recognized as the leading Jewish sage of his day, and his writings were respected by Christian and Muslim thinkers as well. Like Christian scholastics and Muslim philosophers, Maimonides tried to harmonize faith with reason, to reconcile the Hebrew Scriptures and the Talmud (Jewish biblical commentary) with Greek philosophy. In his writings on ethical themes, Maimonides demonstrated piety, wisdom, and humanity.

Care for the poor is ingrained in the Jewish tradition. Rabbis gave the highest value to assistance, given in secret, that helps a poor person to become self-supporting. Maimonides drew upon this rabbinical tradition in his discussion of charity which follows.

CHARITY

The law of the Torah commanded us to practise *tsedakah,*[1] support the needy and help them financially. The command in connection with this duty occurs in various expressions; e.g., "Thou shalt surely open thy hand unto him" (Deut. xv. 8), "Thou shalt uphold him; as a stranger and a settler shall he live with thee" (Lev. xxv. 35). The intention in these passages is identical, viz., that we should console the poor man and support him to the extent of sufficiency. . . .

There are eight degrees in alms-giving, one higher than the other: Supreme above all is to give assistance to a co-religionist who has fallen on evil times by presenting him with a gift or loan, or entering into a partnership with him, or procuring him work, thereby helping him to become self-supporting.

Inferior to this is giving charity to the poor in such a way that the giver and recipient are unknown to each other. This is, indeed, the performance of a commandment from disinterested motives; and it is exemplified by the Institution of the Chamber of the Silent which existed in the Temple,[2] where the righteous secretly deposited their alms and the respectable poor were secretly assisted.*

Next in order is the donation of money to the charitable fund of the Community, to which no contribution should be made without the donors feeling confident that the administration is honest, prudent and capable of proper management.

Below this degree is the instance where the donor is aware to whom he is giving the alms but the recipient is unaware from whom he received them; as, e.g., the great Sages who used to go about secretly throwing money through the doors of the poor. This is quite a proper course to adopt and a great virtue where the administrators of a charitable fund are not acting fairly.

Inferior to this degree is the case where the recipient knows the identity of the donor, but not *vice versa;* as, e.g., the great Sages who used to tie sums of money in linen bundles and throw them behind their backs for poor men to pick up, so that they should not feel shame.

The next four degrees in their order are: the man who gives money to the poor before he is asked; the man who gives money to the poor after he is asked; the man who gives less than he should, but does it with good grace; and lastly, he who gives grudgingly.

---

[1]The term *tsedakah* is derived from *tsédek* (righteousness); it denotes showing kindness to others.

[2]The Temple to which Maimonides refers was the Temple in Jerusalem, destroyed by the Romans in A.D. 70.

---

*This system of charity was adopted by Jews in several Palestinian and Babylonian cities.

REVIEW QUESTIONS

1. What were the apparent motives of those who attacked the Jews at Cologne and elsewhere at the time of the First Crusade?
2. What harassments and abuses were Jews likely to suffer in late medieval society?
3. Why were Christians prone to believe the absurd myth that Jews committed ritual murder?
4. Discuss the role of charity in Jewish medieval culture.

7 Troubadour Love Songs

In the late twelfth century, new kinds of poetry with a distinctive set of themes began to be created at the castles and courts in France, Italy, Spain, and Germany. The poets were themselves knights or noblewomen who composed their poems to be sung or read aloud for the entertainment of fellow feudal nobles. The subject was always that of the love between man and woman.

The original inspiration for the new troubadour poetry was probably the Arab poetry of Spain and Sicily, where the theme of romantic love was developed earlier. What was revolutionary in later European poetry was its treatment of the relationship between men and women. The troubadours reversed the traditional view of men as superior and women as inferior and dependent in their relationships. They introduced what is called "courtly love," a love relationship in which the woman is the superior and dominant figure, the man inferior and dependent. The male courts the lady, paying homage to her beauty and virtue. He suffers humiliation and frustration at her will and expresses the erotic tensions that consume him.

LOVE AS JOYOUS, PAINFUL, AND HUMOROUS

The following poems were all composed by southern French troubadours. In the first selection a poet sings the praises of his beloved.

I wandered through a garden, 'twas
   filled with flowers the rarest,
And of all these brilliant blossoms
   I culled the very fairest;
So fine its shape, so sweet its scent, its
   hues so richly blent,
That heaven, I'm sure, created it itself
   to represent.
My lady is so charming, my lady is so
   meek,
Such tenderness is in her smile, such
   beauty in her cheek;
Such kisses blossom on her lip, such
   love illumines her eye—
Oh, never was there neath the stars a
   man so blest as I!
I gaze, I thrill with joy, I weep, in song
   my feelings flow—
A song of hope, delight, desire, with
   passion all aglow—

A fervent song, a pleading song, a song
   in every line—
Of thanks and praise to her who lists no
   other songs but mine.
Oh, hear me sweet! Oh, kiss me sweet!
   Oh, clasp me tenderly!
Thy beauties many, many touch, but
   none that love like me.

The following two poems tell of a lover's failure to win the affections of his beloved.

Now that the air is fresher
and the world turned green,
I shall sing once more
of the one I love and desire,
but we are so far apart
that I cannot go and witness
how my words might please her.

And nothing can console me
but death, for evil tongues
(may God curse them)
have made us part.
And alas, I so desired her
that now I moan and cry
half mad with grief.

I sing of her, yet her beauty
is greater than I can tell,
with her fresh color, lovely eyes,
and white skin, untanned
and untainted by rouge.
She is so pure and noble
that no one can speak ill of her.

But above all, one must praise,
it seems to me, her truthfulness,
her manners and her gracious speech,
for she never would betray a friend;
and I was mad to believe
what I heard tell of her
and thus cause her to be angry.

I never intended to complain;
and even now, if she so desires,
she could bring me happiness
by granting what I seek.
I cannot go on like this much longer,
for since she's been so far away
I've scarcely slept or eaten.

Love is sweet to look upon
but bitter upon parting;
one day it makes you weep
and another skip and dance,
for now I know that the more
one enters love's service,
the more fickle it becomes.

Messenger, go with Godspeed
and bring this to my lady,
for I cannot stay here much longer
and live, or be cured elsewhere,
unless I have her next to me,
naked, to kiss and embrace
within a curtained room.

———

I said my heart was like to break,
  And that my soul was cast,

By passion's tide, just like a wreck
  Disabled by the blast.

I swore an oath that what I felt
  Was like to turn my head;
I sighed—such sighs!—and then I knelt,
  But not a word she said!

I preached of Grace in moving strain;
  I told her she was fair;
I whispered what renown she'd gain,
  By listening to my prayer.

I spoke of needle and of pole,
  And other things I'd read;
But unto all my rigmarole—
  Why not a word she said!

I prayed her then my love to test,
  To send me near or far—
I'd squelch the dragon in his den,
  I'd yoke him to my car.

I'd risk for her, as faithful knight,
  My eyes, or limbs, or head,
Being quite prepared to fool or fight—
  But not a word she said!

I argued that, if poor in cash,
  Yet I was rich in mind;
Of rivals vowed to make a hash,
  When such I chanced to find.

I knit my brows, I clenched my hand,
  I tried to wake her dread;
In quiet wise, you'll understand—
  But not a word she said!

———

Troubadours could also be playful. Sometimes they mocked women who labored too hard to preserve a youthful beauty.

———

That creature so splendid is but an old jade;
Of ointment and padding her beauty is made;
Unpainted if you had the hap to behold her,
You'd find her all wrinkles from forehead to
    shoulder.

What a shame for a woman who has lost all her
    grace

To waste thus her time in bedaubing her face!
To neglect her poor soul I am sure is not right
   of her,
For a body that's going to corruption
   in spite of her.

Sometimes they even mocked this obsession
with romance.

You say the moon is all aglow,
   The nightingale a-singing—

I'd rather watch the red wine flow,
   And hear the goblets ringing.

You say 'tis sweet to hear the gale
   Creep sighing through the willows—
I'd rather hear a merry tale,
   'Mid a group of jolly fellows!

You say 'tis sweet the stars to view
   Upon the waters gleaming—
I'd rather see, 'twixt me and you
   And the post, my supper steaming.

REVIEW QUESTION

1. What do these troubadours' love songs reveal about the tradition of courtly love?

---

8 The Status of Women in Medieval Society

The precise status of a woman in medieval society differed immensely depending on the time, the place, and her class. The majority of women managed families and households, often taking part in farmwork or other crafts connected with the family livelihood. However, their legal rights, social standing, and power were inferior to those of adult males in their own families. During the High Middle Ages, the Christian church increasingly supported a patriarchal structure of authority in church and civil society that left women effectively under the domination of males, clerical and lay. Although clerical teachings tended to demean women, several church doctrines also recognized the inherent dignity of a woman. The church regarded marriage as a sacrament, considered adultery a sin, and subjected men and women to the same moral standards. Neither sex had any special advantage in attaining salvation.

Despite legal, social, and economic handicaps imposed upon them by males, some women successfully assumed positions of power and achievement. A few ruled kingdoms and principalities or headed convents and religious orders. Others organized guilds; founded nunneries; practiced various crafts; served as teachers, physicians, and midwives; and operated small businesses. Some showed talent as poets, dramatists, and artists.

Christine de Pisan
THE CITY OF LADIES

In the early Renaissance, a remarkable woman took up the task of defending women from their many male detractors. Christine de Pisan (1364–1429?) was born in Venice but moved with her parents to Paris, where her father was court physician and astrologer. She married a court notary when she was fifteen, had three children, and was left a widow and penniless ten years later. She decided to use her unusually good education to become a professional writer, an unheard-of occupation for a woman at that time. She won the patronage and friendship of noble ladies at the French royal court and produced many poems and books, including a biography of King Charles V and several polemical attacks upon the poets who slandered womankind. The most famous of these is *The City of Ladies,* written in 1405. In it Christine de Pisan questioned three allegorical figures—Reason, Rectitude, and Justice—about the lies and slanders of males concerning the virtues and achievements of women. The book is really a history of famous women and their accomplishments in many fields of endeavour. In the following passages, she challenged the traditional medieval attitude toward women. In questioning Lady Reason about the alleged inferiority of women to men, de Pisan cleverly changed the subject to that of virtue, proclaiming the equality of the sexes in attaining it.

"My lady [Lady Reason], according to what I understand from you, woman is a most noble creature. But even so, Cicero [Roman statesman, see page 74] says that a man should never serve any woman and that he who does so debases himself, for no man should ever serve anyone lower than him."

She replied, "The man or the woman in whom resides greater virtue is the higher; neither the loftiness nor the lowliness of a person lies in the body according to the sex, but in the perfection of conduct and virtues. And surely he is happy who serves the Virgin [Mary, the mother of Jesus], who is above all the angels."

"My lady, one of the Catos[1]—who was such a great orator—said, nevertheless, that if this world were without women, we would converse with the gods."

She replied, "You can now see the foolishness of the man who is considered wise, because, thanks to a woman, man reigns with God. And if anyone would say that man was banished because of Lady Eve, I tell you that he gained more through [the Virgin] Mary than he lost through Eve when humanity was conjoined to the Godhead,[2] which would never have taken place if Eve's misdeed [eating the forbidden fruit] had not occurred. Thus man and woman should be glad for this sin, through which such an honor has come about. For as low as human nature fell through this creature woman, was human nature lifted higher by this same creature. And as for conversing with the gods, as this Cato has said, if there had been no woman, he spoke truer than he knew, for he was a pagan, and among those of this belief, gods were thought to reside

[1] Several Roman statesmen bore the name Cato. Cato the Censor (234–149 B.C.) was a vigorous critic of women.

[2] This clause refers to the Christian belief that God became a human being in the person of Jesus Christ.

in Hell as well as in Heaven, that is, the devils whom they called the gods of Hell—so that it is no lie that these gods would have conversed with men, if Mary had not lived."

In this next passage, de Pisan discusses the slander that women are not as intelligent as men.

". . . But please enlighten me again, whether it has ever pleased this God, who has bestowed so many favors on women, to honor the feminine sex with the privilege of the virtue of high understanding and great learning, and whether women ever have a clever enough mind for this. I wish very much to know this because men maintain that the mind of women can learn only a little."

She [Lady Reason] answered, "My daughter, since I told you before, you know quite well that the opposite of their opinion is true, and to show you this even more clearly, I will give you proof through examples. I tell you again—and don't doubt the contrary—if it were customary to send daughters to school like sons, and if they were then taught the natural sciences, they would learn as thoroughly and understand the subtleties of all the arts and sciences as well as sons. And by chance there happen to be such women, for, as I touched on before, just as women have more delicate bodies than men, weaker and less able to perform many tasks, so do they have minds that are freer and sharper whenever they apply themselves."

"My lady, what are you saying? With all due respect, could you dwell longer on this point, please. Certainly men would never admit this answer is true, unless it is explained more plainly, for they believe that one normally sees that men know more than women do."

She answered, "Do you know why women know less?"

"Not unless you tell me, my lady."

"Without the slightest doubt, it is because they are not involved in many different things, but stay at home, where it is enough for them to run the household, and there is nothing which so instructs a reasonable creature as the exercise and experience of many different things."

"My lady, since they have minds skilled in conceptualizing and learning, just like men, why don't women learn more?"

She replied, "Because, my daughter, the public does not require them to get involved in the affairs which men are commissioned to execute, just as I told you before. It is enough for women to perform the usual duties to which they are ordained. As for judging from experience, since one sees that women usually know less than men, that therefore their capacity for understanding is less, look at men who farm the flatlands or who live in the mountains. You will find that in many countries they seem completely savage because they are so simple-minded. All the same, there is no doubt that Nature provided them with the qualities of body and mind found in the wisest and most learned men. . . ."

Next, Christine de Pisan argues in favor of giving young women the same opportunities for learning as men.

Following these remarks, I, Christine, spoke, "My lady, I realize that women have accomplished many good things and that even if evil women have done evil, it seems to me, nevertheless, that the benefits accrued and still accruing because of good women—particularly the wise and literary ones and those educated in the natural sciences whom I mentioned above—outweigh the evil. Therefore, I am amazed by the opinion of some men who claim that they do not want their daughters, wives, or kinswomen to be educated because their mores would be ruined as a result."

She responded, "Here you can clearly see that not all opinions of men are based on reason and that these men are wrong. For it must not be presumed that mores necessarily grow worse from knowing the moral sciences, which teach the virtues, indeed, there is not the slightest doubt that moral education amends and ennobles them. How could anyone think or believe that whoever follows good teaching or doctrine is the worse for it? Such an opinion cannot be expressed or maintained. I do not mean that it would be good for a man or a woman to study the art of divination or those fields of learning which are forbidden—for the holy Church did not remove them from common use without good reason—but it should not be believed that women are the worse for knowing what is good. . . .

". . . To speak of more recent times, without searching for examples in ancient history, Giovanni Andrea, a solemn law professor in Bologna [Italy] not quite sixty years ago, was not of the opinion that it was bad for women to be educated. He had a fair and good daughter, named Novella, who was educated in the law to such an advanced degree that when he was occupied by some task and not at leisure to present his lectures to his students, he would send Novella, his daughter, in his place to lecture to the students from his chair. And to prevent her beauty from distracting the concentration of her audience, she had a little curtain drawn in front of her. In this manner she could on occasion supplement and lighten her father's occupation. . . ."

REVIEW QUESTION

1. Evaluate the arguments used by Christine de Pisan in her defense of women.

9 The Fourteenth Century: An Age of Adversity

During the Late Middle Ages, roughly the fourteenth and early fifteenth centuries, medieval civilization was in decline. The fourteenth century, an age of adversity, was marked by crop failures, famine, population decline, plagues, stagnating production, unemployment, inflation, devastating warfare, and abandoned villages. Violent rebellions by the poor of the towns and countryside were ruthlessly suppressed by the upper classes. The century witnessed flights into mysticism, outbreaks of mass hysteria, and massacres of Jews; it was an age of pessimism and general insecurity. The papacy declined in power, heresy proliferated, and the synthesis of faith and reason, erected by Christian thinkers during the High Middle Ages, began to disintegrate. These developments were signs that the stable and coherent civilization of the thirteenth century was drawing to a close.

Jean de Venette
THE BLACK DEATH

Until the fourteenth century, the population of Europe had increased steadily from its low point in the centuries immediately following the fall of the Roman Empire in the West. Particularly from the eleventh century on, landlords tried to raise their income by bringing new land into cultivation. By improving farming technology, building dikes, draining marshland, and clearing forests, European peasants produced much more food, which permitted more people to survive and multiply. That advance in population tapered off by the early fourteenth century due to many crop failures and wars, which wasted the countryside and led to economic stagnation. But the greatest catastrophe began in the fall of 1347, when sailors returning to Sicily from eastern Mediterranean ports brought with them a new disease, bubonic plague. Within the next three years, from one-quarter to one-third of the population of Europe died from what became known, because of some of its symptoms, as the Black Death. Most who caught the plague died, though some survived. No one knew its cause or cure. We now know that the bacteria were transmitted by fleas from infected rats. The unsanitary living conditions of medieval towns and low standards of personal cleanliness helped to spread the disease. The people were so terrified by the incomprehensible pattern of the disease's progress that superstition, hysteria, and breakdown of civility were common.

The progress of the plague as it made its way through Europe and speculation on its causes, the terrible toll of victims, and various moral responses to the crisis are described in the following reading from the chronicle of Jean de Venette (c. 1308–c. 1368), a French friar who lived through the events described.

In A.D. 1348, the people of France and of almost the whole world were struck by a blow other than war. For in addition to the famine which I described in the beginning and to the wars which I described in the course of this narrative, pestilence and its attendant tribulations appeared again in various parts of the world. . . . All this year and the next, the mortality of men and women, of the young even more than of the old, in Paris and in the kingdom of France, and also, it is said, in other parts of the world, was so great that it was almost impossible to bury the dead. People lay ill little more than two or three days and died suddenly, as it were in full health. He who was well one day was dead the next and being carried to his grave. Swellings appeared suddenly in the armpit or in the groin—in many cases both—and they were infallible signs of death. This sickness or pestilence was called an epidemic by the doctors. Nothing like the great numbers who died in the years 1348 and 1349 has been heard of or seen or read of in times past. This plague and disease came from *ymaginatione* or association and contagion, for if a well man visited the sick he only rarely evaded the risk of death. Wherefore in many towns timid priests withdrew, leaving the exercise of their ministry to such of the religious as were more daring. In many places not two out of

twenty remained alive. So high was the mortality at the Hôtel-Dieu [an early hospital] in Paris that for a long time, more than five hundred dead were carried daily with great devotion in carts to the cemetery of the Holy Innocents in Paris for burial. A very great number of the saintly sisters of the Hôtel-Dieu who, not fearing to die, nursed the sick in all sweetness and humility, with no thought of honor, a number too often renewed by death, rest in peace with Christ, as we may piously believe.

This plague, it is said, began among the unbelievers [Muslims], came to Italy, and then crossing the Alps reached Avignon [site of the papacy in that period], where it attacked several cardinals and took from them their whole household. Then it spread, unforeseen, to France, through Gascony [now part of the south of France] and Spain, little by little, from town to town, from village to village, from house to house, and finally from person to person. It even crossed over to Germany, though it was not so bad there as with us. During the epidemic, God of His accustomed goodness deigned to grant this grace, that however suddenly men died, almost all awaited death joyfully. Nor was there anyone who died without confessing his sins and receiving the holy viaticum [the Eucharistic bread given to the sick or dying]. . . .

Some said that this pestilence was caused by infection of the air and waters, since there was at this time no famine nor lack of food supplies, but on the contrary great abundance. As a result of this theory of infected water and air as the source of the plague the Jews were suddenly and violently charged with infecting wells and water and corrupting the air. The whole world rose up against them cruelly on this account. In Germany and other parts of the world where Jews lived, they were massacred and slaughtered by Christians, and many thousands were burned everywhere, indiscriminately. The unshaken, if fatuous, constancy of the [Jewish] men and their wives was remarkable. For mothers hurled their children first into the fire that they might not be baptized and then leaped in after them to burn with their husbands and children. It is said that many bad Christians were found who in a like manner put poison into wells. But in truth, such poisonings, granted that they actually were perpetrated, could not have caused so great a plague nor have infected so many people. There were other causes; for example, the will of God and the corrupt humors [four elemental body fluids believed to determine a person's physical and mental condition] and evil inherent in air and earth. Perhaps the poisonings, if they actually took place in some localities, reenforced these causes. The plague lasted in France for the greater part of the years 1348 and 1349 and then ceased. Many country villages and many houses in good towns remained empty and deserted. Many houses, including some splendid dwellings, very soon fell into ruins. Even in Paris several houses were thus ruined, though fewer here than elsewhere.

After the cessation of the epidemic, pestilence, or plague, the men and women who survived married each other. There was no sterility among the women, but on the contrary fertility beyond the ordinary. Pregnant women were seen on every side. . . . But woe is me! the world was not changed for the better but for the worse by this renewal of population. For men were more avaricious and grasping than before, even though they had far greater possessions. They were more covetous and disturbed each other more frequently with suits, brawls, disputes, and pleas. Nor by the

mortality resulting from this terrible plague inflicted by God was peace between kings and lords established. On the contrary, the enemies of the king of France and of the Church were stronger and wickeder than before and stirred up wars on sea and on land. Greater evils than before [swarmed] everywhere in the world. And this fact was very remarkable. Although there was an abundance of all goods, yet everything was twice as dear, whether it were utensils, victuals, or merchandise, hired helpers or peasants and serfs, except for some hereditary domains which remained abundantly stocked with everything. Charity began to cool, and iniquity with ignorance and sin to abound, for few could be found in the good towns and castles who knew how or were willing to instruct children in the rudiments of grammar.

Jean de Venette vividly describes one of the more bizarre reactions to the terrible plague, the sudden appearance of the Flagellants. Marching like pilgrims across the countryside, the Flagellants were a group of laymen and laywomen who sought divine pardon for their sins by preaching repentance to others and scourging themselves in a quasi-liturgical ceremony in local churches or marketplaces. The movement foreshadowed events in which moral, social, and economic discontent would increasingly manifest itself in the form of religiously justified popular uprisings against civil and clerical authorities.

In the year 1349, while the plague was still active and spreading from town to town, men in Germany, Flanders, Hainaut [east of Flanders], and Lorraine uprose and began a new sect on their own authority. Stripped to the waist, they gathered in large groups and bands and marched in procession through the crossroads and squares of cities and good towns. There they formed circles and beat upon their backs with weighted scourges, rejoicing as they did so in loud voices and singing hymns suitable to their rite and newly composed for it. Thus for thirty-three days they marched through many towns doing their penance and affording a great spectacle to the wondering people. They flogged their shoulders and arms with scourges tipped with iron points so zealously as to draw blood. But they did not come to Paris nor to any part of France, for they were forbidden to do so by the king of France, who did not want them. He acted on the advice of the masters of theology of the University of Paris, who said that this new sect had been formed contrary to the will of God, to the rites of Holy Mother Church, and to the salvation of all their souls. That indeed this was and is true appeared shortly. For Pope Clement VI was fully informed concerning this fatuous new rite by the masters of Paris through emissaries reverently sent to him and, on the grounds that it had been damnably formed, contrary to law, he forbade the Flagellants under threat of anathema [excommunication] to practise in the future the public penance which they had so presumptuously undertaken.

His prohibition was just, for the Flagellants, supported by certain fatuous priests and monks, were enunciating doctrines and opinions which were beyond measure evil, erroneous, and fallacious. For example, they said that their blood thus drawn by the scourge and poured out was mingled with the blood of Christ. Their many errors showed how little they knew of the Catholic faith. Wherefore, as they had begun fatuously of themselves and not of God, so in a short time they were reduced to nothing. On being warned, they desisted and humbly received absolution and penance at the hands of their prelates as the pope's representatives. Many honorable women and devout matrons, it must be added, had done this penance with scourges, marching and singing through towns and churches like the men, but after a little like the others they desisted.

REVIEW QUESTIONS

1. In the absence of any scientific knowledge about the nature and causes of the bubonic plague, how did the populace react to the mysterious spread of the disease?
2. In the chronicler's opinion, what were some of the long-term moral, social, and economic consequences of the plague?

---

10 The Medieval World-View

The modern world is linked in many ways to the Middle Ages. European cities, the middle class, the state system, English common law, representative institutions, universities—all had their origins in the Middle Ages. Despite these elements of continuity, the characteristic outlook of medieval people is markedly different from that of people today. Whereas science and secularism shape the modern point of view, religion was the foundation of the Middle Ages. Christian beliefs as formulated by the church made life and death purposeful and intelligible.

Medieval thinkers drew a sharp distinction between a higher, spiritual world and a lower, material world. God, the creator of the universe and the source of moral values, dwelled in the higher celestial world, an abode of perfection. The universe was organized as a hierarchy with God at the summit and hell at the other extremity. Earth, composed of base matter, stood just above hell. By believing in Christ and adhering to God's commandments as taught by the church, people could overcome their sinful nature and ascend to God's world. Sinners, on the other hand, would descend to hell, a fearful place the existence of which medieval people never doubted.

Scholastic philosophy, which sought to demonstrate through reason the truth of Christian doctrines, and the Gothic cathedral, which seemed to soar from the material world to heaven, were two great expressions of the medieval mind. A third was *The Divine Comedy* of Dante Alighieri, the greatest literary figure of the Middle Ages.

Lothario dei Segni (Pope Innocent III)
ON THE MISERY OF THE HUMAN CONDITION

At the center of medieval belief was the image of a perfect God and a wretched and sinful human being. God had given Adam and Eve freedom to choose; rebellious and presumptuous, they had used their freedom to disobey God. In doing so, they made evil an intrinsic part of the human personality. But God, who had not stopped loving human beings, showed them the way out of sin. God became man and died so that human beings might be saved. Men and women were weak, egocentric, and sinful. With God's grace they could overcome their sinful nature and gain salvation; without grace they were utterly helpless. A classic expression of this pessimistic view of human nature was written in the late twelfth century by an Italian canon lawyer, Lothario dei Segni (c. 1160–1216), who was later elected pope in 1198, taking the name Innocent III. His *On the Misery of the Human Condition* was enormously popular and inspired numerous rhetorical writings on the same theme as late as the seventeenth century. Scattered excerpts follow.

• For sure man was formed out of earth, conceived in guilt, born to punishment. What he does is depraved and illicit, is shameful and improper, vain and unprofitable. He will become fuel for the eternal fires, food for worms, a mass of rottenness.

I shall try to make my explanation clearer and my treatment fuller. Man was formed of dust, slime, and ashes; what is even more vile, of the filthiest seed. He was conceived from the itch of the flesh, in the heat of passion and the stench of lust, and worse yet, with the stain of sin. He was born to toil, dread, and trouble; and more wretched still, was born only to die. He commits depraved acts by which he offends God, his neighbor, and himself; shameful acts by which he defiles his name, his person, and his conscience; and vain acts by which he ignores all things important, useful, and necessary. He will become fuel for those fires which are forever hot and burn forever bright; food for the worm which forever nibbles and digests; a mass of rottenness which will forever stink and reek.

• A bird is born to fly; man is born to toil. All his days are full of toil and hardship, and at night his mind has no rest.

• How much anxiety tortures mortals! They suffer all kinds of cares, are burdened with worry, tremble and shrink with fears and terrors, are weighted down with sorrow. Their nervousness makes them depressed, and their depression makes them nervous. Rich or poor, master or slave, married or single, good and bad alike—all suffer worldly torments and are tormented by worldly vexations.

• For sudden sorrow always follows worldly joy: what begins in gaiety ends in grief. Worldly happiness is besprinkled indeed with much bitterness.

• Then, suddenly, when least expected, misfortune strikes, a calamity befalls us, disease attacks; or death, which no one can escape, carries us off.

• Men strive especially for three things: riches, pleasures, and honors. Riches lead to immorality, pleasures to shame, and honors to vanity.

• But suppose a man is lifted up high, suppose he is raised to the very peak. At once his cares grow heavy, his worries mount up, he eats less and cannot sleep. And so nature is corrupted, his spirit weakened, his sleep disturbed, his appetite lost; his strength is diminished, he loses weight. Exhausting himself, he scarcely lives half a lifetime and ends his wretched days with a more wretched death.

• Almost the whole life of mortals is full of mortal sin, so that one can scarcely find anyone who does not go astray, does not return to his own vomit and rot in his own dung. Instead they "are glad when they have done evil and rejoice in most wicked things." "Being filled with all iniquity, malice, fornication, avarice, wickedness, full of envy, murders, contention, deceit, evil, being whisperers, detractors, hateful to God, irreverent, proud, haughty, plotters of evil, disobedient to parents, foolish, dissolute, without affection, without fidelity, without mercy." This world is full of such and worse; it abounds in heretics and schismatics [Christians who reject the authority of the pope], traitors and tyrants, simonists [buyers or sellers of spiritual offices or sacred items] and hypocrites; the ambitious and the covetous, robbers and brigands, violent men, extortionists, usurers, forgers; the impious and sacreligious, the betrayers and liars, the flatterers and deceivers; gossips, tricksters, gluttons, drunkards; adulterers, incestuous men, deviates, and the dirty-minded; the lazy, the careless, the vain, the prodigal, the impetuous, the irascible, the impatient and inconstant; poisoners, fortune tellers, perjurers, cursers; men who are presumptuous and arrogant, unbelieving and desperate; and finally those ensnared in all vices together.

THE VANITY OF THIS WORLD

The following poem, written in Latin by an unknown thirteenth-century author, expresses the medieval rejection of earthly pursuits and preoccupation with the world to come.

Why does the world war for glory that's vain?
All its successes wax only to wane;
Quickly its triumphs are frittered away,
Like vessels the potter casts out of frail clay.

As well trust to letters imprinted in ice
As trust the frail world with its treacherous
    device,
Its prizes a fraud and its values all wrong;
Who would put faith in its promise for long?

Rather in hardship's uncertain distress
Trust than in this world's unhappy success;
With dreams and with shadows it leads men
    astray,

A cheat in our work and a cheat at our play.
Where now is Samson's invincible arm,
And where is Jonathan's sweet-natured charm?
Once-famous Solomon, where now is he
Or the fair Absalom, so good to see?[1]

Whither is Caesar the great Emperor fled,
Or Croesus whose show on his table was
    spread?

---

[1]In the Old Testament, Samson was the warrior hero of the Israelites; Jonathan was the son of King Saul and the loving friend of David; Solomon was the king of Israel, famous for his wisdom; and Absalom was the most beloved son of David.

Cicero's eloquence now is in vain;[2]
Where's Aristotle's magnificent brain?

All those great noblemen, all those past days,
All kings' achievements and all prelates' praise,
All the world's princes in all their array—
In the flash of an eye comes the end of the play.

Short is the season of all earthly fame;
Man's shadow, man's pleasure, they both are the
    same,
And the prizes eternal he gives in exchange
For the pleasure that leads to a land that is
    strange.

---

[2]Croesus was a king of ancient Lydia renowned for his wealth. For Cicero, see page 74.

Food for the worms, dust and ashes, O why,
Bubble on water, be lifted so high?
Do good unto all men as long as ye may;
Ye know not your life will last after to-day.

This pride of the flesh which so dearly ye prize,
Like the flower of the grass (says the Scripture),
    it dies,
Or as the dry leaf which the wind whirls away,
Man's life is swept out from the light of the
    day.

Call not your own what one day ye may lose;
The world will take back all it gives you to use.
Let your hearts be in heaven, your thoughts in
    the skies;
Happy is he who the world can despise.

Dante Alighieri
THE DIVINE COMEDY

Dante Alighieri was a poet, political philosopher, soldier, and politician. Born in 1265 in Florence, Italy, he died in exile in 1321. His greatest work, *The Divine Comedy,* was composed of one hundred cantos (individual poems) and written not in Latin, the language of learning, but in the Tuscan Italian dialect of the common people. The poem is an elaborate allegory in which each character and event can be understood on two or more levels—for example, a literal description of the levels of hell and Dante's (and every Christian's) struggle to overcome a flawed human nature and to ward off worldly sin. Dante, representing all human beings, is guided through the afterworlds: hell (inferno), purgatory, and heaven (paradise). The Roman poet Virgil conducts him through hell and purgatory; Beatrice, his long-dead beloved, leads him through heaven to the point where he sees God in all his glory.

In the descent through the nine concentric circles of hell, Virgil describes the nature and significance of each region through which they pass. In each section of hell, sinners are punished in proportion to their earthly sins. Over the entrance gate to hell, Dante reads these words:

THROUGH ME YOU GO INTO THE CITY OF GRIEF,
THROUGH ME YOU GO INTO THE PAIN THAT
    IS ETERNAL,
THROUGH ME YOU GO AMONG PEOPLE LOST.

JUSTICE MOVED MY EXALTED CREATOR;
THE DIVINE POWER MADE ME,

THE SUPREME WISDOM, AND THE PRIMAL
    LOVE.

BEFORE ME ALL CREATED THINGS WERE ETERNAL,
AND ETERNAL I WILL LAST.
ABANDON EVERY HOPE, YOU WHO ENTER
    HERE.

Dante descends from the first circle to the second circle, where he finds the souls of those who had been guilty of sins of the flesh.

Now I begin to hear the sad notes of pain,
now I have come to where
loud cries beat upon my ears.

I have reached a place mute of all light
which roars like the sea in a tempest
when beaten by conflicting winds.

The infernal storm which never stops
drives the spirit in its blast;
whirling and beating, it torments them.

When they come in front of the landslide,
they utter laments, moans, and shrieks;
there they curse the Divine Power.

I learned that to such a torment
carnal sinners are condemned
who subject their reason to desire.

And, as starlings are borne by their wings
in the cold season, in a broad and dense flock,
so that blast carries the evil spirits.

Here, there, up, and down, it blows them;
no hope ever comforts them
of rest or even of less pain.

And as cranes go chanting their lays,
making a long line of themselves in the air,
so I saw coming, uttering laments,
shades borne by that strife of winds.

Finally the two poets reach the ninth and lowest circle, a frozen wasteland reserved for Satan and traitors.

". . . look ahead,"
my master [Virgil] said, "and try to
discern him."

As, when a thick mist covers the land
or when night darkens our hemisphere,
a windmill, turning, appears from afar,

so now I seemed to see such a structure;
then because of the wind, I drew back
behind my guide, for there was no other
    protection.

Already—and with fear I put it into verse—
I was where the shades are covered in the ice
and show through like bits of straw in glass.

Some were lying, some standing erect,
some on their heads, others on their feet,
still others like a bow bent face to toes.

When we had gone so far ahead
that my master was pleased to show me
the creature (Lucifer)[1] that once had been so fair,

he stood from in front of me, and made me stop,
saying, "Behold, Dis![2] Here is the place
where you must arm yourself with courage."

How faint and frozen I then became,
do not ask, Reader, for I do not write it down,
since all words would be inadequate.

I did not die and did not stay alive:
think now for yourself, if you have the wit,
how I became, without life or death.

The emperor of the dolorous [sorrowful] realm
from mid-breast protruded from the ice,
and I compare better in size

with the giants than they do with his arms.
Consider how big the whole must be,
proportioned as it is to such a part.

If he were once as handsome as he is ugly now,
and still presumed to lift his hand against his
    Maker,
all affliction must indeed come from him.

Oh, how great a marvel appeared to me
when I saw three faces on his head!
The one in front (hatred) was fiery red;

---

[1]Lucifer (light-bringer) was an archangel who led a rebellion against God and was cast into hell for punishment. He was identified with Satan.
[2]Dis was another name for Pluto or Hades, the god of the dead and ruler of the underworld.

the two others which were joined to it
over the middle of each shoulder
were fused together at the top.

The right one (impotence) seemed between
    white and yellow;
the left (ignorance) was in color like those
who come from where the Nile rises.

Under each two great wings spread
of a size fitting to such a bird;
I have never seen such sails on the sea.

They had no feathers, and seemed
like those of a bat, and they flapped,
so that three blasts came from them.

Thence all Cocytus[3] was frozen.
With six eyes he wept, and over his three chins
he let tears drip and bloody foam.

In each mouth he chewed a sinner with his teeth
in the manner of a hemp brake,[4]
so that he kept three in pain.

To the one in front the biting was nothing
compared to the scratching, for at times,
his back was stripped of skin.

"The soul up there with the greatest
    punishment,"
said my master, "is Judas Iscariot.[5] His head
is inside the mouth, and he kicks with his legs.

Of the other two whose heads are down,
the one hanging from the black face is Brutus;[6]
see how he twists and says nothing.

The other who seems so heavy set is Cassius.[7]
But night is rising again now,
and it is time to leave, for we have seen all."

---

[3]The Cocytus, a river in western Greece, was alleged to lead to the underworld.

[4]A hemp brake was a tool used to break up hemp fibers so that they could be made into rope.

[5]Judas Iscariot was the disciple who betrayed Jesus to the authorities.

[6]Brutus, a first-century Roman statesman, conspired to murder Julius Caesar.

[7]Cassius, another Roman statesman, was a co-conspirator with Brutus.

Dante and Beatrice make the ascent to the highest heaven, the Empyrean, which is located beyond Saturn, the last of the seven planets, beyond the circle of stars that encloses the planets, and above the Primum Mobile—the outermost sphere revolving around the earth. Here at the summit of the universe is a realm of pure light that radiates truth, goodness, and happiness, where God is found. Dante is permitted to look at God, but words cannot describe "the glory of Him who moves us all."

For my sight, growing pure, penetrated
ever deeper into the rays
of the Light [God] which is true in Itself.

From then on my vision was greater
than our speech which fails at such a sight,
just as memory is overcome by the excess.

As one who in a dream sees clearly,
and the feeling impressed remains afterward,
although nothing else comes back to mind,

so am I; for my vision disappears
almost wholly, and yet the sweetness
caused by it is still distilled within my heart.

Thus, in sunlight, the snow melts away;
thus the sayings of the Sibyl [a Roman
    oracle], written
on light leaves, were lost in the wind.

O Supreme Light that risest so high
above mortal concepts, give back to my mind
a little of what Thou didst appear,

and make my tongue strong,
so that it may leave to future peoples
at least a spark of Thy glory!

For, by returning to my memory
and by sounding a little in these verses
more of Thy victory will be conceived.

By the keenness of the living ray I endured
I believe I would have been dazed
if my eyes had turned away from it;

and I remember that I was bolder
because of that to sustain the view
until my sight *attained* the Infinite Worth
    [God].

O abundant grace through which I presumed
to fix my eyes on the Eternal Light
so long that I consumed my vision on it!

In its depths I saw contained, bound with
    love
in one volume, what is scattered
on leaves throughout the world—

substances (things) and accidents (qualities)
    and their modes
as if fused together in such a way
that what I speak of is a single light.

The universal form (principle) of this unity
I believe I saw, because more abundantly
in saying this I feel that I rejoice.

One moment obscures more for me than
    twenty-five centuries
have clouded since the adventure which made
    Neptune [the sea god]
wonder at the shadow of the Argo (the first
    ship).[8]

Thus my mind with rapt attention
gazed fixedly, motionless and attentive,
continually enflamed by its very gazing.

In that light we become such
that we can never consent
to turn from it for another sight,

inasmuch as the good which is the object
of the will is all in it, and outside of it
whatever is perfect there is defective.

Now my speech, even for what I remember,
will be shorter than that of an infant
who still bathes his tongue at the breast.

Not that more than a single semblance
was in the living light I gazed upon
(for it is always as it was before),

but in my vision which gained strength
as I looked the single appearance,
through a change in me, was transformed.

Within the deep and clear subsistence
of the great light three circles of three colors
and of one dimension (the Trinity) appeared
    to me,

and one (the Son) seemed reflected from the
    other (the Father)
as Iris by Iris,[9] and the third (the Holy
    Spirit)
seemed fire emanating equally from both.

O how poor our speech is and how feeble
for my conception! Compared to what I saw
to say its power is "little" is to say too
    much.

O Eternal Light (Father), abiding in Thyself
    alone,
Thou (Son) alone understanding Thyself, and
    Thou (Holy Spirit)
understood only by Thee, Thou dost love and
    smile!

The circle which appeared in Thee
as a reflected light (the Son)
when contemplated a while

seemed depicted with our image within
    itself
and of its own (the Circle's) color,
so that my eyes were wholly fixed on it.

Like the geometer who strives
to square the circle and cannot find
by thinking the principle he needs

I was at that new sight. I wanted to see
how the (human) image was conformed
to the (divine) circle and has a place in it,

---

[8]The *Argo*, in Greek legends, was the ship in which the hero Jason and his companions sailed in search of the Golden Fleece. A Greek poet, Apollonius of Rhodes, wrote an epic poem, the *Argonautica*, about it in the mid-third century B.C.

[9]Iris, goddess of the rainbow, was the messenger of the gods.

but my own wings were not enough for
   that—
except that my mind was illuminated by a
   flash
(of Grace) through which its wish was
   realized.

For the great imagination here power
   failed;
but already my desire and will (in harmony)
were turning like a wheel moved evenly

by the Love which turns the sun and the other
   stars.

REVIEW QUESTIONS

1. Compare Innocent III's view of the human condition with the classical view.
2. Why does the author of "The Vanity of This World" assert that "happy is he who the world can despise"?
3. How did Dante conceive the nature of evil and the moral ordering of specific sins?

CHAPTER 7

The Renaissance and Reformation

THE TRIUMPH OF GALATEA, Raphael, 1513. This fresco from the Palazzo della Farnesina in Rome exemplifies the Renaissance artist's elevation of the human form. The mythological subject is also humanistic in its evocation of the ancient Greek tradition. *(Giraudon/Art Resource, N.Y.)*

From the fifteenth through the seventeenth centuries, medieval attitudes and institutions broke down, and distinctly modern cultural, economic, and political forms emerged. For many historians, the Renaissance, which originated in the city-states of Italy, marks the starting point of the modern era. The Renaissance was characterized by a rebirth of interest in the humanist culture and outlook of ancient Greece and Rome. Although Renaissance individuals did not repudiate Christianity, they valued worldly activities and interests to a much greater degree than did the people of the Middle Ages, whose outlook was dominated by Christian otherworldliness. Renaissance individuals were fascinated by *this* world and by life's possibilities; they aspired to live a rich and creative life on earth and to fulfill themselves through artistic and literary activity.

During the High Middle Ages there had been a revival of Greek and Roman learning. Yet there were two important differences between the period called the Twelfth-Century Awakening and the Renaissance. First, many more ancient works were restored to circulation during the Renaissance than during the cultural revival of the Middle Ages. Second, medieval scholastics had tried to fit the ideas of the ancients into a Christian framework; they used Greek philosophy to explain Christian teachings. Renaissance scholars, on the other hand, valued ancient works for their own sake, believing that Greek and Roman authors could teach much about the art of living.

A distinguishing feature of the Renaissance period was the humanist movement, an educational and cultural program based on the study of ancient Greek and Latin literature. By studying the humanities—history, literature, rhetoric, moral and political philosophy—humanists aimed to revive the worldly spirit of the ancient Greeks and Romans, which they believed had been lost in the Middle Ages.

Humanists were thus fascinated by the writings of the ancients. From the works of Thucydides, Plato, Cicero, Seneca, and other ancient authors, humanists sought guidelines for living life well in this world and looked for stylistic models for their own literary efforts. To the humanists, the ancients had written brilliantly, in an incomparable literary style, on friendship, citizenship, love, bravery, statesmanship, beauty, excellence, and every other topic devoted to the enrichment of human life.

Like the humanist movement, Renaissance art also marked a break with medieval culture. The art of the Middle Ages had served a religious function; its purpose was to lift the mind to God. It depicted a spiritual universe in which the supernatural was the supreme reality. The Renaissance shattered the dominance of religion over art, shifting attention from heaven to the natural world and to the human being; Renaissance artists often dealt with religious themes, but they placed their subjects in a naturalistic setting.

The Renaissance began in the late fourteenth century in the northern Italian city-states, which had grown prosperous from the revival of trade in the Middle Ages. Italian merchants and bankers had the

176

wealth to acquire libraries and fine works of art and to support art, literature, and scholarship. Surrounded by reminders of ancient Rome—amphitheaters, monuments, and sculpture—the well-to-do took an interest in classical culture and thought. In the late fifteenth and the sixteenth centuries, Renaissance ideas spread to Germany, France, Spain, and England through books available in great numbers due to the invention of the printing press.

The reformation of the church in the sixteenth century was rooted in demands for spiritual renewal. The principal source of the reform spirit was a widespread popular yearning for a more genuine spirituality. It took many forms: the rise of new pious practices; greater interest in mystical experiences and in the study of the Bible; the development of communal ways for lay people to live and work following the apostles' example; and a heightened search for ways within secular society to imitate more perfectly the life of Christ—called the New Devotion movement. This deepening spirituality led many people to criticize the church for its worldliness and materialism—its involvement in European power politics and its pursuit of wealth and luxury.

In Germany, a spirit of discontent with social and economic conditions coincided with the demand for reform of the church and religious life. For several decades before Martin Luther's revolt against the papacy, the economic conditions of the knights, the peasants, and the lower-class urban workers had deteriorated. The knights' grievances included loss of their political power to the centralizing governments of the German princes and increasing restrictions on their customary feudal privileges. Peasants protested that lords had steadily withdrawn certain of their customary rights and had added burdens, increasing the lords' income and control over their estates. The knights and peasants were squeezed into an ever-worsening social and economic niche. In the cities, the lower-class artisans and laborers were similarly oppressed. Those in the urban upper classes, who controlled town governments, enhanced their own economic privileges at the expense of lower-class citizens. The church, which was a major landowner and active in commercial enterprises in the towns, played an important role in these conflicts. All these grievances formed the explosive background to Martin Luther's challenge to the authority of the church and the imperial government.

These divisions in the Christian church marked a turning point in European history and culture, ending forever the coherent worldview of medieval Christendom. The Reformation split the peoples of Europe into two broad political, intellectual, and spiritual camps: Protestant and Catholic. With the moral, political, and ideological power of the church significantly diminished, post-Reformation society was open to increasing secularization on all fronts. By ending the religious unity of the Middle Ages and weakening the Catholic Church, the Reformation contributed significantly to the rise of modernity.

1   The Humanists' Fascination with Antiquity

Humanists believed that a refined person must know the literature of Greece and Rome. They strove to imitate the style of the ancients, to speak and write as eloquently as the Greeks and Romans. Toward these ends, they sought to read, print, and restore to circulation every scrap of ancient literature that could still be found.

Petrarch
THE FATHER OF HUMANISM

During his lifetime, Francesco Petrarca, or Petrarch (1304–1374), had an astounding reputation as a poet and scholar. Often called the "father of humanism," he inspired other humanists through his love for classical learning; his criticism of medieval Latin as barbaric in contrast to the style of Cicero, Seneca, and other Romans; and his literary works based on classical models. Petrarch saw his own age as a restoration of classical brilliance after an interval of medieval darkness.

A distinctly modern element in Petrarch's thought is the subjective and individualistic character of his writing. In talking about himself and probing his own feelings, Petrarch demonstrates a self-consciousness characteristic of the modern outlook.

Like many other humanists, Petrarch remained devoted to Christianity: "When it comes to thinking or speaking of religion, that is, of the highest truth, of true happiness and eternal salvation," he declared, "I certainly am not a Ciceronian or a Platonist but a Christian." Petrarch was a forerunner of the Christian humanism best represented by Erasmus. Christian humanists combined an intense devotion to Christianity with a great love for classical literature, which they much preferred to the dull and turgid treatises written by scholastic philosopher-theologians. In the following passage, Petrarch criticizes his contemporaries for their ignorance of ancient writers and shows his commitment to classical learning.

. . . O inglorious age! that scorns antiquity, its mother, to whom it owes every noble art—that dares to declare itself not only equal but superior to the glorious past. I say nothing of the vulgar, the dregs of mankind, whose sayings and opinions may raise a laugh but hardly merit serious censure. . . .

. . . But what can be said in defense of men of education who ought not to be ignorant of antiquity and yet are plunged in this same darkness and delusion?

You see that I cannot speak of these matters without the greatest irritation and indignation. There has arisen of late a set of dialecticians [experts in logical argument], who are not only ignorant but demented. Like a black army of ants from some old rotten oak, they swarm forth from their hiding places and devastate the fields of sound learning. They condemn Plato and Aristotle, and laugh at Socrates and Pythagoras.[1] And, good God! under what silly and incompetent leaders these opinions are put forth. . . . What shall we say of men who scorn Marcus Tullius Cicero,[2] the bright sun of eloquence? Of those who scoff at Varro and Seneca,[3] and are scandalized at what they choose to call the crude, unfinished style of Livy and Sallust [Roman historians]? . . .

Such are the times, my friend, upon which we have fallen; such is the period in which we live and are growing old. Such are the critics of today, as I so often have occasion to lament and complain—men who are innocent of knowledge and virtue, and yet harbour the most exalted opinion of themselves. Not content with losing the words of the ancients, they must attack their genius and their ashes. They rejoice in their ignorance, as if what they did not know were not worth knowing. They give full rein to their license and conceit, and freely introduce among us new authors and outlandish teachings.

---

[1]The work of Aristotle (384–322 B.C.), a leading Greek philosopher, had an enormous influence among medieval and Renaissance scholars. A student of the philosopher Socrates, Plato (c. 427–347 B.C.) was one of the greatest philosophers of ancient Greece (see Chapter 2). His work grew to be extremely influential in the West during the Renaissance period, as new texts of his writings were discovered and translated into Latin and more Westerners could read the originals in Greek. Pythagoras (c. 582–c. 507 B.C.) was a Greek philosopher whose work influenced both Socrates and Plato.

[2]Cicero (106–43 B.C.) was a Roman statesman and rhetorician. His Latin style was especially admired and emulated during the Renaissance (see p. 74).

[3]Varro (116–27 B.C.) was a Roman scholar and historian. Seneca (4 B.C.–A.D. 65) was a Roman statesman, dramatist, and Stoic philosopher whose literary style was greatly admired during the Renaissance.

Leonardo Bruni
STUDY OF GREEK LITERATURE AND A HUMANIST EDUCATIONAL PROGRAM

Leonardo Bruni (1374–1444) was a Florentine humanist who extolled both intellectual study and active involvement in public affairs, an outlook called civic humanism. In the first reading from his *History of His Own Times in Italy*, Bruni expresses the humanist's love for ancient Greek literature and language.

In a treatise, *De Studiis et Literis* (On Learning and Literature), written around 1405 and addressed to the noble lady Baptista di Montefeltro (1383–1450), daughter of the Count of Urbino, Bruni outlines the basic course of studies that the humanists recommended as the best preparation for a life of wisdom and virtue. In addition to the study of Christian literature, Bruni encourages a wide familiarity with the best minds and stylists of ancient Greek and Latin cultures.

LOVE FOR GREEK LITERATURE

Then first came a knowledge of Greek, which had not been in use among us for seven hundred years. Chrysoloras the Byzantine,[1] a man of noble birth and well versed in Greek letters, brought Greek learning to us. When his country was invaded by the Turks, he came by sea, first to Venice. The report of him soon spread, and he was cordially invited and besought and promised a public stipend, to come to Florence and open his store of riches to the youth. I was then studying Civil Law,[2] but . . . I burned with love of academic studies, and had spent no little pains on dialectic and rhetoric. At the coming of Chrysoloras I was torn in mind, deeming it shameful to desert the law, and yet a crime to lose such a chance of studying Greek literature; and often with youthful impulse I would say to myself: "Thou, when it is permitted thee to gaze on Homer, Plato and Demosthenes,[3] and the other [Greek] poets, philosophers, orators, of whom such glorious things are spread abroad, and speak with them and be instructed in their admirable teaching, wilt thou desert and rob thyself? Wilt thou neglect this opportunity so divinely offered? For seven hundred years, no one in Italy has possessed Greek letters; and yet we confess that all knowledge is derived from them. How great advantage to your knowledge, enhancement of your fame, increase of your pleasure, will come from an understanding of this tongue? There are doctors of civil law everywhere; and the chance of learning will not fail thee. But if this one and only doctor of Greek letters disappears, no one can be found to teach thee." Overcome at length by these reasons, I gave myself to Chrysoloras, with such zeal to learn, that what through the wakeful day I gathered, I followed after in the night, even when asleep.

ON LEARNING AND LITERATURE

. . . The foundations of all true learning must be laid in the sound and thorough knowledge of Latin: which implies study marked by a broad spirit, accurate scholarship, and careful attention to details. Unless this solid basis be secured it is useless to attempt to rear an enduring edifice. Without it the great monuments of literature are unintelligible, and the art of composition impossible. To attain this essential knowledge we must never relax our careful attention to the grammar of the language, but perpetually confirm and extend our acquaintance with it until it is thoroughly our own. . . . To this end we must be supremely careful in our choice of authors, lest an inartistic and debased style infect our own writing and degrade our taste; which danger is best avoided by bringing a keen, critical sense to bear upon select works, observing the sense of each passage, the structure of the sentence, the force of every word down to the least important particle. In this way our reading reacts directly upon our style. . . .

But we must not forget that true distinction is to be gained by a wide and varied range of such studies as conduce to the profitable enjoyment of life, in which, however, we must observe due proportion in the attention and time we devote to them.

First amongst such studies I place History: a subject which must not on any account be neglected by one who aspires to true cultivation. For it is our duty to understand the origins of our own history and its development; and the achievements of Peoples and of Kings.

For the careful study of the past enlarges our foresight in contemporary affairs and affords to citizens and to monarchs lessons of incitement or warning in the ordering of public policy.

---

[1]Chrysoloras (c. 1355–1415), a Byzantine writer and teacher, introduced the study of Greek literature to the Italians, helping to open a new age of Western humanistic learning.

[2]Civil Law refers to the Roman law as codified by Emperor Justinian in the early sixth century A.D. and later studied in medieval law schools.

[3]Demosthenes (384–322 B.C.) was an Athenian statesman and orator whose oratorical style was much admired by Renaissance humanists.

From History, also, we draw our store of examples of moral precepts.

In the monuments of ancient literature which have come down to us History holds a position of great distinction. We specially prize such [Roman] authors as Livy, Sallust and Curtius;[4] and, perhaps even above these, Julius Caesar; the style of whose Commentaries, so elegant and so limpid, entitles them to our warm admiration. . . .

The great Orators of antiquity must by all means be included. Nowhere do we find the virtues more warmly extolled, the vices so fiercely decried. From them we may learn, also, how to express consolation, encouragement, dissuasion or advice. If the principles which orators set forth are portrayed for us by philosophers, it is from the former that we learn how to employ the emotions—such as indignation, or pity—in driving home their application in individual cases. Further, from oratory we derive our store of those elegant or striking turns of expression which are used with so much effect in literary compositions. Lastly, in oratory we find that wealth of vocabulary, that clear easy-flowing style, that verve and force, which are invaluable to us both in writing and in conversation.

I come now to Poetry and the Poets. . . . For we cannot point to any great mind of the past for whom the Poets had not a powerful attraction. Aristotle, in constantly quoting Homer, Hesiod, Pindar, Euripides and other [Greek] poets, proves that he knew their works hardly less intimately than those of the philosophers. Plato, also, frequently appeals to them, and in this way covers them with his approval. If we turn to Cicero, we find him not content with quoting Ennius, Accius,[5] and others of the Latins, but rendering poems from the Greek and employing them habitually. . . . Hence my view that familiarity with the great poets of

antiquity is essential to any claim to true education. For in their writings we find deep speculations upon Nature, and upon the Causes and Origins of things, which must carry weight with us both from their antiquity and from their authorship. Besides these, many important truths upon matters of daily life are suggested or illustrated. All this is expressed with such grace and dignity as demands our admiration. . . . To sum up what I have endeavoured to set forth. That high standard of education to which I referred at the outset is only to be reached by one who has seen many things and read much. Poet, Orator, Historian, and the rest, all must be studied, each must contribute a share. Our learning thus becomes full, ready, varied and elegant, available for action or for discourse in all subjects. But to enable us to make effectual use of what we know we must add to our knowledge the power of expression. These two sides of learning, indeed, should not be separated: they afford mutual aid and distinction. Proficiency in literary form, not accompanied by broad acquaintance with facts and truths, is a barren attainment; whilst information, however vast, which lacks all grace of expression, would seem to be put under a bushel or partly thrown away. Indeed, one may fairly ask what advantage it is to possess profound and varied learning if one cannot convey it in language worthy of the subject. Where, however, this double capacity exists—breadth of learning and grace of style—we allow the highest title to distinction and to abiding fame. If we review the great names of ancient [Greek and Roman] literature, Plato, Democritus, Aristotle, Theophrastus, Varro, Cicero, Seneca, Augustine, Jerome, Lactantius, we shall find it hard to say whether we admire more their attainments or their literary power.

---

[4]Q. Curtius Rufus, a Roman historian and rhetorician of the mid-first century A.D., composed a biography of Alexander the Great.
[5]Ennius (239–169 B.C.) wrote the first great Latin epic

poem, which was based on the legends of Rome's founding and its early history. Accius (c. 170–c. 90 B.C.), also a Roman, authored a history of Greek and Latin literature.

REVIEW QUESTIONS

1. What do historians mean by the term "Renaissance humanism"?
2. What made Petrarch aware that a renaissance, or rebirth, of classical learning was necessary in his time?
3. Why did Leonardo Bruni abandon his earlier course of studies to pursue the study of Greek literature?
4. What subjects made up the basic course of studies advocated by Bruni?

---

2 Human Dignity

In his short lifetime, Giovanni Pico della Mirandola (1463–1494) mastered Greek, Latin, Hebrew, and Arabic and aspired to synthesize the Hebrew, Greek, and Christian traditions. His most renowned work, *Oration on the Dignity of Man,* composed in 1486, has been called the humanist manifesto.

Pico della Mirandola
ORATION ON THE DIGNITY OF MAN

In the opening section of the *Oration,* Pico declares that unlike other creatures, human beings have not been assigned a fixed place in the universe. Our destiny is not determined by anything outside us. Rather, God has bestowed upon us a unique distinction: the liberty to determine the form and value our lives shall acquire. The notion that people have the power to shape their own lives is a key element in the emergence of the modern outlook.

I have read in the records of the Arabians, reverend Fathers, that Abdala the Saracen,[1] when questioned as to what on this stage of the world, as it were, could be seen most worthy of wonder, replied: "There is nothing to be seen more wonderful than man." In agreement with this opinion is the saying of Hermes Trismegistus: "A great miracle, Asclepius, is man."[2] But when I weighed the reason for these maxims, the many grounds for the excellence of human nature reported by many men failed to satisfy me—that

man is the intermediary between creatures, the intimate of the gods, the king of the lower beings, by the acuteness of his senses, by the discernment of his reason, and by the light of his intelligence the interpreter of nature, the interval between fixed eternity and fleeting time, and (as the Persians say) the bond, nay, rather, the marriage song of the world, on David's [biblical king] testimony but little lower than the angels. Admittedly great though these reasons be, they are not the principal grounds, that is, those which may rightfully claim for themselves the privilege of the highest admiration. For why should we not admire more the angels themselves and the blessed choirs of heaven? At last it seems to me I have come to understand why man is the most fortunate of creatures and con-

---

[1]Abdala the Saracen possibly refers to the eighth-century A.D. writer Abd-Allah Ibn al-Muqaffa.

[2]Ancient writings dealing with magic, alchemy, astrology, and occult philosophy were erroneously attributed to an assumed Egyptian priest, Hermes Trismegistus. Asclepius was a Greek god of healing.

sequently worthy of all admiration and what precisely is that rank which is his lot in the universal chain of Being—a rank to be envied not only by brutes but even by the stars and by minds beyond this world. It is a matter past faith and a wondrous one. Why should it not be? For it is on this very account that man is rightly called and judged a great miracle and a wonderful creature indeed. . . .

. . . God the Father, the supreme Architect, had already built this cosmic home we behold, the most sacred temple of His godhead, by the laws of His mysterious wisdom. The region above the heavens He had adorned with Intelligences, the heavenly spheres He had quickened with eternal souls, and the excrementary and filthy parts of the lower world He had filled with a multitude of animals of every kind. But, when the work was finished, the Craftsman kept wishing that there were someone to ponder the plan of so great a work, to love its beauty, and to wonder at its vastness. Therefore, when everything was done (as Moses and Timaeus[3] bear witness), He finally took thought concerning the creation of man. But there was not among His archetypes that from which He could fashion a new offspring, nor was there in His treasurehouses anything which He might bestow on His new son as an inheritance, nor was there in the seats of all the world a place where the latter might sit to contemplate the universe. All was now complete; all things had been assigned to the highest, the middle, and the lowest orders. But in its final creation it was not the part of the Father's power to fail as though exhausted. It was not the part of His wisdom to waver in a needful matter through poverty of counsel. It was not the part of His kindly love that he who was to praise God's divine generosity in regard to others should be compelled to condemn it in regard to himself.

At last the best of artisans [God] ordained that that creature to whom He had been able to give nothing proper to himself should have joint possession of whatever had been peculiar to each of the different kinds of being. He therefore took man as a creature of indeterminate nature and, assigning him a place in the middle of the world, addressed him thus: "Neither a fixed abode nor a form that is thine alone nor any function peculiar to thyself have we given thee, Adam, to the end that according to thy longing and according to thy judgment thou mayest have and possess what abode, what form, and what functions thou thyself shalt desire. The nature of all other beings is limited and constrained within the bounds of laws prescribed by Us. Thou, constrained by no limits, in accordance with thine own free will, in whose hand We have placed thee, shalt ordain for thyself the limits of thy nature. We have set thee at the world's center that thou mayest from thence more easily observe whatever is in the world. We have made thee neither of heaven nor of earth, neither mortal nor immortal, so that with freedom of choice and with honor, as though the maker and molder of thyself, thou mayest fashion thyself in whatever shape thou shalt prefer. Thou shalt have the power to degenerate into the lower forms of life, which are brutish. Thou shalt have the power, out of thy soul's judgment, to be reborn into the higher forms, which are divine."

O supreme generosity of God the Father, O highest and most marvelous felicity of man! To him it is granted to have whatever he chooses, to be whatever he wills. Beasts as soon as they are born (so says Lucilius)[4] bring with them from their mother's womb all they will ever possess. Spiritual beings [angels], either from the beginning or soon thereafter, become what they are to be for ever and ever. On man when he came into life the Father conferred the seeds of all kinds and the germs of every way of life. Whatever seeds each man cultivates will grow to maturity and bear in him their own fruit. If they be

---

[3]Timaeus, a Greek Pythagorean philosopher, was a central character in Plato's famous dialogue *Timaeus*.

[4]Lucilius, a first-century A.D. Roman poet and Stoic philosopher, was a close friend of Seneca, the philosopher-dramatist.

vegetative, he will be like a plant. If sensitive, he will become brutish. If rational, he will grow into a heavenly being. If intellectual, he will be an angel and the son of God. And if, happy in the lot of no created thing, he withdraws into the center of his own unity, his spirit, made one with God, in the solitary darkness of God, who is set above all things, shall surpass them all.

REVIEW QUESTIONS

1. According to Pico della Mirandola, what quality did humans alone possess? What did its possession allow them to do?
2. Compare Pico's view of the individual with that of Saint Augustine (see page 118) and Innocent III (see page 167).

---

3 Break with Medieval Political Theory

Turning away from the religious orientation of the Middle Ages, Renaissance thinkers discussed the human condition in secular terms and opened up possibilities for thinking about moral and political problems in new ways. Thus, Niccolò Machiavelli (1469–1527), a Florentine statesman and political theorist, broke with medieval political theory. Medieval political thinkers held that the ruler derived power from God and had a religious obligation to rule in accordance with God's precepts. Machiavelli, though, ascribed no divine origin to kingship, nor did he attribute events to the mysterious will of God; and he explicitly rejected the principle that kings should adhere to Christian moral teachings. For Machiavelli, the state was a purely human creation. Successful kings or princes, he asserted, should be concerned only with preserving and strengthening the state's power and must ignore questions of good and evil, morality and immorality. Machiavelli did not assert that religion was supernatural in origin and rejected the prevailing belief that Christian morality should guide political life. For him, religion's value derived from other factors: a ruler could utilize religion to unite his subjects and to foster obedience to law.

Niccolò Machiavelli
THE PRINCE

In contrast to medieval thinkers, Machiavelli did not seek to construct an ideal Christian community but to discover how politics was *really* conducted. In *The Prince,* written in 1513 and published posthumously in 1532, he studied politics in the cold light of reason, as the following passage illustrates.

It now remains to be seen what are the methods and rules for a prince as regards his subjects and friends. And as I know that many have written of this, I fear that my writing about it may be deemed presumptuous, differing as I do, especially in this matter, from the opinions of others. But my intention being to write something of use to those who understand, it appears to me more proper to go to the real truth of the matter than to its imagination; and many have imagined republics and principalities which have never been seen or known to exist in reality; for how we live is so far removed from how we ought to live, that he who abandons what is done for what ought to be done, will rather learn to bring about his own ruin than his preservation.

Machiavelli removed ethics from political thinking. A successful ruler, he contended, is indifferent to moral and religious considerations. But will not the prince be punished on the Day of Judgment for violating Christian teachings? In startling contrast to medieval theorists, Machiavelli simply ignored the question. The action of a prince, he said, should be governed solely by necessity.

A man who wishes to make a profession of goodness in everything must necessarily come to grief among so many who are not good. Therefore it is necessary for a prince, who wishes to maintain himself, to learn how not to be good, and to use this knowledge and not use it, according to the necessity of the case.

Leaving on one side, then, those things which concern only an imaginary prince, and speaking of those that are real, I state that all men, and especially princes, who are placed at a greater height, are reputed for certain qualities which bring them either praise or blame. Thus one is considered liberal, another . . . miserly; . . . one a free giver, another rapacious; one cruel, another merciful; one a breaker of his word, another trustworthy; one effeminate and pusillanimous, another fierce and high-spirited; one humane, another haughty; one lascivious, another chaste; one frank, another astute; one hard, another easy; one serious, another frivolous; one religious, another an unbeliever, and so on. I know that every one will admit that it would be highly praiseworthy in a prince to possess all the above-named qualities that are reputed good, but as they cannot all be possessed or observed, human conditions not permitting of it, it is necessary that he should be prudent

enough to avoid the scandal of those vices which would lose him the state, and guard himself if possible against those which will not lose it [for] him, but if not able to, he can indulge them with less scruple. And yet he must not mind incurring the scandal of those vices, without which it would be difficult to save the state, for if one considers well, it will be found that some things which seem virtues would, if followed, lead to one's ruin, and some others which appear vices result in one's greater security and wellbeing. . . .

. . . I say that every prince must desire to be considered merciful and not cruel. He must, however, take care not to misuse this mercifulness. Cesare Borgia was considered cruel, but his cruelty had brought order to the Romagna,[1] united it, and reduced it to peace and fealty. If this is considered well, it will be seen that he was really much more merciful than the Florentine people, who, to avoid the name of cruelty, allowed Pistoia[2] to be destroyed. A prince, therefore, must not mind incurring the charge of cruelty for the purpose of keeping his subjects united and faithful; for, with a very few examples, he will be more merciful than those who, from excess of tenderness, allow disorders to arise, from whence spring bloodshed and rapine; for these as a rule injure the whole community, while the executions carried out by the prince injure only individuals. . . .

Machiavelli's rigorous investigation of politics led him to view human nature from the standpoint of its limitations and imperfections. The astute prince, he said, recognizes that human beings are by nature selfish, cowardly, and dishonest, and regulates his political strategy accordingly.

---

[1]Cesare Borgia (c. 1476–1507) was the bastard son of Rodrigo Borgia, then a Spanish cardinal, and later Pope Alexander VI (1492–1503). With his father's aid he attempted to carve out for himself an independent duchy in north-central Italy, with Romagna as its heart. Through cruelty, violence, and treachery, he succeeded at first in his ambition, but ultimately his principality collapsed. Romagna was eventually incorporated into the Papal State under Pope Julius II (1503–1513).

[2]Pistoia, a small Italian city in Tuscany, came under the control of Florence in the fourteenth century.

From this arises the question whether it is better to be loved more than feared, or feared more than loved. The reply is, that one ought to be both feared and loved, but as it is difficult for the two to go together, it is much safer to be feared than loved, if one of the two has to be wanting. For it may be said of men in general that they are ungrateful, voluble, dissemblers, anxious to avoid danger, and covetous of gain; as long as you benefit them, they are entirely yours; they offer you their blood, their goods, their life, and their children, as I have before said, when the necessity is remote; but when it approaches, they revolt. And the prince who has relied solely on their words, without making other preparations, is ruined; for the friendship which is gained by purchase and not through grandeur and nobility of spirit is bought but not secured, and at a pinch is not to be expended in your service. And men have less scruple in offending one who makes himself loved than one who makes himself feared; for love is held by a chain of obligation which, men being selfish, is broken whenever it serves their purpose; but fear is maintained by a dread of punishment which never fails.

Still, a prince should make himself feared in such a way that if he does not gain love, he at any rate avoids hatred; for fear and the absence of hatred may well go together, and will be always attained by one who abstains from interfering with the property of his citizens and subjects or with their women. And when he is obliged to take the life of any one, let him do so when there is a proper justification and manifest reason for it; but above all he must abstain from taking the property of others, for men forget more easily the death of their father than the loss of their patrimony [inheritance]. Then also pretexts for seizing property are never wanting, and one who begins to live by rapine will always find some reason for taking the goods of others, whereas causes for taking life are rarer and more fleeting.

But when the prince is with his army and has a large number of soldiers under his control, then it is extremely necessary that he should not mind being thought cruel; for without this reputation he could not keep an army united or disposed to any duty. Among the noteworthy actions of Hannibal[3] is numbered this, that although he had an enormous army, composed of men of all nations and fighting in foreign countries, there never arose any dissension either among them or against the prince, either in good fortune or in bad. This could not be due to anything but his inhuman cruelty, which together with his infinite other virtues, made him always venerated and terrible in the sight of his soldiers, and without it his other virtues would not have sufficed to produce that effect. Thoughtless writers admire on the one hand his actions, and on the other blame the principal cause of them. . . .

Again in marked contrast to the teachings of Christian (and ancient) moralists, Machiavelli said that the successful prince will use any means to achieve and sustain political power. If the end is desirable, all means are justified.

How laudable it is for a prince to keep good faith and live with integrity, and not with astuteness, every one knows. Still the experience of our times shows those princes to have done great things who have had little regard for good faith, and have been able by astuteness to confuse men's brains, and who have ultimately overcome those who have made loyalty their foundation.

You must know, then, that there are two methods of fighting, the one by law, the other by force: the first method is that of men, the second of beasts; but as the first method is often insufficient, one must have recourse to the second. It is therefore necessary for a prince to know well how to use both the beast and the man. . . .

---

[3]Hannibal (247–182 B.C.) was a brilliant Carthaginian general whose military victories almost destroyed Roman power. He was finally defeated at the battle of Zama in 202 B.C. by the Roman general Scipio Africanus.

A prince being thus obliged to know well how to act as a beast must imitate the fox and the lion, for the lion cannot protect himself from traps, and the fox cannot defend himself from wolves. One must therefore be a fox to recognise traps, and a lion to frighten wolves. Those that wish to be only lions do not understand this. Therefore, a prudent ruler ought not to keep faith when by so doing it would be against his interest, and when the reasons which made him bind himself no longer exist. If men were all good, this precept would not be a good one; but as they are bad, and would not observe their faith with you, so you are not bound to keep faith with them. Nor have legitimate grounds ever failed a prince who wished to show [plausible] excuse for the non-fulfilment of his promise. Of this one could furnish an infinite number of modern examples, and show how many times peace has been broken, and how many promises rendered worthless, by the faithlessness of princes, and those that have been best able to imitate the fox have succeeded best. But it is necessary to be able to disguise this character well, and to be a great feigner and dissembler; and men are so simple and so ready to obey present necessities, that one who deceives will always find those who allow themselves to be deceived. . . .

. . . Thus it is well to seem merciful, faithful, humane, sincere, religious, and also to be so; but you must have the mind so disposed that when it is needful to be otherwise you may be able to change to the opposite qualities. And it must be understood that a prince, and especially a new prince, cannot observe all those things which are considered good in men, being often obliged, in order to maintain the state, to act against faith, against charity, against humanity, and against religion. And, therefore, he must have a mind disposed to adapt itself according to the wind, and as the variations of fortune dictate, and, as I said before, not deviate from what is good, if possible, but be able to do evil if constrained.

A prince must take great care that nothing goes out of his mouth which is not full of the above-named five qualities, and, to see and hear him, he should seem to be all mercy, faith, integrity, humanity, and religion. And nothing is more necessary than to seem to have this last quality, for men in general judge more by the eyes than by the hands, for every one can see, but very few have to feel. Everybody sees what you appear to be, few feel what you are, and those few will not dare to oppose themselves to the many, who have the majesty of the state to defend them; and in the actions of men, and especially of princes, from which there is no appeal, the end justifies the means. Let a prince therefore aim at conquering and maintaining the state, and the means will always be judged honourable and praised by every one, for the vulgar is always taken by appearances and the issue of the event; and the world consists only of the vulgar, and the few who are not vulgar are isolated when the many have a rallying point in the prince. A certain prince of the present time, whom it is well not to name, never does anything but preach peace and good faith, but he is really a great enemy to both, and either of them, had he observed them, would have lost him state or reputation on many occasions.

REVIEW QUESTIONS

1. In what ways was Niccolò Machiavelli's advice to princes a break from the teachings of medieval political and moral philosophers?
2. How does Machiavelli's image of human nature compare with that of Pico della Mirandola, of Pope Gregory VII (see page 144), and of Innocent III (see page 167).
3. Would Machiavelli's political advice help or hurt a politician in a modern democratic society?

4   The Ideal Gentleman

By the early sixteenth century, the era of the republics had come to an end in Italy, and the princely courts were the new social and political ideal. At the same time that Machiavelli was defining the new *political* ideal in his *Prince,* Baldassare Castiglione (1478–1529) was describing the new *social* ideal—the Renaissance courtier who served princes—in his *Book of the Courtier* (1528). Born into an illustrious Lombard family near Mantua, Castiglione received a humanist education in Latin and Greek, and had a distinguished career serving in the courts of Italian dukes and Charles V in Spain. Castiglione's handbook became one of the most influential books of the day, providing instruction to aristocrats and non-aristocrats alike about how to be the perfect courtier or court lady. By the end of the sixteenth century, it had been translated into every major European language, making Castiglione the arbiter of aristocratic manners throughout Europe.

Like Greco-Roman moralists, Castiglione sought to overcome brutish elements in human nature and to shape a higher type of individual through reason. To structure the self artistically, to live life with verve and style, and to achieve a personal dignity were the humanist values that Castiglione's work spread beyond Italy.

Baldassare Castiglione
THE BOOK OF THE COURTIER

Castiglione chose the court of Urbino as the setting for his *Book of the Courtier,* which he wrote in the form of a conversation among the courtiers and ladies of the court. The participants—such as Guidobaldo, Duke of Urbino; the Duchess, Elisabetta Gonzaga; Count Ludovico da Canossa; and Cardinal Pietro Bembo— were all real people who in Castiglione's day had actual conversations at the court. In the first two books of *The Courtier,* Castiglione describes the ideal courtier as an example of the Renaissance "universal man," a well-rounded person with breadth of interest and versatility of accomplishment. For Castiglione, the courtier is a person of noble birth who is skilled in weaponry, an expert horseman, and adept at all sorts of games. And not only should the courtier be physically gifted; he should be well educated. In the following passages, Count Ludovico declares that he should be learned in the humanities, the new educational curriculum of the Renaissance humanists. Moreover, in the spirit of the "universal man," he should be a musician, and he should display a knowledge of drawing and painting.

"I would have him more than passably learned in letters, at least in those studies which we call the humanities. Let him be conversant not only with the Latin language, but with Greek as well, because of the abundance and variety of things that are so divinely written therein. Let him be versed in the poets, as well as in the orators and historians, and let him be practiced also in writing verse and prose, especially in our own vernacular; for, besides the personal satisfaction he will take in this, in this way he will never want for pleasant entertainment with the ladies, who are usually fond of such things. And if, because of other occupations or lack of study, he does not attain to such a perfection that his writings should merit great praise, let him take care to keep them under cover so that others will not laugh at him, and let him show them only to a friend who can be trusted; because at least they will be of profit to him in that, through such exercise, he will be capable of judging the writing of others. For it very rarely happens that a man who is unpracticed in writing, however learned he may be, can ever wholly understand the toils and industry of writers, or taste the sweetness and excellence of styles, and those intrinsic niceties that are often found in the ancients. . . .

"Gentlemen, you must know that I am not satisfied with our Courtier unless he also be a musician, and unless, besides understanding and being able to read music, he can play various instruments. For, if we rightly consider, no rest from toil and no medicine for ailing spirits can be found more decorous or praiseworthy in time of leisure than this; and especially in courts where, besides the release from vexations which music gives to all, many things are done to please the ladies, whose tender and delicate spirits are readily penetrated with harmony and filled with sweetness. Hence, it is no wonder that in both ancient and modern times they have always been particularly fond of musicians, finding the music a most welcome food for the spirit." . . .

Then the Count said: "Before we enter upon that subject, I would discuss another matter which I consider to be of great importance and which I think must therefore, in no way be neglected by our Courtier: and this is a knowledge of how to draw and an acquaintance with the art of painting itself."

REVIEW QUESTIONS

1. How does Castiglione's ideal gentleman reflect the spirit of Renaissance humanism and art?
2. Compare and contrast Castiglione's ideal courtier with what would be regarded as an ideal type during the Middle Ages.

---

5 The Lutheran Reformation

The reformation of the Western Christian church in the sixteenth century was precipitated by Martin Luther (1483–1546). A pious German Augustinian monk and theologian, Luther had no intention of founding a new church or overthrowing the political and ecclesiastical order of late medieval Europe. He was educated in the tradition of the New Devotion, which called for spiritual renewal, and as a theology professor at the university in Wittenberg, Germany, he opposed rationalistic, scholastic theology. Sympathetic at first to the ideas of Christian humanists like Erasmus, Luther too sought a reform of morals and an end to abusive practices within the church. But a visit to the papal court in Rome in 1510 left him profoundly shocked at its worldliness and disillusioned with the papacy's role in the church's governance.

Martin Luther
ON PAPAL POWER, JUSTIFICATION BY FAITH, THE INTERPRETATION OF THE BIBLE, AND THE NATURE OF THE CLERGY

To finance the rebuilding of the church of St. Peter in Rome, the papacy in 1515 offered indulgences to those who gave alms for this pious work. An indulgence was a mitigation or remission of the penance imposed by a priest in absolving a penitent who confessed a sin and indicated remorse. Indulgences were granted by papal decrees for those who agreed to perform some act of charity, almsgiving, prayer, pilgrimage, or other pious work. Some preachers of this particular papal indulgence deceived people into believing that a "purchase" of this indulgence would win them, or even the dead, a secure place in heaven.

In 1517, Luther denounced the abuses connected with the preaching of papal indulgences. The quarrel led quickly to other and more profound theological issues. His opponents defended the use of indulgences on the basis of papal authority, shifting the debate to questions about the nature of papal power within the church. Luther responded with a vigorous attack on the whole system of papal governance. The principal points of his criticism were set out in his *Address to the Christian Nobility of the German Nation Concerning the Reform of the Christian Estate,* published in August 1520. In the first excerpt that follows, Luther argued that the papacy was blocking any reform of the church and appealed to the nobility of Germany to intervene by summoning a "free council" to reform the church.

A central point of contention between Luther and Catholic critics was his theological teaching on justification (salvation) by faith and on the role of good works in the scheme of salvation. Luther had suffered anguish about his unworthiness before God. Then, during a mystical experience, Luther suddenly perceived that his salvation came not because of his good works but as a free gift from God due to Luther's faith in Jesus Christ.

Thus, while never denying that a Christian was obliged to perform good works, Luther argued that such pious acts were not helpful in achieving salvation. His claim that salvation or justification was attained through faith in Jesus Christ as Lord and Savior, and through that act of faith alone, became the rallying point of the Protestant reformers.

The Catholic position, not authoritatively clarified until the Council of Trent (1545–1563), argued that justification came not only through faith, but through hope and love as well, obeying God's commandments and doing good works. In *The Freedom of a Christian,* published in 1520, Luther outlined his teaching on justification by faith and on the inefficacy of good works; the second excerpt is from this work.

Another dispute between Luther and papal theologians was the question of interpretation of the Bible. In the medieval church, the final authority in any dispute over the meaning of Scriptural texts or church doctrine was ordinarily the pope alone, speaking as supreme head of the church or in concert with the bishops in an ecumenical council. The doctrine of papal infallibility (that the pope could not err in teaching matters of faith and morals) was already well known, but belief in this doctrine had not been formally required. Luther argued that the literal text of Scripture was alone the foundation of Christian truth, not the teaching of popes or councils. Moreover, Luther said that all believers were priests, and the clergy did not hold any power beyond that of the laity; therefore the special privileges of the clergy were unjustified. The third excerpt contains Luther's views on the interpretation of Scripture and the nature of priestly offices.

ON PAPAL POWER

The Romanists [traditional Catholics loyal to the papacy] have very cleverly built three walls around themselves. Hitherto they have protected themselves by these walls in such a way that no one has been able to reform them. As a result, the whole of Christendom has fallen abominably.

In the first place, when pressed by the temporal power they have made decrees and declared that the temporal power had no jurisdiction over them, but that, on the contrary, the spiritual power is above the temporal. In the second place, when the attempt is made to reprove them with the Scriptures, they raise the objection that only the pope may interpret the Scriptures. In the third place, if threatened with a council, their story is that no one may summon a council but the pope.

In this way they have cunningly stolen our three rods from us, that they may go unpunished. They have [settled] themselves within the safe stronghold of these three walls so that they can practice all the knavery and wickedness which we see today. Even when they have been compelled to hold a council they have weakened its power in advance by putting the princes under oath to let them remain as they were. In addition, they have given the pope full authority over all decisions of a council, so that it is all the same whether there are many councils or no councils. They only deceive us with puppet shows and sham fights. They fear terribly for their skin in a really free council! They have so intimidated kings and princes with this technique that they believe it would be an offense against God not to be obedient to the Romanists in all their knavish and ghoulish deceits. . . .

The Romanists have no basis in Scripture for their claim that the pope alone has the right to call or confirm a council. This is just their own ruling, and it is only valid as long as it is not harmful to Christendom or contrary to the laws of God. Now when the pope deserves punishment, this ruling no longer obtains, for not to punish him by authority of a council is harmful to Christendom. . . .

Therefore, when necessity demands it, and the pope is an offense to Christendom, the first man who is able should, as a true member of the whole body, do what he can to bring about a truly free council. No one can do this so well as the temporal authorities, especially since they are also fellow-Christians, fellow-priests, fellow-members of the spiritual estate, fellow-lords over all things. Whenever it is necessary or profitable they ought to exercise the office and work which they have received from God over everyone.

JUSTIFICATION BY FAITH

You may ask, "What then is the Word of God, and how shall it be used, since there are so many words of God?" I answer: The Apostle explains this in Romans 1. The Word is the gospel of God concerning his Son, who was made flesh, suffered, rose from the dead, and was glorified through the Spirit who sanctifies. To preach Christ means to feed the soul, make it righteous, set it free, and save it, provided it believes the preaching. Faith alone is the saving and efficacious use of the Word of God, according to Rom. 10(:9): "If you confess with your lips that Jesus is Lord and believe in your heart that God raised him from the dead, you will be saved." Furthermore, "Christ is the end of the law, that every one who has faith may be justified" (Rom. 10:4). Again, in Rom. 1(:17), "He who through faith is righteous shall live." The Word of God cannot be received and cherished by any works whatever but only by faith. Therefore it is clear that, as the soul needs only the Word of God for its life and righteousness, so it is justified by faith alone and not any works; for if it could be justified by anything else, it would not need the Word, and consequently it would not need faith.

This faith cannot exist in connection with works—that is to say, if you at the same time claim to be justified by works, whatever their character—for that would be the same as "limping with two different opinions" (I Kings 18:21), as worshiping Baal and kissing one's own hand (Job 31:27–28), which, as Job says, is a very great iniquity. Therefore the moment you begin to have faith you learn that all things in you are altogether blameworthy, sinful, and damnable, as the Apostle says in Rom. 3(:23), "Since all have sinned and fall short of the glory of God," and, "None is righteous, no, not one: . . . all have turned aside, together they have gone wrong" (Rom. 3:10–12). When you have learned this you will know that you need Christ, who suffered and rose again for you so that, if you believe in him, you may through this faith become a new man in so far as your sins are forgiven and you are justified by the merits of another, namely, of Christ alone.

Since, therefore, this faith can rule only in the inner man, as Rom. 10(:10) says, "For man believes with his heart and so is justified," and since faith alone justifies, it is clear that the inner man cannot be justified, freed, or saved by any outer work or action at all, and that these works, whatever their character, have nothing

to do with this inner man. On the other hand, only ungodliness and unbelief of heart, and no outer work, make him guilty and a damnable servant of sin. Wherefore it ought to be the first concern of every Christian to lay aside all confidence in works and increasingly to strengthen faith alone and through faith to grow in the knowledge, not of works, but of Christ Jesus, who suffered and rose for him, as Peter teaches in the last chapter of his first Epistle (1 Pet. 5:10). No other work makes a Christian. . . .

Our faith in Christ does not free us from works but from false opinions concerning works, that is, from the foolish presumption that justification is acquired by works. Faith redeems, corrects, and preserves our consciences so that we know that righteousness does not consist in works, although works neither can nor ought to be wanting; just as we cannot be without food and drink and all the works of this mortal body, yet our righteousness is not in them, but in faith; and yet those works of the body are not to be despised or neglected on that account. In this world we are bound by the needs of our bodily life, but we are not righteous because of them. "My kingship is not of this world" (John 18:36), says Christ. He does not, however, say, "My kingship is not here, that is, in this world." And Paul says, "Though we live in the world we are not carrying on a worldly war" (II Cor. 10:3), and in Gal. 2(:20), "The life I now live in the flesh I live by faith in the Son of God." Thus what we do, live, and are in works and ceremonies, we do because of the necessities of this life and of the effort to rule our body. Nevertheless we are righteous, not in these, but in the faith of the Son of God.

THE INTERPRETATION OF THE BIBLE AND THE NATURE OF THE CLERGY

They (the Roman Catholic Popes) want to be the only masters of Scriptures. . . . They assume sole authority for themselves and would persuade us with insolent juggling of words that the Pope, whether he be bad or good, cannot err in matters of faith. . . .

. . . They cannot produce a letter to prove that the interpretation of Scripture . . . belongs to the Pope alone. They themselves have usurped this power . . . and though they allege that this power was conferred on Peter when the keys were given to him, it is plain enough that the keys were not given to Peter alone but to the entire body of Christians (Matt. 16:19; 18:18). . . .

. . . Every baptized Christian is a priest already, not by appointment or ordination from the Pope or any other man, but because Christ Himself has begotten him as a priest . . . in baptism. . . .

The Pope has usurped the term "priest" for his anointed and tonsured hordes [clergy and monks]. By this means they have separated themselves from the ordinary Christians and have called themselves uniquely the "clergy of God," God's heritage and chosen people who must help other Christians by their sacrifice and worship. . . . Therefore the Pope argues that he alone has the right and power to ordain and do what he will. . . .

[But] the preaching office is no more than a public service which happens to be conferred on someone by the entire congregation all the members of which are priests. . . .

. . . The fact that a pope or bishop anoints, makes tonsures, ordains, consecrates [makes holy], and prescribes garb different from those of the laity . . . nevermore makes a Christian and a spiritual man. Accordingly, through baptism all of us are consecrated to the priesthood, as St. Peter says . . . (I Peter 2:9).

To make it still clearer, if a small group of pious Christian laymen were taken captive and settled in a wilderness and had among them no priest consecrated by a bishop, if they were to agree to choose one from their midst, married or unmarried, and were to charge him with the office of baptizing, saying Mass, absolving [forgiving of sins], and preaching, such a man would be as truly a priest as he would if all bishops and popes had consecrated him.

Ulrich von Hutten
RESENTMENT OF ROME

Many Germans were drawn to Luther's message, for it signified a return to the spiritual purity of the first Christians, which had been undermined by a wealthy and corrupt church. Most historians agree that religious considerations—people's yearning for greater holiness and communion with God—were the principal reasons Luther attracted a following. But economic and political factors also drew Germans to him. The urban middle class, in particular, greatly resented the draining of money from German lands in order to provide a luxurious lifestyle for the Roman upper clergy. In a letter written in 1520 to the Elector Frederick of Saxony, Ulrich von Hutten (1488–1523), a distinguished humanist and supporter of Luther, angrily denounced the Roman church for plundering German lands. Hutten's words, excerpted below, also reveal an emerging sense of German national feeling.

We see that there is no gold and almost no silver in our German land. What little may perhaps be left is drawn away daily by the new schemes invented by the council of the most holy members of the Roman curia. What is thus squeezed out of us is put to the most shameful uses. Would you know, dear Germans, what employment I have myself seen that they make at Rome of our money? It does not lie idle! Leo the Tenth gives a part to nephews and relatives (these are so numerous that there is a proverb at Rome, "As thick as Leo's relations"). A portion is consumed by so many most reverend cardinals (of which the holy father created no less than one and thirty in a single day), as well as to support innumerable [auditors, personal secretaries, palace managers, and other high officials] forming the élite of the great head church. These in turn draw after them at untold expense copyists, beadles, messengers, servants, scullions [kitchen help], mule drivers, grooms and an innumerable army of prostitutes and of the most degraded followers. They maintain dogs, horses, monkeys, long-tailed apes and many more such creatures for their pleasure. They construct houses all of marble. They have precious stones, are clothed in purple and fine linen and dine sumptuously, frivolously indulging themselves in every species of luxury. In short, a vast number of the worst of men are supported in Rome in idle indulgence by means of our money. . . . Does not Your Grace perceive how many bold robbers, how many cunning hypocrites commit repeatedly the greatest crimes under the monk's cowl, and how many crafty hawks feign the simplicity of doves, and how many ravening wolves simulate the innocence of lambs? And although there be a few truly pious among them, even they cling to superstition and pervert the law of life which Christ laid down for us.

Now, if all these who devastate Germany and continue to devour everything might once be driven out, and an end made of their unbridled plundering, swindling and deception, with which the Romans have overwhelmed us, we should again have gold and silver in sufficient quantities and should be able to keep it. And then this money, in such supply and value as it may be present, might be put to better uses, for example: to put on foot great armaments and extend the boundaries of the Empire; also that the Turks may be conquered, if this seems desirable; that many who, because of poverty, steal and rob, may honestly earn their living once more, and that those who otherwise must starve may receive from the state contributions to mitigate their need; that scholars may be helped and the study of the arts and sciences, and of good literature advanced; above all that every virtue may receive its reward; want to be relieved at home; indolence banished and deceit killed.

REVIEW QUESTIONS

1. Why did Martin Luther see the papacy as the crucial block to any meaningful reform of the church?
2. How did Luther's teaching undermine the power of the clergy and traditional forms of piety?
3. According to Ulrich von Hutten, why were Germans distressed with the Roman church?

---

6   The Calvinist Reformation

In the first decade of the Lutheran movement, Protestant reform had not spread significantly outside Germany due to suppression by the royal governments in France, Spain, and England. But in 1534 a French clergyman, John Calvin (1509–1564), resigned his church offices and fled to Basel, a Swiss city that had accepted Protestant reforms. There he composed a summary of the new Protestant theology, *The Institutes of the Christian Religion,* which was to be revised four times before his death. Written in the elegant Latin style favored by humanists, the work was translated into French and soon became the principal theological text for French, Scottish, Dutch, and English Protestant reformers. Calvin himself settled in Geneva, Switzerland, where his influence dominated the civil and religious life of the townspeople. From Geneva, Calvin carried on an active mission, spreading his reformed faith throughout his native France and elsewhere.

In 1536, the newly Protestant-controlled government of Geneva asked Calvin to draw up a public confession of the reformed faith, a catechism, and rules for liturgical worship. But the Council of Geneva's demand that all citizens be forced to subscribe to the new confession resulted in a change of government at the elections in 1538. Calvin withdrew to Basel. By 1541, the political situation had changed again; Calvin was recalled, and his recommendations for a new government for the church were put into law. He remained the spiritual leader of Geneva and of many reformed Protestants elsewhere until his death. Calvinism was especially influential in England and Scotland, giving rise to the Puritan movement in seventeenth-century England and the Presbyterian churches in Scotland and Ireland. Both of these religious traditions exercised great influence on the settlers of the English colonies in North America.

John Calvin
THE INSTITUTES
ECCLESIASTICAL ORDINANCES, AND THE OBEDIENCE OWED RULERS

One doctrine that assumed greater and greater importance in the four separate revised editions of Calvin's *Institutes* was predestination: the belief that each person's salvation or damnation was already decided before birth. This doctrine raised a question about whether Christ offered salvation for all human beings or only for the elect—a chosen few who were predestined to be saved by God's sovereign will. Some argued that the latter interpretation, one strongly articulated by Saint Augustine, implied that God was a tyrant who created human beings to be damned and that they were not free to acquire salvation by faith. In effect, salvation and damnation were foreordained. To many Christians, this doctrine diminished the justice and mercy of God, made meaningless the idea of freedom of choice in the process of salvation, and stripped good works of any role in gaining salvation. In the first excerpt (from *The Institutes of the Christian Religion*), Calvin offered his definition of predestination and cited Saint Augustine as an authority.

Calvin's ecclesiastical ordinances became a model for Calvinist churches throughout Europe and America. Each local church was governed by four types of officers: ministers, teachers, elders, and deacons. The ministers preached the Word of God and administered the two sacraments: baptism and the Eucharist. The teachers taught children and candidate members. The elders closely supervised the morals of the congregation. The deacons cared for the poor and the sick. An especially important innovation was the consistory, composed of the ministers and elders who met weekly to hear accusations against and to discipline individuals whose conduct was contrary to the church's moral teachings. Persistent offenders were turned over to the city authorities for punishment.

Like Luther, Calvin had a horror of disobedience of the civil authorities. Although he tended to be skeptical about any good coming from kings, Calvin believed that all authority comes from God and that bad kings or tyrants were to be accepted as an expression of God's wrath and as just punishment for the people's sins.

Yet by 1561 Calvin was forced by circumstance (the severe persecution of his followers in France and elsewhere) to moderate his position. In his *Commentaries on the Book of the Prophet Daniel,* Calvin justified disobeying rulers who deny the rights of God (as understood by the Protestant reformers); an excerpt from this work concludes this selection of Calvin's writings. This teaching would lay the groundwork for Calvinists of France, the Netherlands, England, and Scotland to resist the legitimate Catholic and Anglican kings of those realms to the point of resorting to revolution.

THE INSTITUTES
Predestination

Predestination, by which God adopts some to the hope of life, and adjudges others to eternal death, no one, desirous of the credit of piety, dares absolutely to deny. But it is involved in many [disputes], especially by those who make foreknowledge the cause of [predestination]. We maintain, that both belong to God; but it is preposterous to represent one as dependent on the other. When we attribute foreknowledge to God, we mean that all things have ever been, and perpetually remain, before his eyes, so that to his knowledge nothing is future or past, but all things are present; and present in such a manner, that he does not merely conceive of them from ideas formed in his mind, as things remembered by us appear present to our minds, but really beholds and sees them as if actually placed before him. And this foreknowledge extends to the whole world, and to all the creatures. Predestination we call the eternal decree of God, by which he has determined in himself, what he would have to become of every individual of mankind. For they are not all created with a similar destiny; but eternal life is foreordained for some, and eternal damnation for others.

Every man, therefore, being created for one or the other of these ends, we say, he is predestinated either to life or to death.[1] . . .

The Genevan ecclesiastical ordinances illuminate the character of the Calvinist system of public regulation of morals through community pressure and state power.

ECCLESIASTICAL ORDINANCES
The Duties of Elders, or Presbyters

The office of the elders is to watch over the conduct of every individual, to admonish lovingly those whom they see doing wrong or leading an irregular life. When there is need, they should lay the matter before the body deputed to inflict paternal discipline (i.e. the consistory), of which they are members. . . .

The Consistory, or Session The elders, who have been described, shall assemble once a week with the ministers, namely Thursday morning, to see

---

[1]The phrase "predestinated . . . death" means predestined to be saved (life) or to be damned (death).

if there be any disorders in the Church and discuss together such remedies as shall be necessary. . . . If any one shall in contempt refuse to appear before them, it shall be their duty to inform the [town] council, so that it may supply a remedy. . . .

EXTRACTS FROM CALVIN'S REGULATIONS FOR THE VILLAGES ABOUT GENEVA

The whole household shall attend the sermons on Sunday, except when some one shall be left at home to tend the children or cattle.

If there is preaching on week days, all who can must come,—unless there be some good excuse,—so that at least one from each household shall be present. Those who have menservants or maid-servants shall bring them when it is possible, so that they shall not live like beasts without instruction. . . . Should any one come after the sermon has begun, let him be warned. If he does not amend, let him pay a fine of three sous [coins]. Let the churches be closed except during service, so that no one may enter them at other hours from superstitious motives. If any one be discovered engaged in some superstition within or near the church, let him be admonished. If he will not give up his superstition, let him be punished.

Persecution of Catholics   Those who are found to have rosaries or idols to adore, let them be sent before the consistory, and in addition to the reproof they receive there, let them be sent before the council. Let the same be done with those who go on a pilgrimage. Those who observe feasts or papistical fasts shall only be admonished. Those who go to mass shall, besides being admonished, be sent before the council, and it shall consider the propriety of punishing the offenders by imprisonment or special fines, as it judges best.

He who blasphemes, swearing by the body or blood of our Lord, or in like manner, shall kiss the earth for the first offense, pay five sous for the second and ten for the third. He who contradicts the word of God shall be sent before the consistory for reproof, or before the council for punishment, as the case may require. If any one sings indecent, licentious songs, or dances . . . he shall be kept in prison three days and then sent to the council.*

Commenting on the story of the Hebrew prophet Daniel (who clearly refused to obey the Persian king's order that he not worship the god of Israel) and denying that Daniel had committed any offense against the king, Calvin explains this apparent contradiction. He affirms the traditional Christian view that obedience to divine law takes precedence over obligations to obey the laws of earthly rulers. This view is the Christian basis for civil disobedience and even revolutionary action against a ruler perceived to be an enemy of God. The following passage starts with a biblical quote in which Daniel addresses the Persian king.

RESISTING SECULAR RULERS

. . . *And even before thee, O king, I have committed nothing wrong.* It is clear that the Prophet had violated the king's edict. Why, then, does he not ingenuously confess this? Nay, why does he contend that he has not transgressed against the king? Because he conducted himself with fidelity in all his duties, he could free himself from every [false charge] by which he knew himself oppressed, as if he had despised the king's sovereignty. But Daniel was not so bound to the king of the Persians when [the king] claimed for himself as a god what ought not to be offered to him. We know how earthly empires are constituted by God, only on the condition that [God] deprives himself of nothing, but shines forth alone, and all magistrates must be set in regular order, and every authority in existence must be subject to his glory. Since, therefore, Daniel could not obey the

---

*There are similar provisions for drunkenness, gambling, quarreling, taking more than five per cent interest, etc.

king's edict without denying God, as we have previously seen, he did not transgress against the king by constantly persevering in that exercise of piety to which he had been accustomed, and by calling on his God three times a-day. To make this the more evident, we must remember that passage of [the Apostle] Peter, "Fear God, honour the king" (1 Pet. 2:17). The two commands are connected together, and cannot be separated from one another. The fear of God ought to precede, that kings may obtain their authority. For if any one begins his reverence of an earthly prince by rejecting that of God, he will act preposterously, since this is a complete perversion of the order of nature. Then let God be feared in the first place, and earthly princes will obtain their authority, if only God shines forth, as I have already said. Daniel, therefore, here defends himself with justice, since *he had not committed any crime against the king;* for he was compelled to obey the command of God, and he neglected what the king had ordered in opposition to it. For earthly princes lay aside all their power when they rise up against God, and are unworthy of being reckoned in the number of mankind. We ought rather utterly to defy than to obey them whenever they are so restive and wish to spoil God of his rights, and, as it were, to seize upon his throne and draw him down from heaven.

REVIEW QUESTIONS

1. Why was the doctrine of predestination so troublesome to many Christian theologians?
2. Explain John Calvin's views on the proper relationship between Christians and the state.
3. The close policing of the morals of individuals is characteristic of Calvinist teachings and practice. What role has Calvinism (or Puritanism, as it was called in England and America) played historically in regulating morals in American society?

7   The Catholic Response to Protestantism

The criticisms of Catholic beliefs and practices by Luther, Calvin, and other Protestant reformers generated a host of theological defenses of traditional Catholicism. However, there was a general admission that grave abuses in Catholic clerical morals and discipline had been allowed to go uncorrected. Almost everyone agreed that a new general council of the church was necessary to clarify and affirm Catholic doctrine and institute reforms in clerical discipline and practices. Despite many promises to summon such a council, the popes delayed. Political conditions never seemed right, and the papacy, remembering the challenge to its power attempted by councils in the fifteenth century, feared that prematurely summoning a council could be a disaster for papal authority.

The council was finally convoked in 1545 at the Alpine city of Trent, on the borders between the German lands and Italy. The papacy was firmly in control and no Protestant theologians participated in the conciliar sessions. The council was suspended several times, the longest hiatus lasting for ten years (1552–1562), and concluded its work in 1563.

The council fathers confessed their responsibility for the evils that had grown up in the church and committed themselves to institutional reforms that would raise the standards of morality and learning among future bishops and clergy. The most significant pastoral reforms included creating an official catechism outlining the orthodox beliefs of the Roman church, establishing seminaries to direct the education of future clergy, and reforming the bishop's office by increasing his responsibilities for the pastoral life of his diocese.

CANONS AND DECREES OF THE COUNCIL OF TRENT

On doctrinal matters, the council gave an authoritative Catholic response to Protestant teachings on a host of issues. In the following excerpt from the decrees of the Council of Trent (1545–1563), the council condemned the Protestant view that faith alone was necessary for salvation and insisted on the integration of both faith and good works in the process of salvation. This position allowed the council to defend such traditional Catholic practices as monasticism, indulgences, masses for the dead, almsgiving, pilgrimages, veneration of saints, and other pious works.

THE NECESSITY OF PREPARATION FOR JUSTIFICATION [SALVATION] IN ADULTS, AND WHENCE IT PROCEEDS

It is furthermore declared that in adults the beginning of that justification must proceed from the predisposing grace of God through Jesus Christ, that is, from His vocation, whereby, without any merits on their part, they are called; that they who by sin had been cut off from God, may be disposed through His quickening and helping grace to convert themselves to their own justification by freely assenting to and co-operating with that grace; so that, while God touches the heart of man through the illumination of the Holy Ghost, man himself neither does absolutely nothing while receiving that inspiration, since he can also reject it, nor yet is he able by his own free will and without the grace of God to move himself to justice in His sight. Hence, when it is said in the sacred writings: *Turn ye to me, and I will turn to you* [Zach. 1:3], we are reminded of our liberty; and when we reply: *Convert us, O Lord, to thee, and we shall be con-*

verted [Lam. 5:21], we confess that we need the grace of God. . . .

HOW THE GRATUITOUS JUSTIFICATION OF THE SINNER BY FAITH IS TO BE UNDERSTOOD

But when the Apostle [Paul] says that man is justified by faith and freely, these words are to be understood in that sense in which the uninterrupted unanimity of the Catholic Church has held and expressed them, namely, that we are therefore said to be justified by faith, because faith is the beginning of human salvation, the foundation and root of all justification, *without which it is impossible to please God* [Heb. 11:6] and to come to the fellowship of His sons; and we are therefore said to be justified gratuitously [unearned, as a freely given gift], because none of those things that precede justification, whether faith or works, merit the grace of justification. For, *if by grace, it is not now by works, otherwise,* as the Apostle says, *grace is no more grace* [Rom. 11:6]. . . .

IN WHAT THE JUSTIFICATION OF THE SINNER CONSISTS, AND WHAT ARE ITS CAUSES

. . . For though no one can be just except he to whom the merits of the passion of our Lord Jesus Christ are communicated, yet this takes place in that justification of the sinner, when by the merit of the most holy passion, *the charity of God is poured forth by the Holy Ghost in the hearts* [Rom. 5:5] of those who are justified and inheres in them; whence man through Jesus Christ, [with] whom he is [now one], receives in that justification, together with the remission of sins, all these infused at the same time, namely, faith, hope and charity. For faith, unless hope and charity be added to it, neither unites man perfectly with Christ nor makes him a living member of His body. For which reason it is most truly said that *faith without works is dead* [James 2:17, 20] and of no profit, and *in Christ Jesus neither circumcision availeth anything nor uncircumcision, but faith that worketh by charity* [Gal. 5:6, 6:15]. This faith, conformably to Apostolic tradition, catechumens [candidates for baptism] ask of the Church before the sacrament of baptism, when they ask for the faith that gives eternal life, which without hope and charity faith cannot give. Whence also they hear immediately the word of Christ: *If thou wilt enter into life, keep the commandments* [Matt. 19:17]. . . .

The council also condemned individual interpretation of the Bible and set up controls over the publication and sale of unauthorized religious books. It approved the cult of the saints and the use of images, practices condemned by Calvin and the Anabaptists.

Furthermore, to check unbridled spirits, it [the council] decrees that no one relying on his own judgment shall, in matters of faith and morals pertaining to the edification of Christian doctrine, distorting the Holy Scriptures in accordance with his own conceptions, presume to interpret them contrary to that sense which holy mother Church, to whom it belongs to judge of their true sense and interpretation, has held and

holds, or even contrary to the unanimous teaching of the [church] Fathers, even though such interpretations should never at any time be published. Those who act contrary to this shall be made known by the ordinaries [bishops] and punished in accordance with the penalties prescribed by the law.

And wishing, as is proper, to impose a restraint in this matter on printers also, who, now without restraint, thinking what pleases them is permitted them, print without the permission of ecclesiastical superiors the books of the Holy Scriptures and the notes and commentaries thereon of all persons indiscriminately, often with the name of the press omitted, often also under a fictitious press-name, and what is worse, without the name of the author, and also indiscreetly have for sale such books printed elsewhere, (this council) decrees and ordains that in the future the Holy Scriptures, especially the old Vulgate [Latin] Edition, be printed in the most correct manner possible, and that it shall not be lawful for anyone to print or to have printed any books whatsoever dealing with sacred doctrinal matters without the name of the author, or in the future to sell them, or even to have them in possession, unless they have first been examined and approved by the ordinary [the local bishop], under penalty of anathema [condemnation and excommunication] and fine. . . .

ON THE INVOCATION, VENERATION, AND RELICS OF SAINTS, AND ON SACRED IMAGES

The holy council commands all bishops and others who hold the office of teaching and have charge of the *cura animarum* [care of souls], that in accordance with the usage of the Catholic and Apostolic Church, received from the primitive times of the Christian religion, and with the unanimous teaching of the holy Fathers and the decrees of sacred councils, they above all instruct the faithful diligently in matters relating to intercession and invocation of the saints, the veneration of relics, and the legitimate use of images, teaching them that the saints who reign together with Christ offer up their prayers to God for men, that it is good and beneficial suppliantly to invoke them and to have recourse to their prayers, assistance and support in order to obtain favors from God through His Son, Jesus Christ our Lord, who alone is our redeemer and savior.... Also, that the holy bodies of the holy martyrs and of others living with Christ, which were the living members of Christ and the temple of the Holy Ghost, to be awakened by Him to eternal life and to be glorified, are to be venerated by the faithful, through which many benefits are bestowed by God on men.... Moreover, that the images of Christ, of the Virgin Mother of God, and of the other saints are to be placed and retained especially in the churches, and that due honor and veneration is to be given them....

The Council of Trent condemned the Protestant view that clergy were no different than lay people and reaffirmed the Catholic belief that the clergy, for their administration of the church's sacraments, are specially ordained intermediaries between God and human beings. Whereas Luther admitted only three sacraments—baptism, the Eucharist, and penance or confession—and Calvin only two—baptism and the Eucharist—the Council of Trent decreed that there were seven sacraments in the Catholic Church, including ordination of the clergy.

CANONS ON THE SACRAMENTS IN GENERAL

Canon 1. If anyone says that the sacraments of the New Law were not all instituted by our Lord Jesus Christ, or that there are more or less than seven, namely, baptism, confirmation, Eucharist, penance, extreme unction, order and matrimony, or that any one of these seven is not truly and intrinsically a sacrament, let him be anathema [cursed]. . . .

Can. 10. If anyone says that all Christians have the power to administer the word and all the sacraments, let him be anathema. . . .

CANONS ON THE SACRAMENT OF ORDER

Canon 1. If anyone says that there is not in the New Testament a visible and external priesthood, or that there is no power of consecrating and offering the true body and blood of the Lord and of forgiving . . . sins, but only the office and bare ministry of preaching the Gospel; or that those who do not preach are not priests at all, let him be anathema. . . .

Can. 4. If anyone says that by sacred ordination the Holy [Spirit] is not imparted and that therefore the bishops say in vain: *Receive ye the Holy [Spirit]*, or that by it a character is not imprinted, or that he who has once been a priest can again become a layman, let him be anathema.

Can. 5. If anyone says that the holy unction which the Church uses in ordination is not only not required but is detestable and pernicious, as also are the other ceremonies of order, let him be anathema.

Can. 6. If anyone says that in the Catholic Church there is not instituted a hierarchy by divine ordinance, which consists of bishops, priests and ministers, let him be anathema.

Can. 7. If anyone says that bishops are not superior to priests, or that they have not the power to confirm and ordain, or that the power which they have is common to them and to priests, or that orders conferred by them without the consent or call of the people or of the secular power are invalid, or that those who have been neither rightly ordained nor sent by ecclesiastical and canonical authority, but come from elsewhere, are lawful ministers of the word and of the sacraments, let him be anathema.

REVIEW QUESTIONS

1. What was the Catholic doctrine on justification by faith defined by the Council of Trent, and how did it differ from the views of Luther and Calvin?
2. How did the Council of Trent approach the problem of authoritative interpretation of the Scriptures and of church doctrines?

8   Religious Persecution

The passions aroused by the Reformation culminated in vicious religious persecution. Regarding Protestants as dangerous heretics who had affronted God and threatened his church, Catholic clergy and rulers tried to eliminate them, often by fire and sword. Protestants also engaged in persecution, principally against the Anabaptists, a Protestant sect that deviated from the teachings of the main Protestant reformers.

Chronicle of King Francis I
BURNING OF PROTESTANTS IN PARIS

Fearing that Protestant heresy would prove calamitous to his realm and undermine his authority, Francis I (1515–1547) in 1535 had Protestants publicly burned in Paris as a warning to Protestant dissenters. Following is a contemporary account of the spectacle.

The most Christian king [Francis I], our sovereign lord, knowing that certain damnable heresies and blasphemies swarmed in his kingdom and desiring with the aid of God to extirpate the same decreed that a sacred procession should be held in this city of Paris on the twenty-first day [actually the twenty-ninth] of January 1535. The streets were adorned with gorgeous tapestries and the crowds held in order by archers in uniform. First came the crosses and banners of the Diocese of Paris followed by citizens and merchants carrying torches, then the four monastic orders with relics, next priests and canons of the parochial churches with relics, and the monks of Saint Martin with the head of that saint. Another carried the head of Saint Philip, one of the most precious relics in Paris. The body of Madame Saincte Geneviève was borne by six citizens in their shirts. Then followed the Canons of Notre Dame, the Rector of the University, and the Swiss Guard with their band of violins, trumpets, and cornets. Among the relics were the true cross of Christ and the crown of thorns and the lance that pierced his side. Then came a great number of the archbishops and bishops with the blood of our Saviour, the rod of Moses, and the head of John the Baptist. Next the cardinals. The precious body of our Lord was carried by the archdeacons on a velvet cushion of violet adorned with [flowers]. Following the Holy Sacrament came the King alone with bare head carrying a lighted candle. After him marched Monseigneur the Cardinal of Lorraine, then all the princes and knights and members of the *Parlement,* etc. The Holy Sacrament was taken to the church of Notre Dame and there deposited with great reverence by the Bishop of Paris. Then the King and his children, the Queen and her attendants and many notables had dinner with the Bishop of Paris. After dinner the King made a speech against the execrable and damnable opinions dispersed throughout his kingdom. While the King, the Queen, and their court were with the Bishop of Paris, into their presence were brought six of the said heretics and in front of the church of Notre Dame they were burned alive. A number of other heretics went to the stake during the days following so that all over Paris one saw gibbets [gallows] by which the people were filled with terror.

THE PERSECUTION OF ANABAPTISTS: THE EXAMINATION OF ELIZABETH DIRKS

The break with the Roman church and the rapid growth of a reformed church party in Germany under Luther's leadership was soon complicated by the appearance of other anti-Roman Protestants who differed with both the papacy and Luther on questions of theology and church discipline. In the Swiss city of Zurich, enthusiastic reformers like Ulrich Zwingli (1484–1531) and Conrad Grebel (c. 1500–1526) overthrew the local Catholic authorities but failed to agree fully with Luther or with each other on several theological matters. Grebel and his supporters, called Anabaptists, held that admission to membership in the church must be a voluntary act by adults, and condemned the practice of baptizing infants. When Zwingli insisted that no reforms in ecclesiastical practices should be undertaken without permission of the public authorities, the Zurich Anabaptists refused to comply, declaring the complete freedom of the church from state control. Condemned by Zwingli and forced into exile, the Zurich Anabaptists soon spread their ideas throughout the German-speaking lands.

Although the majority of Anabaptists renounced the use of force to impose any religious practice, the Anabaptist reformers in Münster, a city in northwestern Germany, did not. After winning control of the city council, they expelled all citizens who refused to become Anabaptists. Under the influence of "prophets," some Münster Anabaptists adopted practicing polygamy, communal ownership of property, and violence in anticipation of the imminent end of the world. In 1535, the forces of neighboring German princes captured Münster, slaughtering the Anabaptists.

The excesses of the Münster sect caused both Protestant and Catholic authorities to persecute more peaceful and orthodox Anabaptists wherever they were discovered. The movement remained small, fervent, but oppressed, and was confined to an underground existence. Modern Christian churches that acknowledge the sixteenth-century Anabaptists as their spiritual forebears are the Mennonites and Amish, the Plymouth (Pilgrim) Separatists, and the English and American Baptists.

In January 1549, Elizabeth Dirks was arrested in Holland, at that time under Catholic control. A former nun, she had come to doubt whether monastic life was truly Christian and fled the monastery. Following is a verbatim account of her trial before Catholic examiners. Condemned to death, Elizabeth Dirks was drowned in a sack.

EXAMINERS: We understand that you are a teacher and have led many astray. We want to know who your friends are.

ELIZABETH: I am commanded to love the Lord my God and honor my parents. Therefore I will not tell you who my parents are. That I suffer for Christ is damaging to my friends.

EXAMINERS: We will let that rest for the present, but we want to know whom you have taught.

ELIZABETH: No, my Lords, do not press me on this point. Ask me about my faith and I will answer you gladly.

EXAMINERS: We will make it so tough that you will tell us.

ELIZABETH: I hope through the grace of God to guard my tongue that I shall not be a traitor and deliver my brother [in faith] to death.

EXAMINERS: What persons were with you when you were baptized?

ELIZABETH: Christ said, "Ask those who were present." (John 18:21).

EXAMINERS: Now we see that you are a teacher because you make yourself equal to Christ.

ELIZABETH: No indeed. Far be it from me, for I count myself no better than the [refuse] from the house of the Lord.

EXAMINERS: What do you mean by the house of the Lord? Don't you consider our church to be the house of the Lord?

ELIZABETH: I do not, my Lords. For it is written, "You are the temple of the living God" (2 Cor. 6:16). As God said, "I will dwell with you" (Lev. 26:11).

EXAMINERS: What do you think of our Mass?

ELIZABETH: My Lords, I have no faith in your Mass but only in that which is in the Word of God.

EXAMINERS: What do you believe about the Holy Sacrament?

ELIZABETH: I have never in my life read in Scripture about a Holy Sacrament, but only of the Supper of the Lord.

EXAMINERS: Shut your mouth. The devil speaks through it.

ELIZABETH: Yes, my Lords, this is a little matter, for the servant is not greater than his Lord (Matt. 10:24).

EXAMINERS: You speak with a haughty tongue.

ELIZABETH: No, my Lords, I speak with a free tongue.

EXAMINERS: What did the Lord say when he gave the supper to his disciples?

ELIZABETH: What did he give them, flesh or bread?

EXAMINERS: He gave them bread.

ELIZABETH: Did not the Lord continue to sit there? How then could they eat his flesh?

EXAMINERS: What do you believe about the baptism of children, seeing that you have had yourself baptized again?

ELIZABETH: No, my Lords, I have not had myself baptized again. I have been baptized once on my faith, because it is written, "Baptism belongs to believers." [She deduces this from Peter's confession, Matt. 16:15-16.]

EXAMINERS: Are our children then damned because they are baptized?

ELIZABETH: No, my Lords. Far be it from me to judge the children.

EXAMINERS: Do you not think that you are saved by baptism?

ELIZABETH: No, my Lords. All the water in the sea cannot save me. All my salvation is in Christ, who has commanded me to love the Lord, my God, and my neighbor as myself.

EXAMINERS: Do priests have the power to forgive sins?

ELIZABETH: No, my Lords. How should I believe that? I say that Christ is the only priest through whom sins are forgiven.

EXAMINERS: You say that you accept everything in accord with Holy Scripture. Do you not then hold to the word of James?

ELIZABETH: How can I not hold to it?

EXAMINERS: Did he not say, "Go to the elders of the congregation that they should anoint you and pray for you"? (James 5:13).

ELIZABETH: Yes, but would you say, my Lords, that you are such a congregation?

EXAMINERS: The Holy Ghost has made you so holy that you don't need penance or the sacrament.

ELIZABETH: No, my Lords. I freely confess that I have transgressed the ordinances of the pope which the emperor has confirmed with placards. But if you can show me that in any articles I have transgressed against the Lord, my God, I will wail over myself as a miserable sinner.

This was her first hearing.

Then they took her again before the council and brought her to the torture room. Hans, the executioner, was there. The Lords said, "So far we have treated you gently. Since you won't confess we will put you to the torture." The Procurator General said, "Mr. Hans, take hold of her." Mr. Hans answered, "Oh no, my Lords, she will confess voluntarily." But since she would not, he put screws on her thumbs and on two forefingers till the blood spurted from the nails.

EXAMINERS: Confess and we will ease your pain. We told you to confess and not to call upon the Lord, your God!

But she held steadfastly to the Lord, her God, as above related. Then they eased her pain and she said, "Ask me. I will answer, for I feel no pain any more at all as I did."

EXAMINERS: Then won't you confess?

ELIZABETH: No, my Lords.

Then they put two screws on her legs and she said, "Oh my Lords, do not put me to shame. No man has ever touched my bare body." The Procurator General said, "Miss Elizabeth, we will not treat you dishonorably." Then she fainted and one said, "Maybe she's dead." Reviving she said, "I'm alive. I'm not dead." Then they took off the screws and tried to bend her by blandishments.

ELIZABETH: Why do you try me with candied speech as one does with children?

So they could get from her not a word against her brothers in the faith, nor against any one.

EXAMINERS: Will you recant everything you have said?

ELIZABETH: No, my Lords. I will not, but I will seal it with my blood.

EXAMINERS: We will not torture you any more. Will you now tell us in good faith who baptized you?

ELIZABETH: Oh no, my Lords. I have told you all along that I will not do it.

Then, on March 27, 1549, Elizabeth was condemned to death and drowned in a sack. And thus she offered up her life to God.

REVIEW QUESTIONS

1. Why was the burning of heretics treated as a public festival?
2. Why were Anabaptists like Elizabeth Dirks considered dangerous to both Catholic and Protestant authorities?

CHAPTER 8

Early Modern Society and Politics

HENRY HUDSON/DUTCH EAST INDIA COMPANY. The Dutch East India Company was the foundation on which the Dutch built their colonial empire. The company hired Henry Hudson (d. 1611), English explorer and navigator, to find a quicker passage to the Spice Islands of the Pacific than the long and expensive voyage around the Cape of Good Hope. Hudson's quest for a northwest passage through North America was doomed to fail. In this picture, officials of the East India Company are conferring with Hudson. *(The Granger Collection, New York.)*

The period from the Renaissance through the Scientific Revolution saw the breakdown of distinctively medieval cultural, political, and economic forms. The Renaissance produced a more secular attitude and expressed confidence in human capacities. Shortly afterward, the Protestant Reformation ended the religious unity of medieval Latin Christendom and weakened the political power of the church. At the same time the discovery of new trade routes to East Asia and of new lands across the Atlantic widened the imagination and ambitions of Christian Europeans and precipitated a commercial revolution. This great expansion of economic activity furthered capitalism and initiated a global economy—two developments associated with the modern world. The European economy was tied to Asian spices, African slaves, and American silver. A wide variety of goods circulated all over the globe. From the West Indies and East Asia, sugar, rice, tea, cacao, and tobacco flowed into Europe. From the Americas, potatoes, corn, sweet potatoes, and manioc (from which tapioca is made) spread to the rest of the world. Europeans paid for Asian silks and spices with American silver.

The increasing demand for goods and a rise in prices produced more opportunities for the accumulation and investment of capital by private individuals, which is the essence of capitalism. State policies designed to increase national wealth and power also stimulated the growth of capitalism. Governments subsidized new industries, chartered joint-stock companies to engage in overseas trade, and struck at internal tariffs and guild regulations that hampered domestic economic growth. Improvements in banking, shipbuilding, mining, and manufacturing further stimulated economic growth.

In the sixteenth and seventeenth centuries the old medieval political order dissolved, and the modern state began to emerge. The modern state has a strong central government that issues laws that apply throughout the land and a permanent army of professional soldiers paid by the state. Trained bureaucrats, responsible to the central government, collect taxes, enforce laws, and administer justice. The modern state has a secular character; promotion of religion is not the state's concern, and churches do not determine state policy. These features of the modern state were generally not prevalent in the Middle Ages, when the nobles, church, and towns possessed powers and privileges that impeded central authority, and kings were expected to rule in accordance with Christian principles. In the sixteenth and seventeenth centuries, monarchs were exercising central authority with ever-greater effectiveness at the expense of nobles and clergy. The secularization of the state became firmly established after the Thirty Years' War (1618–1648); with their states worn out by Catholic–Protestant conflicts, kings came to act less for religious motives than for reasons of national security and power.

1   Toward the Modern Economy: The Example of Holland

The Spanish and Portuguese monopoly of trade was challenged in the late sixteenth century, first by English privateers who preyed on the Spanish fleets crossing the Atlantic and then by the Dutch who were in revolt against their sovereign, the Spanish king Philip II (1556–1598). Earlier, the Dutch had traded with both Spanish and Portuguese ports, but were not allowed to seek markets directly with the Americas or the East Indies. When Philip II, who was also king of Portugal from 1580, excluded the rebellious Dutch from trading in his ports— a policy that was renewed by his son, Philip III (1598–1621)—Dutch merchants decided to break the Portuguese monopoly over trade with the East Indies. In doing so, they launched the first of many commercial wars designed to win control over world trade markets.

To encourage trade with the East Indies, the Dutch government established a private limited stockholding company, the East India Company, and granted it a monopoly over trade and colonization anywhere east of the Cape of Good Hope or beyond the Straits of Magellan at the southern tip of South America. The company was granted the right to build fortresses, to raise armies, to establish laws and courts in territories it captured from the Spanish or the Portuguese, and to enter into diplomatic alliances with other princes. The East India Company was the foundation on which the Dutch built their colonial empire. Other European states established similar corporations to further trade and colonization.

William Carr
THE DUTCH EAST INDIA COMPANY

In 1693, William Carr, the English consul at Amsterdam, wrote a travelers' guide to the leading cities of Holland, Flanders, northern Germany, and Scandinavia. Of these, the largest and wealthiest was Amsterdam in Holland. In less than a century, this once small medieval city had grown to become the most important commercial port in the West and the center of European financial capitalism. In the following selection, Carr describes the commercial trading system of the famous Dutch East India Company, which established trading posts in South Africa, the Persian Gulf area, India, Ceylon, Bangladesh, Indonesia, China, and Japan. Although not mentioned by Carr, the Dutch West India Company conducted similar operations in the Caribbean and North America. The Dutch trading post of New Amsterdam at the mouth of the Hudson River would become the city of New York, the world center of finance capitalism in the twentieth century.

... The East India Company of the Netherlands is said to be a commonwealth within a commonwealth, and this is true when you consider the sovereign power and privileges the company has been granted by the States General [the ruling council of the Dutch Republic] and also consider its riches and vast number of subjects, and the many territories and colonies it possesses in the East Indies. The company is said to have 30,000 men in its constant employ and more than 200 capital ships, in addition to its sloops, ketches, and yachts. The company possesses many colonies formerly belonging to Spain, Portugal, and various Indian princes, and as good Christians company members have spread the Gospel of Christ in these lands, printing the Bible, prayer books, and catechisms in Indian languages and maintaining ministers and teachers to instruct those that are converted to the faith. Having said that this company is so extensive—as it were a commonwealth apart—I will demonstrate that it is a commonwealth first by its power, riches, and strength in the East Indies, and second, by its position in Europe.... But I will begin at the Cape of Good Hope [Africa] where the company has built a fort where it maintains a garrison to defend its ships when they stop there for fresh water. From there let us view the company on the island of Java, where it has built a fair city called Batavia and fortified it with bastions like those in Amsterdam. This city is the residence of the company's grand minister of state, called the General of the Indies. He has six privy counsellors (ordinary) and two extraordinary; they oversee the concerns of the company throughout the Indies, including matters of war and peace.... The General of the Indies has horse and foot soldiers, officers, and servants—as if he were a sovereign prince—all paid for by the company.... So formidable is the company in the East Indies that it looks as though it aims to rule the South Seas. It also has a great trade with China and Japan.... With Persia also it has great commerce and is so confident that it wages war with the Persian monarch if he wrongs it in trade. It also has several colonies on the coast of Malabar and Coromandel [west coast of India] and in the country of the Great Mogul.... But especially let us examine the company on the rich island of Ceylon [Sri Lanka] where it controls the plains, so the king of the island is forced to live in the mountains while the company possesses the city of Colombo.... I will say no more of the company's power in the Indies, but let us examine its position in Europe. To begin with, in Amsterdam the company has two large stately palaces, one being in the old part of the city, and the other in the new; in the old part it keeps its court—where the Resident Committee of the company sits—and sells the company's goods.

REVIEW QUESTION

1. What evidence of the Dutch East India Company's power does Carr provide?

2   The Atlantic Slave Trade

As the first Portuguese merchants began to penetrate southward along the coast of western Africa, they found that the local African societies engaged in an extensive trade in slave laborers. Like slaves in the Mediterranean region, African slaves were prisoners of war, criminals, or victims of violence and kidnapping. The Portuguese ships began carrying slaves from one local market to another along the

African coast. Some slaves were taken back to Europe, but after 1500 the trade shifted largely to the Portuguese colony in Brazil and the Spanish colonies in the West Indies. In addition, Arabs and Portuguese competed in conveying slaves from East Africa to the markets of the Middle East. The widespread use of African slaves marked a new stage in the history of slavery. In the western world slavery became identified with race; the myth emerged that blacks were slaves by nature.

In the seventeenth century, the Dutch and English entered the West African slave trade, ousting the Portuguese as the principal slave traders to the West Indies and North America. The supply of laborers from Africa was essential to the New World's successful economic development. The Africans proved themselves to be skilled farmers and artisans who could endure the heavy labor of plantation life without the high rate of sickness and death that afflicted the local Indian populations. The Atlantic slave trade continued for more than three hundred years until finally suppressed by European governments in the nineteenth century. During that period, it is estimated that between 9.5 and 12 million African men, women, and children were shipped to the New World as slaves.

Seventeenth-Century Slave Traders
BUYING AND TRANSPORTING AFRICANS

Dealing in slaves was a profitable business that attracted numerous entrepreneurs. Following are two accounts written by slave traders in the seventeenth century.

As the slaves come down to Fida from the inland country, they are put into a booth, or prison, built for that purpose, near the beach, all of them together; and when the Europeans are to receive them, they are brought out into a large plain, where the surgeons examine every part of every one of them, to the smallest member, men and women being all stark naked. Such as are allowed good and sound, are set on the one side, and the others by themselves; which slaves so rejected are there called Mackrons, being above thirty five years of age, or defective in their limbs, eyes or teeth; or grown grey, or that have the venereal disease, or any other imperfection. These being so set aside, each of the others, which have passed as good, is marked on the breast, with a red-hot iron, imprinting the mark of the French, English, or Dutch companies, that so each nation may distinguish their own, and to prevent their being chang'd by the natives for worse, as they are apt

enough to do. In this particular, care is taken that the women, as tenderest, be not burnt too hard.

The branded slaves, after this, are returned to their former booth, where the factor [buyer] is to subsist them at his own charge, which amounts to about two-pence a day for each of them, with bread and water, which is all their allowance. There they continue sometimes ten or fifteen days, till the sea is still enough to send them aboard; for very often it continues too boisterous for so long a time, unless in January, February and March, which is commonly the calmest season: and when it is so, the slaves are carried off by parcels, in bar-canoes, and put aboard the ships in the road. Before they enter the canoes, or come out of the booth, their former Black masters strip them of every rag they have, without distinction of men or women; to supply which, in orderly ships, each of them as they come aboard is allowed a piece of canvas, to wrap around their waist, which is very acceptable to those poor wretches. . . . [I]n the aforesaid months of January, February and March, which are the good season, ships are for the most part soon dispatched, if there be a good number of slaves at hand; so that they need not stay above four weeks for their cargo, and sometimes it is done in a fortnight.

The Blacks of Fida are so expeditious at this trade of slaves that they can deliver a thousand every month. . . . If there happens to be no stock of slaves at Fida, the factor must trust the Blacks with his goods, to the value of a hundred and fifty, or two hundred slaves; which goods they carry up into the inland, to buy slaves, at all the markets, for above two hundred leagues up the country, where they are kept like cattle [are kept] in Europe; the slaves sold there being generally prisoners of war, taken from their enemies, like other booty, and perhaps some few sold by their own countrymen, in extreme want, or upon a famine; as also some as a punishment of heinous crimes: tho' many Europeans believe that parents sell their own children, men their wives and relations, which, if it ever happens, is so seldom, that it cannot justly be charged upon a whole nation, as a custom and common practice.

A second slaver describes the loading and transporting of the newly acquired slaves.

When our slaves were come to the seaside, our canoes were ready to carry them off to the longboat, if the sea permitted, and she convey'd them aboard ship, where the men were all put in irons, two and two shackled together, to prevent their mutiny, or swimming ashore.

The negroes are so wilful and loth to leave their own country, that they have often leap'd out of the canoes, boat and ship, into the sea, and kept under water till they were drowned, to avoid being taken up and saved by our boats, which pursued them; they having a more dreadful apprehension of Barbadoes than we can have

of hell, tho' in reality they live much better there than in their own country; but home is home, etc: we have likewise seen [many] of them eaten by the sharks, of which a prodigious number [swam] about the ships in this place, and I have been told will follow her hence to Barbadoes, for the dead negroes that are thrown over-board in the passage. I am certain in our voyage there we did not [lack] the sight of some every day, but that they were the same I can't affirm.

We had about 12 negroes did wilfully drown themselves, and others starv'd themselves to death; for 'tis their belief that when they die they return home to their own country and friends again.

I have been inform'd that some commanders have cut off the legs and arms of the most wilful, to terrify the rest, for they believe if they lose a member, they cannot return home again: I was advis'd by some of my officers to do the same, but I could not be perswaded to entertain the least thought of it, much less put in practice such barbarity and cruelty to poor creatures, who, excepting their want of christianity and true religion (their misfortune more than fault) are as much the works of God's hands, and no doubt as dear to him as ourselves; nor can I imagine why they should be despis'd for their colour, being what they cannot help, and the effect of the climate it has pleas'd God to appoint them. I can't think there is any intrinsick value in one colour more than another, nor that white is better than black, only we think so because we are so, and are prone to judge favourably in our own case, as well as the blacks, who in odium of the colour, say, the devil is white, and so paint him. . . .

When our slaves are aboard we shackle the men two and two, while we lie in port, and in sight of their own country, for 'tis then they attempt to make their escape, and mutiny; to prevent which we always keep centinels upon the hatchways, and have a chest full of small arms, ready loaden and prim'd, constantly lying at hand upon the quarter-deck, together with some granada shells; and two of our quarter-deck guns, pointing on the deck thence, and two more out of the steerage, the door of which is always kept shut, and well barr'd; they are fed twice a day, at 10 in the morning, and 4 in the evening, which is the time they are aptest to mutiny, being all upon deck; therefore all that time, what of our men are not employ'd in distributing their victuals to them, and settling them, stand to their arms; and some with lighted matches at the great guns that [yawn] them, loaden with partridge, till they have done and gone down to their kennels between decks. . . .

When we come to sea we let them all out of irons, they never attempting then to rebel, considering that should they kill or master us, they could not tell how to manage the ship, or must trust us, who would carry them where we pleas'd; therefore the only danger is while we are in sight of their own country, which they are loth to part with; but once out of sight out of mind: I never heard that they mutiny'd in any ships of consequence, that had a good number of men, and the least care; but in small tools [vessels] where they had but few men, and those negligent or drunk, then they surpriz'd and butcher'd them, cut the cables, and let the vessel drive ashore, and every one shift for himself. However, we have some 30 or 40 gold coast[1] negroes, which we buy, and are

---

[1]The Gold Coast was a section of coastal western Africa along the Gulf of Guinea, known for its trade in gold.

procur'd us there by our factors, to make guardians and overseers of the Whidaw negroes, and sleep among them to keep them from quarrelling; and in order, as well as to give us notice, if they can discover any caballing or plotting among them, which trust they will discharge with great diligence: they also take care to make the negroes scrape the decks where they lodge every morning very clean, to eschew any distempers that may engender from filth and nastiness; when we constitute a guardian, we give him a cat of nine tails [whip] as a badge of his office, which he is not a little proud of, and will exercise with great authority. We often at sea in the evenings would let the slaves come up into the sun to air themselves, and make them jump and dance for an hour or two to our bag-pipes, harp, and fiddle, by which exercise to preserve them in health; but notwithstanding all our endeavour, 'twas my hard fortune to have great sickness and mortality among them.

Having bought my compliment of 700 slaves, *viz.* 480 men and 220 women, and finish'd all my business at Whidaw, I took my leave of the old king . . . and parted, with many affectionate expressions on both sides, being forced to promise him that I would return again the next year, with several things he desired me to bring him from England. . . .

Malachy Postlethwayt
SLAVERY DEFENDED

While some people attacked African bondage as morally repugnant, its proponents argued that it was a boon to shipping and manufacturing and also benefited Africans by liberating them from oppressive African rulers, who had captured and enslaved them, and placing them in the care of more humane Christian masters, who instructed them in Christian ideals. Malachy Postlethwayt (c. 1707–1767), an English economist, defended slavery in the following excerpt written in 1746.

The most approved judges of the commercial interests of these Kingdoms have ever been of the opinion, that our West-India and African trades are the most nationally beneficial of any we carry on. It is also allowed on all hands, that the trade to Africa is the Branch which renders our American colonies and plantations so advantageous to Great Britain, that traffic only affording our planters a constant supply of negro servants for the culture of their lands in the produce of sugars, tobacco, rice, rum, cotton, pimento, and all other our plantation-produce: so that the extensive employment of our shipping in, to, and from America, the great brood of Seamen consequent thereupon, and the daily bread of the most considerable part of our British manufactures, are owing primarily to the labours of Negroes; who, as they were the first happy instruments of raising our plantations; so their labour only can support and preserve them, and render them still more and more profitable to their mother-kingdom.

The negro-trade, therefore, and the national consequences resulting from it, may be justly esteemed an inexhaustible fund of wealth and naval power to this nation. And by the surplus of negroes above what have served our own plantations, we have drawn likewise no inconsiderable quantities of treasure from the Spaniards, who are settled on the continent of America, . . . for Negroes furnished them from Jamaica. . . .

What renders the negro trade still more estimable and important, is, that near nine-tenths of those negroes are paid for in Africa with British produce and manufactures only; and the remainder with East-India commodities. We send no specie or bullion [coined money] to pay for the products of Africa but, 'tis certain, we bring from thence very large quantities of gold. . . .

And it may be worth consideration that while our plantations depend only on planting by negro servants, they will neither depopulate our own country, become independent of her dominion, or any way interfere with the interests of the British manufacturer, merchant, or landed gentleman: whereas were we under the necessity of supplying our colonies with white-men instead of blacks, they could not fail being in a capacity to interfere with the manufactures of this nation, in time to shake off their dependency thereon, and prove as injurious to the landed, and trading interests as ever they have hitherto been beneficial.

Many are prepossessed against this trade, thinking it a barbarous, inhuman and unlawful traffic for a Christian country to trade in Blacks; to which I would beg leave to observe; that though the odious appellation of slaves is annexed to this trade, it being called by some the slave-trade, yet it does not appear from the best enquiry I have been able to make, that the state of those people is changed for the worse, by being servants to our British planters in America; they are certainly treated with great lenity and humanity: and as the improvement of the planter's estates depends upon due care being taken of their healths and lives, I cannot but think their condition is much bettered to what it was in their own country.

Besides, the negro princes in Africa, 'tis well known, are in perpetual war with each other, and since before they had this method of disposing of their prisoners of war to Christian merchants, they were wont not only to be applied to inhuman sacrifices, but to extreme torture and barbarity, their transportation must certainly be a melioration [improvement] of their condition; provided living in a civilized Christian country, is better than living among savages: Nay, if life be preferable to torment and cruel death, their state cannot, with any color of reason, be presumed to be worsened. . . .

As the present prosperity and splendor of the British colonies have been owing to negro labor, so not only their future advancement, but even their very being depends [on it]. That our colonies are capable of very great improvements, by the proper application of the labour of blacks, has been urged by the most experienced judges of commerce.

The negro princes and chiefs in Africa are generally at war with each other on the continent; and the prisoners of war, instead of being slain, or applied to inhuman sacrifices, are carefully preserved and sold to those Europeans only, who have established interest and power among the natives, by means of forts and settlements; or to such who are admitted to traffic with the natives, by virtue, and under the sanction and protection of such European settlements; which is the case of all the British merchants who trade to Africa at present, at full liberty, under the authority and protection of our Royal African Company's rights and privileges, interest and power among the natives. . . .

John Wesley
THOUGHTS UPON SLAVERY

John Wesley (1703–1791) was, with his brother Charles, the founder of the evangelical Methodist movement in England. Inspired by the Great Awakening in the American colonies, he launched a successful revival of Christianity in England in 1739. The rest of his long life was devoted to leadership of the Methodist movement.

Wesley's eyes were opened to the evils of slavery by reading an indictment of the slave trade by a French Quaker, Anthony Benezet. In 1774 he published the tract *Thoughts upon Slavery,* from which the extracts below are taken. Wesley drew heavily on Benezet's writings for his facts, but in warning participants in the slave trade of divine retribution, he spoke in the cadences of the inspired evangelical preacher.

Wesley became one of the leaders in the movement against slavery and his pioneering work, in which he was supported by the Methodist movement, helped bring about the abolition of slavery in England in 1807.

I would inquire whether [the abuses of slavery] can be defended on the principles of even heathen honesty, whether they can be reconciled (setting the Bible out of question) with any degree of either justice or mercy.

The grand plea is, "They are authorized by law." But can law, human law, change the nature of things? Can it turn darkness into light or evil into good? By no means. Notwithstanding ten thousand laws, right is right, and wrong is wrong still. There must still remain an essential [difference] between justice and injustice, cruelty and mercy. So that I still ask, who can reconcile this treatment of the Negroes first and last, with either mercy or justice? . . . Yea, where is the justice of taking away the lives of innocent, inoffensive men, murdering thousands of them in their own land, by the hands of their own countrymen, many thousands year after year on shipboard, and then casting them like dung into the sea and tens of thousands in that cruel slavery to which they are so unjustly reduced? . . .

But if this manner of procuring and treating Negroes is not consistent either with mercy or justice, yet there is a plea for it which every man of business will acknowledge to be quite sufficient. . . . "D—n justice, it is necessity. . . . It is necessary that we should procure slaves, and when we have procured them, it is necessary to use them with severity, considering their stupidity, stubbornness and wickedness."

I answer you stumble at the threshold. I deny that villainy is ever necessary. It is impossible that it should ever be necessary for any reasonable creature to violate all the laws of justice, mercy, and truth. No circumstances can make it necessary for a man to burst in sunder all the ties of humanity. It can never be necessary for a rational being to sink himself below a brute. A man can be under no necessity of degrading himself into a wolf. The absurdity of the supposition is so glaring that one would wonder anyone can help seeing it. . . .

"But the furnishing us with slaves is necessary for the trade, and wealth, and glory of our nation." Here are several mistakes. For first wealth is not necessary to the glory of any nation, but wisdom, virtue, justice, mercy, generosity, public spirit, love of our country. These are necessary to the real glory of a nation, but abundance of wealth is not.

. . . But, secondly, it is not clear that we should have either less money or trade (only less of that detestable trade of man—stealing), if there was not a Negro in all our islands or in all English America. It is demonstrable, white men inured to it by degrees can work as well as they, and they would do it, were Negroes out of the way, and proper encouragement given them. However, thirdly, I come back to the same point: Better no trade than trade procured by villainy. It is far better to have no wealth than to gain wealth at the expense of virtue. Better is honest poverty than all the riches bought by the tears, and sweat, and blood of our fellow creatures.

"However this be, it is necessary, when we have slaves, to use them with severity." What, to whip them for every petty offence, till they are all in gore blood? To take that opportunity of rubbing pepper and salt into their raw flesh? To drop burning wax upon their skin? To castrate them? To cut off half their foot with an axe? To hang them on gibbets [gallows], that they may die by inches with heat, and hunger, and thirst? To pin them down to the ground, and then burn them by degrees from the feet to the head? To roast them alive? When did a Turk or heathen find it necessary to use a fellow-creature thus?

I pray, to what end is this usage necessary? "Why to prevent their running away, and to keep them constantly to their labour, that they may not idle away their time. So miserably stupid is this race of men, yea, so stupid and so wicked." Allowing them to be as stupid as you say, to whom is that stupidity owing? Without question it lies at the door of their inhuman masters who give them no means, no opportunity of improving their understanding. . . . Consequently it is not their fault but yours: you must answer for it before God and man. . . .

And what pains have you taken, what method have you used, to reclaim them from their wickedness? Have you carefully taught them, "That there is a God, a wise, powerful, merciful being, the creator and governor of heaven and earth? That he has appointed a day wherein he will judge the world, will take account of all our thoughts, words and actions? That in that day he will reward every child of man according to his works: that 'Then the righteous shall inherit the kingdom prepared for them from the foundation of the world: and the wicked shall be cast into everlasting fire, prepared for the devil and his angels.'" If you have not done this, if you have taken no pains or thought about the matter, can you wonder at their wickedness? What wonder if they should cut your throat? And if they did, whom could you thank for it but yourself? You first acted the villain in making them slaves (whether you stole them or bought them). You kept them stupid and wicked by cutting them off from all opportunities of improving either in knowledge or virtue. And now you assign their want of wisdom and goodness as the reason for using them worse than brute beasts. . . .

It remains only to make a little application of the preceding observations. . . . I therefore add a few words to those who are more immediately concerned, . . . and first to the captains employed in this trade. . . .

Is there a God? You know there is. Is he a just God? Then there must be a state of retribution; a state wherein the just God will reward every man according to his works. Then what reward will he render to you? O think betimes! Before you drop into eternity! Think now: he shall have judgment without mercy, that showed no mercy.

Are you a man? . . . Have you no sympathy? No sense of human woe? No pity for the miserable? . . . When you squeezed the agonizing creatures down in the ship, or when you threw their poor mangled remains into the sea, had you no [compassion]? Did not one tear drop from your eye, one sigh escape from your breast? Do you feel no [compassion] now? If you do not, you must go on till the measure of your iniquities is full. Then will the great God deal with *you,* as you have dealt with *them,* and require all their blood at your hands. . . .

Today resolve, God being your helper, to escape for your life. Regard not money! All that a man hath will he give for his life! Whatever you lose, lose not your soul; nothing can countervail that loss. Immediately quit the horrid trade. At all events, be an honest man.

This equally concerns every merchant who is engaged in the slave-trade. It is you that induce the African villain, to sell his countrymen, and in order thereto, to steal, rob, murder men, women and children without number. By enabling the English villain to pay him for so doing, whom you overpay for his execrable [detestable] labour. It is your money that is the spring of all, that impowers him to go on. . . . And is your conscience quite reconciled to this? Does it never reproach you at all? Has gold entirely blinded your eyes, and stupefied your heart? . . . Have no more part in this detestable business. Be you a man! Not a wolf, a devourer of the human species. Be merciful that you may obtain mercy.

And this equally concerns every gentleman that has an estate in our African plantations. Yea, all slave-holders of whatever rank and degree, seeing men-buyers are exactly at a level with men-sellers. Indeed you say, "I pay honestly for my goods, and am not concerned to know how they are come by." Nay, but . . . you know they are not honestly come by. . . .

If therefore you have any regard to justice (to say nothing of mercy, nor of the revealed law of God) render unto all their due. Give liberty to whom liberty is due, that is, to every child of man, to every partaker of human nature. Let none serve you but by his own act and deed, by his own voluntary choice. Away with all whips, all chains, all compulsion. Be gentle toward all men. And see that you invariably do unto every one, as you would he should do unto you.

O thou God of love, thou who art loving to every man, and whose mercy is over all thy works: Thou who art the father of the spirits of all flesh, and who art rich in mercy unto all: Thou who hast mingled in one blood all the nations upon earth: have compassion upon these outcasts of men, who are trodden down as dung upon the earth. Arise and help these who have no helper, whose blood is spilt upon the ground like water! Are not these also the work of thine own hands, the purchase of thy Son's blood? Stir them up to cry unto thee in the land of their captivity; and let their complaint come up before thee; let it enter into thine ears! Make even those that lead them away captive to pity them. . . . O burst thou all their chains in sunder; more especially the chains of their sins: Thou, Saviour of all, make them free, that they may be free indeed!

REVIEW QUESTIONS

1. When were the African slaves most likely to try to escape? How did the slave traders try to prevent this?
2. How did each of the slave traders regard the captive Africans?
3. What was Malachy Postlethwayt's argument in defense of slavery? What is your response?
4. To whom did Wesley address his arguments against the slave trade?
5. What were the commercial justifications for slavery that Wesley disputed? How did he account for the seeming inferiority of the slaves?

3 The Court of Louis XIV

During his seventy-two-year reign, Louis XIV (1643–1715) gave France greater unity and central authority than it had ever known. To prevent the great nobles from challenging royal authority, Louis XIV chose many of his ministers and provincial administrators from the middle class. The great nobles, "princes of the blood," enjoyed considerable social prestige but exercised no real power in the government. The king encouraged these "people of quality" to live at court, where they contended with each other for his favor.

As the symbol of France and the greatest ruler of Europe, Louis insisted that the social life at Versailles provide an appropriate setting for his exalted person. During his long reign, France set the style for the whole of Europe. The splendor of Versailles was the talk of Europe, and other monarchs sought to imitate the fashions and manners of the Sun King's court.

Duc de Saint-Simon
AN ASSESSMENT OF LOUIS XIV

Louis de Rouvroi, duc de Saint-Simon (1675–1755), was an astute observer of Louis XIV and his court. The following description of Louis XIV comes from Saint-Simon's extensive *Memoirs*.

Louis XIV was made for a brilliant Court. In the midst of other men, his figure, his courage, his grace, his beauty, his grand mien, even the tone of his voice and the majestic and natural charm of all his person, distinguished him till his death. . . . The superior ability of his early ministers and his early generals soon wearied him. He liked nobody to be in any way superior to him. Thus he chose his ministers, not for their knowledge, but for their ignorance; not for their capacity, but for their want of it. He liked to form them, as he said; liked to teach them even the most trifling things. It was the same with his generals. He took credit to himself for instructing them; wished it to be thought that from his cabinet he commanded and directed all his armies. Naturally fond of trifles, he unceasingly occupied himself with the most petty details of his troops, his household, his mansions. This vanity, this unmeasured and unreasonable love of admiration, was his ruin. His ministers, his generals, his mistresses, his courtiers, soon perceived his weakness. They praised him with emulation and spoiled

him. Those whom he liked owed his affection for them, to their untiring flatteries. This is what gave his ministers so much authority, and the opportunities they had for adulating him, of attributing everything to him, and of pretending to learn everything from him. Suppleness, meanness, an admiring, dependent, cringing manner—above all, an air of nothingness—were the sole means of pleasing him.

Though his intellect, as I have said, was beneath mediocrity, it was capable of being formed. He loved glory, was fond of order and regularity; was by disposition prudent, moderate, discreet, master of his movements and his tongue. Will it be believed? He was also by disposition good and just! God had sufficiently gifted him to enable him to be a good King; perhaps even *a tolerably great King!* All the evil came to him from elsewhere. His early education was . . . neglected. He was scarcely taught how to read or write, and remained so ignorant, that the most familiar historical and other facts were utterly unknown to him! He fell, accordingly, and sometimes even in public, into the grossest absurdities.

He was exceedingly jealous of the attention paid him. Not only did he notice the presence of the most distinguished courtiers, but those of inferior degree also. He looked to the right and to the left, not only upon rising but upon going to bed, at his meals, in passing through his apartments, or his gardens of Versailles, where alone the courtiers were allowed to follow him; he saw and noticed everybody; not one escaped him, not even those who hoped to remain unnoticed. He marked well all absentees from the court, found out the reason of their absence, and never lost an opportunity of acting towards them as the occasion might seem to justify. With some of the courtiers (the most distinguished), it was a demerit not to make the court their ordinary abode; with others 'twas a fault to come but rarely; for those who never or scarcely ever came it was certain disgrace. When their names were in any way mentioned, "I do not know them," the King would reply haughtily. Those who presented themselves but seldom were thus characterised: "They are people I never see"; these decrees were irrevocable. He could not bear people who liked Paris [better than Versailles].

Louis XIV took great pains to be well informed of all that passed everywhere; in the public places, in the private houses, in society and familiar intercourse. His spies and tell-tales were infinite. He had them of all species; many who were ignorant that their information reached him; others who knew it; others who wrote to him direct, sending their letters through channels he indicated; and all these letters were seen by him alone, and always before everything else; others who sometimes spoke to him secretly in his cabinet, entering by the back stairs. These unknown means ruined an infinite number of people of all classes, who never could discover the cause; often ruined them very unjustly; for the King, once prejudiced, never altered his opinion, or so rarely, that nothing was more rare. He had, too, another fault, very dangerous for others and often for himself, since it deprived him of good subjects. He had an excellent memory; in this way, that if he saw a man who, twenty years before, perhaps, had in some manner offended him, he did not forget the man, though he might forget the offence. This was enough, however, to exclude the person from all favour. The representations of a minister, of a general, of his confessor even, could not move the King. He would not yield.

The most cruel means by which the King was informed of what was passing—for many years before anybody knew it—was that of opening letters. The promptitude and dexterity with which they were opened passes understanding. He saw extracts from all the letters in which there were passages that the chiefs of the post-office, and then the minister who governed it, thought ought to go before him; entire letters, too, were sent to him, when their contents seemed to justify the sending. Thus the chiefs of the post, nay, the principal clerks were in a position to suppose what they pleased and against whom they pleased. A word of contempt against the King or the government, a joke, a detached phrase, was enough. It is incredible how many people, justly or unjustly, were more or less ruined, always without resource, without trial, and without knowing why. . . .

Never was man so naturally polite, or of a politeness so measured, so graduated, so adapted to person, time, and place. Towards women his politeness was without parallel. Never did he pass the humblest petticoat without raising his hat; even to chambermaids, that he knew to be such, as often happened at Marly. For ladies he took his hat off completely. . . . He took it off for the princes of the blood, as for the ladies. If he accosted ladies he did not cover himself until he had quitted them. All this was out of doors, for in the house he was never covered. . . .

The King loved air and exercise very much, as long as he could make use of them. He had excelled in dancing, and at tennis and mall [a game played on grass with a mallet]. On horseback he was admirable, even at a late age. He liked to see everything done with grace and address. To acquit yourself well or ill before him was a merit or a fault. . . . He was very fond of shooting, and there was not a better or more graceful shot than he. He had always in his cabinet seven or eight pointer bitches, and was fond of feeding them, to make himself known to them. He was very fond, too, of stag hunting. . . .

He liked splendour, magnificence, and profusion in everything: you pleased him if you shone through the brilliancy of your houses, your clothes, your table, your equipages [horse-drawn carriages].

As for the King himself, nobody ever approached his magnificence. His buildings, who could number them? At the same time, who was there who did not deplore the pride, the caprice, the bad taste seen in them? St. Germains, a lovely spot, with a marvellous view, rich forest, terraces, gardens, and water he abandoned for Versailles; the dullest and most ungrateful of all places, without prospect, without wood, without water, without soil; for the ground is all shifting sand or swamp, the air accordingly bad. . . .

Let me now speak of the amours of the King which were even more fatal to the state than his building mania.

Louis XIV in his youth was more made for love than any of his subjects—being tired of gathering passing sweets, fixed himself at last upon La Vallière.[1] The progress and the result of his love are well known. . . .

When the King travelled his coach was always full of women; his mistresses, afterwards his bastards, his daughters-in-law, sometimes *Madame,* and other ladies when there was room. In the coach, during his journeys, there were always all sorts of things to eat, as meat, pastry, fruit. A quarter of a league was not passed over before the King asked if somebody would not eat. He never ate anything between meals himself, not even fruit; but he amused himself by seeing others do so, aye, and to bursting. You were obliged to be hungry, merry, and to eat with appetite, otherwise he was displeased and even showed it. And yet after this, if you supped with him at table the same day, you were compelled to eat with as good a countenance as though you had tasted nothing since the previous night. He was as inconsiderate in other and more delicate matters; and ladies, in his long drives and stations, had often occasion to curse him. The Duchesse de Chevreuse once rode all the way from Versailles to Fontainebleau in such extremity, that several times she was well-nigh losing consciousness. . . .

At ten o'clock his supper was served. The captain of the guard announced this to him. A quarter of an hour after the King came to supper, and from the ante-chamber of Madame de Maintenon[2] to the table again, any one spoke to him who wished. This supper was always on a grand scale, the royal household (that is, the sons and daughters of France), at table, and a large number of courtiers and ladies present, sitting or standing. . . .

During all his life, the King failed only once in his attendance at mass. It was with the army, during a forced march; he missed no fast day, unless really indisposed. Some days before Lent, he publicly declared that he should be very much displeased if any one ate meat or gave it to others, under any pretext.

---

[1]Françoise-Louise de La Vallière was Louis XIV's mistress from 1661 to 1667; she held great influence over him and was the mother of four of his children. After being discarded as his mistress she retired to a convent in 1674.

[2]Françoise d'Aubigné (Madame de Maintenon) was the widow of a celebrated poet when she became governess to two of the king's children in 1669. He provided her with an estate and later married her secretly.

REVIEW QUESTION

1. According to Saint-Simon, what were Louis XIV's likes and dislikes?

4 Justification of Absolute Monarchy

Effectively blocking royal absolutism in the Middle Ages were the dispersion of power between kings and feudal lords, the vigorous sense of personal freedom and urban autonomy of the townspeople, and the limitations on royal power imposed by the church. However, by the late sixteenth century, monarchs were asserting their authority over competing groups with ever-greater effectiveness. In this new balance of political forces, European kings implemented their claim to absolute power as monarchs chosen by and responsible to God alone. This theory, called the divine right of kings, became the dominant political ideology of seventeenth- and eighteenth-century Europe.

James I
". . . KINGS ARE GOD'S LIEUTENANTS UPON EARTH. . . ."

One of the most articulate defenders of the divine right of monarchy was James VI, who was king of Scotland (1567–1625) and as James I (1603–1625) also was king of England. A scholar as well as a king, James in 1598 anonymously published a widely read book called the *True Law of Free Monarchies.* He claimed that the king alone was the true legislator. James's notions of the royal prerogative and of the role of Parliament are detailed in the following passages from the *True Law* and a speech to Parliament.

TRUE LAW
Prerogative and Parliament

According to these fundamental laws already alleged, we daily see that in the parliament (which is nothing else but the head court of the king and his vassals) the laws are but craved by his subjects, and only made by him at their [proposal] and with their advice: for albeit the king make daily statutes and ordinances, [imposing] such pains thereto as he thinks [fit], without any advice of parliament or estates, yet it lies in the power of no parliament to make any kind of law or statute, without his sceptre [that is, authority] be to it, for giving it the force of a law. . . . And as ye see it manifest that the king is over-lord of the whole land, so is he master over every person that inhabiteth the same, having power over the life and death of every one of them: for although a just prince will not take the life of any of his subjects without a clear law, yet the same laws whereby he taketh them are made by himself or his predecessors; and so the power flows always from himself. . . . Where he sees the law doubtsome or rigorous, he may interpret or mitigate the same, lest otherwise *summum jus* be *summa injuria* [the greatest right be the greatest wrong]: and therefore general laws made publicly in parliament may upon . . . [the king's] authority be mitigated and suspended upon causes only known to him.

As likewise, although I have said a good king will frame all his actions to be according to the law, yet is he not bound thereto but of his good will, and for good example-giving to his subjects [?] . . . So as I have already said, a good king, though he be above the law, will subject and frame his actions thereto, for example's sake to his subjects, and of his own free will, but not as subject or bound thereto. . . .

In a speech before the English Parliament in March 1610, James elaborated on his exalted theory of the monarch's absolute power.

A SPEECH TO PARLIAMENT

. . . The state of monarchy is the supremest thing upon earth: for kings are not only God's lieutenants upon earth and sit upon God's throne, but even by God himself they are called gods. There be three principal [comparisons] that illustrate the state of monarchy: one taken out of the word of God, and the two other out of the grounds of policy and philosophy. In the Scriptures kings are called gods, and so their power after a certain relation compared to the Divine power. Kings are also compared to fathers of families: for a king is truly *parens patriae* [parent of the country], the politic father of his people. And lastly, kings are compared to the head of this microcosm of the body of man. . . .

I conclude then this point touching the power of kings with this axiom of divinity, That as to dispute what God may do is blasphemy, . . . so is it sedition in subjects to dispute what a king may do in the height of his power. But just kings will ever be willing to declare what they will do, if they will not incur the curse of God. I will not be content that my power be disputed upon; but I shall ever be willing to make the reason appear of all my doings, and rule my actions according to my laws. . . .

Now the second general ground whereof I am to speak concerns the matter of grievances. . . . First then, I am not to find fault that you inform yourselves of the particular just grievances of the people; nay I must tell you, ye can neither be just nor faithful to me or to your countries that trust and employ you, if you do it not. . . . But I would wish you to be careful to avoid [these] things in the matter of grievances.

First, that you do not meddle with the main points of government: that is my craft . . . to meddle with that, were to lessen me. I am now an old king . . .; I must not be taught my office.

Secondly, I would not have you meddle with such ancient rights of mine as I have received from my predecessors, possessing them *more majorum* [as ancestral customs]: such things I would be sorry should be accounted for grievances. All novelties are dangerous as well in a politic as in a natural body: and therefore I would be loath to be quarrelled in my ancient rights and possessions: for that were to judge me unworthy of that which my predecessors had and left me.

Thomas Hobbes
LEVIATHAN

Thomas Hobbes (1588–1679), a British philosopher and political theorist, witnessed the agonies of the English civil war, including the execution of Charles I in 1649. These developments fortified Hobbes's conviction that absolutism was the most desirable and logical form of government. Only the unlimited power of a sovereign, said Hobbes, could contain human passions that disrupt the social order and threaten civilized life; only absolute rule could provide an environment secure enough for people to pursue their individual interests.

Leviathan (1651), Hobbes's principal work of political thought, broke with medieval political theory. Medieval thinkers assigned each group of people— clergy, lords, serfs, guildsmen—a place in a fixed social order; an individual's social duties were set by ancient traditions believed to have been ordained by God. During early modern times, the great expansion of commerce and capitalism spurred the new individualism already pronounced in Renaissance culture; group ties were shattered by competition and accelerating social mobility. Hobbes gave expression to a society where people confronted each other as competing individuals.

Hobbes was influenced by the new scientific thought that saw mathematical knowledge as the avenue to truth. Using geometry as a model, Hobbes began with what he believed were self-evident axioms regarding human nature, from which he deduced other truths. He aimed at constructing political philosophy on a scientific foundation and rejected the authority of tradition and religion as inconsistent with a science of politics. Thus, although Hobbes supported absolutism, he dismissed the idea advanced by other theorists of absolutism that the monarch's power derived from God. He also rejected the idea that the state should not be obeyed when it violated God's law. *Leviathan* is a rational and secular political statement. In this modern approach, rather than in Hobbes's justification of absolutism, lies the work's significance.

Hobbes had a pessimistic view of human nature. Believing that people are innately selfish and grasping, he maintained that competition and dissension, rather than cooperation, characterize human relations. Even when reason teaches that cooperation is more advantageous than competition, Hobbes observed that people are reluctant to alter their ways, because passion, not reason, governs their behavior. In the following passages from *Leviathan,* Hobbes describes the causes of human conflicts.

Nature hath made men so equall, in the faculties of body, and mind; as that though there bee found one man sometimes manifestly stronger in body, or of quicker mind than another; yet when all is reckoned together, the difference between man, and man, is not so considerable, as that one man can thereupon claim to himselfe any benefit, to which another may not pretend, as well as he. For as to the strength of body, the weakest has strength enough to kill the strongest, either by secret machination, or by confederacy with others, that are in the same danger with himselfe. . . .

And as to the faculties of the mind . . . men are . . . [more] equall than unequall. . . .

From this equality of ability, ariseth equality of hope in the attaining of our Ends. And therefore if any two men desire the same thing, which neverthelesse they cannot both enjoy, they become enemies; and in the way to their End, . . . endeavour to destroy, or subdue one another. . . . If one plant, sow, build, or possesse a convenient Seat, others may probably be expected to come prepared with forces united, to dispossesse, and deprive him, not only of the fruit of his labour, but also of his life, or liberty. . . .

So that in the nature of man, we find three principall causes of quarrell. First, Competition; Secondly, Diffidence [unsureness]; Thirdly, Glory.

The first, maketh men invade for Gain; the second, for Safety; and the third, for Reputation. The first use Violence, to make themselves Masters of other men's persons, wives, children, and cattell; the second, to defend them; the third, for trifles, as a word, a smile, a different opinion, and any other signe of undervalue, either direct in their Persons, or by reflexion in their Kindred, their Friends, their Nation, their Profession, or their Name.

Hereby it is manifest, that during the time men live without a common Power to keep them all in awe, they are in that condition which is called Warre; and such a warre, as is of every man, against every man. . . .

Hobbes then describes a state of nature—the hypothetical condition of humanity prior to the formation of the state—as a war of all against all. For Hobbes, the state of nature is a logical abstraction, a device employed to make his point. Only a strong ruling entity—the state—will end the perpetual strife and provide security. For Hobbes, the state is merely a useful arrangement that permits individuals to exchange goods and services in a secure environment. The ruling authority in the state, the sovereign, must have supreme power, or society will collapse and the anarchy of the state of nature will return.

Whatsoever therefore is consequent to a time of Warre, where every man is Enemy to every man; the same is consequent to the time, wherein men live without other security, than what their own strength, and their own invention shall furnish them withall. In such condition, there is no place for Industry; because the fruit thereof is uncertain: and consequently no Culture of the Earth; no Navigation, nor use of the commodities that may be imported by Sea; no commodious Building; no Instruments of moving, and removing such things as require much force; no Knowledge of the face of the Earth; no account of Time; no Arts; no Letters; no Society; and which is worst of all, continuall feare, and danger of violent death; And the life of man, solitary, poore, nasty, brutish, and short. . . .

The Passions that encline men to Peace, are Feare of Death; Desire of such things as are necessary to commodious living; and a Hope by their Industry to obtain them. And Reason suggesteth convenient Articles of Peace, upon which men may be drawn to agreement. . . .

And because the condition of Man, (as hath been declared in the precedent Chapter) is a condition of Warre of every one against every one; in which case every one is governed by his own Reason; and there is nothing he can make use of, that may not be a help unto him, in preserving his life against his enemyes; It followeth, that in such a condition, every man has a Right to every thing; even to one another's body. And therefore, as long as this naturall Right of every man to every thing

endureth, there can be no security to any man, (how strong or wise soever he be,) of living out the time, which Nature ordinarily alloweth men to live. . . .

. . . If there be no Power erected, or not great enough for our security; every man will and may lawfully rely on his own strength and art, for caution against all other men. . . .

The only way to erect . . . a Common Power, as may be able to defend them from the invasion of [foreigners] and the injuries of one another, and thereby to secure them in such sort, as that by their owne industrie, and by the fruites of the Earth, they may nourish themselves and live contentedly; is, to conferre all their power and strength upon one Man, or upon one Assembly of men, that may reduce all their Wills, by plurality of voices, unto one Will . . . and therein to submit their Wills, every one to his Will, and their Judgements, to his Judgement. This is more than Consent, or Concord; it is a reall Unitie of them all, in one and the same Person, made by Covenant of every man with every man, in such manner, as if every man should say to every man, *I Authorise and give up my Right of Governing my selfe, to this Man, or to this Assembly of men, on this condition, that thou give up thy Right to him, and Authorise all his Actions in like manner.* This done, the Multitude so united in one Person, is called a COMMON-WEALTH. . . . For by this Authoritie, given him by every particular man in the Common-wealth, he hath the use of so much Power and Strength . . . conferred on him, that by terror thereof, he is inabled to forme the wills of them all, to Peace at home, and mutuall [aid] against their enemies abroad. And in him consisteth the Essence of the Common-wealth; which (to define it,) is *One Person, of whose Acts a great Multitude, by mutuall Covenants one with another, have made themselves every one the Author, to the end he may use the strength and means of them all, as he shall think expedient, for their Peace and Common Defence.*

And he that carryeth this Person, is called SOVERAIGNE, and said to have *Soveraigne Power;* and every one besides, his SUBJECT. . . .

. . . They that have already Instituted a Common-wealth, being thereby bound by

Covenant . . . cannot lawfully make a new Covenant, amongst themselves, to be obedient to any other, in any thing whatsoever, without his permission. And therefore, they that are subjects to a Monarch, cannot without his leave cast off Monarchy, and return to the confusion of a disunited Multitude; nor transferre their Person from him that beareth it, to another Man, or other Assembly of men: for they . . . are bound, every man to every man, to [acknowledge] . . . that he that already is their Soveraigne, shall do, and judge fit to be done; so that [those who do not obey] break their Covenant made to that man, which is injustice: and they have also every man given the Soveraignty to him that beareth their Person; and therefore if they depose him, they take from him that which is his own, and so again it is injustice. . . . And whereas some men have pretended for their disobedience to their Soveraigne, a new Covenant, made, not with men, but with God; this also is unjust: for there is no Covenant with God, but by mediation of some body that representeth God's Person; which none doth but God's Lieutenant, who hath the Soveraignty under God. But this pretence of Covenant with God, is so evident a [lie], even in the pretenders own consciences, that it is not onely an act of an unjust, but also of a vile, and unmanly disposition. . . .

. . . Consequently none of [the sovereign's] Subjects, by any pretence of forfeiture, can be freed from his Subjection.

REVIEW QUESTIONS

1. What was the theory of kingship by divine authority embraced by King James I of England?
2. What was the proper role of Parliament for James I?
3. What was Thomas Hobbes's view of human nature and what conclusions did he draw from it about the best form of government?
4. What has been the political legacy of Hobbes's notion of the state?

---

5 The Triumph of Constitutional Monarchy in England: The Glorious Revolution

The struggle against absolute monarchy in England during the early seventeenth century reached a climax during the reign of Charles I (1625–1649). Parliament raised its own army as civil war broke out between its supporters and those of the king. Captured by the Scottish Presbyterian rebels in 1646 and turned over to the English parliamentary army in 1647, Charles was held prisoner for two years until the Puritan parliamentary general Oliver Cromwell (1599–1658) decided to put him on trial for treason. The king was found guilty and executed in 1649.

The revolutionary parliamentary regime evolved into a military dictatorship headed by Cromwell. After Cromwell's death, Parliament in 1660 restored the monarchy and invited the late king's heir to end his exile and take the throne. Charles II (1660–1685), by discretion and skillful statesmanship, managed to evade many difficulties caused by the hostility of those who opposed his policies. He attempted to ease religious discrimination by ending the laws that penalized dissenters who rejected the official Church of England. But the religious prejudices of Parliament forced the king to desist, and the laws penalizing both Protestant dissenters and Roman Catholics remained in force. The king's motives for establishing religious toleration were suspect, since he himself was married to a French Catholic and his brother and heir James, Duke of York, was also a staunch Catholic.

When James II (1685–1688) succeeded to the throne, he tried unsuccessfully to get Parliament to repeal the Test Act, a law that forbade anyone to hold a civil or military office or to enter a university unless he was a member in good standing of the Church of England. This law effectively barred both Catholics and Protestant dissenters from serving in the king's government. When Parliament refused to act, James got the legal Court of the King's Bench to approve his decree suspending the Test Act. The court affirmed that the king, due to his sovereign authority, had absolute power to suspend any law at his sole discretion. The prerogatives claimed by the king were seen by many as an attempt to impose absolute monarchy on the English people.

King James further roused enemies by appointing many Catholics to high government posts and by issuing his Declaration of Indulgence for Liberty of Conscience on April 4, 1687. This declaration established complete freedom of worship for all Englishmen, ending all civil penalties and discriminations based on religious dissent. Instead of hailing the declaration as a step forward in solving the religious quarrels within the kingdom, many persons viewed this suspension of the laws as a further act of absolutism because James acted unilaterally without consulting Parliament. This act united the king's enemies and alienated his former supporters.

When the king's wife gave birth to a son, making the heir to the throne another Catholic, almost all factions (except the Catholics) abandoned James II and invited the Dutch Protestant Prince William of Orange and his wife Mary, James II's Protestant daughter, to come to England. James and his Catholic family and friends fled to France. Parliament declared the throne vacant and offered it to William and Mary as joint sovereigns. As a result of the "Glorious Revolution," the English monarchy became clearly limited by the will of Parliament.

THE ENGLISH DECLARATION OF RIGHTS

In depriving James II of the throne, Parliament had destroyed forever in Britain the theory of divine right as an operating principle of government and had firmly established a limited constitutional monarchy. The appointment of William and Mary was accompanied by a declaration of rights (later enacted as the Bill of Rights), which enumerated and declared illegal James II's arbitrary acts. The Declaration of Rights, excerpted below, compelled William and Mary and future monarchs to recognize the right of the people's representatives to dispose of the royal office and to set limits on its powers. These rights were subsequently formulated into laws passed by Parliament. Prior to the American Revolution, colonists protested that British actions in the American colonies violated certain rights guaranteed in the English Bill of Rights. Several of these rights were later included in the Constitution of the United States.

And whereas the said late king James the Second having abdicated the government and the throne being thereby vacant, His Highness

the prince of Orange (whom it hath pleased Almighty God to make the glorious instrument of delivering this kingdom from popery and arbitrary power) did (by the advice of the lords spiritual and temporal and divers principal persons of the commons)[1] cause letters to be written to the lords spiritual and temporal, being Protestants; and other letters to the several counties, cities, universities, boroughs and Cinque ports[2] for the choosing of such persons to represent them, as were of right to be sent to parliament, to meet and sit at Westminster upon the two and twentieth day of January in this year one thousand six hundred eighty and eight,[3] in order to [guarantee] . . . that their religion, laws and liberties might not again be in danger of being subverted; upon which letters elections having been accordingly made.

And thereupon the said lords spiritual and temporal and commons pursuant to their respective letters and elections being now assembled in a full and free representative of this nation, taking into their most serious consideration the best means for attaining the ends aforesaid, do in the first place (as their ancestors in like case have usually done) for the vindicating and asserting their ancient rights and liberties, declare:

That the pretended power of suspending of laws or the execution of laws by regal authority without consent of parliament is illegal.

That the pretended power of dispensing with laws or the execution of laws by regal authority as it hath been assumed and exercised of late is illegal.

That the commission for erecting the late court of commissioners for ecclesiastical causes and all other commissions and courts of like nature are illegal and pernicious.

That the levying money for or to the use of the crown by pretence of prerogative without grant of parliament for a longer time or in other manner than the same is or shall be granted is illegal.

That it is the right of the subjects to petition the king and all commitments and prosecutions for such petitioning are illegal.

That the raising or keeping a standing army within the kingdom in time of peace unless it be with consent of parliament is against the law.

That the subjects which are Protestants may have arms for their defence suitable to their conditions and as allowed by law.

That election of members of parliament ought to be free.

That the freedom of speech and debates or proceedings in parliament ought not to be impeached or questioned in any court or place out of parliament.

That excessive bail ought not to be required nor excessive fines imposed nor cruel and unusual punishments inflicted.

That jurors ought to be duly impanelled and returned and jurors which pass upon men in trials for high treason ought to be freeholders [landholders].

That all grants and promises of fines and forfeitures of particular persons before conviction are illegal and void.

And that for redress of all grievances and for the amending, strengthening and preserving of the laws parliaments ought to be held frequently.

And they do claim, demand and insist upon all and singular the premises as their undoubted rights and liberties and that no declarations, judgments, doings or proceedings to the prejudice of the people in any of the said premises ought in any wise to be drawn hereafter into consequence or example.

---

[1]"The lords spiritual" refers to the bishops of the Church of England who sat in the House of Lords, and "the lords temporal" refers to the nobility entitled to sit in the House of Lords. "The commons" refers to the elected representatives in the House of Commons.

[2]The Cinque ports along England's southeastern coast (originally five in number) enjoyed special privileges because of their military duties in providing for coastal defense.

[3]The year was in fact 1689 because until 1752, the English used March 25 as the beginning of the new year.

REVIEW QUESTIONS

1. How did the Declaration of Rights limit royal authority? With what result?
2. In what ways did the Glorious Revolution impact upon the American rebellion in the 1770s?

CHAPTER 9

Intellectual Revolutions

GALILEO GALILEI'S (1564–1642) support of Copernicanism and rejection of the medieval division of the universe into higher and lower realms make him a principal shaper of modern science. *(The Granger Collection, New York.)*

The Scientific Revolution of the sixteenth and seventeenth centuries replaced the medieval view of the universe with a new cosmology and produced a new way of investigating nature. It overthrew the medieval conception of nature as a hierarchical order ascending toward a realm of perfection. Rejecting reliance on authority, the thinkers of the Scientific Revolution affirmed the individual's ability to know the natural world through the method of mathematical reasoning, the direct observation of nature, and carefully controlled experiments.

The medieval view of the universe had blended the theories of Aristotle and Ptolemy, two ancient Greek thinkers, with Christian teachings. In that view, a stationary earth stood in the center of the universe just above hell. Revolving around the earth were seven planets: the moon, Mercury, Venus, the sun, Mars, Jupiter, and Saturn. Because people believed that earth did not move, it was not considered a planet. Each planet was attached to a transparent sphere that turned around the earth. Encompassing the universe was a sphere of fixed stars; beyond the stars lay three heavenly spheres, the outermost of which was the abode of God. An earth-centered universe accorded with the Christian idea that God had created the universe for men and women and that salvation was the aim of life.

Also agreeable to the medieval Christian view was Aristotle's division of the universe into a lower, earthly realm and a higher realm beyond the moon. Two sets of laws operated in the universe, one on earth and the other in the celestial realm. Earthly objects were composed of four elements: earth, water, fire, and air; celestial objects were composed of the divine ether—a substance too pure, too clear, too fine, too spiritual to be found on earth. Celestial objects naturally moved in perfectly circular orbits around the earth; earthly objects, composed mainly of the heavy elements of earth and water, naturally fell downward, whereas objects made of the lighter elements of air and fire naturally flew upward toward the sky.

The destruction of the medieval world picture began with the publication in 1543 of *On the Revolutions of the Heavenly Spheres,* by Nicolaus Copernicus, a Polish mathematician, astronomer, and clergyman. In Copernicus's system, the sun was in the center of the universe, and the earth was another planet that moved around the sun. Most thinkers of the time, committed to the Aristotelian–Ptolemaic system and to the biblical statements that seemed to support it, rejected Copernicus's conclusions.

The work of Galileo Galilei, an Italian mathematician, astronomer, and physicist, was decisive in the shattering of the medieval cosmos and the shaping of the modern scientific outlook. Galileo advanced the modern view that knowledge of nature derives from direct observation and from mathematics. For Galileo, the universe was a "grand book which . . . is written in the language of mathematics, and its characters are triangles, circles, and other geometric figures without which it is humanly impossible to understand a single word of it." Galileo also pioneered experimental physics, advanced the modern idea that nature is uniform throughout the universe, and attacked reliance on scholastic authority rather than on experimentation in resolving scientific controversies.

Johannes Kepler (1571–1630), a contemporary of Galileo, discovered three laws of planetary motion that greatly advanced astronomical knowledge. Kepler showed that the path of a planet was an ellipse, not a circle as Ptolemy (and Copernicus) had believed, and that planets do not move at uniform speed but accelerate as they near the sun. He devised formulas to calculate accurately both a planet's speed at each point in its orbit around the sun and a planet's location at a particular time. Kepler's laws provided further evidence that Copernicus had been right, for they made sense only in a sun-centered universe, but Kepler could not explain why planets stayed in their orbits rather than flying off into space or crashing into the sun. The resolution of that question was left to Sir Isaac Newton.

Newton's great achievement was integrating the findings of Copernicus, Galileo, and Kepler into a single theoretical system. In *Principia Mathematica* (1687), he formulated the mechanical laws of motion and attraction that govern celestial and terrestrial objects.

The Scientific Revolution was instrumental in shaping the modern outlook. It destroyed the medieval conception of the universe and established the scientific method as the means for investigating nature and acquiring knowledge, even in areas having little to do with the study of the physical world. By demonstrating the powers of the human mind, the Scientific Revolution gave thinkers great confidence in reason and led eventually to a rejection of traditional beliefs in magic, astrology, and witches. In the eighteenth century, this growing skepticism led thinkers to question miracles and other Christian beliefs that seemed contrary to reason.

The Enlightenment of the eighteenth century culminated the movement toward modernity that started in the Renaissance era. The thinkers of the Enlightenment, called *philosophes,* attacked medieval otherworldliness, dethroned theology from its once-proud position as queen of the sciences, and based their understanding of nature and society on reason alone, unaided by revelation or priestly authority.

From the broad spectrum of Western history, several traditions flowed into the Enlightenment: the rational spirit born in classical Greece, the Stoic emphasis on natural law that applies to all human beings, and the Christian belief that all individuals are equal in God's eyes. A more immediate influence on the Enlightenment was Renaissance humanism, which focused on the individual and worldly human accomplishments and which criticized medieval theology-philosophy for its preoccupation with questions that seemed unrelated to the human condition. In many ways, the Enlightenment grew directly out of the Scientific Revolution. The philosophes praised both Newton's discovery of the mechanical laws that govern the universe and the scientific method that made this discovery possible. They wanted to transfer the scientific method—the reliance on experience and the critical use of the intellect—to the realm of society. They maintained that independent of clerical authority, human beings through reason could grasp the natural laws that govern the social world, just as Newton had uncovered the laws of nature that operate in the physical world. The philosophes said that those institutions and traditions that could not meet the test of reason, because they were based on authority, ignorance, or superstition, had to be reformed or dispensed with.

For medieval philosophers, reason had been subordinate to revelation; the Christian outlook determined the medieval concept of nature, morality, government, law, and life's purpose. During the Renaissance and Scientific Revolution, reason increasingly asserted its autonomy. For example, Machiavelli rejected the principle that politics should be based on Christian teachings; he recognized no higher world as the source of a higher truth. Galileo held that on questions regarding nature, one should trust to observation, experimentation, and mathematical reasoning and should not rely on Scripture. Descartes rejected reliance on past authority and maintained that through thought alone one could attain knowledge that has absolute certainty. Agreeing with Descartes that the mind is self-sufficient, the philosophes rejected the guidance of revelation and its priestly interpreters. They believed that through the use of reason, individuals could comprehend and reform society.

The Enlightenment philosophes articulated basic principles of the modern outlook: confidence in the self-sufficiency of the human mind, belief that individuals possess natural rights that governments should not violate, and the desire to reform society in accordance with rational principles. Their views influenced the reformers of the French Revolution and the founding fathers of the United States.

---

1 Expanding the New Astronomy

The brilliant Italian scientist Galileo Galilei (1564–1642) rejected the medieval division of the universe into higher and lower realms and proclaimed the modern idea of nature's uniformity. Learning that a telescope had been invented in Holland, Galileo built one for himself and used it to investigate the heavens. Through his telescope, Galileo saw craters and mountains on the moon; he concluded that celestial bodies were not pure, perfect, and immutable, as had been believed. There was no difference in quality between heavenly and earthly bodies; nature was the same throughout.

Galileo appealed to the Roman Catholic authorities asking them to halt their actions against the theories of Copernicus, but was unsuccessful. His support of Copernicus aroused the ire of both clergy and scholastic philosophers. In 1616, the church placed Copernicus's book on the index of forbidden books, and Galileo was ordered to cease his defense of the Copernican theory. In 1632, Galileo published *Dialogue Concerning the Two Chief World Systems* in which he upheld the Copernican view. Widely distributed and acclaimed, the book antagonized Galileo's enemies, who succeeded in halting further printing. Summoned to Rome, the aging and infirm scientist was put on trial by the Inquisition and ordered to renounce the Copernican theory. Galileo bowed to the Inquisition, which condemned the *Dialogue* and sentenced him to life imprisonment—largely house arrest at his own villa near Florence, where he was treated humanely.

Galileo Galilei
THE STARRY MESSENGER

In the following reading from *The Starry Messenger* (1610), Galileo reported the findings observed through his telescope, which led him to proclaim the uniformity of nature, a key principle of modern science.

About ten months ago a report reached my ears that a certain Fleming [a native of Flanders]* had constructed a spyglass by means of which visible objects, though very distant from the eye of the observer, were distinctly seen as if nearby. Of this truly remarkable effect several experiences were related, to which some persons gave credence while others denied them. A few days later the report was confirmed to me in a letter from a noble Frenchman at Paris, Jacques Badovere,† which caused me to apply myself wholeheartedly to inquire into the means by which I might arrive at the invention of a similar instrument. This I did shortly afterwards, my basis being the theory of refraction. First I prepared a tube of lead, at the ends of which I fitted two glass lenses, both plane on one side while on the other side one was spherically convex and the other concave. Then placing my eye near the concave lens I perceived objects satisfactorily large and near, for they appeared three times closer and nine times larger than when seen with the naked eye alone. Next I constructed another one, more accurate, which represented objects as enlarged more than sixty times. Finally, sparing neither labor nor expense, I succeeded in constructing for myself so excellent an instrument that objects seen by means of it appeared nearly one thousand times larger and over thirty times closer than when regarded with our natural vision.

It would be superfluous to enumerate the number and importance of the advantages of such an instrument at sea as well as on land. But forsaking terrestrial observations, I turned to celestial ones, and first I saw the moon from as near at hand as if it were scarcely two terrestrial radii [a measure of distance, obscure today] away. After that I observed often with wondering delight both the planets and the fixed stars, and since I saw these latter to be very crowded, I began to seek (and eventually found) a method

---

*Credit for the original invention is generally assigned to Hans Lipperhey, a lens grinder in Holland who chanced upon this property of combined lenses and applied for a patent on it in 1608.

†Badovere studied in Italy toward the close of the sixteenth century and is said to have been a pupil of Galileo's in about 1598. When he wrote concerning the new instrument in 1609, he was in the French diplomatic service at Paris, where he died in 1620.

by which I might measure their distances apart. . . .

Now let us review the observations made during the past two months, once more inviting the attention of all who are eager for true philosophy to the first steps of such important contemplations. Let us speak first of that surface of the moon which faces us. For greater clarity I distinguish two parts of this surface, a lighter and a darker; the lighter part seems to surround and to pervade the whole hemisphere, while the darker part discolors the moon's surface like a kind of cloud, and makes it appear covered with spots. Now those spots which are fairly dark and rather large are plain to everyone and have been seen throughout the ages; these I shall call the "large" or "ancient" spots, distinguishing them from others that are smaller in size but so numerous as to occur all over the lunar surface, and especially the lighter part. The latter spots had never been seen by anyone before me. From observations of these spots repeated many times I have been led to the opinion and conviction that the surface of the moon is not smooth, uniform, and precisely spherical as a great number of philosophers believe it (and the other heavenly bodies) to be, but is uneven, rough, and full of cavities and prominences, being not unlike the face of the earth, relieved by chains of mountains and deep valleys. . . .

With his telescope, Galileo discovered four moons orbiting Jupiter, an observation that overcame a principal objection to the Copernican system. Galileo showed that a celestial body could indeed move around a center other than the earth; that earth was not the common center for all celestial bodies; that a celestial body (earth's moon or Jupiter's moons) could orbit a planet at the same time that the planet revolved around another body (namely, the sun).

On the seventh day of January in this present year 1610, at the first hour of night, when I was viewing the heavenly bodies with a telescope, Jupiter presented itself to me; and because I had prepared a very excellent instrument for myself, I perceived (as I had not before, on account of the weakness of my previous instrument) that beside the planet there were three starlets, small indeed, but very bright. Though I believed them to be among the host of fixed stars, they aroused my curiosity somewhat by appearing to lie in an exact straight line parallel to the ecliptic, and by their being more splendid than others of their size. Their arrangement with respect to Jupiter and each other was the following:

East   *   *   **O**   *   *West*

that is, there were two stars on the eastern side and one to the west. The most easterly star and the western one appeared larger than the other. I paid no attention to the distances between them and Jupiter, for at the outset I thought them to be fixed stars, as I have said.‡ But returning to the same investigation on January eighth—led by what, I do not know—I found a very different arrangement. The three starlets were now all to the west of Jupiter, closer together, and at equal intervals from one another as shown in the following sketch:

East   **O**   *   *   *   *West*

On the tenth of January, however, the stars appeared in this position with respect to Jupiter:

East   *   *   **O**   *West*

that is, there were but two of them, both easterly, the third (as I supposed) being hidden behind Jupiter. . . . There was no way in which such al-

---

‡The reader should remember that the telescope was nightly revealing to Galileo hundreds of fixed stars never previously observed. His unusual gifts for astronomical observation are illustrated by his having noticed and remembered these three merely by reason of their alignment, and recalling them so well that when by chance he happened to see them the following night he was certain that they had changed their positions.

terations could be attributed to Jupiter's motion, yet being certain that these were still the same stars I had observed . . . my perplexity was now transformed into amazement. I was sure that the apparent changes belonged not to Jupiter but to the observed stars, and I resolved to pursue this investigation with greater care and attention. . . .

I had now decided beyond all question that there existed in the heavens three stars wandering about Jupiter as do Venus and Mercury about the sun, and this became plainer than daylight from observations on similar occasions which followed. Nor were there just three such stars; four wanderers complete their revolutions about Jupiter. . . .

Here we have a fine and elegant argument for quieting the doubts of those who, while accepting with tranquil mind the revolutions of the planets about the sun in the Copernican system, are mightily disturbed to have the moon alone revolve about the earth and accompany it in an annual rotation about the sun. Some have believed that this structure of the universe should be rejected as impossible. But now we have not just one planet rotating about another while both run through a great orbit around the sun; our own eyes show us four stars which wander around Jupiter as does the moon around the earth, while all together trace out a grand revolution about the sun in the space of twelve years.

Galileo Galilei
LETTER TO THE GRAND DUCHESS CHRISTINA AND *DIALOGUE CONCERNING THE TWO CHIEF WORLD SYSTEMS— PTOLEMAIC AND COPERNICAN*

The first reading illustrates Galileo's active involvement in a struggle for freedom of inquiry many years before the *Dialogue* was published. In 1615, in a letter addressed to Grand Duchess Christina of Tuscany, Galileo argued that passages from the Bible had no authority in scientific disputes.

The second reading (from the *Dialogue*) reveals Galileo's views on Aristotle. Medieval scholastics regarded Aristotle as the supreme authority on questions concerning nature, an attitude that was perpetuated by early modern scholastics. Galileo insisted that such reliance on authority was a hindrance to scientific investigation, that it is through observation, experiment, and reason that one arrives at physical truth.

BIBLICAL AUTHORITY

Some years ago, as Your Serene Highness well knows, I discovered in the heavens many things that had not been seen before our own age. The novelty of these things, as well as some consequences which followed from them in contradic-

tion to the physical notions commonly held among academic philosophers, stirred up against me no small number of professors—as if I had placed these things in the sky with my own hands in order to upset nature and overturn the sciences. They seemed to forget that the increase of known truths stimulates the investigation, establishment, and growth of the arts; not their diminution or destruction.

Showing a greater fondness for their own opinions than for truth, they sought to deny and disprove the new things which, if they had cared to look for themselves, their own senses would have demonstrated to them. To this end they hurled various charges and published numerous writings filled with vain arguments, and they made the grave mistake of sprinkling these with passages taken from places in the Bible which they had failed to understand properly, and which were ill suited to their purposes. . . .

. . . Men who were well grounded in astronomical and physical science were persuaded as soon as they received my first message. There were others who denied them or remained in doubt only because of their novel and unexpected character, and because they had not yet had the opportunity to see for themselves. These men have by degrees come to be satisfied. But some, besides allegiance to their original error, possess I know not what fanciful interest in remaining hostile not so much toward the things in question as toward their discoverer. No longer being able to deny them, these men now take refuge in obstinate silence, but being more than ever exasperated by that which has pacified and quieted other men, they divert their thoughts to other fancies and seek new ways to damage me. . . .

. . . Possibly because they are disturbed by the known truth of other propositions of mine which differ from those commonly held, and therefore mistrusting their defense so long as they confine themselves to the field of philosophy, these men have resolved to fabricate a shield for their fallacies out of the mantle of pretended religion and the authority of the Bible. These they apply, with little judgment, to the refutation of arguments that they do not understand and have not even listened to.

First they have endeavored to spread the opinion that such propositions in general are contrary to the Bible and are consequently damnable and heretical. . . . Hence they have had no trouble in finding men who would preach the damnability and heresy of the new doctrine from their very pulpits with unwonted confidence, thus doing impious and inconsiderate injury not only to that doctrine and its followers but to all mathematics and mathematicians in general. . . .

. . . They go about invoking the Bible, which they would have minister to their deceitful purposes. Contrary to the sense of the Bible and the intention of the holy [Church] Fathers, if I am not mistaken, they would extend such authorities until even in purely physical matters—where faith is not involved—they would have us altogether abandon reason and the evidence of our senses in favor of some biblical passage, though under the surface meaning of its words this passage may contain a different sense.

I hope to show that I proceed with much greater piety than they do, when I argue not against condemning [Copernicus's] book, but against condemning it in the way they suggest—that is, without understanding it, weighing it, or so much as reading it. For Copernicus never discusses matters of religion or faith, nor does he use arguments that depend in any way upon the authority of sacred writings which he might have interpreted erroneously. He stands always upon physical conclusions pertaining to the celestial motions, and deals with them by astronomical and geometrical demonstrations, founded primarily upon sense experiences and very exact observations. He did not ignore the Bible, but he knew very well that if his doctrine were proved, then it could not contradict the Scriptures when they were rightly understood. . . .

The reason produced for condemning the opinion that the earth moves and the sun stands still is that in many places in the Bible one may read that the sun moves and the earth stands still. Since the Bible cannot err, it follows as a necessary consequence that anyone takes an erroneous and heretical position who maintains that the sun is inherently motionless and the earth movable.

With regard to this argument, I think in the first place that it is very pious to say and prudent to affirm that the holy Bible can never speak untruth—whenever its true meaning is understood. But I believe nobody will deny that it is often very abstruse, and may say things which are quite different from what its bare words signify. Hence in expounding the Bible if one were always to confine oneself to the unadorned grammatical meaning, one might fall into error. . . .

. . . Now the Bible, merely to condescend to popular capacity, has not hesitated to obscure some very important pronouncements, attributing to God himself some qualities extremely remote from (and even contrary to) His essence. Who, then, would positively declare that this principle has been set aside, and the Bible has confined itself rigorously to the bare and restricted sense of its words, when speaking but casually of the earth, of water, of the sun, or of any other created thing? Especially in view of the fact that these things in no way concern the primary purpose of the sacred writings, which is the service of God and the salvation of souls— matters infinitely beyond the comprehension of the common people.

This being granted, I think that in discussions of physical problems we ought to begin not from the authority of scriptural passages, but from sense-experiences and necessary demonstrations. . . . Nothing physical which sense-experience sets before our eyes, or which necessary demonstrations prove to us, ought to be called in question (much less condemned) upon the testimony of biblical passages which may have some different meaning beneath their words. . . .

. . . I do not feel obliged to believe that that same God who has endowed us with senses, reason, and intellect has intended to forgo their use and by some other means to give us knowledge which we can attain by them. He would not require us to deny sense and reason in physical matters which are set before our eyes and minds by direct experience or necessary demonstrations. . . .

It is obvious that such [anti-Copernican] authors, not having penetrated the true senses of Scripture, would impose upon others an obligation to subscribe to conclusions that are repugnant to manifest reason and sense, if they had any authority to do so. God forbid that this sort of abuse should gain countenance and authority, for then in a short time it would be necessary to proscribe [banish] all the contemplative sciences. People who are unable to understand perfectly both the Bible and the sciences far outnumber those who do understand. The former, glancing superficially through the Bible, would arrogate to themselves the authority to decree upon every question of physics on the strength of some word which they have misunderstood, and which was employed by the sacred authors for some different purpose. And the smaller number of understanding men could not dam up the furious torrent of such people, who would gain the majority of followers simply because it is much more pleasant to gain a reputation for wisdom without effort or study than to consume oneself tirelessly in the most laborious disciplines.

Galileo attacked the unquestioning acceptance of Aristotle's teachings in his *Dialogue Concerning the Two Chief World Systems— Ptolemaic and Copernican.* In the *Dialogue,* Simplicio is an Aristotelian and Salviati is a spokesman for Galileo; Sagredo, a third participant, introduces the problem of relying on the authority of Aristotle.

ARISTOTELIAN AUTHORITY

SAGREDO One day I was at the home of a very famous doctor in Venice, where many persons came on account of their studies, and others occasionally came out of curiosity to see some anatomical dissection performed by a man who was truly no less learned than he was a careful and expert anatomist. It happened on this day that he was investigating the source and origin of the nerves, about which there exists a notorious controversy between the Galenist and Peripatetic doctors.[1] The anatomist showed that

---

[1]Galenist doctors followed the medical theories of Galen (A.D. 130–c. 200), a Greek anatomist and physician whose writings had great authority among medieval and early modern physicians. Peripatetic doctors followed Aristotle's teachings.

the great trunk of nerves, leaving the brain and passing through the nape, extended on down the spine and then branched out through the whole body, and that only a single strand as fine as a thread arrived at the heart. Turning to a gentleman whom we knew to be a Peripatetic philosopher, and on whose account he had been exhibiting and demonstrating everything with unusual care, he asked this man whether he was at last satisfied and convinced that the nerves originated in the brain and not in the heart. The philosopher, after considering for awhile, answered: "You have made me see this matter so plainly and palpably that if Aristotle's text were not contrary to it, stating clearly that the nerves originate in the heart, I should be forced to admit it to be true." . . .

SIMPLICIO But if Aristotle is to be abandoned, whom shall we have for a guide in philosophy? Suppose you name some author.

SALVIATI We need guides in forests and in unknown lands, but on plains and in open places only the blind need guides. It is better for such people to stay at home, but anyone with eyes in his head and his wits about him could serve as a guide for them. In saying this, I do not mean that a person should not listen to Aristotle; indeed, I applaud the reading and careful study of his works, and I reproach only those who give themselves up as slaves to him in such a way as to subscribe blindly to everything he says and take it as an inviolable decree without looking for any other reasons. This abuse carries with it another profound disorder, that other people do not try harder to comprehend the strength of his demonstrations. And what is more revolting in a public dispute, when someone is dealing with demonstrable conclusions, than to hear him interrupted by a text (often written to some quite different purpose) thrown into his teeth by an opponent? If, indeed, you wish to continue in this method of studying, then put aside the name of philosophers and call yourselves historians, or memory experts; for it is not proper that those who never philosophize should usurp the honorable title of philosopher.

REVIEW QUESTIONS

1. What methods did Galileo Galilei use in his scientific investigations?
2. What was the implication for modern astronomy of Galileo's observation of the surface of the moon? Of the moons of Jupiter?
3. What was Galileo Galilei's objection to using the Bible as a source of knowledge of physical things? According to him, how did one acquire knowledge of nature?
4. What point was Galileo making in telling the story of the anatomical dissection?
5. What was Galileo's view on the use of Aristotle's works as a basis for scientific endeavors?

2 The Autonomy of the Mind

René Descartes (1596–1650), a French mathematician and philosopher, united the new currents of thought initiated during the Renaissance and the Scientific Revolution. Descartes said that the universe was a mechanical system whose inner laws could be discovered through mathematical thinking and formulated in mathematical terms. With Descartes' assertions on the power of thought, human beings became fully aware of their capacity to comprehend the world through their mental powers. For this reason he is regarded as the founder of modern philosophy.

The deductive approach stressed by Descartes presumes that inherent in the mind are mathematical principles, logical relationships, the principle of cause and effect, concepts of size and motion, and so on—ideas that exist independently of human experience with the external world. Descartes, for example, would say that the properties of a right-angle triangle ($a^2 + b^2 = c^2$) are implicit in human consciousness prior to any experience one might have with a triangle. These innate ideas, said Descartes, permit the mind to give order and coherence to the physical world. Descartes held that the mind arrives at truth when it "intuits" or comprehends the logical necessity of its own ideas and expresses these ideas with clarity, certainty, and precision.

René Descartes
DISCOURSE ON METHOD

In the *Discourse on Method* (1637), Descartes proclaimed the mind's autonomy and importance, and its ability and right to comprehend truth. In this work he offered a method whereby one could achieve certainty and thereby produce a comprehensive understanding of nature and human culture. In the following passage from the *Discourse on Method,* he explained the purpose of his inquiry. How he did so is almost as revolutionary as the ideas he wished to express. He spoke in the first person, autobiographically, as an individual employing his own reason, and he addressed himself to other individuals, inviting them to use their reason. He brought to his narrative an unprecedented confidence in the power of his own judgment and a deep disenchantment with the learning of his times.

PART ONE

From my childhood I lived in a world of books, and since I was taught that by their help I could gain a clear and assured knowledge of everything useful in life, I was eager to learn from them. But as soon as I had finished the course of studies which usually admits one to the ranks of the learned, I changed my opinion completely. For I found myself saddled with so many doubts and errors that I seemed to have gained nothing in trying to educate myself unless it was to discover more and more fully how ignorant I was.

Nevertheless I had been in one of the most celebrated schools in Europe, where I thought there should be wise men if wise men existed anywhere on earth. I had learned there everything that others learned, and, not satisfied with merely the knowledge that was taught, I had perused as many books as I could find which contained more unusual and recondite [obscure] knowledge. . . . And finally, it did not seem to me that our times were less flourishing and fertile than were any of the earlier periods. All this led me to conclude that I could judge others by myself, and to decide that there was no such wisdom in the world as I had previously hoped to find. . . .

I revered our theology, and hoped as much as anyone else to get to heaven, but having learned on great authority that the road was just as open to the most ignorant as to the most learned, and that the truths of revelation which lead thereto are beyond our understanding, I would not have dared to submit them to the weakness of my reasonings. I thought that to succeed in their examination it would be necessary to have some extraordinary assistance from heaven, and to be more than a man.

I will say nothing of philosophy except that it has been studied for many centuries by the most outstanding minds without having produced anything which is not in dispute and consequently doubtful. I did not have enough presumption to hope to succeed better than the others; and when I noticed how many different opinions learned men may hold on the same subject, despite the fact that no more than one of them can ever be right, I resolved to consider almost as false any opinion which was merely plausible. . . .

This is why I gave up my studies entirely as soon as I reached the age when I was no longer under the control of my teachers. I resolved to seek no other knowledge than that which I might find within myself, or perhaps in the great book of nature. I spent a few years of my adolescence traveling, seeing courts and armies, living with people of diverse types and stations of life, acquiring varied experience, testing myself in the episodes which fortune sent me, and, above all, thinking about the things around me so that I could derive some profit from them. For it seemed to me that I might find much more of the truth in the cogitations [reflections] which each man made on things which were important to him, and where he would be the loser if he judged badly, than in the cogitations of a man of letters in his study, concerned with speculations which produce no effect, and which have no consequences to him. . . .

. . . After spending several years in thus studying the book of nature and acquiring experience, I eventually reached the decision to study my own self, and to employ all my abilities to try to choose the right path. This produced much better results in my case, I think, than would have been produced if I had never left my books and my country. . . .

PART TWO

. . . As far as the opinions which I had been receiving since my birth were concerned, I could

not do better than to reject them completely for once in my lifetime, and to resume them afterwards, or perhaps accept better ones in their place, when I had determined how they fitted into a rational scheme. And I firmly believed that by this means I would succeed in conducting my life much better than if I built only upon the old foundations and gave credence to the principles which I had acquired in my childhood without ever having examined them to see whether they were true or not. . . .

. . . Never has my intention been more than to try to reform my own ideas, and rebuild them on foundations that would be wholly mine. . . . The decision to abandon all one's preconceived notions is not an example for all to follow. . . .

As for myself, I should no doubt have . . . [never attempted it] if I had had but a single teacher or if I had not known the differences which have always existed among the most learned. I had discovered in college that one cannot imagine anything so strange and unbelievable but that it has been upheld by some philosopher; and in my travels I had found that those who held opinions contrary to ours were neither barbarians nor savages, but that many of them were at least as reasonable as ourselves. I had considered how the same man, with the same capacity for reason, becomes different as a result of being brought up among Frenchmen or Germans than he would be if he had been brought up among Chinese or cannibals; and how, in our fashions, the thing which pleased us ten years ago and perhaps will please us again ten years in the future, now seems extravagant and ridiculous; and I felt that in all these ways we are much more greatly influenced by custom and example than by any certain knowledge. Faced with this divergence of opinion, I could not accept the testimony of the majority, for I thought it worthless as a proof of anything somewhat difficult to discover, since it is much more likely that a single man will have discovered it than a whole people. Nor, on the other hand, could I select anyone whose opinions seemed to me to be preferable to those of others, and I was thus constrained to embark on the investigation for myself.

Nevertheless, like a man who walks alone in the darkness, I resolved to go so slowly and circumspectly that if I did not get ahead very rapidly I was at least safe from falling. Also, I did not want to reject all the opinions which had slipped irrationally into my consciousness since birth, until I had first spent enough time planning how to accomplish the task which I was then undertaking, and seeking the true method of obtaining knowledge of everything which my mind was capable of understanding. . . .

Descartes' method consists of four principles that place the capacity to arrive at truth entirely within the province of the human mind. First one finds a self-evident principle, such as a geometric axiom. From this general principle, other truths are deduced through logical reasoning. This is accomplished by breaking a problem down into its elementary components and then, step by step, moving toward more complex knowledge.

. . . I thought that some other method [besides that of logic, algebra, and geometry] must be found to combine the advantages of these three and to escape their faults. Finally, just as the multitude of laws frequently furnishes an excuse for vice, and a state is much better governed with a few laws which are strictly adhered to, so I thought that instead of the great number of precepts of which logic is composed, I would have enough with the four following ones, provided that I made a firm and unalterable resolution not to violate them even in a single instance.

The first rule was never to accept anything as true unless I recognized it to be evidently such: that is, carefully to avoid precipitation and prejudgment, and to include nothing in my conclusions unless it presented itself so clearly and distinctly to my mind that there was no occasion to doubt it.

The second was to divide each of the difficulties which I encountered into as many parts as possible, and as might be required for an easier solution.

The third was to think in an orderly fashion, beginning with the things which were simplest and easiest to understand, and gradually and by degrees reaching toward more complex knowledge, even treating as though ordered materials which were not necessarily so.

The last was always to make enumerations so complete, and reviews so general, that I would be certain that nothing was omitted. . . .

What pleased me most about this method was that it enabled me to reason in all things, if not perfectly, at least as well as was in my power. In addition, I felt that in practicing it my mind was gradually becoming accustomed to conceive its objects more clearly and distinctly. . . .

Descartes was searching for an incontrovertible truth that could serve as the first principle of philosophy. His arrival at the famous dictum "I think, therefore I am" marks the beginning of modern philosophy.

PART FOUR

. . . As I desired to devote myself wholly to the search for truth, I thought that I should . . . reject as absolutely false anything of which I could have the least doubt, in order to see whether anything would be left after this procedure which could be called wholly certain. Thus, as our senses deceive us at times, I was ready to suppose that nothing was at all the way our senses represented them to be. As there are men who make mistakes in reasoning even on the simplest topics in geometry, I judged that I was as liable to error as any other, and rejected as false all the reasoning which I had previously accepted as valid demonstration. Finally, as the same precepts which we have when awake may come to us when asleep without their being true, I decided to suppose that nothing that had ever entered my mind was more real than the illusions of my dreams. But I soon noticed that while I thus wished to think everything false, it was necessarily true that I who thought so was something. Since this truth, *I think, therefore I am,* was so firm and assured that all the most extrava-gant suppositions of the sceptics[1] were unable to shake it, I judged that I could safely accept it as the first principle of the philosophy I was seeking.

---

[1]The skeptics belonged to the ancient Greek philosophic school that held true knowledge to be beyond human grasp and treated all knowledge as uncertain.

REVIEW QUESTIONS

1. Why was René Descartes critical of the learning of his day?
2. What are the implications of Descartes' famous words: "I think, therefore I am"?
3. Compare Descartes' method with the approach advocated by Francis Bacon.

---

3 The Mechanical Universe

By demonstrating that all bodies in the universe—earthly objects as well as moons, planets, and stars—obey the same laws of motion and gravitation, Sir Isaac Newton (1646–1723) completed the destruction of the medieval view of the universe. The idea that the same laws governed the movement of earthly and heavenly bodies was completely foreign to medieval thinkers, who drew a sharp division between a higher celestial world and a lower terrestrial one. In the *Principia Mathematica* (1687), Newton showed that the same forces that hold celestial bodies in their orbits around the sun make apples fall to the ground. For Newton, the universe was like a giant clock, all of whose parts obeyed strict mechanical principles and worked together in perfect precision. To Newton's contemporaries, it seemed as if mystery had been banished from the universe.

Isaac Newton
PRINCIPIA MATHEMATICA

In the first of the following passages from *Principia Mathematica,* Newton stated the principle of universal law and lauded the experimental method as the means of acquiring knowledge.

RULES OF REASONING
IN PHILOSOPHY

Rule I.   We are to admit no more causes of natural things than such as are both true and sufficient to explain their appearances.

To this purpose the philosophers say that Nature does nothing in vain, and more is in vain when less will serve; for Nature is pleased with simplicity, and affects not the pomp of superfluous causes.

Rule II.   Therefore to the same natural effects we must, as far as possible, assign the same causes.

As to respiration in a man and in a beast; the descent of stones [meteorites] in *Europe* and in *America*; the light of our culinary fire and of the sun; the reflection of light in the earth, and in the planets.

Rule III. The qualities of bodies, which admit neither [intensification] nor remission of degrees, and which are found to belong to all bodies within the reach of our experiments, are to be esteemed the universal qualities of all bodies whatsoever.

For since the qualities of bodies are only known to us by experiments, we are to hold for universal all such as universally agree with experiments; and such as are not liable to diminution can never be quite taken away. We are certainly not to relinquish the evidence of experiments for the sake of dreams and vain fictions of our own devising; nor are we to recede from the analogy of Nature, which [is] . . . simple, and always consonant to itself. We no other way know the extension of bodies than by our senses, nor do these reach it in all bodies; but because we perceive extension in all that are sensible, therefore, we ascribe it universally to all others also. That abundance of bodies are hard, we learn by experience; and because the hardness of the whole arises from the hardness of the parts, we, therefore, justly infer the hardness of the undivided particles not only of the bodies we feel but of all others. That all bodies are impenetrable, we gather not from reason, but from sensation. The bodies which we handle we find impenetrable, and thence, conclude impenetrability to be an universal property of all bodies whatsoever. That all bodies are moveable, and endowed with certain powers (which we call . . . {*inertia*}) of persevering in their motion, or in their rest, we only infer from the like properties observed in the bodies which we have seen. The extension, hardness, impenetrability, mobility, . . . of the whole, result from the extension, hardness, impenetrability, mobility, . . . of the parts; and thence we conclude the least particles of all bodies to be also all extended, and hard and impenetrable, and moveable. . . . And this is the foundation of all philosophy. . . .

Lastly, if it universally appears, by experiments and astronomical observations, that all bodies about the earth gravitate towards the earth, and that in proportion to the quantity of matter which they severally contain; that the moon likewise, according to the quantity of its matter, gravitates towards the earth; that, on the other hand, our sea gravitates towards the moon; and all the planets mutually one towards another; and the comets in like manner towards the sun; we must, in consequence of this rule, universally allow that all bodies whatsoever are endowed with a principle of mutual gravitation. . . .

Rule IV. In experimental philosophy we are to look upon propositions collected by general induction from phenomena as accurately or very nearly true, notwithstanding any contrary hypotheses that may be imagined, till such time as other phenomena occur, by which they may either be made more accurate, or liable to exceptions.

This rule we must follow, that the argument of induction may not be evaded by hypotheses.

Newton describes further his concepts of gravity and scientific methodology.

GRAVITY

Hitherto, we have explained the phenomena of the heavens and of our sea by the power of gravity, but have not yet assigned the cause of this power. This is certain, that it must proceed from a cause that penetrates to the very centres of the sun and planets, without suffering the least diminution of its force; that operates not according to the quantity of the surfaces of the particles upon which it acts (as mechanical causes used to do) but according to the quantity of the solid matter which they contain, and propagates its virtue on all sides to immense distances, decreasing always in the duplicate portion of the distances. . . .

Hitherto I have not been able to discover the cause of those properties of gravity from the phenomena, and I frame no hypothesis; for whatever is not deduced from the phenomena is to be called an hypothesis; and hypotheses, whether metaphysical or physical, whether of occult qualities or mechanical, have no place in experimental philosophy. In this philosophy particular propositions are inferred from the phenomena, and afterward rendered general by induction. Thus it was the impenetrability, the mobility, and the impulsive forces of bodies, and the laws of motion and of gravitation were discovered. And to us it is enough that gravity does really exist, and acts according to the laws which we have explained, and abundantly serves to account for all the motions of the celestial bodies, and of our sea.

A devout Anglican, Newton believed that God had created this superbly organized universe. The following selection is also from the *Principia*.

GOD AND THE UNIVERSE

This most beautiful system of the sun, planets, and comets could only proceed from the counsel and dominion of an intelligent and powerful Being. And if the fixed stars are the centers of other like systems, these, being formed by the like wise counsel, must be all subject to the dominion of One, especially since the light of the fixed stars is of the same nature with the light of the sun and from every system light passes into all the other systems; and lest the systems of the fixed stars should, by their gravity, fall on each other mutually, he hath placed those systems at immense distances from one another.

This Being governs all things not as the soul of the world, but as Lord over all; and on account of his dominion he is wont to be called "Lord God" . . . or "Universal Ruler." . . . It is the dominion of a spiritual being which constitutes a God. . . . And from his true dominion it follows that the true God is a living, intelligent and powerful Being. . . . [H]e governs all things, and knows all things that are or can be done. . . . He endures for ever, and is every where present; and by existing always and every where, he constitutes duration and space. . . . In him are all things contained and moved; yet neither affects the other: God suffers nothing from the motion of bodies; bodies find no resistance from the omnipresence of God. . . . As a blind man has no idea of colors so we have no idea of the manner by which the all-wise God preserves and understands all things. He is utterly void of all body and bodily figure, and can therefore neither be seen, nor heard, nor touched; nor ought to be worshipped under the representation of any corporeal thing. We have ideas of his attributes, but what the real substance of any thing is we know not. . . . Much less, then, have we any idea of the substance of God. We know him only by his most wise and excellent contrivances of things. . . . [W]e reverence and adore him as his servants; and a god without dominion, providence, and final causes, is nothing else but Fate and Nature. Blind metaphysical necessity, which is certainly the same always and everywhere, could produce no variety of things. All that diversity of natural things which we find suited to different times and places could arise from nothing but the ideas and will of a Being necessarily existing. . . . And thus much concerning God; to discourse of whom from the appearances of things does certainly belong to Natural Philosophy.

REVIEW QUESTIONS

1. What did Isaac Newton mean by universal law? What examples of universal law did he provide?
2. What method for investigating nature did Newton advocate?
3. Summarize Newton's arguments for God's existence.
4. For Newton, what is God's relationship to the universe?

4 Political Liberty

John Locke (1632–1704), a British statesman, philosopher, and political theorist, was a principal source of the Enlightenment. Eighteenth-century thinkers were particularly influenced by Locke's advocacy of religious toleration, his reliance on experience as the source of knowledge, and his concern for liberty. In his first *Letter Concerning Toleration* (1689), Locke declared that Christians who persecute others in the name of religion vitiate Christ's teachings. Locke's political philosophy as formulated in the *Two Treatises on Government* (1690) was a rational and secular attempt to understand and improve the human condition. The Lockean spirit pervades the American Declaration of Independence, the Constitution, and the Bill of Rights and is the basis of the liberal tradition that aims to protect individual liberty from despotic state authority.

Viewing human beings as brutish and selfish, Thomas Hobbes (see page 221) had prescribed a state with unlimited power; only in this way, he said, could people be protected from each other and civilized life preserved. Locke, regarding people as essentially good and humane, developed a conception of the state differing fundamentally from Hobbes's. Locke held that human beings are born with natural rights of life, liberty, and property; they establish the state to protect these rights. Consequently, neither executive nor legislature, neither king nor assembly has the authority to deprive individuals of their natural rights. Whereas Hobbes justified absolute monarchy, Locke explicitly endorsed constitutional government in which the power to govern derives from the consent of the governed and the state's authority is limited by agreement.

John Locke
SECOND TREATISE ON GOVERNMENT

Locke said that originally, in establishing a government, human beings had never agreed to surrender their natural rights to any state authority. The state's founders intended the new polity to preserve these natural rights and to implement the people's will. Therefore, as the following passage from Locke's *Second Treatise on Government* illustrates, the power exercised by magistrates cannot be absolute or arbitrary.

. . . *Political power* is that power, which every man having in the state of nature, has given up into the hands of the society, and therein to the governors, whom the society hath set over itself, with this express or tacit trust, that it shall be employed for their good, and the preservation of their property: now this *power,* which every man has *in the state of nature,* and which he parts with to the society in all such cases where the society can secure him, is to use such means, for the preserving of his own property, as he thinks good, and nature allows him;

and to punish the breach of the law of nature in others, so as (according to the best of his reason) may most conduce to the preservation of himself, and the rest of mankind. So that the *end and measure of this power,* when in every man's hands in the state of nature, being the preservation of all of his society, that is, all mankind in general, it can have no other *end or measure,* when in the hands of the magistrate, but to preserve the members of that society in their lives, liberties, and possessions; and so cannot be an absolute, arbitrary power over their lives and fortunes, which are as much as possible to be preserved; but a *power to make laws,* and annex such *penalties* to them, as may tend to the preservation of the whole, by cutting off those parts, and those only, which are so corrupt, that they threaten the sound and healthy, without which no severity is lawful. And this *power has its original only from compact,* and agreement, and the mutual consent of those who make up the community. . . .

These are the *bounds,* which the trust, that is put in them by the society, and the law of God and nature, have *set to the legislative* power of every common-wealth, in all forms of government.

First, They are to govern by *promulgated established laws,* not to be varied in particular cases, but to have one rule for rich and poor, for the favourite at court, and the country man at plough.

Secondly, These *laws* also ought to be designed *for* no other end ultimately, but *the good of the people.*

Thirdly, They must *not raise taxes* on the *property of the people, without the consent of the people,* given by themselves, or their deputies. And this properly concerns only such governments, where the *legislative* is always in being, or at least where the people have not reserved any part of the legislative to deputies, to be from time to time chosen by themselves.

Fourthly, The *legislative* neither must *nor can transfer the power of making laws* to any body else, or place it any where, but where the people have. . . .

> If government fails to fulfill the end for which it was established—the preservation of the individual's right to life, liberty, and property—the people have a right to dissolve that government.

. . . The *legislative acts against the trust* reposed in them, when they endeavour to invade the property of the subject, and to make themselves, or any part of the community, masters, or arbitrary disposers of the lives, liberties, or fortunes of the people.

The reason why men enter into society, is the preservation of their property; and the end why they chuse and authorize a legislative, is, that there may be laws made, and rules set, as guards and fences to the properties of all the members of the society, to limit the power, and moderate the dominion of every part and member of the society: for since it can never be supposed to be the will of the society, that the legislative should have a power to destroy that which every one designs to secure, by entering into society, and for which the people submitted themselves to legislators of their own making; whenever the *legislators endeavour to take away, and destroy the property of the people,* or to reduce them to slavery under arbitrary power, they put themselves into a state of war with the people, who are thereupon absolved from any farther obedience, and are left to the common refuge, which God hath provided for all men, against force and violence. Whensoever therefore the *legislative* shall transgress this fundamental rule of society; and either by ambition, fear, folly or corruption, *endeavour to grasp* themselves, *or put into the hands of any other, an absolute power* over the lives, liberties, and estates of the people; by this breach of trust they *forfeit the power* the people had put into their hands for quite contrary ends, and it devolves to the people, who have a right to resume their original liberty, and, by the establishment of a new legislative, (such as they shall think fit) provide for their own safety and security, which is the end for which they are in society. What I have said here, concerning the legislative in general, holds true also concerning the supreme executor, who having a double trust put in him, both to have a part in the legislative, and the supreme execution of the law, acts against both, when he goes about to set up his own arbitrary will as the law of the society. He *acts* also *contrary to his trust,* when he either employs the force, treasure, and offices of the society, to corrupt the *representatives,* and gain them to his purposes; or openly pre-engages the *electors,* and prescribes to their choice, such, whom he has, by sollicitations, threats, promises, or otherwise, won to his designs; and employs them to bring in such, who have promised beforehand what to vote, and what to enact. . . .

Locke responds to the charge that his theory will produce "frequent rebellion." Indeed, says Locke, the true rebels are the magistrates who, acting contrary to the trust granted them, violate the people's rights.

. . . Such *revolutions happen* not upon every little mismanagement in public affairs. *Great mistakes* in the ruling part, many wrong and inconvenient laws, and all the *slips* of human frailty, will be *borne by the people* without mutiny or murmur. But if a long train of abuses, prevarications [lies] and artifices [tricks], all tending the same way, make the design visible to the people, and they cannot but feel what they lie under, and see whither they are going; it is not to be wondered at, that they should then rouze themselves, and endeavour to put the rule into

such hands which may secure to them the ends for which government was at first erected. . . .

. . . I answer, that *this doctrine* of a power in the people of providing for their safety a-new, by a new legislative, when their legislators have acted contrary to their trust, by invading their property, is *the best defence against rebellion,* and the probablest means to hinder it: for *rebellion* being an opposition, not to persons, but authority, which is founded only in the constitutions and laws of the government; those, whoever they be, who by force break through, and by force justify their violation of them, are truly and properly *rebels:* for when men, by entering into society and civil government, have excluded force, and introduced laws for the preservation of property, peace, and unity amongst themselves, those who set up force again in opposition to the laws, do [rebel], that is, bring back again the state of war, and are properly rebels: which they who are in power, (by the pretence they have to authority, the temptation of force they have in their hands, and the flattery of those about them) being likeliest to do; the properest way to prevent the evil, is to shew them the danger and injustice of it, who are under the greatest temptation to run into it.

The end of government is the good of mankind; and which is *best for mankind,* that the people should always be exposed to the boundless will of tyranny, or that the rulers should be sometimes liable to be opposed, when they grow exorbitant in the use of their power, and employ it for the destruction, and not the preservation of the properties of their people?

Thomas Jefferson
DECLARATION OF INDEPENDENCE

Written in 1776 by Thomas Jefferson (1743–1826) to justify the American colonists' break with Britain, the Declaration of Independence enumerated principles that were quite familiar to English statesmen and intellectuals. The preamble to the Declaration, excerpted below, articulated clearly Locke's philosophy of natural rights. Locke had viewed life, liberty, and property as the individual's essential natural rights; Jefferson substituted the "pursuit of happiness" for property.

A DECLARATION BY THE REPRESENTATIVES OF THE UNITED STATES OF AMERICA, IN GENERAL CONGRESS ASSEMBLED.

When in the Course of human Events, it becomes necessary for one People to dissolve the Political Bands which have connected them with another, and to assume among the Powers of the Earth, the separate and equal Station to which the Laws of Nature and of Nature's God entitle them, a decent Respect to the Opinions of Mankind requires that they should declare the causes which impel them to the Separation.

We hold these Truths to be self-evident, that all Men are created equal, that they are endowed by their Creator with certain unalienable Rights, that among these are Life, Liberty, and the Pursuit of Happiness—That to secure these Rights, Governments are instituted among Men, deriving their just Powers from the Consent of the Governed, That whenever any Form of Government becomes destructive of these Ends, it is the Right of the People to alter or to abolish it, and to institute new Government, laying its Foundation on such Principles, and organizing its Powers in such Form, as to them shall seem most likely to effect their Safety and Happiness. Prudence, indeed, will dictate that Governments long established should not be changed for light and transient Causes; and accordingly all Experience hath shewn, that Mankind are more disposed to suffer, while Evils are sufferable, than to right themselves by abolishing the Forms to which they are accustomed. But when a long Train of Abuses and Usurpations, pursuing invariably the same Object, evinces a Design to reduce them under absolute Despotism, it is their right, it is their duty, to throw off such Government, and to provide new Guards for their future Security. Such has been the patient Sufferance of these Colonies; and such is now the Necessity which constrains them to alter their former Systems of Government. The History of the present King of Great-Britain is a History of repeated Injuries and Usurpations, all having in direct Object the Establishment of an absolute Tyranny over these States. . . .

REVIEW QUESTIONS

1. Compare the views of John Locke with those of Thomas Hobbes (see page 221) regarding the character of human nature, political authority, and the right to rebellion.
2. Compare Locke's theory of natural rights with the principles stated in the American Declaration of Independence.

---

5 Attack on Religion

Christianity came under severe attack during the eighteenth century. The philosophes rejected Christian doctrines that seemed contrary to reason. Deism, the dominant religious outlook of the philosophes, taught that religion should accord with reason and natural law. To deists, it seemed reasonable to believe in God, for this superbly constructed universe required a creator in the same manner that a watch required a watchmaker. But, said the deists, after God had constructed the universe, he did not interfere in its operations; the universe was governed by mechanical laws. Deists denied that the Bible was God's work, rejected clerical authority, and dismissed miracles—like Jesus walking on water—as incompatible with natural law. To them, Jesus was not divine but an inspired teacher of morality. Many deists still considered themselves Christians; the clergy, however, viewed the deists' religious views with horror.

Voltaire
A PLEA FOR TOLERANCE AND REASON

François Marie Arouet (1694–1778), known to the world as Voltaire, was the recognized leader of the French Enlightenment. Few of the philosophes had a better mind, and none had a sharper wit. A relentless critic of the Old Regime (the social structure in prerevolutionary France), Voltaire attacked superstition, religious fanaticism and persecution, censorship, and other abuses of eighteenth-century French society. Spending more than two years in Great Britain, Voltaire acquired a great admiration for English liberty, toleration, commerce, and science. In *Letters Concerning the English Nation* (1733), he drew unfavorable comparisons between a progressive Britain and a reactionary France.

Voltaire's angriest words were directed against established Christianity, to which he attributed many of the ills of modern society. Voltaire regarded Christianity as "the Christ-worshiping superstition" that someday would be destroyed "by the weapons of reason." He rejected revelation and the church hierarchy and was repulsed by Christian intolerance, but he accepted Christian morality and believed in God as the prime mover who set the universe in motion.

The following passages compiled from Voltaire's works—grouped according to topic—provide insight into the outlook of the philosophes. The excerpts come from sources that include his *Treatise on Tolerance* (1763), *The Philosophical Dictionary* (1764), and *Commentary on the Book of Crime and Punishments* (1766).

TOLERANCE

It does not require any great art or studied elocution to prove that Christians ought to tolerate one another. I will go even further and say that we ought to look upon all men as our brothers. What! call a Turk, a Jew, and a Siamese, my brother? Yes, of course; for are we not all children of the same father, and the creatures of the same God?

———

What is tolerance? . . . We are all full of weakness and errors; let us mutually pardon our follies. This is the last law of nature. . . .

It is clear that every private individual who persecutes a man, his brother, because he is not of the same opinion, is a monster. . . .

Of all religions, the Christian ought doubtless to inspire the most tolerance, although hitherto the Christians have been the most intolerant of all men.

———

. . . Tolerance has never brought civil war; intolerance has covered the earth with carnage. . . .

What! Is each citizen to be permitted to believe and to think that which his reason rightly or wrongly dictates? He should indeed, provided that he does not disturb the public order; for it is not contingent on man to believe or not to believe; but it is contingent on him to respect the [practices] of his country; and if you say that it is a crime not to believe in the dominant religion, you accuse then yourself the first Christians, your ancestors, and you justify those whom you accuse of having martyred them.

You reply that there is a great difference, that all religions are the work of men, and that the Apostolic Roman Catholic Church is alone the work of God. But in good faith, ought our religion because it is divine reign through hate, violence, exiles, usurpation of property, prisons, tortures, murders, and thanksgivings to God for these murders? The more the Christian religion is divine, the less it pertains to man to require it; if God made it, God will sustain it without you. You know that intolerance produces only hypocrites or rebels; what distressing alternatives! In short, do you want to sustain through executioners the religion of a God whom executioners have put to death and who taught only gentleness and patience?

———

I shall never cease, my dear sir, to preach tolerance from the housetops, despite the complaints of your priests and the outcries of ours, until persecution is no more. The progress of reason is slow, the roots of prejudice lie deep. Doubtless, I shall never see the fruits of my efforts, but they are seeds which may one day germinate.

DOGMA

. . . Is Jesus the Word? If He be the Word, did He emanate from God in time or before time? If He emanated from God, is He co-eternal and consubstantial with Him, or is He of a similar substance? Is He distinct from Him, or is He not? Is He made or begotten? Can He beget in His turn? Has He paternity? or productive virtue without paternity? Is the Holy Ghost made? or begotten? or produced? or proceeding from the Father? or proceeding from the Son? or proceeding from both? Can He beget? can He produce? is His hypostasis consubstantial with

the hypostasis of the Father and the Son? and how is it that, having the same nature—the same essence as the Father and the Son, He cannot do the same things done by these persons who are Himself?

Assuredly, I understand nothing of this; no one has ever understood any of it, and that is why we have slaughtered one another.

The Christians tricked, cavilled [faulted frivolously], hated, and excommunicated one another, for some of these dogmas inaccessible to human intellect.

FANATICISM

Fanaticism is to superstition what delirium is to fever, what rage is to anger. He who has ecstasies and visions, who takes dreams for realities, and his own imaginations for prophecies is an enthusiast; he who reinforces his madness by murder is a fanatic. . . .

The most detestable example of fanaticism is that exhibited on the night of St. Bartholomew,[1] when the people of Paris rushed from house to house to stab, slaughter, throw out of the window, and tear in pieces their fellow citizens who did not go to mass.

There are some cold-blooded fanatics; such as those judges who sentence men to death for no other crime than that of thinking differently from themselves. . . .

Once fanaticism has infected a brain, the disease is almost incurable. I have seen convulsionaries who, while speaking of the miracles of Saint Paris [a fourth-century Italian bishop], gradually grew heated in spite of themselves. Their eyes became inflamed, their limbs shook, fury disfigured their face, and they would have killed anyone who contradicted them.

There is no other remedy for this epidemic malady than that philosophical spirit which, extending itself from one to another, at length softens the manners of men and prevents the access of the disease. For when the disorder has

———

[1]"St. Bartholomew" refers to the day of August 24, 1572, when the populace of Paris, instigated by King Charles IX at his mother's urging, began a week-long slaughter of Protestants.

made any progress, we should, without loss of time, flee from it, and wait till the air has become purified.

PERSECUTION

What is a persecutor? He whose wounded pride and furious fanaticism arouse princes and magistrates against innocent men, whose only crime is that of being of a different opinion. "Impudent man! you have worshipped God; you have preached and practiced virtue; you have served man; you have protected the orphan, have helped the poor; you have changed deserts, in which slaves dragged on a miserable existence, into fertile lands peopled by happy families; but I have discovered that you despise me, and have never read my controversial work. You know that I am a rogue; that I have forged G[od]'s signature, that I have stolen. You might tell these things; I must anticipate you. I will, therefore, go to the confessor [spiritual counselor] of the prime minister, or the magistrate; I will show them, with outstretched neck and twisted mouth, that you hold an erroneous opinion in relation to the cells in which the Septuagint was studied; that you have even spoken disrespectfully ten years ago of Tobit's dog,[2] which you asserted to have been a spaniel, while I proved that it was a greyhound. I will denounce you as the enemy of God and man!" Such is the language of the persecutor; and if precisely these words do not issue from his lips, they are engraven on his heart with the pointed steel of fanaticism steeped in the bitterness of envy. . . .

O God of mercy! If any man can resemble that evil being who is described as ceaselessly employed in the destruction of your works, is it not the persecutor?

---

[2]The Septuagint, the version of the Hebrew Scriptures used by Saint Paul and other early Christians, was a Greek translation done by Hellenized Jews in Alexandria sometime in the late third or the second century B.C. *Tobit's dog* appears in the Book of Tobit, a Hebrew book contained in the Catholic version of the Bible.

SUPERSTITION

In 1749 a woman was burned in the Bishopric of Würzburg [a city in central Germany], convicted of being a witch. This is an extraordinary phenomenon in the age in which we live. Is it possible that people who boast of their reformation and of trampling superstition under foot, who indeed supposed that they had reached the perfection of reason, could nevertheless believe in witchcraft, and this more than a hundred years after the so-called reformation of their reason?

In 1652 a peasant woman named Michelle Chaudron, living in the little territory of Geneva [a major city in Switzerland], met the devil going out of the city. The devil gave her a kiss, received her homage, and imprinted on her upper lip and right breast the mark that he customarily bestows on all whom he recognizes as his favorites. This seal of the devil is a little mark which makes the skin insensitive, as all the demonographical jurists of those times affirm.

The devil ordered Michelle Chaudron to bewitch two girls. She obeyed her master punctually. The girls' parents accused her of witchcraft before the law. The girls were questioned and confronted with the accused. They declared that they felt a continual pricking in certain parts of their bodies and that they were possessed. Doctors were called, or at least, those who passed for doctors at that time. They examined the girls. They looked for the devil's seal on Michelle's body—what the statement of the case called *satanic marks*. Into them they drove a long needle, already a painful torture. Blood flowed out, and Michelle made it known, by her cries, that satanic marks certainly do not make one insensitive. The judges, seeing no definite proof that Michelle Chaudron was a witch, proceeded to torture her, a method that infallibly produces the necessary proofs: this wretched woman, yielding to the violence of torture, at last confessed every thing they desired.

The doctors again looked for the satanic mark. They found a little black spot on one of her thighs. They drove in the needle. The torment of the torture had been so horrible that the poor creature hardly felt the needle; thus the crime was established. But as customs were becoming somewhat mild at that time, she was burned only after being hanged and strangled.

In those days every tribunal of Christian Europe resounded with similar arrests. The [twigs] were lit everywhere for witches, as for heretics. People reproached the Turks most for having neither witches nor demons among them. This absence of demons was considered an infallible proof of the falseness of a religion.

A zealous friend of public welfare, of humanity, of true religion, has stated in one of his writings on behalf of innocence, that Christian tribunals have condemned to death over a hundred thousand accused witches. If to these judicial murders are added the infinitely superior number of massacred heretics, that part of the world will seem to be nothing but a vast scaffold covered with torturers and victims, surrounded by judges, guards and spectators.

Thomas Paine
THE AGE OF REASON

Exemplifying the deist outlook was Thomas Paine (1737–1809), an Englishman who moved to America in 1774. Paine's *Common Sense* (1776) was an eloquent appeal for American independence. Paine is also famous for *The Rights of Man* (1791–1792), in which he defended the French Revolution. In *The Age of Reason* (1794–1796), he denounced Christian mysteries, miracles, and prophecies as superstition and called for a natural religion that accorded with reason and science.

I believe in one God, and no more; and I hope for happiness beyond this life.

I believe in the equality of man; and I believe that religious duties consist in doing justice, loving mercy, and endeavoring to make our fellow-creatures happy.

But, lest it should be supposed that I believe many other things in addition to these, I shall, in the progress of this work, declare the things I do not believe, and my reasons for not believing them.

I do not believe in the creed professed by the Jewish church, by the Roman church, by the Greek church, by the Turkish church, by the Protestant church, nor by any church that I know of. My own mind is my own church. . . .

When Moses told the children of Israel that he received the two tablets of the [Ten] commandments from the hands of God, they were not obliged to believe him, because they had no other authority for it than his telling them so;

and I have no other authority for it than some historian telling me so. The commandments carry no internal evidence of divinity with them; they contain some good moral precepts, such as any man qualified to be a lawgiver, or a legislator, could produce himself, without having recourse to supernatural intervention. . . .

When also I am told that a woman called the Virgin Mary, said, or gave out, that she was with child without any cohabitation with a man, and that her betrothed husband, Joseph, said that an angel told him so, I have a right to believe them or not; such a circumstance required a much stronger evidence than their bare word for it; but we have not even this—for neither Joseph nor Mary wrote any such matter themselves; it is only reported by others that *they said so*—it is hearsay upon hearsay, and I do not choose to rest my belief upon such evidence.

It is, however, not difficult to account for the credit that was given to the story of Jesus Christ being the son of God. He was born when the heathen mythology had still some fashion and repute in the world, and that mythology had prepared the people for the belief of such a story. Almost all the extraordinary men that lived under the heathen mythology were reputed to be the sons of some of their gods. It was not a new thing, at that time, to believe a man to have been celestially begotten; the intercourse of gods with women was then a matter of familiar opinion. Their Jupiter [chief Roman god], according to their accounts, had cohabited with hundreds: the story, therefore, had nothing in it either new, wonderful, or obscene; it was conformable to the opinions that then prevailed among the people called Gentiles, or Mythologists, and it was those people only that believed it. The Jews who had kept strictly to the belief of one God, and no more, and who had always rejected the heathen mythology, never credited the story. . . .

Nothing that is here said can apply, even with the most distant disrespect, to the real character of Jesus Christ. He was a virtuous and an amiable man. The morality that he preached and practised was of the most benevolent kind; and though similar systems of morality had been preached by Confucius [Chinese philosopher], and by some of the Greek philosophers, many years before; by the Quakers [members of the Society of Friends] since; and by many good men in all ages, it has not been exceeded by any. . . .

. . . The resurrection and ascension [of Jesus Christ], supposing them to have taken place, admitted of public and ocular demonstration, like that of the ascension of a balloon, or the sun at noon-day, to all Jerusalem at least. A thing which everybody is required to believe, requires that the proof and evidence of it should be equal to all, and universal; and as the public visibility of this last related act was the only evidence that could give sanction to the former part, the whole of it falls to the ground, because that evidence never was given. Instead of this, a small number of persons, not more than eight or nine, are introduced as proxies for the whole world, to say they saw it, and all the rest of the world are called upon to believe it. But it appears that Thomas [one of Jesus' disciples] did not believe the resurrection, and, as they say, would not believe without having ocular and manual demonstration himself. *So neither will I,* and the reason is equally as good for me, and for every other person, as for Thomas.

It is in vain to attempt to palliate [conceal] or disguise this matter. The story, so far as relates to the supernatural part, has every mark of fraud and imposition stamped upon the face of it. Who were the authors of it is as impossible for us now to know, as it is for us to be assured that the books in which the account is related were written by the persons whose names they bear; the best surviving evidence we now have respecting this affair is the Jews. They are regularly descended from the people who lived in the times this resurrection and ascension is said to have happened, and they say, *it is not true.*

REVIEW QUESTIONS

1. What arguments did Voltaire offer in favor of religious toleration?
2. Why did Voltaire ridicule Christian theological disputation?
3. What did Voltaire mean by the term *fanaticism?* What examples did he provide? How was it to be cured?
4. What Christian beliefs did Thomas Paine reject? Why?

6 Compendium of Knowledge

A 38-volume *Encyclopedia,* whose 150 or more contributors included leading Enlightenment thinkers, was undertaken in Paris during the 1740s as a monumental effort to bring together all human knowledge and to propagate Enlightenment ideas. The *Encyclopedia*'s numerous articles on science and technology and its limited coverage of theological questions attest to the new interests of eighteenth-century intellectuals. Serving as principal editor, Denis Diderot (1713–1784) steered the project through difficult periods, including the suspension of publication by French authorities. After the first two volumes were published, the authorities denounced the work for containing "maxims that would tend to destroy royal authority, foment a spirit of independence and revolt, . . . and lay the foundations for the corruption of morals and religion." In 1759, Pope Clement XIII condemned the *Encyclopedia* for having "scandalous doctrines [and] inducing scorn for religion." It required careful diplomacy and clever ruses to finish the project and still incorporate ideas considered dangerous by religious and governmental authorities. With the project's completion in 1772, Diderot and Enlightenment opinion triumphed over clerical censors and powerful elements at the French court.

Denis Diderot
ENCYCLOPEDIA

The *Encyclopedia* was a monument to the Enlightenment, as Diderot himself recognized. "This work will surely produce in time a revolution in the minds of man, and I hope that tyrants, oppressors, fanatics, and the intolerant will not gain thereby. We shall have served humanity." Some articles from the *Encyclopedia* follow.

Encyclopedia . . . In truth, the aim of an *encyclopedia* is to collect all the knowledge scattered over the face of the earth, to present its general outlines and structure to the men with whom we live, and to transmit this to those who will come after us, so that the work of past centuries may be useful to the following centuries, that our children, by becoming more educated, may at the same time become more virtuous and happier, and that we may not die without having deserved well of the human race. . . .

. . . We have seen that our *Encyclopedia* could only have been the endeavor of a philosophical century. . . .

I have said that it could only belong to a philosophical age to attempt an *encyclopedia;* and I have

said this because such a work constantly demands more intellectual daring than is commonly found in [less courageous periods]. All things must be examined, debated, investigated without exception and without regard for anyone's feelings. . . . We must ride roughshod over all these ancient puerilities [foolishnesses], overturn the barriers that reason never erected, give back to the arts and sciences the liberty that is so precious to them. . . . We have for quite some time needed a reasoning age when men would no longer seek the rules in classical authors but in nature. . . .

Fanaticism . . . is blind and passionate zeal born of superstitious opinions, causing people to commit ridiculous, unjust, and cruel actions, not only without any shame or remorse, but even with a kind of joy and comfort. *Fanaticism,* therefore, is only superstition put into practice. . . .

Fanaticism has done much more harm to the world than impiety. What do impious people claim? To free themselves of a yoke, while *fanatics* want to extend their chains over all the earth. Infernal zealomania! . . .

Government . . . The good of the people must be the great purpose of the *government.* The governors are appointed to fulfill it; and the civil constitution that invests them with this power is bound therein by the laws of nature and by the law of reason, which has determined that purpose in any form of *government* as the cause of its welfare. The greatest good of the people is its liberty. Liberty is to the body of the state what health is to each individual; without health man cannot enjoy pleasure; without liberty the state of welfare is excluded from nations. A patriotic governor will therefore see that the right to defend and to maintain liberty is the most sacred of his duties. . . .

If it happens that those who hold the reins of *government* find some resistance when they use their power for the destruction and not the conservation of things that rightfully belong to the people, they must blame themselves, because the public good and the advantage of society are the purposes of establishing a *government.* Hence it necessarily follows that power cannot be arbitrary and that it must be exercised according to the established laws so that the people may know its duty and be secure within the shelter of laws, and so that governors at the same time should be held within just limits and not be tempted to employ the power they have in hand to do harmful things to the body politic. . . .

History . . . *On the usefullness of history.* The advantage consists of the comparison that a statesman or a citizen can make of foreign laws, morals, and customs with those of his country. This is what stimulates modern nations to surpass one another in the arts, in commerce, and in agriculture. The great mistakes of the past are useful in all areas. We cannot describe too often the crimes and misfortunes caused by absurd quarrels. It is certain that by refreshing our memory of these quarrels, we prevent a repetition of them. . . .

Humanity . . . is a benevolent feeling for all men, which hardly inflames anyone without a great and sensitive soul. This sublime and noble enthusiasm is troubled by the pains of other people and by the necessity to alleviate them. With these sentiments an individual would wish to cover the entire universe in order to abolish slavery, superstition, vice, and misfortune. . . .

Intolerance . . . Any method that would tend to stir up men, to arm nations, and to soak the earth with blood is impious.

It is impious to want to impose laws upon man's conscience: this is a universal rule of conduct. People must be enlightened and not constrained. . . .

What did Christ recommend to his disciples when he sent them among the Gentiles? Was it to kill or to die? Was it to persecute or to suffer? . . .

Which is the true voice of humanity, the persecutor who strikes or the persecuted who moans?

Peace . . . War is the fruit of man's depravity; it is a convulsive and violent sickness of the body politic. . . .

If reason governed men and had the influence over the heads of nations that it deserves, we would never see them inconsiderately surrender themselves to the fury of war; they would not show that ferocity that characterizes wild beasts. . . .

Political Authority No man has received from nature the right to command others. Liberty is a gift from heaven, and each individual of the same species has the right to enjoy it as soon as he enjoys the use of reason. . . .

The prince owes to his very subjects the *authority* that he has over them; and this *authority* is limited by the laws of nature and the state. The laws of nature and the state are the conditions under which they have submitted or are supposed to have submitted to its government. . . .

Moreover the government, although hereditary in a family and placed in the hands of one person, is not private property, but public property that consequently can never be taken from the people, to whom it belongs exclusively, fundamentally, and as a freehold. Consequently it is always the people who make the lease or the agreement: they always intervene in the contract that adjudges its exercise. It is not the state that belongs to the prince, it is the prince who belongs to the state: but it does rest with the prince to govern in the state, because the state has chosen him for that purpose: he has bound himself to the people and the administration of affairs, and they in their turn are bound to obey him according to the laws. . . .

The Press [*press* includes newspapers, magazines, books, and so forth] . . . People ask if freedom of the *press* is advantageous or prejudicial to a state. The answer is not difficult. It is of the greatest importance to conserve this practice in all states founded on liberty. I would even say that the disadvantages of this liberty are so inconsiderable compared to its advantages that this ought to be the common right of the universe, and it is certainly advisable to authorize its practice in all governments. . . .

REVIEW QUESTIONS

1. Why was the publication of the *Encyclopedia* a vital step in the philosophes' hopes for reform?
2. To what extent were John Locke's political ideals reflected in the *Encyclopedia*?
3. Why was freedom of the press of such significance to the enlightened philosophes?

7 Humanitarianism

A humanitarian spirit pervaded the philosophes' outlook. Showing a warm concern for humanity, they attacked militarism, slavery, religious persecution, torture, and other violations of human dignity, as can be seen in passages from the *Encyclopedia* and Voltaire's works earlier in this chapter. Through reasoned arguments they sought to make humankind recognize and renounce its own barbarity. In the following selections, other eighteenth-century reformers denounce judicial torture and slavery.

Caesare Beccaria
ON CRIMES AND PUNISHMENTS

In *On Crimes and Punishments* (1764), Caesare Beccaria (1738–1794), an Italian economist and criminologist, condemned torture, commonly used to obtain confessions in many European countries, as irrational and inhuman.

The true relations between sovereigns and their subjects, and between nations, have been discovered. Commerce has been reanimated by the common knowledge of philosophical truths diffused by the art of printing, and there has sprung up among nations a tacit rivalry of industriousness that is most humane and truly worthy of rational beings. Such good things we owe to the productive enlightenment of this age. But very few persons have studied and fought against the cruelty of punishments and the irregularities of criminal procedures, a part of legislation that is as fundamental as it is widely neglected in almost all of Europe. Very few persons have undertaken to demolish the accumulated errors of centuries by rising to general principles, curbing, at least, with the sole force that acknowledged truths possess, the unbounded course of ill-directed power which has continually produced a long and authorized example of the most cold-blooded barbarity. And yet the groans of the weak, sacrificed to cruel ignorance and to opulent indolence; the barbarous torments, multiplied with lavish and useless severity, for crimes either not proved or wholly imaginary; the filth and horrors of a prison, intensified by that cruellest tormentor of the miserable, uncertainty— all these ought to have roused that breed of magistrates who direct the opinions of men. . . .

But what are to be the proper punishments for such crimes?

Is the death-penalty really *useful* and *necessary* for the security and good order of society? Are torture and torments *just,* and do they attain the *end* for which laws are instituted? What is the best way to prevent crimes? Are the same punishments equally effective for all times? What influence have they on customary behavior? These problems deserve to be analyzed with that geometric precision which the mist of sophisms [false arguments], seductive eloquence, and timorous doubt cannot withstand. If I could boast only of having been the first to present to Italy, with a little more clarity, what other nations have boldly written and are beginning to practice, I would account myself fortunate. But if, by defending the rights of man and of unconquerable truth, I should help to save from the spasm and agonies of death some wretched victim of tyranny or of no less fatal ignorance, the thanks and tears of one innocent mortal in his transports of joy would console me for the contempt of all mankind. . . .

A cruelty consecrated by the practice of most nations is torture of the accused during his trial, either to make him confess the crime or to clear up contradictory statements, or to discover accomplices, or to purge him of infamy in some metaphysical and incomprehensible way, or, finally, to discover other crimes of which he might be guilty but of which he is not accused.

No man can be called *guilty* before a judge has sentenced him, nor can society deprive him of public protection before it has been decided that he has in fact violated the conditions under which such protection was accorded him. What right is it, then, if not simply that of might, which empowers a judge to inflict punishment on a citizen while doubt still remains as to his guilt or innocence? Here is the dilemma, which is nothing new: the fact of the crime is either certain or uncertain; if certain, all that is due is the punishment established by the laws, and tortures are useless because the criminal's confession is useless; if uncertain, then one must not torture the innocent, for such, according to the laws, is a man whose crimes are not yet proved. . . .

. . . The impression of pain may become so great that, filling the entire sensory capacity of the tortured person, it leaves him free only to choose what for the moment is the shortest way of escape from pain. The response of the accused is then as inevitable as the impressions of fire and water. The sensitive innocent man will then confess himself guilty when he believes that, by so doing, he can put an end to his torment. Every difference between guilt and innocence disappears by virtue of the very means one pretends to be using to discover it. [Torture] is an infallible means indeed—for absolving robust scoundrels and for condemning innocent persons who happen to be weak. Such are the fatal defects of this so-called criterion of truth, a criterion fit for a cannibal. . . .

Of two men, equally innocent or equally guilty, the strong and courageous will be acquitted, the weak and timid condemned, by virtue of this rigorous rational argument: "I, the judge, was supposed to find you guilty of such and such a crime; you, the strong, have been able to resist the pain, and I therefore absolve you; you, the weak, have yielded, and I therefore condemn you. I am aware that a confession wrenched forth by torments ought to be of no weight whatsoever, but I'll torment you again if you don't confirm what you have confessed."

A strange consequence that necessarily follows from the use of torture is that the innocent person is placed in a condition worse than that of the guilty, for if both are tortured, the circumstances are all against the former. Either he confesses the crime and is condemned, or he is declared innocent and has suffered a punishment he did not deserve. The guilty man, on the contrary, finds himself in a favorable situation; that is, if, as a consequence of having firmly resisted the torture, he is absolved as innocent, he will have escaped a greater punishment by enduring a lesser one. Thus the innocent cannot but lose, whereas the guilty may gain. . . .

It would be superfluous to [cite] . . . the innumerable examples of innocent persons who have confessed themselves criminals because of the agonies of torture; there is no nation, there is no age that does not have its own to cite.

Denis Diderot
ENCYCLOPEDIA
"MEN AND THEIR LIBERTY ARE NOT OBJECTS OF COMMERCE. . . ."

Montesquieu, Voltaire, David Hume, Benjamin Franklin, Thomas Paine, and several other philosophes condemned slavery and the slave trade. In Book 15 of *The Spirit of the Laws* (1748), Montesquieu scornfully refuted all justifications for slavery. Ultimately, he said, slavery, which violates the fundamental principle of justice underlying the universe, derived from base human desires to dominate and exploit other human beings. In 1780, Paine helped draft the act abolishing slavery in Pennsylvania. Five years earlier, he wrote:

> Our Traders in Men . . . must know the wickedness of that SLAVE-TRADE, if they attend to reasoning, or the dictates of their own hearts, and [those who] shun and stifle all these willfully sacrifice Conscience, and the character of integrity to that Golden Idol. . . . Most shocking of all is the alleging the sacred Scriptures to favour this wicked practice.

The *Encyclopedia* denounced slavery as a violation of the individual's natural rights.

[This trade] is the buying of unfortunate Negroes by Europeans on the coast of Africa to use as slaves in their colonies. This buying of Negroes, to reduce them to slavery, is one business that violates religion, morality, natural laws, and all the rights of human nature.

Negroes, says a modern Englishman full of enlightenment and humanity, have not become slaves by the right of war; neither do they deliver themselves voluntarily into bondage, and consequently their children are not born slaves. Nobody is unaware that they are bought from their own princes, who claim to have the right to dispose of their liberty, and that traders have them transported in the same way as their other goods, either in their colonies or in America, where they are displayed for sale.

If commerce of this kind can be justified by a moral principle, there is no crime, however atrocious it may be, that cannot be made legitimate. Kings, princes, and magistrates are not the proprietors of their subjects: they do not, therefore, have the right to dispose of their liberty and to sell them as slaves.

On the other hand, no man has the right to buy them or to make himself their master. Men and their liberty are not objects of commerce; they can be neither sold nor bought nor paid for at any price. We must conclude from this that a man whose slave has run away should only blame himself, since he had acquired for money illicit goods whose acquisition is prohibited by all the laws of humanity and equity.

There is not, therefore, a single one of these unfortunate people regarded only as slaves who does not have the right to be declared free, since he has never lost his freedom, which he could not lose and which his prince, his father, and any person whatsoever in the world had not the power to dispose of. Consequently the sale that has been completed is invalid in itself. This Negro does not divest himself and can never divest himself of his natural right; he carries it everywhere with him, and he can demand everywhere that he be allowed to enjoy it. It is, therefore, patent inhumanity on the part of judges in free countries where he is transported, not to emancipate him immediately by declaring him free, since he is their fellow man, having a soul like them.

REVIEW QUESTIONS

1. What were Caesare Beccaria's arguments against the use of torture in judicial proceedings? In your opinion, can torture ever be justified?
2. What ideals of the Enlightenment philosophes are reflected in Beccaria's arguments?

---

8 Literature as Satire: Critiques of European Society

The French philosophes, particularly Voltaire, Diderot, and Montesquieu, often used the medium of literature to decry the ills of their society and advance Enlightenment values. In the process they wrote satires that are still read and admired for their literary merits and insights into human nature and society. The eighteenth century also saw the publication of Jonathan Swift's *Gulliver's Travels* (1726), one of the greatest satirical works written in English.

Voltaire
CANDIDE

Several eighteenth-century thinkers, including German philosopher Gottfried Wilhelm Leibnitz (1646–1716) and English poet Alexander Pope, subscribed to the view that God had created the best of all possible worlds, that whatever evil or misfortune existed served a purpose—it contributed to the general harmony of the universe. This is the meaning of Pope's famous lines in his *Essay on Man:* "One truth is clear, WHATEVER IS IS RIGHT." This view, known as philosophical optimism, implied that individuals must accept their destiny and make no attempt to change it. In *Candide* (1759), his most important work of fiction, Voltaire bitterly attacked and ridiculed philosophical optimism. In effect Voltaire asked: "In a world where we constantly experience cruelty, injustice, superstition, intolerance, and a host of other evils, how can it be said that this is the best of all possible worlds?" But Voltaire does not resign himself to despair, for he is an ardent reformer who believes that through reason human beings can improve society.

An immediate inspiration for Voltaire's response to philosophical optimism was the catastrophic earthquake that struck Lisbon, Portugal, on November 1, 1755, claiming sixty thousand victims. How does such a catastrophe fit into the general harmony of things in this best of all possible worlds? Like the biblical Book of Job, *Candide* explored the question: Why do the innocent suffer? And because Voltaire delved into this mystery with wit, irony, satire, and wisdom, the work continues to be hailed as a literary masterpiece.

The illegitimate Candide (son of the sister of the baron in whose castle he lives in Westphalia) is tutored by the philosopher Pangloss, a teacher of "metaphysico-theologo-cosmolonigology": that is, a person who speaks nonsense. The naive Pangloss clings steadfastly to the belief that all that happens, even the worst misfortunes, are for the best.

Candide falls in love with Cunegund, the beautiful daughter of the baron of the castle; but the baron forcibly removes Candide from the castle when he discovers their love. Candide subsequently suffers a series of disastrous misfortunes, but he continues to adhere to the belief firmly instilled in him by Pangloss, that everything happens for the best and that this is the best of all possible worlds. Later, he meets an old beggar, who turns out to be his former teacher, Pangloss, who tells Candide that the Bulgarians have destroyed the castle and killed Cunegund and her family. Candide and Pangloss then travel together to Lisbon, where they survive the terrible earthquake, only to have Pangloss hanged (but he escapes death) by the Inquisition. Soon thereafter, Candide is reunited with Cunegund, who, despite having been raped and sold into prostitution, has not been killed. Following further adventures and misfortunes, the lovers are again separated when Cunegund is captured by pirates.

After experiencing more episodes of human wickedness and natural disasters, Candide abandons the philosophy of optimism, declaring "that we must cultivate our gardens." By this Voltaire meant that we can never achieve utopia, but neither should we descend to the level of brutes. Through purposeful and honest work, and the deliberate pursuit of virtue, we can improve, however modestly, the quality of human existence.

The following excerpt from Candide starts with Candide's first misfortune after being driven out of the castle at Westphalia. In addition to ridiculing philosophical optimism, Voltaire expresses his revulsion for militarism.

CHAPTER II

What Befell Candide Among the Bulgarians

Candide, thus driven out of this terrestrial paradise, wandered a long time, without knowing where he went; sometimes he raised his eyes, all bedewed with tears, toward Heaven, and sometimes he cast a melancholy look toward the magnificent castle where dwelt the fairest of young baronesses. He laid himself down to sleep in a furrow, heartbroken and supperless. The snow fell in great flakes, and, in the morning when he awoke, he was almost frozen to death; however, he made shift to crawl to the next town, which was called Waldberghoff-trarbk-dikdorff, without a penny in his pocket, and half dead with hunger and fatigue. He took up his stand at the door of an inn. He had not been long there before two men dressed in blue fixed their eyes steadfastly upon him.

"Faith, comrade," said one of them to the other, "yonder is a well-made young fellow, and of the right size."

Thereupon they went up to Candide, and with the greatest civility and politeness invited him to dine with them.

"Gentlemen," replied Candide, with a most engaging modesty, "you do me much honor, but, upon my word, I have no money."

"Money, sir!" said one of the men in blue to him. "Young persons of your appearance and merit never pay anything. Why, are you not five feet five inches high?"

"Yes, gentlemen, that is really my size," replied he with a low bow.

"Come then, sir, sit down along with us. We will not only pay your reckoning, but will never suffer such a clever young fellow as you to want money. Mankind were born to assist one another."

"You are perfectly right, gentlemen," said Candide; "that is precisely the doctrine of Master Pangloss; and I am convinced that everything is for the best."

His generous companions next entreated him to accept a few crowns, which he readily complied with, at the same time offering them his note for the payment, which they refused, and sat down to table.

"Have you not a great affection for—"

"Oh, yes!" he replied. "I have a great affection for the lovely Miss Cunegund."

"Maybe so," replied one of the men, "but that is not the question! We are asking you whether you have not a great affection for the King of the Bulgarians?"*

"For the King of the Bulgarians?" said Candide. "Not at all. Why, I never saw him in my life."

"Is it possible! Oh, he is a most charming king! Come, we must drink his health."

"With all my heart, gentlemen," Candide said, and he tossed off his glass.

"Bravo!" cried the blues. "You are now the support, the defender, the hero of the Bulgarians; your fortune is made; you are on the high road to glory."

So saying, they put him in irons and carried him away to the regiment. There he was made to wheel about to the right, to the left, to draw his ramrod, to return his ramrod, to present, to fire, to march, and they gave him thirty blows with a cane. The next day he performed his exercise a little better, and they gave him but twenty. The day following he came with ten and was looked upon as a young fellow of surprising genius by all his comrades.

Candide was struck with amazement and could not for the soul of him conceive how he came to be a hero. One fine spring morning, he took it into his head to take a walk, and he marched straight forward, conceiving it to be a privilege of the human species, as well as of the brute creation, to make use of their legs how and when they pleased. He had not gone above two leagues when he was overtaken by four other heroes, six feet high, who bound him neck and heels, and carried him to a dungeon. A court-martial sat upon him, and he was asked which he liked best, either to run the gauntlet six and thirty times through the whole regiment, or to

---

*I.e., Prussians.

have his brains blown out with a dozen musket balls. In vain did he remonstrate to them that the human will is free, and that he chose neither. They obliged him to make a choice, and he determined, in virtue of that divine gift called free will, to run the gauntlet six and thirty times. He had gone through his discipline twice, and the regiment being composed of two thousand men, they composed for him exactly four thousand strokes, which laid bare all his muscles and nerves, from the nape of his neck to his rump. As they were preparing to make him set out a third time, our young hero, unable to support it any longer, begged as a favor they would be so obliging as to shoot him through the head. The favor being granted, a bandage was tied over his eyes, and he was made to kneel down. At that very instant, his Bulgarian Majesty, happening to pass by, inquired into the delinquent's crime, and being a prince of great penetration, he found, from what he heard of Candide, that he was a young meta-physician, entirely ignorant of the world. And, therefore, out of his great clemency, he condescended to pardon him, for which his name will be celebrated in every journal, and in every age. A skillful surgeon made a cure of Candide in three weeks by means of emollient unguents prescribed by Dioscorides. His sores were now skinned over, and he was able to march when the King of the Bulgarians gave battle to the King of the Abares.[†]

CHAPTER III

How Candide Escaped from the Bulgarians, and What Befell Him Afterwards

Never was anything so gallant, so well accoutered, so brilliant, and so finely disposed as the two armies. The trumpets, fifes, oboes, drums, and cannon, made such harmony as never was heard in hell itself. The entertainment began by a discharge of cannon, which, in the twinkling of an eye, laid flat about six thousand men on each side. The musket bullets swept away, out of the best of all possible worlds, nine or ten thousand scoundrels that infested its surface. The bayonet was next the sufficient reason for the deaths of several thousands. The whole might amount to thirty thousand souls. Candide trembled like a philosopher and concealed himself as well as he could during this heroic butchery.

At length, while the two kings were causing *Te Deum*[‡] to be sung in each of their camps, Candide took a resolution to go and reason somewhere else upon causes and effects. After passing over heaps of dead or dying men, the first place he came to was a neighboring village, in the Abarian territories, which had been burned to the ground by the Bulgarians in accordance with international law. Here lay a number of old men covered with wounds, who beheld their wives dying with their throats cut, and hugging their children to their breasts all stained with blood. There several young virgins, whose bellies had been ripped open after they had satisfied the natural necessities of the Bulgarian heroes, breathed their last; while others, half burned in the flames, begged to be dispatched out of the world. The ground about them was covered with the brains, arms, and legs of dead men.

Candide made all the haste he could to another village, which belonged to the Bulgarians, and there he found that the heroic Abares had treated it in the same fashion. From thence continuing to walk over palpitating limbs or through ruined buildings, at length he arrived beyond the theater of war, with a little provision in his pouch, and Miss Cunegund's image in his heart.

[†] I.e., French. The Seven Years' War had begun in 1756.

[‡] A Te Deum ("We praise thee, God") is a special liturgical hymn praising and thanking God for granting some special favor, like a military victory or the end of a war.

Denis Diderot
SUPPLEMENT TO THE VOYAGE OF BOUGANVILLE

Enlightenment thinkers often used examples from the non-European world in order to attack European values that seemed contrary to nature and reason. Denis Diderot reviewed Louis Antoine de Bouganville's *Voyage Around the World* (1771) and in the next year wrote *Supplement to the Voyage of Bouganville* (published posthumously in 1796). In this work, Diderot explored some ideas, particularly the sex habits of Tahitians, treated by the French explorer. Diderot also denounced European imperialism and the exploitation of non-Europeans, and questioned traditional Christian sexual standards. In *Supplement,* Diderot constructed a dialogue between a Tahitian (Orou), who possesses the wisdom of a French philosophe, and a chaplain, whose defense of Christian sexual mores reveals Diderot's critique of the Christian view of human nature. Diderot thus used a representative of an alien culture to attack those European customs and beliefs that the philosophes detested. In the opening passage, before Orou's dialogue, a Tahitian elder rebukes Bouganville and his companions for bringing the evils of European civilization to his island.

"We [Tahitians] are free—but see where you [Europeans] have driven into our earth the symbol of our future servitude. You are neither a god nor a devil—by what right, then, do you enslave people? Orou! You who understand the speech of these men, tell every one of us, as you have told me, what they have written on that strip of metal—'This land belongs to us.' This land belongs to you! And why? Because you set foot in it? If some day a Tahitian should land on your shores, and if he should engrave on one of your stones or on the bark of one of your trees: 'This land belongs to the people of Tahiti,' what would you think? You are stronger than we are! And what does that signify? When one of our lads carried off some of the miserable trinkets with which your ship is loaded, what an uproar you made, and what revenge you took! And at that very moment you were plotting, in the depths of your hearts, to steal a whole country! You are not slaves; you would suffer death rather than be enslaved, yet you want to make slaves of us! Do you believe, then, that the Tahitian does not

know how to die in defense of his liberty? This Tahitian, whom you want to treat as a chattel, as a dumb animal—this Tahitian is your brother. You are both children of Nature—what right do you have over him that he does not have over you?

"You came; did we attack you? Did we plunder your vessel? Did we seize you and expose you to the arrows of our enemies? Did we force you to work in the fields alongside our beasts of burden? We respected our own image in you. Leave us our own customs, which are wiser and more decent than yours. We have no wish to barter what you call our ignorance for your useless knowledge. We possess already all that is good or necessary for our existence. Do we merit your scorn because we have not been able to create superfluous wants for ourselves? When we are hungry, we have something to eat; when we are cold, we have clothing to put on. You have been in our huts—what is lacking there, in your opinion? You are welcome to drive yourselves as hard as you please in pursuit of what you call the comforts of life, but allow sensible people to stop when they see they have nothing to gain but imaginary benefits from the continuation of their painful labors. If you persuade us to go beyond the bounds of strict necessity, when shall we come to the end of our labor? When shall we have time for enjoyment? We have reduced our daily and yearly labors to the least possible amount, because to us nothing seemed more desirable than leisure. Go and bestir yourselves in your own country; there you may torment yourselves as much as you like; but leave us in peace, and do not fill our heads with a hankering after your false needs and imaginary virtues. Look at these men—see how healthy, straight and strong they are. See these women— how straight, healthy, fresh and lovely they are. Take this bow in your hands—it is my own— and call one, two, three, four of your comrades to help you try to bend it. I can bend it myself. I work the soil, I climb mountains, I make my way through the dense forest, and I can run four leagues [about 12 miles] on the plain in less than an hour. Your young comrades have been hard put to it to keep up with me, and yet I have passed my ninetieth year. . . .

"Woe to this island! Woe to all the Tahitians now living, and to all those yet to be born, woe from the day of your arrival! We used to know but one disease—the one to which all men, all animals and all plants are subject—old age. But you have brought us a new one [venereal disease]: you have infected our blood. We shall perhaps be compelled to exterminate with our own hands some of our young girls, some of our women, some of our children, those who have lain with your women, those who have lain with your men. Our fields will be spattered with the foul blood that has passed from your veins into ours. Or else our children, condemned to die, will nourish and perpetuate the evil disease that you have given their fathers and mothers, transmitting it forever to their descendants." . . .

Before the arrival of Christian Europeans, lovemaking was natural and enjoyable. Europeans introduced an alien element, guilt.

But a while ago, the young Tahitian girl blissfully abandoned herself to the embraces of a Tahitian youth and awaited impatiently the day when her mother, authorized to do so by her having reached the age of puberty, would remove her veil and uncover her breasts. She was proud of her ability to excite men's desires, to attract the amorous looks of strangers, of her own relatives, of her own brothers. In our presence, without shame, in the center of a throng of innocent Tahitians who danced and played the flute, she accepted the caresses of the young man whom her young heart and the secret promptings of her senses had marked out for her. The notion of crime and the fear of disease have come among us only with your coming. Now our enjoyments, formerly so sweet, are attended with guilt and terror. That man in black [a priest], who stands near to you and listens to me, has spoken to our young men, and I know not what he has said to our young girls, but our youths are hesitant and our girls blush. Creep away into the dark forest, if you wish, with the perverse companion of your pleasures, but allow the good, simple Tahitians to reproduce themselves without shame under the open sky and in broad daylight.

In the following conversation between Orou and the chaplain, Christian sexual mores and the concept of God are questioned. Orou addresses the chaplain.

[OROU] "You are young and healthy and you have just had a good supper. He who sleeps alone, sleeps badly; at night a man needs a woman at his side. Here is my wife and here are my daughters. Choose whichever one pleases you most, but if you would like to do me a favor, you will give your preference to my youngest girl, who has not yet had any children."

The mother said: "Poor girl! I don't hold it against her. It's no fault of hers."

The chaplain replied that his religion, his holy orders, his moral standards and his sense of decency all prevented him from accepting Orou's invitation.

Orou answered: "I don't know what this thing is that you call 'religion,' but I can only have a low opinion of it because it forbids you to partake of an innocent pleasure to which Nature, the sovereign mistress of us all, invites everybody. It seems to prevent you from bringing one of your fellow creatures into the world, from doing a favor asked of you by a father, a mother and their children, from repaying the kindness of a host, and from enriching a nation by giving it an additional citizen. I don't know what it is that you call 'holy orders,' but your chief duty is to be a man and to show gratitude. . . . I hope that you will not persist in disappointing us. Look at the distress you have caused to appear on the faces of these four women—they are afraid you have noticed some defect in them that arouses your distaste. But even if that were so, would it not be possible for you to do a good deed and have the pleasure of honoring one of my daughters in the sight of her sisters and friends? Come, be generous!"

THE CHAPLAIN "You don't understand—it's not that. They are all four of them equally beautiful. But there is my religion! My holy orders! . . .

. . . [God] spoke to our ancestors and gave them laws; he prescribed to them the way in which he wishes to be honored; he ordained that certain actions are good and others he forbade them to do as being evil."

OROU "I see. And one of these evil actions which he has forbidden is that of a man who goes to bed with a woman or girl. But in that case, why did he make two sexes?"

THE CHAPLAIN "In order that they might come together—but only when certain conditions are satisfied and only after certain initial ceremonies have been performed. By virtue of these ceremonies one man belongs to one woman and only to her; one woman belongs to one man and only to him."

OROU "For their whole lives?"

THE CHAPLAIN "For their whole lives."

OROU "So that if it should happen that a woman should go to bed with some man who was not her husband, or some man should go to bed with a woman that was not his wife . . . but that could never happen because the workman [God] would know what was going on, and since he doesn't like that sort of thing, he wouldn't let it occur."

THE CHAPLAIN "No. He lets them do as they will, and they sin against the law of God (for that is the name by which we call the great workman) and against the law of the country; they commit a crime."

OROU "I should be sorry to give offense by anything I might say, but if you don't mind, I'll tell you what I think."

THE CHAPLAIN "Go ahead."

OROU "I find these strange precepts contrary to nature, and contrary to reason. . . . Furthermore, your laws seem to me to be contrary to the general order of things. For in truth is there anything so senseless as a precept that forbids us to heed the changing impulses that are inherent in our being, or commands that require a degree of [steadfastness] which is not possible, that violate the liberty of both male and female by chaining them perpetually to one another? Is there anything more unreasonable than this perfect fidelity that would restrict us, for the enjoyment of pleasures so capricious, to a single partner—than an oath of immutability taken by two individuals made of flesh and blood under a sky that is not the same for a moment, in a cavern that threatens to collapse upon them, at the foot of a cliff that is crumbling into dust, under a tree that is withering, on a bench of stone that is being worn away? Take my word for it, you have reduced human beings to a worse condition than that of the animals. I don't know what your great workman is, but I am very happy that he never spoke to our forefathers, and I hope that he never speaks to our children, for if he does, he may tell them the same foolishness, and they may be foolish enough to believe it." . . .

Orou "Are monks faithful to their vows of sterility?"

The chaplain "No."

Orou "I was sure of it. Do you also have female monks?"

The chaplain "Yes."

Orou "As well behaved as the male monks?"

The chaplain "They are kept more strictly in seclusion, they dry up from unhappiness and die of boredom."

Orou "So nature is avenged for the injury done to her! Ugh! What a country! If everything is managed the way you say, you are more barbarous than we are."

REVIEW QUESTIONS

1. What does *Candide* reveal about Voltaire's general outlook?
2. How did Diderot attempt to use the Tahitians to criticize the sexual morals of Europeans?
3. How did Diderot use the concept of the law of nature to undermine Christian sexual morality?

Credits continued from page ii.

Chapter 1

Section 6–8 pp. 18–23: *Revised Standard Version of the Bible,* copyright 1946, 1952 (2nd edition, 1971) by the Division of Christian Education of the National Council of the Churches of Christ in the United States of America. Used by permission. All rights reserved.

Chapter 2

Section 1 p. 28: From "The Iliad" by Homer, translated by E. V. Rieu. Copyright © the Estate of E. V. Rieu, 1946. Reprinted by permission of the Estate of E. V. Rieu and Penguin Books, Ltd. *Section 2* p. 31: Reprinted by permission of the publishers and the Trustees of the Loeb Classical Library from *Hippocrates: Volume II,* Loeb Classical Library Volume L 148, translated by W. H. S. Jones, Cambridge, Mass.: Harvard University Press, 1923. The Loeb Classical Library® is a registered trademark of the President and Fellows of Harvard College. *Section 2, 4, 6* pp. 32, 39, 47: From *History of the Peloponnesian War* by Thucydides, translated by Rex Warner (Penguin Classics, 1954). Translation copyright Rex Warner, 1954. Reproduced by permission of Penguin Books, Ltd. p. 33: From Critias, "Religion as a Human Invention," reprinted by permission of the publishers from *Ancilla to the Pre-Socratic Philosophers* by Kathleen Freeman, Cambridge, Mass.: Harvard University Press, 1948. *Section 3* p. 34: Excerpt from *The Three Theban Plays: Antigone, Oedipus the King, and Oedipus at Colonus* by Sophocles, edited by Theodore Howard Banks. Copyright © 1956 by Oxford University Press, Inc. Used by permission of Oxford University Press, Inc. *Section 5* p. 42: From: *The Medea,* translated by Rex Warner in Euripides, Vol. 3 of Richard Lattimore, *The Complete Greek Tragedies,* p. 96, 101. Copyright © 1959 by The Bodley Head. p. 43: From *Lysistrata* by Aristophanes, English translation copyright © 1991 by Nicholas Rudall, all rights reserved, by permission of Ivan R. Dee, Publisher. *Section 7* p. 50: From *The Trial and Death of Socrates,* trans. F. J. Church (London: Macmillan, 1880), pp. 37–41, 50–53, 56–57. *Section 8* p. 54: From *The Republic of Plato,* translated by F. M. Cornford, 1941, pp. 178–179, 181, 190–192, 228–231, 282–283, 286, 288–289. Reprinted by permission of Oxford University Press. *Section 9* p. 59: Excerpt from Aristotle, "The History of Animals, Politics, and Nicomachean Ethics" from *The Oxford Translation Of Aristotle,* edited by W. D. Ross (1925). *Section 10* p. 64: Plutarch, "Cultural Fusion," from *Plutarch, Moralia,* Vol. IV, translated by Frank C. Babbit, Cambridge, Mass: Harvard University Press, 1948. p. 66: Excerpt from Epicurus, "Self-Sufficiency" from *Epicurus: The Extant Remains,* translated by Cyril Bailey (Oxford University Press, 1926), pp. 53, 83, 85, 89, 97, 101, 115, 117, 119. Reprinted by permission of Oxford University Press, UK.

Chapter 3

Section 1 p. 70: Excerpt from Polybius, "The Roman Army," in The Rise of the Roman Empire, translated and edited by Ian Scott-Kilvert (Penguin Books, Ltd., UK, 1979). Copyright © Ian Scott-Kilvert, 1979. Reprinted by permission of Penguin UK. p. 73: Livy, *The War with Hannibal,* translated by Audrey de Selincourt. Copyright © 1965 the Estate of Audrey de Selincourt. Reprinted by permission of Penguin Books, Ltd., UK. *Section 2* p. 75: From *Selected Works* by Cicero, translated by Michael Grant (Penguin Classics, 1963, revised edition 1971). Copyright © Michael Grant 1980, 1971, 1955. Reproduced by permission of Penguin Books, Ltd. p. 76: Plutarch, *Plutarch's Lives: The Translation Called Dryden's,* corrected from the Greek and revised by A. H. Clough, Boston: Little, Brown, & Company, 1875, Vol. II, pp. 345–347. *Section 3* p. 78: Reprinted by permission of the publishers and the Trustees of the Loeb Classical Library from *Diodorus Siculus: Volume II,* Library of History, Loeb Classical Library Vol. L340, translated by C. H. Oldfather, pp. 195, 197, 199, 201, Cambridge, Mass: Harvard University Press, 1939. The Loeb Classical Library® is a registered trademark of the President and Fellows of Harvard College. *Section 4* p. 81: From *A Source Book of Roman History,* ed. Dana C. Monro (Boston: D. C. Heath, 1904), pp. 201–204. *Section 5* p. 84: Excerpt from Plutarch, "Tiberius Gracchus," from *Plutarch, Volume X—Parallel Lives,* Loeb Classical Library, Volume L 102, translated by B. Perrin, Cambridge, Mass: Harvard University Press, 1921. The Loeb Classical Library® is a registered trademark of the President and Fellows of Harvard College. p. 85: From *Selected Works* by Cicero, translated by Michael Grant (Penguin Classics, 1963, revised edition 1971). Reproduced by permission of Penguin Books, Ltd. p. 86: From *The Jugurthine War/The Conspiracy of Catiline* by Sallust, translated by S. A. Handford. Copyright © The Estate of S. A. Handford, 1963. Reproduced by permission of Penguin Books, Ltd. *Section 6* p. 88: Moses Hadas, *The History of Rome.* Copyright © 1956 by Doubleday Company, Inc. Used with permission. p. 90: "The Other Side of the Pax Romana" by Tacitus from *On Britain and Germany* translated by H. Mattingly (Penguin Classics, 1948). Copyright © the Estate of H. Mettingly, 1948. Reproduced by permission of Penguin Books, Ltd. p. 92: From *The Aeneid* by Virgil, translated by Robert Fitzgerald, Random House, Inc., 1983. p. 92: Adapted from *The Satires of Juvenal,* translated by Hubert Creekmore (New York: The New American Library, 1963). Permission granted courtesy of Schaffner Agency, Inc. for the estate of Hubert Creekmore. p. 95: From S. P. Scott, tr., *Corpus Juris Civilis* (The Civil Law), 17 Volumes, 1932 by The Central Trust Company. p. 98: Salvian, *The Writings of Salvian, the Presbyter.* Copyright © 1962 by The Catholic University of America Press. Used with permission. p. 99: From James Harvey Robinson, *Readings in European History* (Boston: Ginn, 1904), pp. 23–24. p. 100: From Gregory the Great, *Homiliarum in Ezechielem* in *Gregory the Great,* translated by F. Homes Dudden (New York: Longmans, Green and Co., 1905), II, 18–20.

Chapter 4

Section 1 pp. 105–106: *Revised Standard Version of the Bible,* copyright 1946, 1952 (2nd edition, 1971) by the Division of Christian Education of the National Council of the Churches of Christ in the United States of America. Used by permission. All rights reserved. *Section 2* p. 107: From *Early Latin Theology,* translated and edited by S. L. Greenslade (Volume V: The Library of Christian Classics). Published simultaneously in Great Britain and the USA by the SCM Press, Ltd., London, and the Westminster/John Knox Press, Louisville, KY. p. 108: From Clement of Alexandria, *Christ the Educator,* translated by Simon P. Wood, C. P., 1954, pp. 128–130 (New York: Fathers of the Church, Inc.). *Section 3* p. 109: Excerpt from *The Desert Fathers* by Helen Waddell, 1936. Reprinted with permission of Constable & Robin, Ltd. pp. 110: From Oliver J. Thatcher, *Library of Original Sources* (Milwaukee, WI: University Research Extension Co., 1907), Vol. 4, pp. 130–133, 136–139, 144, 147–148, 153, 155. *Section 4* p. 113: From Oliver J. Thatcher, *Library of Original Sources* (Milwaukee, WI: University Research Extension Co., 1907), Vol. 4, pp. 133–134. p. 115: From Saint John Chrysostom, *Discourses Against Judaizing Christians,* translated by Paul W. Harkins, 1979. Used with permission from The Catholic University of America Press, Fathers of the Church Series, Washington, D.C. *Section 6* p. 118: St. Augustine, *The City of God.* Copyright © 1858 by Catholic University Press of America. Used with permission.

Chapter 5
Section 1 p. 124: Excerpt from Theophylact Simocattes, *Byzantium: Church, Society, and Civilization Seen Through Contemporary Eyes,* edited by Deno John Geanakoplos, 1984. Reprinted with permission of The University of Chicago Press. *Section 2* p. 125: From *The Koran* by Muhammad, translated by N. J. Dawood (Penguin Classics, 1958, Fifth Revised Edition, 1990), pp. 27, 38, 46–47, 64, 78, 376, 378–380. *Section 3* p. 129: From *Avicenna on Theology* by Arthur J. Arberry, pp. 9–13. Copyright © 1951. Reprinted by permission of John Murray (Publishers) Ltd. *Section 4* p. 131: From *A History of the English Church and People,* by Bede, translated by Leo Sherley-Price (Penguin Classics 1955, revised edition 1968). Copyright © 1955, 2968 Leo Sherley-Price. Used with permission. *Section 4* p. 132: Hroswitha, "Abraham," from *The Plays of Roswitha,* translated by Christopher St. John (New York: Benjamin Bloom, 1966). *Section 5* p. 134–136: Excerpt from Einhard, *Life of Charlemagne,* translated by Samuel E. Turner, 1960, pp. 30–32, 53–54 (University of Michigan Press, 1960). *Section 6* p. 137–138: From Galbert, ommendation and Oath of Fealty" and Fulbert, "Obligations of Lords and Vassals" from *Translations and Reprints from the Original Sources of European History,* ed. E. P. Cheyney (Philadelphia: University of Pennsylvania Press, 1895), Vol. 4, No. 3, pp. 18, 23–24.

Chapter 6
Section 1 p. 141: Larson, *The King's Mirror.* Copyright © 1917 by The Scandinavian Foundation. Used with permission. *Section 2* p. 144: Ephraim Emerton, editor and translator, *The Correspondence of Pope Gregory VII.* Copyright © 1932, renewed 1960 Columbia University Press.

Reprinted by permission of Columbia University Press. *Section 3* p. 148: From *Translations and Reprints from the Original Sources of European History,* ed. D. C. Munro (Philadelphia: University of Pennsylvania, 1897), pp. 5–8. *Section 4* p. 150: From *The Liber Augustalis* or *Constitutions of Melfi Promulgated* by the Emperor Frederick II for the Kingdom of Sicily in 1231, translated with an Introduction and Notes by James M. Powell, 1971 Syracuse University Press. Reprinted with permission. *Section 5* p. 152: Anton Pegis, editor and translator, *The Basic Writings of St. Thomas Aquinas.* Copyright © 1945. Used with permission. *Section 6* p. 154: Excerpt from Albert of Aix-la-Chapelle, "Massacre of the Jews of Mainz" in August C. Krey, *The First Crusade* (Princeton University Press, 1921). p. 156: From Joseph Jacobs, *The Jews of Angevin England* (London: David Nutt, 1893), p. 45. p. 156: From *The Teachings of Maimonides,* ed. A. Cohen, 1968, pp. 289–293. *Section 7* p. 158: "Love as Joyous, Painful, and Humorous," from Anthony Bonner, *Songs of the Troubadours* (Schoken Books, 1972). *Section 8* p. 161: From *The Book of the City of Ladies* by Christine de Pisan, translated by Earl Jeffrey Richards. Copyright © 1982, 1998 by Persea Books, Inc. Reprinted by permission of Persea Books, Inc., New York. *Section 9* p. 164: Excerpt from Jean de Venette, *The Black Death,* trans. by Jean Birdsall in *The Chronicle of Jean De Venette,* pp. 48–52, 128–129 (Columbia University Press, 1953). Reprinted by permission of the author. *Section 10* p. 167: Excerpt from Lothario dei Segni (Pope Innoncent III), "On the Misery of the Human Condition," from *On the Misery of the Human Condition,* edited by Donald R. Howard, translated by Margaret Mary Dietz, (Indianapolis, Bobbs-Merrill 1969), pp. 6, 13, 16, 25, 29, 33, 54, 68. p. 168: "The Vanity of this World" from *Twenty-One Medieval Latin Poems,* edited by E.J. Martin (London, Scholartis Press, 1931). p. 169: From Dante, *The Divine Comedy,* PB*72* 1st edition by Huse, H. R. © 1954. Reprinted with permission of Heinle, a division of Thomson Learning: www.thomsonrights.com. Fax 800-730-2215.

Chapter 7
Section 1 p. 178: From J. H. Robinson and H. W. Rolfe, *Petrarch, the First Modern Scholar and Man of Letters* (New York: G. P. Putnam's Son, 1909), pp. 208, 210, 213. p. 179: Excerpt from Leonardo Bruni, "Study of Greek Literature and a Humanist Educational Program," translated in Henry Osborn Taylor, *Thought and Expression in the Sixteenth Century,* Second Revised Edition (NY: Frederick Ungar, 1930, republished 1959). *Section 2* p. 182: Pico della Mirandola, translated by Elizabeth L. Forbes from *The Renaissance Philosophy of Man,* edited by Ernst Cassirer, Paul Oskar Kristeller, and John H. Randall, Jr., 1948. Reprinted with permission of The University of Chicago Press. *Section 3* p. 184: From *The Prince,* by Niccolò Machiavelli, translated by Luigi, revised by E. R. P. Vincent, 1935, pp. 92–93, 97, 98–99, 101–103. Reprinted by permission of Oxford University Press. *Section 4* p. 188: From *The Book of the Courtier* by Baldassare Castiglione, Illus. Edited by Edgar Mayhew, translated by Charles Singleton. Copyright © 1959 by Charles S. Sin-

gleton and Edgar de N. Mayhew. Used by permission of Doubleday, a division of Random House, Inc. **Section 5** p. 190: From *Luther's Works*, Vol. 44, edited by James Atkinson, copyright © 1966 Fortress Press. Used by permission of Augsburg Fortress. p. 193: Ulrich von Hutten, *Resentment of Rome.* Translations and reprints from the *Original Sources of European History*, Vol. 11 (Philadelphia: University of Pennsylvania, 1897), pp. 13–14. **Section 6** p. 196: Excerpt from John Calvin, "The Institutes," "Ecclesiastical Ordiances," and "The Obedience Owed Rulers," translated in John Allen, *Institues of the Christian Religion by John Calvin*, Vol. 2 (Westminster/John Knox Press, 1928). Used by permission of Westminster/John Knox Press. **Section 7** p. 199: Excerpt from "Canons and Decrees of the Council of Trent" from H. J. Schroeder, tr., *Canons and Decrees of the Council of Trent* (TAN Books and Publications, Inc., 1979). Reprinted courtesy of TAN Books and Publishers, Inc. **Section 8** p. 202: "Catholic Persecution of Protestants," in Roland H. Bainton, ed., *The Age of Reformation* (Princeton: Van Nostrand, 1956), pp. 180–181. Translated from Cronique du Francoys Premiere, ed. Geroge Guiffrey (Paris: Renouard, 1860), pp. 113–129. p. 203: From *Women of the Reformation in Germany and Italy* by Roland H. Bainton. Copyright © 1971 Fortress Press. Used by permission of Augsburg Fortress.

Chapter 8

Section 1 p. 209: From William Carr, *Travels Through Holland, Germany, Sweden, and Denmark by an English Gentleman* (London: Randall Taylor, 1693), pp. 14–18, 33–34, 60–64. **Section 2** p. 210: From *Documents Illustrative of the History of the Slave Trade to America*, Vol. 1, edited by Elizabeth Donnan. Copyright © 1935, published by Carnegie Institution. Reprinted by permission of Carnegie Institution of Washington. p. 213: Malachy Postlethwayt, *The Nation and Private Advantages of the African Trade Considered: Being an Enquiry How Far It Concerns the Trading Interest of Great Britain, Effactually to Support and Maintain the Forts and Settlements in Africa; Belonging to the Royal African Company of England*, London, printed for John and Paul Knapton, 1746, pp. 1–6, 40–41. p. 214: John Wesley, *Thoughts Upon Slavery* (London: R. Hawes, 1774), pp. 29–30, 34–35, 38–44, 47–49, 52–53. **Section 3** p. 217: From *Memoirs of the Duc de Saint-Simon*, edited by W. H. Lewis. Copyright © 1964. **Section 4** p. 220: From *Select Statutes and Other Constitutional Documents Illustrative of the Reigns of Elizabeth and James I*, 3rd ed., ed. G. W. Prothero (Oxford: Clarendon Press, 1906), pp. 293–294, 400–401. p. 222: From *The English Works of Thomas Hobbes of Malmesbury, Leviathan, or the Matter Form and Power of a Commonwealth Ecclesiastical and Civil,* collected and edited by Sir William Molesworth (London: John Bohn, 1839), Vol. 3, pp. 110–113, 116, 117, 154, 157–158, 160–161. **Section 5** p. 225: From *Select Douments of English Constitutional History*, eds. George Burton Adams and H. Morse Stephens (New York: Macmillan Company, 1902), pp. 464–465.

Chapter 9

Section 1 p. 231: From *Discoveries and Opinions of Galileo Galilei* by Galileo Galilei, pp. 28–31, 51–53, 57. Copyright © 1957 by Stillman Drake. Used by permission of Doubleday, a division of Bantam Doubleday Dell Publishing Group, Inc. p. 233: Galileo Galilei, *Dialogue Concerning the Two Chief World Systems*, translated by Stillman Drake (University of California Press, 1962). Reprinted with permission of University of California Press. **Section 2** p. 237: From René Descartes, *Philosophical Writings*, translated by Norman Kemp Smith. Reprinted by permission of Macmillan Press Ltd. **Section 3** p. 240: From Sir Isaac Newton, *The Mathematical Principles of Natural Philosophy, Book III*, trans. Andrew Motte (London: H. D. Symonds, 1803), II, 160–162, 310–314. **Section 4** p. 243: From John Locke, *Two Treatises on Civil Government* (London: 1688, 7th reprinting by J. Whiston et al., 1772), pp. 292, 315–316, 354–355, 358–359, 361–362. **Section 5** p. 247: From *Candide and Other Writings* by Voltaire, edited by Haskell M. Block. Copyright © 1956 and renewed 1984 by Random House, Inc. p. 250: From Thomas Paine, *Age of Reason Being an Investigation of True and Fabulous Theology* (New York: Peter Eckler, 1892), pp. 5–11. **Section 6** p. 252–254: From Denis Diderot, *The Encyclopedia Selections*, ed. and trans. Stephen J. Gendzier, pp. 92–93, 104, 124–125, 134, 136, 153, 156, 183–187, 199, 229–230. Reprinted by permission of Stephen J. Gendzier. **Section 7** p. 255: Extracts reprinted with permission of Macmillan Publishing Company from Caesare Beccaria, *On Crimes and Punishments*, translated by Henry Paolucci, copyright © 1963 by Macmillan Publishing Company. p. 256: From Denis Diderot, *The Encyclopedia Selections*, ed. and trans. Stephen J. Gendzier, pp. 229–230. p. 259: Reprinted with permission of Pocket Books, an imprint of Simon & Schuster from Voltaire, *Candide*, from *Candide & Zadig* translated by Tobias George Smollett. Edited by Lester G. Croker. Copyright © 1962 by Washington Square Press. Copyright renewed 1990 by Lester G. Crocker. p. 261: From Denis Diderot, *Romeau's Nephew and Other Works*, translated by Jacques Barzun and Ralph H. Bowen. Copyright © 1956 by Jacque Barzun and Ralph H. Bowen; copyright renewed 1984; pp. 188–190, 194–195, 197–199, 213.